Shrubs

for gardens, agroforestry & permaculture

MARTIN CRAWFORD

Permanent Publications

Published by
Permanent Publications
Hyden House Ltd
The Sustainability Centre
East Meon
Hampshire GU32 1HR
United Kingdom
Tel: 01730 776 582
or +44 (0)1730
Email: enquiries@permaculture.co.uk
Web: www.permanentpublications.co.uk

Distributed in North America by
Chelsea Green Publishing Company, PO Box 428, White River Junction, VT 05001
www.chelseagreen.com

Designed by Two Plus George Limited, www.TwoPlusGeorge.co.uk

Printed in the UK by Bell & Bain, Thornliebank, Glasgow

MIX Paper from responsible sources FSC® C007785 www.fsc.org

All paper from FSC certified mixed sources

The Forest Stewardship Council (FSC) is a non-profit international organisation established to promote the responsible management of the world's forests. Products carrying the FSC label are independently certified to assure consumers that they come from forests that are managed to meet the social, economic and ecological needs of present and future generations.

British Library Cataloguing-in-Publication Data
A catalogue record for this book is available from the British Library

ISBN 978 1 85623 333 0

Contents

Index of Latin names

Martin's new book is an utterly indispensable guide to growing shrubs and small trees, no matter how limited or expansive your space. There are some commonly known edible and otherwise useful trees – grapes, currants, raspberries, etc. – as well as the best of the less familiar – honeyberry, saskatoon, Siberian ginseng among them. The book is full of Martin's unique knowledge and experience – the best cultivars, how to care for each species, and a wealth of other useful and perfectly laid out information. Martin's writing is lively and the design and photography superb. I'm one of many who are grateful to Martin for blazing a trail and sharing what he discovers. An essential guide for all tree lovers.

Rob Hopkins

Transition Network cofounder
and author of *From What Is to What If*

I've been inspired by Martin's pioneering work for 20 years, and his new book places much of his wisdom in our hands. Focusing on beautifully diverse shrubs – from American allspice to yellowhorn – this book shows us how to enrich our patch and be part of a people-driven response to climate change in the process. Beautifully designed, thorough and fascinating, this is an essential for climate-minded gardeners wanting to grow delicious, useful perennials at any scale.

Mark Diacono

experimental gardener, journalist
and author of *The New Kitchen Garden*

Martin has been a leader in choosing and growing plants for our gardens of the future. This ethnobotanical volume on shrubs is as expected, researched with immense detail mirroring his own practical trials. Filled with useful tables that will answer every gardeners questions on soil type, aspect, flowering and fruiting times, frost hardiness, fertility and many more. The section on climatic zones is particularly pertinent as we plan planting schemes for climate change.

Ben Law

woodsman and author of several books,
including *The Woodland Way*

Martin Crawford does it again, with another in his series of useful guides to forest garden plants of all kinds. The book is well organized, the photographs beautiful, the descriptions brief yet informative, with Martin's direct experience shining through. The listings of cultivars and their qualities are especially welcome. Covers an array of shrub and vine species for a range of climates and growing conditions, for edible, medicinal, soil improvement and other uses. A worthy reference and a great introduction to a wealth of woody plants!

Dave Jacke

Dynamics Ecological Design
and co-author of *Edible Forest Gardens volume 1 and 2*

You cannot help but admire Martin Crawford's work. His exhaustive research is remarkable. His lists of varieties and comments speak to many hours of detailed study. In this latest work it's great to hear a much more personal voice coming through in the opening pages reflecting his concerns about the state of the planet. When he says "Nothing we do in terms of land use is an action in isolation", I'm with him all the way. This is not a beginner's book, but for convinced forest gardeners it's a great addition. I learnt lots. Goji berry leaves are edible – so it doesn't matter if they don't fruit (which they'll never do in the frozen North)! Great to see RHS hardiness ratings not just USDA – more sense for European growers…

Graham Bell

creator of the oldest food forest in Britain,
permaculture teacher and author of
The Permaculture Garden

Crawford sets out his vision of forest gardens being like orchards enriched with shrubs and other productive plants, before urging us to 'get planting'. The introduction includes some very timely and interesting information on carbon sequestration and the final section has highly helpful plant lists. Crawford has clearly done the research to ensure his plant information is relevant to a geographically diverse readership with variable growing conditions. It's pure escapism for plant geeks and an absolute must for the design and plant selection stage of any forest gardening project.

Jo Homan

Edible Landscapes London

A great deal of what I know about forest gardens I've learnt from Martin Crawford. Each year I take several permaculture design course groups for a tour of his flagship two acre site in Devon and I always learn something new. I'm very fortunate, and even with this regular face-to-face contact I'm excited to hold another of his books in my hands. Martin is a prolific writer, which is a great gift for us all. *Shrubs for Gardens, Agroforestry and Permaculture* follows up his excellent reference on trees. Again, most of the book is given over to the plants, providing as much detail as most of us are ever likely to need to propagate and grow them, including in an agroforestry context. Unusual species are found amongst the familiar and, where relevant, cultivars are recommended. This is another fine volume to educate and inspire and the only problem I have now is that I want to grow them all!

Aranya
permaculture teacher and author of
Permaculture Design: A Step-by-Step Guide

Martin Crawford has done it again. I have been following Martin's work for many years. This book on shrubs fills in the vertical gap alongside his marvellous books on trees and perennial vegetables. Along with his forest garden studies, those that live in temperate climes now have a complete set of texts for developing a forest garden. In point of fact, these may very well be the only manuals that you will need, not only to get started, but to learn the complexities of proper maintenance and management. I cannot say enough about Martin's ability to organize an incredibly wide range of plant species and techniques into a working whole that makes sense to the beginner and the experienced gardener or farmer. Thanks Martin for your perseverance through the years to inform, educate, implement and put the word out, tirelessly!

Wayne Weiseman
co-author of *Integrated Forest Gardening: the Complete Guide to Polycultures and Plant Guilds in Permaculture Systems*

This book, like Martin's previous books, is brilliantly clear and comprehensive, a testament to his years of extensive research. The shrub layer can often get a little lost between the planning of the canopy and ground cover layers, and become a 'soft fruit' layer by default. Martin's ongoing search for useful plants that will thrive in our climate presents us with a list which increases the potential for this intermediate layer, and for perennial systems as a whole to meet our human needs - food, materials, medicines, etc while also meeting the needs of the ecosystem which supports us. This book will be particularly useful for those wanting a forest garden on a small domestic scale who may not have space for trees, and is a great resource for all forest garden designers.

Caroline Aitken
Director of Whitefield Permaculture
co-author of *Food from your Forest Garden*

It is clear that if we are to survive on this small planet, future generations will need to leave behind the era of oil and fossil fuel dependence and look to low carbon, living and local solutions to meet our needs in terms of food, fibre, energy, shelter, medicine and culture. Packed with knowledge, information and wisdom drawn from over three decades of pioneering research and first hand observation, Martin's wonderful books will become key texts as we learn how to live abundantly in the coming age of the tree.

Graham Burnett
permaculture teacher, forest gardener
and author of *The Vegan Book of Permaculture*

About the Author

After a brief spell messing about with computers, Martin Crawford has spent the last three decades on the land, starting with organic horticulture but soon becoming entranced by the beauty and potential of trees and perennial plants. He founded the Agroforestry Research Trust in 1991 and has been the director since, setting up one of the best established temperate forest gardens and experimenting with tree, shrub and perennial crops on 8 hectares (20 acres) of land in Devon, UK.

The Agroforestry Research Trust (ART) is a non-profit-making charity that researches into temperate agroforestry and all aspects of plant cropping and uses. Martin runs the nursery at ART which propagates and sells a wide range of perennial plants and trees.

Martin has published multiple journals through ART on fruit and nut trees, useful plants and agroforestry and offers consultancy for orchards, forest gardens and other agroforestry techniques. He is also the author of four bestselling books: *Creating a Forest Garden*, *How to Grow Perennial Vegetables*, *Food From The Forest Garden* and *Trees for Gardens, Orchards and Permaculture*.

INTRODUCTION

The world is changing. Underlying the economic, social and political upheavals is the biggest factor that is affecting us and will affect our children and grandchildren: climate change. Despite increasingly urgent clarion calls from scientists, the not-fit-for-purpose economic and political systems we live in cannot be relied upon to implement the carbon emission reductions needed. This is where you come into it: it is up to every single one of us – farmer, gardener or plant dabbler – to minimise our carbon footprint and ideally live a carbon-negative life.

This is where woody crops become very important. Woody crops sequester carbon in their biomass, but can also lead to the storage of large amounts of carbon into the soil. In fact, I believe that agriculture cannot possible reduce its carbon emissions enough without a large scale shift towards perennial and woody species.

This book focusses on shrubs – smaller woody plants up to about 3m in height, usually with multiple stems, and complements its companion volume *Trees for Gardens, Orchards and Permaculture*. For many people it won't be a choice of whether to grow trees or shrubs, but more a choice of which trees and which shrubs to mix together in the growing system. Thankfully, negative interactions between trees and shrubs (apart from shading) are minimal and almost unlimited possibilities abound for mixing them together.

This book of useful shrubs includes species for using in many different situations. It includes, of course, common fruit bushes like currants and gooseberries, but includes many other less well-known shrubs with edible fruits, nuts, leaves, or other parts; spice trees; shrubs with medicinal parts, also shrubs for nitrogen-fixation to help fertilise other plants.

Diversity in our growing systems will become increasingly important. The word 'sustainable' is much misused these days but in terms of gardens, smallholdings or farms, ecological sustainability also requires much greater diversity both of species and structure of growing systems. Plant diversity is one of the main ways we can make our garden or farm systems more resilient in the face of floods, droughts, new pests and diseases and warming temperatures.

Even the tiniest garden (or balcony) has room for shrubs which can be just 30cm high. British allotment gardens – often with restrictions on tree planting – often have some shrubs like blackcurrants, and the possibilities of diversifying are enormous.

Agroforestry is a term which encompasses forest gardens, orchards, alley cropping and wood pasture. Forest gardens are like highly diversified orchards, with underplanting of trees with shrubs and perennial plants, and sometimes overplanting with larger scattered trees too. Traditional orchards do not have much in the way of plant diversity, but the possibilities for diversifying are enormous, using larger shrubs between trees or smaller ones beneath.

Alley cropping is farm-scale agroforestry with lines of woody plants, in between which are alleys still cultivated for annual grains or vegetables. The lines of plants can be single or multiple rows of trees and/or shrubs. One obvious way to incorporate shrubs is to have a single line of trees flanked either side by a line of shrubs – so a three-line system with alleys between, thereby allowing the shrubs plenty of light from one side at least.

Wood pasture (or silvopasture) is a system of scattered trees beneath which are grazed grasses or other forage plants. The role of shrubs in wood pastures is less than in the other types of agroforestry, simply because most shrubs are much too vulnerable to browsing damage from herbivores.

Shrubs can also be of great value in windbreaks. For garden-scale systems, windbreaks are often desired that are not too tall, so 2-3m shrubs can be ideal. Some can be made of spiny shrubs to keep out four-legged or two-legged pests. Larger-scale windbreaks may sometimes consist of a line of trees plus one or two lines of shrubs, the latter to keep the windbreak functioning well as the trees get larger and perhaps become thin low down as lower branches naturally die off.

Some shrubs can also be incorporated into existing hedgerows to increase their diversity and productivity.

Nothing we do in terms of land use is an act in isolation. Every shrub and every tree planted may give us a crop and make us feel better, but it will also help wildlife and the planet. Just get planting!

Carbon storage in the ART Forest Garden

I started our forest garden in Dartington, UK, in 1994, and it is now a resilient mature growing system which sees several thousand visitors per year.

One of the more exciting developments in the last few years has been the use of the garden for researchers to measure and quantify aspects of the system, including carbon storage in woody crops and in the soil.

Measuring carbon storage in trees and shrubs involves measuring them, estimating or measuring the wood density and then coming up with a measure of the carbon content. This is fine for the above-ground parts, but nobody wants their trees destroyed in such measurements, so the root biomass has to be estimated (the aerial:root biomass ratio is known for some species and estimated for others).

Measuring carbon in soil has other challenges. The vast majority of scientific papers on soil only sample the top 20cm (8ins) of soil, but what happens in lower layers? Again, to accurately sample down to (say) 3m (10ft) depth, would require the effective destruction of the site. But some work has been done on deep carbon storage. The figures measured at Dartington show that the forest garden is amongst the fastest carbon accumulation techniques in temperate climates, exceeding the estimated carbon sequestration predicted for woodland regeneration in the UK.

The amount of carbon stored in growing systems increases with species diversity, so that forest garden systems, probably with more diversity than any other, are likely to maximise carbon storage in this aspect. Soils with a high biological activity also have a higher carbon storage potential.

Deep carbon storage is also affected by the type of growing system: whereas in forests about 50% of soil organic carbon is in the top 20cm (8ins), in shrublands (which forest gardens are more akin to) only 33% of soil organic carbon is in the top 20cm (8ins), meaning the deeper layers store about twice as much as the top sampled layer.

Deadwood and twig/leaf litter are often ignored in scientific analyses – but these can add significant quantities of carbon stored, especially if pruning techniques are encouraged for the express purpose. The figure in the table above is estimated from our regular pruning of green manure trees and shrubs like alders, which add about 800kg (1760lb) material per year, although it only lasts for 7-10 years.

Our 25-year-old forest garden in Dartington

Carbon storage in the ART Forest Garden

	Tonnes carbon stored per hectare per year
Trees[1]	1.80
Shrubs[2]	0.17
Topsoil (top 20cm / 8ins)[3]	0.87
Deep soil (beneath 20cm / 8ins) – estimated	1.77
Deadwood on surface – estimated	0.16
TOTAL	4.77

These figures do not include litter and deadwood, of which there will be considerable quantities in forest gardens.

The forest garden itself is 0.84 hectares in size (2.1 acres), so over its first 25 years it has stored about 100 tonnes of carbon.

The figures above exceed those measured for more 'mainstream' agroforestry systems in temperate climates, which can store 1-4 tonnes carbon per hectare per year.

Carbon stored won't increase forever. Nobody knows the limits of forest gardens, but in forestry the carbon storage tails off at around 100 years of age – with carbon in woody plants reaching an equilibrium earlier than that in soil.

Because a forest garden is more open and less densely planted with trees than a forest, the carbon accumulation in woody plants is less than that in a new forest, although soil accumulation appears greater. Overall, a new forest is likely to sequester more carbon, however apart from timber you won't get many useful crops from it. A forest garden is likely to be the growing system that stores most carbon while at the same time giving many productive crops.

Maximising carbon sequestration in your garden or farm

There are many techniques which will help increase either the rate and/or overall total of carbon storage in growing systems. I don't claim that this list is exhaustive, but you'll see that if you seriously want to store carbon, you need to be thinking about woody and perennial cropping systems.

Maximising sequestration

- High density planting using nurse trees/shrubs.
- Thinning of nurse trees/shrubs, leaving branchwood on the soil surface.
- Minimal soil disturbance prior to or during planting.
- Return of all woody prunings and other plant debris to soil surface.
- Use of woodchip/high carbon mulches.
- Use of especially deep rooted trees/plants (mineral accumulators) to aid transport of carbon deep into the soil.
- Maximising use of perennial crops.
- Maximising diversity of plant species – higher plant diversity increases rhizosphere carbon inputs.
- Aiding establishment of mycorrhizal fungal layer because more mycorrhizae leads to more carbon storage and also increases stable aggregates in soil.
- Use of animals in system e.g. birds:
  - Could attract birds into area to deposit droppings (high in N, low in C, but extra N may increase C sequestration) – though they may be a pest on your crops.
  - Introduce poultry e.g. ducks. Manure high in N, low in C, but extra N may increase C sequestration. Sensible to keep to a low density, as too many will increase NOx emissions which will outweigh carbon stored in terms of greenhouse gas budget.

Maximising rate of sequestration

Choice of species of nurse:

- Fast growing
- Pioneer
- Often nitrogen-fixing (nurses to increase nitrogen circulation and therefore sequestration rate)
- Denser leaf canopy
- Low tannin in wood/leaves to increase decomposition rate (most pioneers are low tannin) and increase sequestration in soil
- High tannin to increase sequestration in dead wood/litter
- Possibly use poor coppicers so root biomass starts to decompose and get recycled quickly
- Trimming of woody debris into sections that lie flat on the soil surface, increasing rate of decomposition
- Good spread of woody debris because the carbon stored in soil as it decomposes is within 1m (3ft) of deadwood
- Use of 30-100cm (1-3ft) high ground covering plants to cover/shade woody debris and increase rate of decomposition by keeping it more moist; and also to keep soil shaded and cooler, reducing C oxidation in soil.

Minimising carbon losses

- Site choice – avoid steep sites (best forested) to avoid erosion by heavy rain.
- Site remediation:
  - Swales / terraces to avoid erosion especially on fine sandy or coarse silt soils where risk is highest.
  - Riparian buffers along streams and rivers to reduce soil erosion.
  - Windbreaks to reduce wind erosion.
  - Decompaction of compacted soils to improve soil health.
  - Good design of paths and tracks to minimise erosion.
  - Minimal soil disturbance from cultivation.
  - Minimising use of annual crops requiring soil cultivation (no dig systems are better).
  - Ground covering plants – evergreen where possible – to minimise soil carbon losses from heavy rain, drought etc.
  - Mulches of organic materials over any bare soil.
  - Leaving stumps in place to decompose.
  - No use of inorganic amendments/fertilisers (manufacture causes high carbon losses).
  - Use of biochar particularly in warmer climates and on soils low in carbon. Residence time in soil may be medium to very long, also has liming benefit, but also may negatively add long-lived toxins to the soil. (If feed source of biochar is on-site wood then might be minimal extra carbon stored.)
  - Minimal use of liming. Liming using calcium oxide compounds does produce CO_2. Only lime to reach pH 6.0 for example.
  - Use of silicates, e.g. Olivine, mg2sio4, for liming which does not produce CO_2 at all. E.g. from igneous rock quarry fines (rock dust).

Woody brash chopped and lying close to soil surface

Hardiness systems

I have used two different systems to give a rating of plant hardiness. The first is the USDA zone system that is widely used in North America and also applicable to much of continental Europe. The second is the newer RHS hardiness rating system, which is better suited to British conditions where the great variability of winter temperatures and generally cooler summers means the USDA system does not work so well.

USDA hardiness zone system

This system has simply divided zones into areas with average minimum temperatures within a 10°F range. Initially defined as 10 zones (1-10) this has recently been expanded to 14 zones, and also with subdivisions a and b (so zone 5a, 5b, 6a, 6b etc.) which each cover a 5°F range. The USDA has published a zone map for the USA using this new scale at https://planthardiness.ars.usda.gov however for most other parts of the world the original 10 zone system is still used and that is what is used in this book.

The zones are defined as:

Zone number	Min average temp (°C)	Min average temp (°F)	Equivalent RHS rating
1	-51 to -46	-60 to -50	H7
2	-46 to -40	-50 to -40	H7
3	-40 to -34	-40 to -30	H7
4	-34 to -29	-30 to -20	H7
5	-29 to -23	-20 to -10	H7
6	-23 to -18	-10 to 0	H6 to H7
7	-18 to -12	0 to 10	H5 to H6
8	-12 to -7	10 to 20	H4 to H5
9	-7 to -1	20 to 30	H3 to H4
10	-1 to 4	30 to 40	H2 to H3

Maps showing USDA hardiness zones in the USA, Canada, Europe, Australia and Japan are also available online.[4]

These maps should be used as a guide to which plants will survive where you are, however in urban areas, near buildings and on a sheltered southern hillside you may 'gain' a whole hardiness zone, whereas in hollows, valleys and northern hillsides you may 'lose' a zone of hardiness. Plants near rivers that do not freeze benefit from the extra warmth, worth up to half a zone of extra hardiness.

Plant hardiness in any particular year is also affected by seasonal conditions – a dry autumn leads to better hardening off of growth and greater winter hardiness than a mild, wet autumn.

RHS hardiness ratings

As well as being based on minimum winter temperatures, this hardiness rating system also takes into account temperature swings, especially in spring and autumn, which are common in Britain and other temperate maritime regions. Hence the common damage associated with late spring frosts, and in autumn the problem of new growth being cut back by frosts before it ripens properly. The ratings are H1 to H7 (H1 and its sub-ratings are not included here as all are very tender).

Rating	Min average temp (°C)	Min average temp (°F)	Category	Definition
H2	1 to 5	34 to 41	Tender	Tolerant of low temperatures, but will not survive being frozen. Except in frost-free inner-city areas or coastal extremities, requires glasshouse conditions in winter, but can be grown outdoors once risk of frost is over.
H3	-5 to 1	23 to 34	Half hardy – mild winter	Hardy in coastal/mild areas, except in hard winters and at risk from sudden (early) frosts. May be hardy elsewhere with wall shelter or good microclimate. Likely to be damaged or killed in cold winters, particularly with no snow cover or if potted. Can survive with artificial winter protection.
H4	-10 to -5	14 to 23	Hardy – average winter	Hardy through most of the UK apart from inland valleys, at altitude and central/northerly locations. May suffer foliage damage and stem dieback in harsh winters in cold gardens. Some normally hardy plants may die in long, wet winters in heavy or poorly drained soil. Plants in pots are more vulnerable.
H5	-15 to -10	5 to 14	Hardy – cold winter	Hardy in most places throughout the UK even in severe winters. May not withstand open/exposed sites or central/northern locations. Many evergreens suffer foliage damage, and plants in pots will be at increased risk.
H6	-20 to -15	-4 to 5	Hardy – very cold winter	Hardy across the UK and Northern Europe. Many plants grown in containers will be damaged unless given protection.
H7	< -20	< -4	Very hardy	Hardy in the severest European continental climates including exposed upland locations in the UK.

Notes

[1] Tree layer carbon stock quantification in a temperate food forest: A periurban polyculture case study. Luke J. Schafer, Marin Lysák, Christian B. Henriksen. Urban Forestry & Urban Greening 45 (2019)

[2] Quantification of the understorey contribution to carbon storage in a periurban temperate food forest. Lisa Molgaard Lehmann, Marin Lysák, Luke Schafer, Christian Bugge Henriksen. Urban Forestry & Urban Greening 45 (2019)

[3] Soil fitness in consciously designed agricultural ecosystems: Sustainability indicators and best practice ecological engineering. Conor Kendrew. MRes Thesis, Plymouth University, 2018.

[4] http://jelitto.com/Plant-Information/Plant-Hardiness-Zones

AMERICAN ALLSPICE / SPICEBUSH
Calycanthus species

Zone 5-7, H6-7
Deciduous
Spice plant
California allspice / spicebush, *Calycanthus occidentalis*, Zone 7, H6
Carolina allspice / spicebush, *Calycanthus floridus*, Zone 5, H6-7

Origin and history

The American allspice or spicebush shrubs get their name from the aromatic scent given off by their crushed leaves and stems. There are five American species (and one from China), of which three are fairly easily available. They are deciduous shrubs with aromatic bark and opposite, glossy green leaves. The flowers of all species are similar, and the bushy shrubs are mid to late summer flowering, multistemmed and sometimes suckering in habit. In warm areas (rarely in Britain), the flowers become hard elliptic capsule-shaped fruit with many brown seeds.

These species have a very long history of culinary and medicinal use by Native North Americans, and are still commercially harvested from the wild to a small degree.

Description

California allspice, from California, is a straggly shrub up to 4m (13ft) high by up to 10m (33ft) wide, with flowers, purple-brown fading to yellow, opening to 7cm (3ins) across, strongly scented, from June-August. Leaves are 8-20cm (3-8ins) long.

Carolina allspice is from the southeastern USA (Virginia to Florida, west to Alabama and West Virginia), growing 1-3m (3-10ft) high. Leaves are 5-12cm (2-5ins) long, grey-green and downy beneath, rough above, turning yellow in autumn. Flowers are reddish-purple, to 5cm (2ins) across, with a fruity strawberry scent, in June-July.

Uses

The bark, wood, roots, shoots and leaves of both species smell strongly of cloves and can be used as a cinnamon substitute (the economic use of the dried bark is the reason Carolina allspice was introduced to Kew around 1789).

The Cherokee used the plant medicinally in several ways – mostly using the bark as an eye medicine (*C. floridus*) and for chesty colds and sore throats (*C. occidentalis*) and the roots (strongly diuretic) for urinary problems. The seeds contain toxic alkaloids and are poisonous to animals.

The leaves can be used as an insect repellent and disinfectant.

The wood and bark from fresh shoots of California allspice was used in basket work, and the pithy shoots used to make arrows.

A light brown dye is obtained from the flowers.

Varieties/Cultivars

Several ornamental varieties of Carolina allspice exist with flowers of good fragrance and colour.

Cultivation

The spice bushes are hardy and long-lived but are intolerant of summer drought; in their native habitat they are always found close to river or stream margins or in wet areas in woodland and mountain regions. They prefer sun in a temperate climate like Britain, where their wood ripens best, but can be grown in shadier spots in warmer climates.

All grow better in acid or neutral soils, though they are tolerant of alkaline soils as long as they are water retentive and of good depth.

Plants in this genus are notably resistant to honey fungus.

The foliage is generally unpalatable to deer and other grazing animals.

Growing from seed is fairly easy. Dry seed requires about three months of cold stratification. Semi-ripe heel cuttings can be taken in midsummer. Suckers can be removed arising at the edge of the shrub; If not yet well rooted, notch the stem and re-bury for a season before removing.

Pests and diseases

There are none of note.

Related species

Calycanthus fertilis, from the southeastern USA, is very similar to Carolina allspice but with inferior flavour.

Calycanthus mohrii, from the southeastern USA, is similar to Carolina allspice but only 1m high, with similar uses.

PART 1 | THE SHRUBS

Carolina allspice

AMERICAN ELDER, *Sambucus canadensis*

Zone 3, H7
Deciduous
Edible fruit, flowers

Origin and history

American elder (sometimes called Canadian or sweet elder) has recently been placed by botanists as a subspecies of the larger European elder (*Sambucus nigra*), however it is a plant of very different character and I think in this case the botanists are probably wrong!

In North America, this species has been used for food and medicine for a very long time, just as European elder has in Europe.

Description

It is a slowly suckering shrub growing 2.4-3.5m (8-12ft) high, becoming a herbaceous perennial at its northern limits. It has shiny young branches and leaves usually with seven leaflets, each to 14 x 6.5cm (5.5 x 2.5ins). Flowers are ivory coloured, pleasantly-scented, in large spreading heads to 20-25cm (8-10ins) in diameter. Flowering starts in July (after European elder has finished flowering) and continues well into autumn (up until December sometimes in Britain, especially where a single selection is planted so no fruit set). Plants are not self-fertile (unlike European elder); two different selections are required for fruiting. Heads of purple-black fruit each 5mm (0.2ins) in diameter ripen from September onwards.

Uses

Fruits are similar to those of European elder and are edible raw or cooked: somewhat bittersweet. They can also be dried. Usually used in bread, jellies, jams, pies, sauces and wines. They are rich in vitamin C.

Flowers are edible raw or cooked. They can be battered and made into fritters, like those of European elder. They can be soaked in cold water to make a drink and also used to make a tea. They can also be picked young (unopened) and pickled.

The flowers are used medicinally, being stimulant, diuretic, diaphoretic and carminative. The inner bark has also been used medicinally.

The leaves repel insects; they have insecticidal and fungicidal properties. The roots are insecticidal, active against mosquitoes (*Culex* spp.).

The bark and roots contain tannins and were used for tanning leather.

The bark has been used as a black dye; the leaves, flowers and fruit can also be used for dyeing.

The wood has been used in watchmaking. The stems can be hollowed and were used as tapping drains for sap tapping, and used to make whistles and flutes.

Varieties/Cultivars

Various fruiting selections of American elder were made in the USA during the 20th century and these tend to be the main varieties grown for flowers or fruit.

Cultivar	Description
Adams	Fruiting cultivar, bearing large clusters of large fruit. Quite late ripening. Vigorous and productive plants.
Aurea	Ornamental cultivar with pale green shoots and golden-yellow leaves. Fruit is red and sweet tasting.
Ebony King	Fruiting cultivar with waxy black fruit. Very productive tree which can produce 11kg (25lb) of fruit annually; evergreen in mild climates.
Hidden Springs	Fruiting cultivar with evenly ripening clusters.
Johns	Fruiting cultivar, bearing huge clusters of large, tasty fruit. Very vigorous plants. Mid season ripening.
Kent	Fruiting cultivar, bearing large fruit. Very early ripening. Of secondary value.
Maxima	Ornamental cultivar which has huge flower heads, to 40cm (16ins) across.
Nova	Fruiting cultivar, with large fruit. Ripens evenly in cluster, mid to late season. Heavy yielding.
Scotia	Fruiting cultivar, with medium sized fruit ripening mid to late season and evenly in the cluster. Fruit is high in soluble solids.
Victoria	Fruiting cultivar with large fruit, very early ripening. Moderately vigorous. Of secondary value.
York	Fruiting cultivar bearing large clusters of very large, juicy fruit, the largest of all *S. canadensis* cultivars. Vigorous. Late ripening.

Cultivation

American elder tolerates a wide range of soils, including chalk; also atmospheric pollution, coastal exposure and shade. It prefers rich, moist but well-drained soil and sun or part shade (deep shade is tolerated but flowering and fruiting will be greatly restricted).

Elder roots grow very near the surface of the soil and are easily damaged by tillage implements; such damage may also encourage suckering.

Can be used in hedging and windbreaks as it is very wind tolerant. Flowers are insect-pollinated by flies, bees and others.

The fruits are edible both raw and cooked, but care should be taken with most not to eat vast quantities raw as this may cause stomach upsets. Remove as much stem as possible before using fruits and flowers as this is not pleasant tasting. The leaves, stems and bark are all poisonous.

Flowers and fruit are borne on the current season's wood, so if you need to prune, just cut back as much as necessary in winter: plants will soon put out numerous strong shoots in the spring. American elder can even be cut back right to the ground and it will recover.

If a single selection is planted, flowering continues longer into the autumn, which may be most desirable if the flowers are the required crop. When cross-pollination occurs, yields of up to 7kg (15lb) of fruit per tree can be achieved.

Commercial plantations in North America use plants spaced at 2 x 3m (6 x 10ft) spacing, with regular pruning, and achieve yields of 7.5-10 tonnes/hectare (3-4 tonnes/acre).

Hardwood cuttings are the easiest method of propagation, taken in winter from the current season's growth. They do not need rooting powder or other special treatment. Softwood cuttings in summer can also succeed, whilst seeds need lengthy stratification (warm for three months then cold for six months) and are slow to germinate.

Pests and diseases

Rarely affected by diseases, just occasionally by verticillium wilt. American elder is resistant to honey fungus (*Armillaria* spp.)

Aphids are a very common pest on the young shoots, particularly blackfly. As long as you have predator-attracting plants in your growing system, these should not ever become a problem.

If growing for fruit, then birds are likely to be a significant pest. Birds love elder fruit and bird-deterrents may need to be utilised as fruit begin to ripen until harvest is finished.

Related species

Several other species have similar uses including:

Blue elder, *Sambucus caerulea*, is more tree-like with similar edible flowers and fruit.

European elder, *Sambucus nigra*, is more tree-like and described in *Trees for Gardens, Orchards and Permaculture* (see Bibliography, p.234).

European red elder, *Sambucus racemosa*, is a similar sized shrub with similar edible flowers and fruit.

BAMBOOS

Zone 5-8, H4-7
Evergreen
Edible shoots
Canes for garden uses, construction etc.

Origin and history

Bamboos are one of those plants that should be growing in every garden, both for their beauty and their useful canes and edible shoots.

The majority of hardier species come from China, and across Asia there is a very long history of using bamboos for food, as a building material and for many other uses.

Description

Bamboos are a subfamily of the grasses, with tree-like or shrubby forms and woody stems. According to the latest classification there are some 115 bamboo genera and over a thousand species. The main useful hardier genera described here are *Arundinaria*, *Chusquea*, *Drepanostachyum*, *Fargesia*, *Indocalamus*, *Phyllostachys*, *Pleioblastus*, *Pseudosasa*, *Semiarundinaria*, *Thamnocalamus* and *Yushania*. Other genera that can be grown include *Brachystachyum*, *Chimonobambusa*, *Clavinodum*, *Himalayacalamus* and *Sinobambusa*. In this book we don't cover the small/dwarf bamboos that are of limited use as crops.

Bamboos are generally very hardy and vigorous, evergreen, shrub-like grasses with extensive root systems. The main structural parts – rhizomes, aerial culms (canes) and culm branches – are all formed according to the same principle: an alternating series of nodes and internodes. As bamboo grows,

Phyllostachys viridiglaucescens

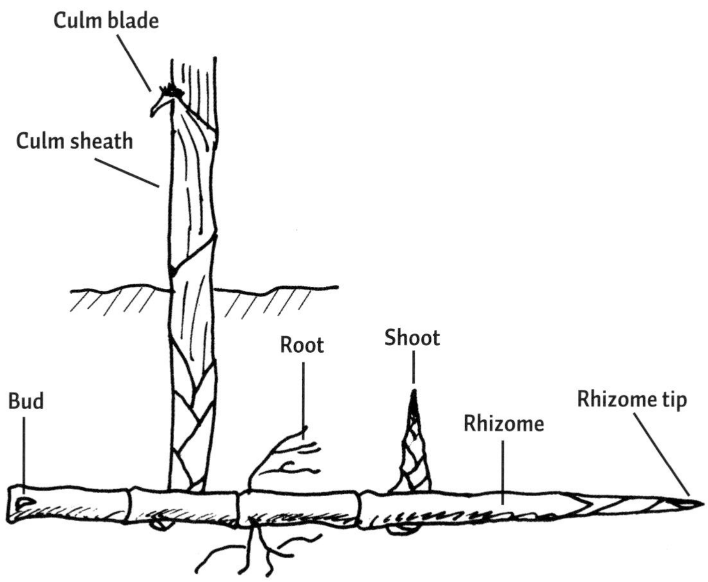

Leptomorph (monopedial/running) bamboo

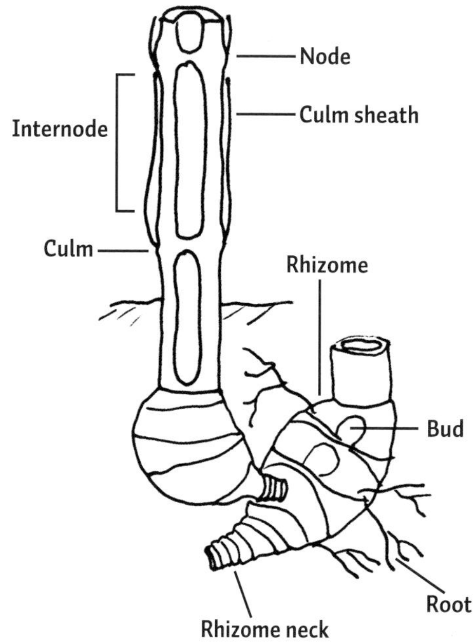

Pachymorph (sympodial/clumping) bamboo with culms in cross section

each new internode is wrapped in a protective sheath, itself attached to the preceding node at the sheath ring.

The young shoots which emerge from the ground maintain their initial diameter, and this will be the diameter the culm remains throughout its life; bamboos do not grow in width like trees do. Similarly, the length that a shoot reaches in its growth season is its final length; there is no yearly increase.

Branches are formed on culms at the nodes, and leaves on the branches. The number of branches and leaves on each culm do increase each year. New young leaves are usually produced in spring at the same time as old leaves are gradually lost.

Young developing bamboo plants produce progressively thicker and taller stems each year, until the clump reaches maturity.

Rhizomes

Rhizomes are the underground stems which grow and branch away from the bamboo plant, colonising new territory. Each year, culms arise from the rhizomes to form the aerial parts of the plant.

Rhizomes are often tightly packed in the soil, most (some 80%) in the top 30cm (1ft), rarely deeper than 50cm (20ins) but occasionally as deep as 1m (3ft). Growth only takes place at the tip of the rhizome, which is the site of cell division. Rhizomes grow on, continually branching and producing new tissue, which differentiates alternately as node or internode. The growing point is very hard, facilitating penetration through the soil; it is formed of tightly overlapping sheaths which enclose each developing internode as the rhizome moves forward. These sheaths are very short-lived, quickly dying and rotting away once the new internodes have hardened.

Rhizomes can be broadly divided into two growth types: pachymorph (clumping) and leptomorph (running); this determines whether the grove will be invasive or clump-forming, and also the distance between individual culms. Most hardier bamboos have leptomorph rhizomes, so they are running bamboos which try and expand their area every year. This is why bamboos have a reputation of being invasive. However, if you are growing bamboo as a crop, there is no need to fear their spread: harvesting maintains the clump size within bounds. Taller running bamboos tend to be less spreading and grow in tighter clumps.

Culms (canes)

In summer and autumn the rhizomes build up and store all the material required for rapid growth in the following spring. The shoots begin to develop underground in the autumn and contain all the basic organs of the culm. In running bamboos, shooting is initiated by temperature, so mostly occurs in the spring from April to June or July. When shoots appear, their diameter indicates the diameter of the culm which will develop from them; the eventual number of internodes (and thus the height of the culm) is predetermined in the shoot, which grows out telescopically with great speed, to full height in around 4-6 weeks. In Britain, culms can grow up to 25cm (10ins) per day.

Culms may be erect or curving, and are normally green but may also be yellow, brown, black or red and may be spotted or striped. Culms are divided into many segments comprising alternate nodes and internodes; as in cereals, the culm is stabilised by the tough nodes. Most culms are circular in section, and have hollow internodes. Hardened culms consist of cellulose fibres up to 10mm (0.4ins) long (as opposed to 1mm in tree woods) and contain both lignin and silica, giving them great strength and resilience. Individual culms may live for 5-10 years or more, depending on the species.

In some species (e.g. *Chimonobambusa*) plants produce a culm with no branches or leaves in the first season of growth, with branches developing in the next season; others produce branches and leaves on the culm in its season of growth.

Leaves and flowers

Bamboo leaves (or more strictly, leaf blades) don't simply grow out from buds as in trees, but develop from a sheath which encircles the stem called a leaf sheath. The leaf blades are attached to their sheaths by short, stalk-like projections of their midribs.

Leaves are thin, elongated and lanceolate, rounded at the base and pointed at the tip. The length and breadth vary widely with species. Individual leaves live for up to two years, usually falling in the spring. In some species, an extreme drought causes a complete shedding of the leaves.

Bamboos in general come into flower only very rarely. Some species flower frequently (e.g. some *Fargesia*) but most only at intervals of up to or over 100 years.

Flowers are similar to other grass flowers and are wind-pollinated. The seeds produced are most commonly the size and appearance of a grain of wheat (and indeed have often been used as a grain), and if fertile will germinate readily; seeds only remain viable for a short period. After flowering, it is common for plants to die because all their energy has been used up and too few leaves have been produced during flowering to facilitate photosynthesis. In the wild, profuse regeneration by seed would be expected.

Uses

Edible shoots

Shoots of most (probably all) hardy species are edible. The following table gives more information on the time of shoot emergence (early spring = April, mid spring = May, late spring = June in southern England) and shoot quality where known.

Species	Emergence	Comments on shoots
Phyllostachys angusta	Mid spring	Free of bitterness
Phyllostachys aureosulcata	Mid spring	Free of bitterness
Phyllostachys bambusoides	Late spring	Bitter when raw
Phyllostachys dulcis	Early spring	Prized, major Chinese edible shoot
Phyllostachys edulis	Mid spring	Prized, major Japanese edible shoot
Phyllostachys flexuosa	Mid spring	Acrid when raw
Phyllostachys glauca	Mid spring	Fairly free of bitterness
Phyllostachys nidularia	Early spring	
Phyllostachys nigra	Late spring	Bitter when raw
Phyllostachys nuda	Spring	Fairly free of bitterness raw; good quality
Phyllostachys rubromarginata	Late spring	Good quality
Phyllostachys sulphurea viridis	Mid spring	Fairly free of bitterness; quite good quality
Phyllostachys viridiglaucescens	Early spring	Fairly free of bitterness
Phyllostachys vivax	Late spring	Free of bitterness
Pleioblastus simonii	Spring	Fair quality
Pseudosasa japonica		Early spring

Canned bamboo shoots are usually from *Phyllostachys edulis*.

Canes

The culms (canes) of most bamboo species can be cut and used (before or after drying), especially the erect species. For production of 2-3m length canes, vigorous species that send up lots of new shoots each year are preferable. The most highly recommended species are:

Phyllostachys violascens
Phyllostachys viridiglaucescens
Phyllostachys vivax
Pleioblastus simonii
Pseudosasa japonica
Semiarundinaria fastuosa
Yushiana maculata
Yushiana maling

Hedging

Species that tolerate some wind exposure can be used for hedging but note that bamboo will not work well in really exposed hedges, where the canes tend to sway excessively and break at the base. Plants should be spaced at about 1m (3ft) apart to grow into an effective hedge. Bamboo hedges are 50-60% permeable which is ideal to reduce wind speeds. The main drawback of using bamboos in quantity in hedges is their price: they are very expensive to buy because of the time involved in propagation.

Yushania maculata

Other uses

The importance of bamboo has not been diminished in Asia by the introduction of modern substitutes. Bamboo is light and hard, flexible and tough, hard to set on fire, bendable under heat, splittable into fine fibres. A bamboo pipe is as strong as steel, but more malleable and doesn't rust.

Bamboo can be drilled by drilling from the outside with a steel bit; to saw, use a very fine hacksaw; to split, knock a knife through the cane (split cane can be flattened with a very hot flat iron); to bend thin fresh canes, just bend into circles and tie (they keep their shape after a few days); thicker pieces of bamboo become soft and pliable at about 150°C and can be worked over a gas flame or heat of glowing charcoal; to paint, first use fine sandpaper.

Many or all species of bamboo can be put to numerous different uses, including:

- Harvested and pulped to make paper and bamboo cloth (the bamboo fibres are long). The leaves as well as the culms have been used to make paper.
- Animal fodder – the leaves and young shoots are relished by ruminants.
- Soil stabilisers, controlling erosion – the root systems are good soil binders.
- The seeds, probably of all species, are edible in the same way as other grass seeds (e.g. wheat, rice), and are used as a cereal crop in China when flowering occurs (irregularly). They are also brewed into a bamboo beer and sake.
- Ground cover – several smaller species make excellent ground cover in shady sites, particularly the *Pleioblastus*, *Sasa* and *Sasaella* species. To make a good cover, 8-12 plants/m^2 will take 1-2 years; 5-7 plants/m^2 will take 2-3 years; three plants/m^2 will take 3-4 years; one plant/m^2 will take 4-5 years.
- Utensils and implements both domestic and agricultural, e.g. cups, pipes, rakes, brooms, ladders, brushes, carts, furniture, wheelbarrows.
- Bicycle frames (much used and manufactured in Europe in the late 1800s).
- Musical instruments such as flutes.
- Matting, screening, fencing, etc. often split and used like basketry willow.
- Ropes, made by splitting culms into fine fibres, then twisting. Often used in conjunction with canes for making bridges.
- Weapons – bows, arrows, blowpipes.
- Baskets – very widespread in Asia, used for all carrying tasks and even for cooking (steaming), made from split culms.
- Construction – used for all aspects in Asia, including house foundations, flooring, walls, blinds, roof frames. Also used for scaffolding on larger concrete buildings, and for shuttering. Used to make bamboo reinforced concrete.

Varieties/Cultivars

KEY TO SPECIES TABLE

Size: S = small, up to 1.5m; M = medium, 1.5-3m; L = large (3-6m); VL = very large (over 6m).

Width: Culm width at ground level: S = slender, 5-15 mm; M = medium, 15-25mm; T = thick, 25-45mm; VT = very thick, over 45mm.

Culm: Culm habit: E = erect/straight, A = arching, Z = zig-zag.

Habit: Rhizome habit: C= clumping, MI = moderately invasive, I = invasive, VI = very invasive.

Hardy: Minimum winter temperature survivable in °C.

Hedge: Can be used for hedging – tolerates some exposure.

Canes: Noted as providing good straight cut canes. (Most erect species will also do so.)

Edible: Young shoots have been particularly noted as edible (but all hardy species probably have edible shoots).

Species	Size	Width	Culm	Habit	Hardy	Hedge	Canes	Edible
Arundinaria gigantea	M	M	E	MI	-10			✓
Chimonobambusa marmoreal	S-M	S	E	I	-15		✓	
Chimonobambusa microphylla	M	S		MI	-15		✓	
Chimonobambusa quadrangularis	M	M	E	I	-15		✓	✓
Chusquea culeou	L	T	.	C	-15	✓		✓
Chusquea culeou tenuis	S	M	A	C	-15	✓		✓
Chusquea ramosissima	L	T	A	C	-10		✓	
Drepanostachyum falcatum	L	M	A	C	-12		✓	
Drepanostachyum khasianum	L	M		C	-10		✓	
Drepanostachyum microphyllum	L	M		C	-10		✓	
Fargesia dracocephala	L	S	A	C	-20	✓		
Fargesia murieliae	L	S	A	C	-25	✓	✓	
Fargesia nitida	L	S	A	C	-20	✓	✓	
Himalayacalamus falconeri	L	M	E	C	-8		✓	
Himalaycalamus hookerianus	L	M	E	C	-10		✓	
Phyllostachys angusta	L	T	E	MI	-17		✓	✓
Phyllostachys arcana	L	T	E,Z	MI	-15		✓	
Phyllostachys atrovaginata	L	T	E	MI	-15		✓	
Phyllostachys aurea	L	T	E	MI	-20	✓	✓	✓
Phyllostachys aureosulcata	L	T	E	MI	-20	✓	✓	✓
Phyllostachys bambusoides	VL	VT	E	MI	-18		✓	✓
Phyllostachys bissettii	L	T	E	MI	-21	✓	✓	
Phyllostachys decora	L	T	E	MI	-21		✓	
Phyllostachys dulcis	L	T	A	MI	-10		✓	✓
Phyllostachys edulis	VL	VT	E	MI	-16		✓	✓
Phyllostachys edulis heterocycla	L	T	E	MI	-16		✓	✓
Phyllostachys flexuosa	M-L	M	A	MI	-17	✓	✓	✓
Phyllostachys fulva	L	S	E	MI	-15		✓	
Phyllostachys glauca	L	M-T	A	MI	-20		✓	✓
Phyllostachys heteroclada	L	M-T	E	MI	.		✓	
Phyllostachys humilis	M	S	E	MI	-13	✓		
Phyllostachys iridescens	L	T	Z	MI	.		✓	
Phyllostachys makinoi	L	T	E	MI	-12		✓	
Phyllostachys mannii	L	T	E	MI	-15		✓	
Phyllostachys marliacea	M	M		MI	-20		✓	

Species	Size	Width	Culm	Habit	Hardy	Hedge	Canes	Edible
Phyllostachys meyeri	L	T	E	MI	-18		✓	✓
Phyllostachys nidularia	L	T	E	MI	-12		✓	✓
Phyllostachys nigra	L	M-T	A	MI	-18	✓	✓	✓
Phyllostachys nigra 'Boryana'	VL	T	A	MI	-20	✓	✓	✓
Phyllostachys nigra f. punctata	L	T	A	C	-17		✓	✓
Phyllostachys nigra henonis	L-VL	T	A	C	-20	✓	✓	✓
Phyllostachys nuda	L	T	E	MI	-24		✓	✓
Phyllostachys propinqua	L	T	E	MI	-15		✓	
Phyllostachys rubromarginata	VL	T	E	MI	-15		✓	✓
Phyllostachys sulphurea	L	VT	E	MI	-20		✓	
Phyllostachys sulphurea viridis	L	VT	E	MI	-20		✓	✓
Phyllostachys violascens	L	T	E	I	-20		✓	
Phyllostachys viridiglaucescens	L-VL	T	E	MI	-20	✓	✓	✓
Phyllostachys vivax	VL	T-VT	E	MI	-12		✓	✓
Pleioblastus chino angustifolius	M	M		VI	-15		✓	
Pleioblastus gramineus	L	M	A	MI	-15		✓	
Pleioblastus hindsii	L	M	E	MI	-15		✓	
Pleioblastus linearis	L	M	A	MI	-15	✓	✓	
Pleioblastus oleosus	L	M	.	MI	.		✓	
Pleioblastus shibuyanus	S	S	.	I	.			
Pleioblastus simonii	L	M	E	MI	-23	✓	✓	✓
Pleioblastus variegatus	S	VS	.	MI	-20			
Pseudosasa amabilis	L	M	E	MI	-10		✓	
Pseudosasa japonica	L	M	E	MI	-24	✓	✓	✓
Pseudosasa owatarii	S	VS	.	I	-15			
Pseudosasa pleioblastoides	L	M	E	MI	-15	✓	✓	
Semiarundinaria fastuosa	VL	T	E	MI	-22	✓	✓	✓
Semiarundinaria kagamaniana	L-VL	T	E	MI	-20	✓	✓	✓
Semiarundinaria yamadorii	M-L	M	E,Z	MI	-15		✓	✓
Semiarundinaria yashadake	L	T	E	MI	-20		✓	
Sinobambusa tootsik	L	T	.	MI	-10		✓	
Thamnocalamus spathiflorus	L	M	A	C	-12		✓	
Thamnocalamus tessellatus	L	M	E	C	-15		✓	
Yushiana anceps	L	M	E	I	-20	✓	✓	
Yushiana anceps 'Pitt White'	VL	M	E	I	-15	✓	✓	
Yushiana maculata	L	M-T	E	MI	-15	✓	✓	
Yushiana maling	L	M-T	E	I	-10		✓	

New shoots of *Phyllostachys edulis*

Bamboo shoot emerging

Cultivation

Bamboos are easily cultivated. They need a moist soil, preferably fairly rich; they cannot tolerate waterlogging, and in dry sites the shoots can wither. A wide range of soil pH is tolerated. Shelter from strong cold winds is essential for most species, although those recommended for hedging here tolerate exposure. Ground preparation need not be too deep, as bamboos are relatively shallow rooted.

Most of hardier species prefer a position in sun but easily tolerate some shade and just about survive in deeper shade. In hot summer climates they prefer a part shady position.

To prevent plants running where they are not desired, simply harvest the shoots where they emerge. Once severed, a shoot will not usually resprout in that season, and the rhizome extension is halted. Hence to control the size of a clump, the important thing is to define a boundary for it, and harvest shoots to eat that come up beyond the boundary through spring. In larger spaces, a root barrier is unnecessary, but in a small garden, especially if you are planting near your boundary, a root barrier installed 50cm (20ins) deep may be a good idea to stop the plant spreading to your neighbour's. You can buy root barrier material made for bamboos.

Regular harvesting of shoots or culms will necessitate feeding the plants, particularly with a nitrogen source, otherwise you'll see a reduction in culm width/height. Nearby (overhead) nitrogen-fixing trees can be very effective.

Each year after planting, the culms that emerge will be thicker and grow higher until a maximum is reached (after 8-10 years) which depends on the species and your climate. The same species will grow bigger in a warmer climate.

Edible shoot production

Cut shoots at around 25-30cm (10-12ins) high, at ground level (or you can dig down a bit to get a longer crop).

Shoots are prepared by cutting off the woody proportion at the base, then a slit is made lengthwise through the outer papery sheaths, which are removed to expose the white/pale green flesh. Cut these into pieces and steam for five minutes to remove any bitterness before eating. Steamed bamboo shoots have a flavour reminiscent of steamed courgette with a little pea flavour added in.

Cane production

Fresh cut canes can be used immediately outside but won't be very durable. To increase durability (to about five years) the canes should be dried. Only ripe canes should be cut for drying; culms take three years to mature and lignify. You need to be systematic and paint a dot of colour on each year's growth, so you can easily identify the three-year-old canes. These should be severed close to the ground; you need heavy duty branch cutters for large canes. Cut off any stub left, otherwise someone will trip over it.

Once the cane is cut, all branches should be cut off close to the stem, and the fine whippy top cut off. These are discarded or perhaps used for fine basketry. Dry slowly, laid flat under cover but in good ventilation, turning occasionally. Each 4mm of diameter requires about one month of drying, thus 12mm (0.5ins) canes need three months of drying and 25mm (1ins) canes need six months drying.

Commercial plantations plant running species at 2.4-3m (8-10ft) spacing (i.e. around 450-550 per acre, 1100-1400 per hectare) in rich, well-drained soils. While the plants establish, considerable labour is needed for hand weeding. Cutting proceeds as above, but care is taken not to cut too many culms at the edges of the grove, for this can lead to a band of dead rhizomes which restrict living rhizomes, forcing them back into the grove. Kiln drying is often used to cure canes, though it can't be too rapid as this splits the outer membrane of several species.

Propagation

Propagation is usually by dividing existing clumps in spring. You are likely to need axes, saws and maybe a pickaxe and it is quite tough work! Pot up the new clump for a year before planting out.

Occasionally seed is produced and this should be sown immediately. Protect against rodents. Germination is fast.

Pests and diseases

Bamboos are naturally robust plants, suffering from few diseases. The young shoots are attractive to rabbits, squirrels and deer, so young plants may need protection for a few years.

BARBERRIES, *Berberis* species

Zone 3-8, H4-7
Deciduous, evergreen, semi-evergreen
Bee plant, edible fruit, hedging

Origin and history

The barberries are a group of evergreen and deciduous thorny shrubs, with some 450 species in Europe, North Africa, the Americas and Asia. They are found wild in or by light woodlands. Most are small or large shrubs up to 3m (10ft) high.

Description

General characteristics are: wood and inner bark is yellow; leaves, often with spiny margins, are borne in clusters, and on long shoots often develop three-parted thorns; flowers, often borne in profusion in spring or summer, are normally yellow or orange, and pollinated by insects, often by bees; fruits are richly-coloured berries, sometimes persisting into winter, with one or more small seeds. Fruits mostly ripen in late summer, September onwards. Many of the deciduous species have brightly coloured autumn leaves.

Uses

Uses of individual species are summarised in the table below and detailed in the species descriptions later.

Berberis flowers are highly desirable for bees, including wild bumblebees and honey bees.

The fruits of many species have been used for food either raw, cooked or in preserves but are usually rather acid and best cooked. Some are grown commercially for the fruit to be used fresh or cooked, or for the fruit juice to be used as a food colouring.

Yellow dyes are obtained from the roots (and sometimes the stems/bark) of most species due to the yellow wood.

Medicinal uses for various extracts are common. The compounds berbamine and berberine are present in the roots and stem bark and, sometimes, other parts of most species. Berbamine is leukogenic in effect and used in chemotherapy and radiotherapy (see *B. vulgaris* below for further uses). Several species are used medicinally in China to treat insomnia, feverish delirium, inflammation of the mouth and tongue, and diarrhoea caused by enteritis and dysentery.

The alkaloids found in most species have potential uses in disease and pest control; *B. aristata*, *B. thunbergii* and *B. vulgaris* can all be used in this way.

Most species make good hedges (including many not listed below), being prickly and generally impenetrable to people and livestock.

Most species provide good nesting sites for birds and the berries may be taken by birds; if so they may be useful as sacrificial crops.

Common barberry (*Berberis vulgaris*)

Varieties/Cultivars

Note that in the following species descriptions, simply ornamental varieties have not been listed; those listed have good, larger, or abundant fruit, or some other advantage.

The table below summarises the main characteristics and uses of the most useful *Berberis* species.

Species	Deciduous/ evergreen	Height (m)	Hardiness	Flowering (UK)	Fruit size (mm)	Edible fruit	Medicinal	Ground cover
B. aggregata	Deciduous	2.5	Z6/H6	May-Jun	4-5 x 5-7	✓		
B. amurensis	Deciduous	3.5	Z6/H6	May	10	✓	✓	
B. angulosa	Deciduous	1.5	Z6/H6	Jul-Aug	12-15	✓		
B. aristata	Deciduous	3.0	Z6/H6	May	4-6 x 7-12	✓	✓	
B. asiatica	Evergreen	3.0	Z7/H5-6	May-Jun	8	✓	✓	
B. buxifolia	Evergreen	3.0	Z6-7/H6	Apr-May	8	✓		✓
B. calliantha	Evergreen	0.7	Z7/H5-6	May	10			✓
B. canadensis	Deciduous	1.3	Z5-6/H7	May-Jun	7-10	✓		
B. candidula	Evergreen	0.5	Z5-6/H7	May	9-12			✓
B. x carminea	Semi-evergreen	1.0	Z6/H6	Jun-Jul	5-8 x 8-9	✓		
B. chengii	Deciduous		Z6/H6			✓	✓	
B. chinensis	Deciduous	3.0	Z5/H7	May		✓		
B. chitria	Semi-evergreen	3.0	Z7-8/H5	May	8-12	✓	✓	
B. cooperi	Deciduous	2.0			8	✓		
B. coxii	Evergreen	1.5	Z6/H6	May	10			✓
B. darwinii	Evergreen	3.0	Z7/H5-6	Apr-May	7	✓	✓	
B. empetrifolia	Evergreen	0.3	Z7/H5-6	May	7	✓		✓
B. fendleri	Deciduous	1.5	Z6/H6	May	5	✓		
B. flexuosa	Deciduous					✓		
B. francisci-fernandi	Deciduous	3.0	Z6/H6	May	12	✓		
B. gagnepainii	Evergreen	1.5	Z6/H6	May-Jun	10	✓		
B. georgii	Deciduous	3.0	Z3/H7	May		✓		
B. heterophylla	Semi-evergreen	1.5	Z7/H5-6	Apr-May	6-7	✓		
B. hookeri	Evergreen	0.5	Z6/H6	May	15 x 8			✓
B. integerrima	Deciduous	3.0				✓	✓	
B. jaeschkeana	Deciduous	1.0	Z6/H6			✓		
B. julianae	Evergreen	3.0	Z5-6/H7	May-Jun	8			
B. koreana	Deciduous	2.0	Z4/H7	May	8	✓		
B. x laxiflora	Deciduous	2.5	Z5/H7			✓		
B. lyceum	Semi-evergreen	3.5	Z6/H6	May-Jun	8-12	✓	✓	
B. poiretii	Deciduous	2.0	Z5-6/H7	May	10	✓		
B. polyantha	Semi-evergreen	2.0+	Z5-6/H6		8 x 4	✓		

Species	Deciduous/ evergreen	Height (m)	Hardiness	Flowering (UK)	Fruit size (mm)	Edible fruit	Medicinal	Ground cover
B. prattii	Deciduous	3.0	Z5-6/H7	Jul-Aug	8			
B. x rubrostylla	Deciduous	1.0	Z6/H6	Jun	10-17	✓		
B. ruscifolia	Evergreen	2.0	Z6/H6		6-7	✓		
B. sargentiana	Evergreen	2.0	Z6/H6	May-Jun	6-7		✓	
B. sherriffii	Deciduous	3.0	Z6/H6	Jun-Jul	6-8	✓		
B. sibirica	Deciduous	0.5	Z3/H7	May	7	✓		
B. sieboldii	Deciduous	1.0	Z5-6/H7	May	5	✓		
B. soulieana	Evergreen	1.5	Z6/H6	May		✓		
B. x stenophylla	Evergreen	3.0	Z7/H5-6	Apr-May	7-15	✓		✓
B. thunbergii	Deciduous	1.0	Z5/H7	Apr-May	8	✓	✓	✓
B. tomentosa	Evergreen		Z8/H4-5			✓		
B. verruculosa	Evergreen	1.5	Z6/H6	June	10-12	✓		✓
B. vulgaris	Deciduous	3.0	Z3/H7	May-Jun	9-12	✓	✓	
B. wilsoniae	Deciduous	1.0	Z6/H6	May-Jun	6-8	✓		✓

B. aggregata – Salmon berberis, Salmon barberry

Native to Western China; a densely-branched shrub with light yellow flowers and masses of cinnamon-red fruit. Hybridises, especially freely with *B. wilsoniae*.

Fruits are edible raw or cooked; they have a fairly acid, lemon flavour.

Crimson Bead – bears numerous oblong, carmine fruit slightly smaller than normal (5 x 4mm).

Sibbertoft Coral – has larger red fruit (7 x 5mm).

B. amurensis – Amur barberry

Native to northeastern Asia. A narrow upright shrub with huge drooping racemes of flowers and elliptical bright red fruit.

Fruits are edible, usually cooked and used in preserves. They are high in organic acids. Leaves also reportedly edible. The roots are used in traditional medicine as an antirheumatic, and the plant against cancer.

B. angulosa

Native to the Himalayas. Small with elliptical scarlet fruit, freely borne.

Fruits are edible raw or cooked (slightly sour). They are more palatable than most barberries.

B. aristata – Indian barberry, Nepal barberry

Native to Nepal. Yellow and reddish flowers are followed by reddish fruit.

Fruits are edible raw or cooked; they have a good sweet-acid flavour with slightly bitter seeds. Fruits are sometimes sold in India where they are often dried (they can dry on the bush) and used like raisins. One bush can yield about 650g fruit. Fruits are high in organic acids, and contain 2.3% protein, 12% sugars, 0.6% tannins, 0.4% pectin and 6.4mg/100ml juice vitamin C. Flower buds are also edible, often added to sauces.

The stem bark is used in traditional medicine for eye infections, fevers, skin diseases, jaundice, malarial fever and as an anti-inflammatory.

Extracts from the roots and stems are also used for tanning.

The stems and branches have an insecticidal effect against mosquitoes.

B. asiatica – Asiatic barberry, Himalayan barberry, Raisin barberry

Native to the Himalayas, an evergreen shrub with branches often twining with yellow flowers that are followed by roundish red-black fruit. Tolerates deep shade. Plants are apt to be cut down to the ground in severe winters, but resprout well from the base.

Fruits are edible raw or dried as 'raisins'.

The root bark is used in traditional medicine.

B. buxifolia – Magellan barberry

Native to southern Chile, an evergreen shrub which in severe winters may be deciduous. Orange-yellow flowers are followed by freely borne reddish-black rounded fruit.

Fruits, of pleasant flavour, are edible raw or cooked in preserves. The unripe green fruit may also be cooked in pies etc.

Nana (*B. buxifolia nana*) – a dwarf cultivar with dense growth, seldom reaching 30cm, makes a good low hedging plant or ground cover. It flowers but may be self-sterile, without fruit.

B. calliantha

Native to Tibet, an evergreen shrub with clusters of yellow flowers and ovoid purple-black fruit. Suckering freely and forming thickets.

Makes a good ground cover plant.

B. canadensis – Alleghany barberry, American barberry

Native to eastern North America, a small shrub with reddish-brown pendulous branches; leaves turn a magnificent scarlet-red in autumn. Yellow flowers are followed by elliptical, deep red fruit. An alternate host of black stem rust of cereals.

Fruits are edible raw or cooked – agreeably acid. Used in preserves. Leaves are also edible raw, and the flowers are also reported to be edible.

B. candidula

Native to eastern North America, a dwarf, dense, rounded shrub with solitary yellow flowers and greyish ovoid fruit. Slow growing.

Makes a good ground cover plant.

B. x carminea

A group of hybrids of *B. aggregata* and *B. wilsoniae*. Shrubs with yellow branches and a profusion of carmine-red, ovate fruit.

Fruits are edible, raw or cooked.

Aurora – fruit vermillion, roundish, 8 x 8mm. A medium sized shrub with dark red twigs.

Barbarossa – semi-evergreen, medium sized shrub with dark red branches. Fruit in profusion, scarlet, oblong, 7mm long.

Bountiful – semi-evergreen shrub with dark red branches. Fruits are scarlet, roundish, to 8.5mm.

Buccaneer – semi-evergreen shrub with round, whitish turning shiny red fruit, to 9mm, in large clusters persisting into December.

B. chengii

Native to China.

Fruits edible raw or cooked.

The plant is used medicinally in China, being antibacterial, anti-inflammatory, antipyretic, and depurative. Used for abscesses, boils, burns, enteritis, fevers, gastritis, laryngitis.

B. chinensis

Native to China.

Fruits, dark red, are edible raw or cooked.

B. chitria

Native to Nepal and the Himalayas. Shrub, often semi-evergreen, with yellow flowers followed by bright red oblong fruit.

Fruits are edible raw or cooked.

A root/stem extract is used in traditional medicine for eye infections.

B. cooperi

Native to Bhutan.

Fruits are edible raw or cooked, acid, but pleasant in small quantities.

B. coxii

Native to Tibet. A vigorous evergreen shrub with clusters of pale yellow flowers followed by blue egg-shaped fruit. Spreading by suckers and forming thickets.

Makes a good ground cover.

B. darwinii – Darwin's barberry

Native to Chile and Patagonia. A dense evergreen shrub with tiny holly-like leaves. Golden-yellow flowers are followed by round bluish-green to black fruit ripening in July and August. Succeeds on chalky soils but prefers acid soils; tolerates exposure, flowering and fruiting well.

Fruits are edible raw or cooked; used in preserves. Rather acid and seedy but quite good.

Roots and bark are traditionally used medicinally as a tonic.

Berberis 'Buccaneer' in flower

Gold – grows 1-1.5m high; numerous golden-yellow flowers followed by fruit. Early flowering in mild regions (from February to May).

Prostrata – a dwarf cultivar, growing 40-50cm high. Makes a good ground cover and low hedging plant. Flowers abundantly.

B. empetrifolia – Fuegian barberry

Native to Chile and Tierra del Fuego, this is a prostrate evergreen shrub. Golden-yellow flowers are followed by round blue-black fruit. Needs a well-drained site; intolerant of shallow chalk soils.

Edible fruit, raw or cooked.

B. fendleri

Native to western North America, a shrub with glossy reddish-brown branches. Orange-yellow flowers are followed by roundish red fruit.

Edible fruit, raw or cooked.

B. flexuosa

Native to South America.

Edible fruit, raw or cooked.

B. francisci-fernandi

Native to western China, a vigorous drooping shrub with yellow flowers followed by abundant scarlet ellipsoid fruit.

Fruits are very high in organic acids (14.25%) which are extracted for food use.

B. gagnepainii

Native to western China, an evergreen small shrub. Small groups of golden-yellow flowers are followed by blue-black ovate fruit.

Edible fruit, raw or cooked.

Makes an impenetrable hedge.

B. georgii

A hybrid of unknown origin (probably includes *B. vulgaris*). A shrub with arching branches, yellow flowers and profuse crimson berries in large clusters. Exceptionally free-fruiting.

An alternate host of black stem rust of wheat.

Edible fruit, raw or cooked: very acid, mainly used in preserves. A refreshing lemon-like drink can be made from the fruit.

B. heterophylla

Native to western Chile and Tierra del Fuego, this is a semi-evergreen shrub, spreading via suckers. Solitary orange-yellow flowers are followed by round black fruit.

Edible fruit, raw or cooked.

B. hookeri

Native to the Himalayas. An evergreen shrub with green or pale yellow flowers followed by large mauve-black, glossy oblong fruit. Thicket-forming.

Makes a good ground cover.

B. integerrima (synonym *B. densiflora*) – Zereshk

Originating from North Africa, Iranian seedless barberry has long been cultivated along with *B. vulgaris* for its fruit in South Khorasan, Iran. There are more than 11,000ha under production producing more than 9,200 tonnes of dried fruit, annually. All orchards are established from sucker propagation. Cold hardy and drought tolerant. Shrubs are planted 2m x 3m apart and trained to a multiple-trunk system to facilitate harvest. Biennial bearing is a problem and sometimes no fruit is harvested in the off year. Fruits are harvested in the autumn and sun drying is used.

The plant and its fruits have long been used in traditional medicine – it is well documented for its anti-diabetic, anti-cancer, and antimicrobial activities with berberine as the main active constituent.

The fruits are used for food, and anthocyanins from fruit are useful as a natural colouring agent in food industries.

B. jaeschkeana

Native to Kashmir.

Edible fruit, raw or cooked.

B. julianae

Native to central China. A vigorous, upright, densely-branched, robust evergreen shrub with yellow flowers followed by blue-black oblong fruit.

Makes an excellent hedging shrub.

B. koreana – Korean barberry

Native to Korea. A very hardy shrub with numerous flowers followed by bright red, glossy fruit. Suckers freely.

Edible fruit, raw or cooked; very high in vitamin C (72.5mg/100g), and high in organic acids. One of the best quality *Berberis* fruit for fresh eating. Young leaves are edible when cooked.

Red Tears – vigorous growing to 2m; fruit in long racemes (10cm), 12 x 7mm, long-lasting.

B. x laxiflora

A hybrid, probably of *B. chinensis* and *B. vulgaris*.

Fruits are high in sugars and extracts are used in the food industry.

B. lycium – Indian barberry

Native to the Himalayas from Kashmir to Nepal. Often semi-evergreen, with golden-yellow flowers followed by elliptic purple fruit.

Edible fruit, raw or cooked; made into preserves. Fairly juicy with a nice slightly acid flavour. If left will often dry on the bush.

Flowers of Korean barberry

Berries of Korean barberry

Leaves and young shoots are edible cooked; leaves have been used as a tea substitute.

Roots are traditionally used medicinally, being aperient, carminative, febrifuge, and ophthalmic; they are used for fevers and haemorrhoids.

B. poiretii

Native to northern China, this is a dwarf shrub with nodding branches, abundant light yellow and reddish flowers and oblong light red fruit.

Fruits are edible.

B. polyantha

Native to western China. An erect, semi-evergreen shrub, with abundant flowers followed by grape-like clusters of narrowly ovoid red fruit.

Fruits are very high in organic acids (14.36%) and extracts are used in the food industry.

B. prattii

Native to western China. Has numerous flowers followed by salmon-red fruit. Fruits ripen in late autumn (November) and persist through the winter; not taken by birds.

A good bee plant, supplying nectar and pollen to honey and bumblebees in early summer.

B. x *rubrostilla*

A group of hybrids, probably of *B. wilsoniae* with *B. aggregata*. Shrubs with light yellow flowers followed by scarlet ovate or pear-shaped fruit.

Edible fruit, raw or cooked: acid flavour.

Chealii – fruits are dark red, oblong, 10 x 8mm. Borne abundantly.

Crawleyensis – fruits are oval, bright red, up to 17mm long and 5mm thick, borne abundantly.

B. ruscifolia

Native to Chile and Argentina, an evergreen shrub with blue-black fruit.

Edible fruit when cooked – somewhat bitter.

B. sargentiana – Chinese barberry

Native to central China, an evergreen, densely branching shrub with yellow flowers and purple-black oblong fruit. Sometimes semi-evergreen in cultivation.

Used in traditional Chinese medicine.

B. sherriffii

Native to Tibet, a shrub bearing masses of blue-black oblong fruit.

Edible fruit, raw or cooked.

B. sibirica – Siberian barberry

Native to Siberia. A very hardy, rounded shrub with pale yellow flowers followed by masses of green or red fruit.

Edible fruit, raw or cooked.

B. sieboldii

Native to Japan, a shrub closely related to *B. vulgaris* with light yellow flowers followed by round, light red, glossy fruit. May be an alternate host for black stem rust in wheat. Plants sucker freely, forming thickets.

Edible fruit, raw or cooked.

B. soulieana

Native to China, an evergreen shrub with mauve-black fruit.

Edible fruit, raw or cooked.

B. x *stenophylla*

Hybrids of *B. darwinii* and *B. empetrifolia*, evergreen shrubs with yellowish-orange flowers followed by round black fruit. Prefers part shade; tolerates maritime exposure; fairly slow growing. Very ornamental, many named varieties. Plants sucker freely, forming thickets. Fruits are not always freely borne; may do better when cross-pollinated with another species.

Edible fruit, raw or cooked: a delicious sub-acid flavour, but quite seedy.

A good bee plant – very fragrant flowers in April and May are visited by honey and bumblebees for nectar and pollen.

Makes an excellent prickly, impenetrable, informal hedge that tolerates maritime exposure.

Autumnalis – to 1m high. Flowers in the autumn.

Compacta – good ground cover, 40-60cm high, fruit as well.

Corallina – good ground cover, 70-120cm high, fruit as well.

Corallina Compacta – good ground cover, 30cm high, fruit as well.

Etna – glossy leaves; flowers in April are orange and extremely abundant. Fruit as well.

Gracilis Nana – good ground cover, 30cm high.

B. thunbergii – Green Japanese barberry

Native to Japan, a shrub with yellow flowers followed by elliptic red fruit. Many ornamental varieties.

Edible fruit, raw or cooked: dry, very poor flavour. Leaves are edible when cooked.

Used in traditional medicine.

A good bee plant in April and May when the nectar and pollen attract honey and bumblebees.

Makes a good hedge, very prickly; also an effective ground cover.

The fruits have antibacterial effects on a number of plant diseases.

Green Ornament – a dense upright shrub to 1.5m. Fruits are red, glossy, borne abundantly.

Kobold – dwarf form to 40cm high with a dense, rounded habit. Free-fruiting.

B. tomentosa – Hairy barberry

An evergreen shrub from Chile.

Edible fruit.

B. verruculosa

Native to western China, a slow-growing evergreen shrub with golden-yellow flowers followed by black, bottle-shaped fruit. Does well on chalk. Very ornamental.

Edible fruit, raw or cooked: poor.

Makes an effective dense hedge, and a ground cover.

B. vulgaris – Common barberry, European barberry, Jaundice berry, Pipperidge bush, Zereshk

Native to Europe and North Africa, this is an upright, heavily-branched bush, with abundant yellow flowers followed by oblong, blood-red fruit. Fruits average 0.12g in weight, ripening in September to October. It is frost, drought and heat resistant, disliking wet locations. It tolerates deep shade but then requires a moist soil, and then doesn't set fruit freely. Very ornamental. For a long time, *B. vulgaris* has been known to be an alternate host of black stem rust of wheat (*Puccinia graminis*) and for this reason the advice has been not to cultivate it near to wheat fields.

Iran is the biggest producer of *B. vulgaris* fruit in the world, with 11,000 hectares (27,500 acres) of land under cultivation jointly with the cultivation of saffron. Over 10,000 tonnes of dried *B. vulgaris* fruit (mainly from seedless varieties propagated by cuttings) are produced per year. See *B. integerrima* above.

Edible fruit, raw or cooked: very acid, best used in preserves where they add a good flavour. A refreshing lemon-like drink can be made from the fruit, and the juice from fruit can be used as a lemon juice substitute. Fruit can also be made into wine, liqueurs, compotes etc. Dried fruit can be used as a flavouring for soups, sauces and meat; however when they are used, it is best not to crush the seeds as they contain higher levels of alkaloids. Fruits contain 4.6-12.1% sugars, 0.92% pectin, 3.8-6.7% organic acids, 13-33mg/100g vitamin C, vitamins A and E. Zereshk is the Kurdish and Persian name for the dried fruit of *B. vulgaris*. Zereshk is widely used in Iranian cooking, imparting a tart flavour to chicken dishes. It is usually cooked with rice, called Zereshk polo.

The leaves can be used as a flavouring or as an acid nibble. Dried young leaves and shoot tips make a refreshing tea. (Leaves/shoots should only be used in small amounts.) Flowers are also edible.

Root, stem and fruit extracts have long been used in traditional medicine and in recent decades, extracts, such as the alkaloid berberine, have been confirmed to have anti-fungal, antibiotic and antiseptic properties, and are used in mainstream medicine.

Makes a good hedge in exposed positions; doesn't like extreme maritime exposure.

A good bee plant, flowering in May producing nectar and pollen for honey and bumblebees. Nectar production ranges from 0.49 to 2.35mg per flower. Total nectar produced per plant has been measured as 210g.

The bark is rich in tannins and was formerly used for tanning leather in Poland.

The wood is yellow, fine grained and very hard; it is sometimes used for carving, toothpicks, turnery, mosaic work etc.

Alba – fruits are white or yellow-white. May be less susceptible to bird predation.

Asperma – fruits are seedless, larger and borne abundantly. Was used in Britain and France to make jam.

Dulcis – fruits are sweet or slightly sour.

Lutea – fruits are light yellow. May be less susceptible to bird predation.

Macrocarpa – has larger fruit.

B. wilsoniae –Wilson's barberry

Native to western China, this is a dense, very spiny, spreading shrub with light yellow flowers followed by round, salmon-red fruit. Very ornamental – many named hybrids exist.

Edible fruit, raw or cooked: very acid with a lemony flavour.

A good bee plant, supplying nectar and pollen to honey and bumblebees in July.

A useful ground cover plant.

Comet – fruit rounded, scarlet, 6-6.5mm across.

Fireball – fruit oval-conical, vermillion, 7-8 x 6-7mm.

Firefly – fruit oval-conical, vermillion, 7-8 x 6-7mm.

Joke – wide, upright habit; fruit carmine and salmon, very large and numerous.

Orangeade – low and wide growing. Fruits are carmine and orange, very large and numerous.

Cultivation

Berberis will thrive on all but waterlogged soils, including thin, shallow and dry soils and heavy clays. The optimum is a warm, fairly moist loam.

Deciduous species prefer sun (tolerate part shade); a sunny location encourages fruiting. Evergreen and semi-evergreen species prefer part shade (tolerate full shade), with a moist soil.

Cold tolerance varies widely, though the evergreen/semi-evergreen species are less hardy and in cold areas should be sheltered from cold winter winds. Most species thrive in Britain, fruiting abundantly.

The spines are sometimes formidable, so plants should be sited with care; this characteristic can be utilised in making virtually impenetrable, stock proof hedges.

Plants can be rejuvenated by pruning back severely (to within 30cm/12ins of the ground) and will resprout from the base, though in general, pruning isn't needed. Any trimming should be undertaken in late summer (deciduous species) or after flowering (evergreens).

Propagation methods include:

- By seed: best sown when ripe in summer/autumn; it will germinate next spring. Stored seed will need 6-13 weeks of cold stratification. Seedlings are susceptible to damping off. Most species hybridise freely, so seed may not be true to type if several species are nearby.
- Cuttings: of half-ripe wood taken in July-August, or of mature wood of the current season's growth taken in October-November. Treat with a hormone rooting powder, and place in a frame or greenhouse.
- Layering.
- Suckers can be removed in late autumn to early winter and planted out.
- Air layering in June.

Pests and diseases

The only serious disease of barberries is honey fungus (*Armillaria* spp.), to which some are somewhat prone; *B. darwinii*, *B. polyantha*, *B. thunbergii* and *B. wilsoniae* are resistant.

Some *Berberis* species, but mainly *B. vulgaris*, are alternate hosts for *Puccinia graminis*, the black stem rust of wheat. Laws in the past have even forced the grubbing up of many *B. vulgaris* plants in cereal growing areas, and even now cereal growers worldwide will often remove berberis plants nearby to reduce infection risk.

Berries may be taken by birds, or damaged by a fruit fly, the berberis seed fly (*Phagocarpus permunda*). Foliage may be infested with the barberry aphid (*Liosomaphis berberidis*), or be affected by a black spot (*Pseudomonas berberidis*) which can cause early leaf fall; a powdery mildew (*Microsphaera berberidis*) may also affect leaves.

Related species

Oregon grapes (p.154).

BLACKBERRY and **HYBRID BERRIES**, *Rubus* spp.

Zone 5-7, H5-7
Deciduous and evergreen
Edible fruit

Origin and history

Blackberries and hybrid berries like loganberries are an important fruit crop both commercially and in home gardens in many parts of the world.

In Britain, most commercial production is located in Kent, eastern England and the West Midlands (with about 400 hectares / 1,000 acres of blackberries and 150 hectares / 380 acres of loganberries), although PYO (Pick Your Own) farms are now quite common throughout the country. Most plantations are small (0.4-1 hectares / 1-2.5 acres) and form one of several crops grown. In the USA, the Pacific coast states of Oregon and California are the most important growing regions. The majority of blackberries and hybrid berries grown commercially are destined for the processing industry (including freezing); the demand for blackberries for the dessert trade is very limited and only the first few picks meet the quality requirements.

One of the serious problems for commercial growers has been the thorniness/spinyness of standard varieties, however in the last few decades numerous spineless varieties have been bred which make training, picking and management of the crop much easier.

Description

Blackberry varieties have been derived from several *Rubus* species native to Britain and other temperate climates. There are several thousand species of blackberry now recognised from all regions of the world, and *Rubus fruticosus*, the wild bramble, is divided into thousands of 'microspecies'. In North America, dewberry is the name used for the trailing species native to the eastern states; there are also erect growing species and these are called high-bush or erect blackberries. All blackberry plants have fairly flexible woody stems, usually with spines or thorns and compound toothed leaves; pink or white clustered flowers in mid-late summer are followed by the characteristic fruit.

Blackberries are excellent pioneer species, quickly colonising abandoned and burnt land. Once a thicket is established, trees can grow through the brambles untroubled by browsing animals. They have high wildlife value as a source of food and shelter.

The most important domesticated European blackberry is *Rubus laciniatus*, the 'cut-leaf', 'parsley-leaf' or 'evergreen' blackberry. Seedlings from this species are almost identical to the parent. This species is the main blackberry grown on the North American Pacific coast (as the variety 'Evergreen Thornless' = 'Oregon Thornless').

Important North American domesticated species include *R. allegheniensis*, the eastern North American erect blackberry with stout thorns; *R. baileyanus*, the American dewberry; and *R. ursinus*, the Pacific dewberry. The latter is involved in many of the recent hybrid selections released.

In blackberries, like all *Rubus* species, the real fruits are actually separate miniature drupes or drupelets each with a single seed; these drupelets adhere to one another to form what is called an 'aggregate fruit'.

Uses

Blackberries are high in vitamins A and C, with an average nutritional composition (per 100g) of:

Carbohydrate	12.9g
Vitamin	200 I.U.A
Calcium	32mg
Potassium	170mg
Protein	1.2g
Vitamin B	0.4mg
Phosphorus	19mg
Sodium	1mg
Fat	0.9g
Vitamin C	21mg
Iron	0.9mg
	58 calories

The fruits can be eaten in many ways: fresh, cooked, in preserves, as juice, in jams, in puddings, compotes, syrups, ice creams and yoghurt, in wines and liqueurs etc. They are good added to breakfast cereals and are traditionally cooked with apples. They can also be added to homemade soft drinks, e.g. lemonade. Fresh fruits are best eaten at room temperature; cooling them in a fridge causes a deterioration in flavour and sweetness. Fruits freeze quite well, although a loss of colour often occurs when the frozen berries thaw out.

The flower petals are edible, usually added to salads for a visual effect. Young shoots, peeled of their thorns, are edible, but often astringent. The young roots can be eaten if boiled for a long time as a famine food.

The leaves have medicinal properties, being mildly astringent, bactericidal, antidiarrhoeal and diuretic; the dried leaves are used as an infusion for cystitis, diarrhoea, dysentery, haemorrhoids and stomach disorders (and are found in several proprietary medicines); and for sore throats, mouth ulcers and gum inflammations; they also stimulate the metabolism and are therefore used for metabolic disorders. They contain 9-14% tannins and are high in vitamin C. The dried and also fermented leaves are used in tea mixtures, for example with raspberry leaves and sweet woodruff tops.

Dyes can be obtained from several parts: the fruits dye wool grey and silk slate blue; and a greyish-black dye can be obtained from the shoots (with alum mordant).

Ripening blackberries

The stems (canes) of flexible species/varieties are strong and can be used for basketry; thorny canes must be despined, for example by pulling them through a hole made in a metal can. In the past they have also been processed to make a fibre and twine.

Blackberries are good bee plants (both hive and wild bumblebees), providing nectar and honeydew (the latter if aphids are present).

Thorny varieties and species make an excellent secure barrier against animals (including humans). They can be trained around and up tree trunks to deter two-legged climbers.

Prunings burn well and make very good kindling.

Varieties/Cultivars

Spineless (thornless) cultivars are often planted these days, for obvious reasons; picking and pruning thorny varieties can be painful work. They are the best choice in forest gardens where wild blackberries are likely to be a weed species, so that these thorny invaders can easily be identified and pulled out. Be aware, though, that thornlessness may have disadvantages – particularly in that canes may need more tying than thorny varieties.

Primocane varieties have been bred in the last decade, which fruit on one-year wood. These can be cut back in winter if desired and will fruit early, and some fruit a second time later in the season. Cultivars include Babycakes, Little Black Prince, Montblanc, Prime-Ark 45, Prime-Ark Traveler, Reuben.

KEY TO CULTIVAR TABLE

Cane characteristics: Use the vigour and type to work out planting distances as described in 'cultivation' on p.27.

Vigour: Cane vigour: mod = moderate, vig = vigorous, v.vig = very vigorous.

Type: → means trailing, ↗ means semi-erect/semi-upright, ↑ means erect.

Spines: 'no' means canes are spineless.

Ripening times are average times for the UK. In regions with hotter summers, these dates will be brought forward into June or even May. E = early, M = mid, L = late. Late ripening cultivars will cease fruiting at the first frost, which may be before mid/late October in some areas.

Fruit characteristics:
Colour
Flavour: exc = excellent, v.gd = very good etc.
Size: XL = extremely large (40mm long), VL = very large (32m), L = large (25mm), ML = medium-large (22mm), M = medium (18mm), SM = small-medium (15mm), S = small (under 15mm).
Yield: VH = very high, H = high, MH = moderate to high, M = moderate, LM = low to moderate.

				JULY			AUGUST			SEPTEMBER			OCTOBER					
Cultivar	Vigour	Type	Spines	E	M	L	E	M	L	E	M	L	E	M	Colour	Flavour	Size	Yield
Adrienne	vig	→	no		✓	✓	✓	✓	✓						black	exc	L	H
Apache								✓	✓	✓	✓				black	good	L	H
Arapaho	mod		no												black	good	M	
Ashton Cross	v.vig	→					✓	✓	✓	✓	✓	✓			black	acid	SM	VH
Asterina	v.vig	→	no			✓	✓	✓	✓	✓					black	exc	VL	H
Austin			no															
Babycakes	Low		No	✓	✓					✓	✓							
Bedford Giant	vig	→				✓	✓	✓	✓						black	sweet	VL	H
Bigandearly	low	↑	no	✓	✓	✓	✓								black	good	L	H
Black Beaute	vig	→				✓	✓	✓	✓						black	good	VL	H
Black Butte	v.vig	→			✓	✓	✓	✓	✓	✓					black	good	XL	H
Black Cascade	low	↗						✓	✓	✓	✓				black		M	M
Black Satin	vig	↗	no				✓	✓	✓	✓	✓				black	acid	L	H
Boatsberry		→					✓	✓	✓	✓	✓				dark red	good	VL	
Boysenberry	vig	→				✓	✓	✓	✓	✓					dark red	exc	VL	VH
Brazos	vig	↗														acid	L	H
Brison																good	L	
Buckingham Tayberry	mod	→		✓	✓	✓	✓	✓							purple	v.gd	VL	VH
Cacanska Bestrna	v.vig	→	no						✓	✓	✓	✓			black	acid	L	H
Carolina	vig	→		✓	✓	✓	✓									good		H
Cherokee	vig	↑													black	v.gd	SM	H
Chester Thornless	vig	→	no						✓	✓	✓	✓	✓		black	exc	ML	H
Cheyenne		↑														good	M	
Choctaw	vig	↑													black	mild	ML	H
Columbia Star	vig	→	no	✓	✓	✓	✓	✓	✓	✓					black	good	L	H
Comanche	vig	↑													black	v.gd	L	H
Darrow	vig	→					✓	✓	✓	✓	✓				black	sweet	L	H
Dirksen Thornless	mod	↗	no				✓	✓	✓	✓	✓				black	good	L	M
Douglas Balsg		↗	no						✓	✓	✓	✓	✓		black	acid	ML	MH
Douglass	vig	→					✓	✓	✓	✓	✓				black	exc	ML	
Ebano	vig	→	no						✓	✓	✓	✓	✓		black	good	L	VH
Ebony King		→													purple	good	L	
Eldorado		→													black	good	L	H
Fantasia	v.vig	→					✓	✓	✓	✓	✓	✓			black	good	L	H
Fertodi Botermo	mod					✓	✓	✓	✓	✓					red	acid	L	H
Fertodi Hungaria		→				✓	✓	✓	✓	✓					red	mild	L	
Flordagrand	vig	→													black	good	L	H
Gardena		→	no												black	good	L	
Gem	vig	→														good	L	H

				JULY			AUGUST			SEPTEMBER			OCTOBER					
Cultivar	Vigour	Type	Spines	E	M	L	E	M	L	E	M	L	E	M	Colour	Flavour	Size	Yield
Georgia Thornless		→	no			✓	✓	✓	✓	✓						good	L	H
Helen	mod	→	no	✓	✓	✓	✓								black	v.gd	L	
Hildaberry		→																
Himalaya	v.vig	→						✓	✓	✓	✓	✓	✓	✓	black	mod	M	M
Hull	vig	↗	no					✓	✓	✓	✓	✓			purple	v.gd	ML	H
Humble	mod	→													purple	sweet	S	M
Illini Hardy	v.vig	→													black	good	M	
John Innes	vig	→								✓	✓	✓	✓	✓	black	good	L	H
Kaiteri	mod	→			✓	✓	✓	✓	✓						red	acid	M	
Karaka Back	low	↑	no		✓	✓	✓	✓	✓						black	v,gd	VL	H
Kings Acre Berry	mod	→					✓	✓	✓	✓	✓				black	fair	ML	H
Kiowa	mod	↗													black	exc	VL	MH
Kotata	v.vig	→			✓	✓	✓	✓							black	v.gd	L	VH
Lawton	vig	↑													black	good	ML	H
Laxtonberry	v.vig	→					✓	✓	✓	✓	✓				red	sweet	M	M
Little Black Prince	low	↑	no					✓	✓	✓	✓				black	good	M	M
Loch Maree	low	↗	no			✓	✓	✓	✓						black	good	M	H
Loch Ness	mod	↗	no					✓	✓	✓	✓	✓			black	fair	L	H
Loch Tay	mod	↗	no			✓	✓	✓	✓	✓					black	good	S	H
Loganberry LY 59	mod	→				✓	✓	✓	✓	✓	✓				claret	exc	L	H
Loganberry LY 654	vig	→	no			✓	✓	✓	✓	✓	✓				claret	exc	L	H
Lowberry	v.vig	→					ü	ü	ü	ü	ü				black	good	L	H
Lucretia	vig	→					✓	✓	✓	✓	✓				black	good	ML	H
Mahana	vig	→			✓	✓	✓	✓	✓						red	strong	VL	VH
Mapua	vig	→	no			✓	✓	✓	✓	✓					dark red	exc	VL	H
Marion	vig	→			✓	✓	✓	✓	✓	✓	✓	✓			black	v.gd	L	M
Merton Early	mod	→				✓	✓	✓	✓	✓					black	v.gd	L	H
Merton Thornless	mod	→	no				✓	✓	✓	✓	✓				black	good	L	M
Montblanc	mod	↑						✓	✓	✓	✓				black	good	L	M
Murrindindi	mod	→	no		✓	✓	✓	✓	✓						purple	exc	ML	
Natchez	v.vig	↗	no		✓	✓	✓	✓	✓						black	good	VL	VH
Navaho		↑	no			✓	✓	✓	✓	✓					black	exc	SM	
Nectarberry	vig	→				✓	✓	✓							dark red	fair	L	
No Thorn	vig	→	no													good	L	
Obsidian	vig	→		✓	✓	✓	✓	✓	✓						black	good	M	H
Oklawaha	vig	↑													dark red	good	M	
Olallie	vig	→													black	mild	L	H
Opal	low	↑	no				✓	✓	✓	✓	✓	✓			black	exc	L	H
Oregon Thornless	mod	→							✓	✓	✓	✓	✓		black	good	M	H

Cultivar	Vigour	Type	Spines	JULY			AUGUST			SEPTEMBER			OCTOBER		Colour	Flavour	Size	Yield
				E	M	L	E	M	L	E	M	L	E	M				
Osage		↑			✓	✓	✓	✓							black	exc	M	H
Ouchita		↑	no			✓	✓	✓	✓						black	exc	L	H
Parsley-Leafed	mod	→					✓	✓	✓	✓	✓				black	good	M	MH
Perron's Black	vig	→	no												black	sweet	L	
Phenomenal	mod	→					✓	✓	✓	✓	✓				dark red	good	L	H
Pink Crystal		↑													pink	sweet	M	
Polarberry	vig	→			✓	✓	✓	✓	✓	✓					white	mild	M	H
Prime-Ark 45		↑		✓	✓	✓	✓								black	exc	L	H
Prime-Ark Freedom		↑	no	✓	✓	✓	✓								black	good	VL	H
Prime-Ark Traveler		↑	no												black	mild	M	H
Ranui	mod	→		✓	✓	✓	✓	✓							red	good	ML	LM
Reuben	vig	↗						✓	✓	✓	✓				black	mild	M	L
Riwaka Tahi	mod	→			✓	✓	✓	✓	✓						red	exc	M	MH
Rosborough		↑													black	good	L	H
Shawnee	vig	↑													black	exc	VL	H
Silvan	vig	→		✓	✓	✓	✓	✓	✓	✓					purple	mild	L	H
Smoothstem	v.vig	↑	no						✓	✓	✓	✓	✓		black	good	L	VH
Snyder	vig	↑													dark red	poor	S	
Sunberry	v.vig	↗		✓	✓	✓	✓	✓	✓						purple	good	ML	VH
Taranaki	mod	→			✓	✓	✓	✓	✓						black	good	M	MH
Tasman	vig	→	no			✓	✓	✓	✓	✓	✓				dark red	exc	VL	H
Tayberry	mod	→		✓	✓	✓	✓	✓							purple	v.gd	VL	VH
Theodor Reimers	v.vig	→						✓	✓	✓	✓				black	good	M	H
Thornfree	vig	↗	no						✓	✓	✓	✓	✓		black	good	L	VH
Thornless Boysenberry	v.vig	→	no			✓	✓	✓	✓	✓					dark red	exc	L	M
Thornless Loganberry	mod	→	no		✓	✓	✓	✓	✓						claret	exc	M	H
Thornless Nectarberry	mod	→	no												dark red	fair	L	
Thornless Tayberry	mod	→	no	✓	✓	✓	✓								purple	v.gd	VL	H
Thornless Youngberry	mod	→	no			✓	✓	✓	✓	✓					black	fair	VL	H
Triple Crown	vig	→	no								✓	✓	✓	✓	black	good	L	MH
Tummelberry	mod	↗		ü	✓	✓	✓	✓	✓						dk red	good	L	MH
Veitchberry	mod	↗				✓	✓	✓	✓	✓					purple	good	ML	H
Veronique	low	↗	no					✓	✓	✓	✓	✓			black	good	L	H
Von		↑	no			✓	✓	✓	✓	✓					black	exc	M	H
Waldo	mod	↗	no		✓	✓	✓	✓	✓						black	good	VL	H
White	v.vig	↑													white	sweet	SM	H
Womack																good	L	
Youngberry	v.vig	→				✓	✓	✓	✓	✓					black	sweet	VL	H

Cultivation

Blackberries and hybrid berries are tolerant of a wide range of soil types and tolerate quite poor drainage, but do best on light and medium textured soils high in organic matter. Blackberries grow well in a soil of pH 5.0-7.0, hybrid berries in soils of pH 5.5-7.0; a slightly acid soil (pH 6.0-6.5) is ideal.

Canes should be sited away from frost pockets and with shelter from cold northerly and easterly winds. Winter frosts and cold drying winds can damage the immature tips of canes.

In larger-scale growing, rows are best oriented north-south for even fruit ripening. Fruiting is best in full sun, but blackberries do tolerate deep shade and continue to fruit in moderate shade, albeit in lesser amounts. Hybrid berries are less tolerant of shade. Fruits are sweeter in a sunny site.

Recommended companion plants for blackberries include *Allium* spp., marigolds (*Tagetes* spp.), tansy (*Tanacetum vulgare*) and stinging nettle (*Urtica dioica*).

For trailing types, rows are generally spaced 1.8-3m (6-10ft) apart (the larger spacing for mechanised access), with varieties of moderate vigour and semi-erect varieties at a lesser spacing and vigorous plants at a greater. If in doubt it may be wise to choose a greater spacing. Within rows, spacing between plants is 2.1-2.4m (7-8ft) for weak or moderate growing varieties, rising to 3-4m (10-13ft) for vigorous plants.

Erect growing types in North America need less space than trailing types and do not require the support of wires; they are planted at 60-90cm (2-3ft) apart within rows, the lesser distance for root cuttings and the larger for rooted suckers. Rows are usually 3m (10ft) apart.

Immediately after planting, canes are cut down to within 20-30cm (8-12ins) of the ground to encourage the development of new growth from basal buds. Mulching with an organic mulch will improve establishment.

There are many different ways of training and supporting fruiting canes, either individually or in groups. Canes may be tied to wires fastened between posts or tied in groups around individual posts, although it is normal to provide a permanent post and wire support. In less intensive systems like food forests, they can be tied up to low branches of trees or shrubs.

Erect blackberries in North America grow as a suckering shrub much like raspberries and are trained in the same ways. Suckers may need to be managed as well.

Flowering occurs from late May through June, so frost damage is rarely a problem. Blackberries and hybrid berries are self-fertile and set fruit with their own pollen, hence a single variety can be grown on its own. Pollination is greatly aided by bees (both honey and wild).

Fruits are borne on one-year-old canes, thus high yields are dependent on the annual production of a satisfactory number of canes of reasonable vigour. It is very beneficial to increase the water-holding capacity of soils by adding manures or other bulky organic matter before planting, and by using organic mulches after planting.

Hardiness: Most trailing types are hardy to zone 7/ H5-6, with the very hardy ones and some of the erect spiny types surviving down to zone 5-6 / H6-7.

Blackberries and hybrid berries can be propagated by several methods. Varieties do not come true from seed, so vegetative methods are used, mainly the first three below:

- Tip layering (in the field)
- Softwood cuttings using mist
- Hardwood cuttings
- Root cuttings and suckers – used for erect blackberries
- Micro propagation.

Pests and diseases

Blackberries are most affected by grey mould and purple blotch. Loganberries and hybrid berries are most affected by grey mould, cane spot and spur blight. Commercial growers use numerous applications of fungicides to control these diseases. All species are also susceptible to honey fungus (*Armillaria mellea*) so do not plant near any source of infection of this.

Grey mould (of fruit) (*Botrytis cinerea*): Can cause a serious loss of fruit, especially when wet or humid weather occurs during flowering and fruit ripening, under which conditions grey spore masses are produced on affected flowers and fruit and the disease spreads rapidly. Remove infected parts promptly.

Spur blight (*Didymella applanata*): An important disease of loganberries and hybrid berries. Signs of infection appear on leaf nodes or canes, purple at first, then the lesions extend along the cane and become greyish-white, within which black fruiting bodies are formed which can themselves release spores and infect other canes. Leaves can brown and shrivel. Can be serious in wet springs, where plants are overcrowded or where nitrogen application is too high.

Purple blotch (*Spetocyta ramealis*): Produces large purple blotches on the canes which in severe actions coalesce to envelop the whole of the base of the cane. In severe attacks the canes are weakened but not killed, but where blotches occur at leaf nodes, the buds may fail to develop. Symptoms are generally more severe after a hard winter or when the plantation is in a frost pocket.

Cane spot or Anthracnose (*Elsinoe veneta*): Can occasionally occur on some blackberries and hybrid berries, especially loganberries and tayberries. Sunken spots appear on canes, initially purple then turning grey; these enlarge and crack and girdle canes, sometimes killing them; fruit can be infected and distorted, and a tip dieback is also common. Canes showing severe spotting or cracking should be cut out and burned.

Blackberry and hybrid berry pests of importance include several aphids, raspberry beetle and raspberry midge; however, no cultivars are known to be resistant to these, and in any case the damage caused is not usually as severe as with raspberries. Aphids are often responsible for transmitting viruses which can weaken plants and reduce their life. Sustainable growing systems with high diversity, including plants to attract aphid predators, are the best defence. Birds may eat the ripening fruit. They tend to prefer raspberries and other red-berried fruit.

The harvest season can stretch from July until September. For an individual variety, harvesting continues over about 4-5 weeks, sometimes more.

Annual fruit yields can average 5-10kg (11-22lb) per plant with very heavy croppers sometimes reaching 14kg (30lb). Erect types in North America average yields are about 2.5kg (6lb) per plant. Commercial yields for blackberries are typically 5-15 tonnes / hectare (2-6 tonnes / acre); for loganberries 5-7 tonnes / hectare (2-2.8 tonnes / acre).

Related species

Raspberry (page 166).

BLACKCURRANT

Ribes nigrum

Zone 4, H7
Deciduous
Edible fruit

Origin and history

Blackcurrants are known for their strong flavour, which delayed their widespread use for eating, and they were more often used for colouring and flavouring (for example, in wines). The eighteenth and nineteenth century saw many new cultivars introduced in England, France and Holland. In the last 50 years, most breeding has concentrated on introducing genes from other species to improve characteristics such as larger fruit, disease resistance and longer harvesting periods.

Since the 1950s, the demand for blackcurrant juice, very high in vitamin C, has dominated commercial growing which is highly mechanised. Major producers are now West Germany, Poland and Norway (and the UK for one commercial brand of drink).

In North America, there has been less interest in growing blackcurrants because the plant is an alternative host to the 'white pine blister rust' fungus; but as white pine is becoming less widespread, interest is now growing.

Description

The blackcurrant, *Ribes nigrum*, is a medium sized deciduous shrub growing to 1.2-2m (4-6ft) high and wide, originating from Europe to Asia and the Himalayas. Leaves are alternate, 3-5 lobed; flowers are white or pink, 6-8mm (0.25ins) in diameter, bell shaped and produced in drooping racemes of 5-10. Fruits, produced from midsummer to early autumn, are black, 7-15mm (0.3-0.6ins) in diameter, with a strong flavour.

Uses

Fruits can be used fresh raw or cooked, becoming sweeter the longer they hang on the bushes (some recent cultivars are also much sweeter). Fruits also freeze well and are excellent for jams, jellies, juices, compotes and liqueurs.

The fruits are very high in vitamin C, having some 4% by weight (5-10 times that of lemons). They also contain rutin, bioflavonoids, a large amount of pectin, cellulose, tannins, a volatile oil, 4% organic acids, 8-16% saccharides (mainly fruit sugars), potassium, calcium, iron and magnesium. The calorific value is relatively low. The vitamin C is in a fairly resistant form so that a high percentage may be preserved on cooking.

Fruits continue to be used as a wine colourant, and are used to make the liqueur cassis.

Blackcurrant

Fresh leaves and flower buds are traditionally used in Central Europe as a flavouring in pickles and sauerkraut. They are also used in an infusion as a herbal tea and as a flavouring in soups. Leaves, bark and fruit are sometimes used medicinally.

The seeds contain gamma-linoleic acid, which is used in cosmetic preparations, and can also be used medicinally.

The fruit/juice can be used for dyeing: with an alum mordant it gives a good lilac dye. The leaves can be used to dye yellow.

Blackcurrants can be used for hedging, being very hardy, although fruiting in an exposed position will be much reduced.

Varieties/Cultivars

Much of the recent work on breeding new cultivars has taken place in Eastern Europe and the countries of the former USSR. Many of these cultivars require a high winter chilling, and in the mild climate of Britain will not crop reliably. However, many are being used in breeding programmes combining their disease resistance with the good cropping characteristics of better-known UK cultivars. The following cultivar list has been limited to the most commonly available cultivars in Western Europe and North America.

Flowering and ripening time tables

Times of flowering and ripening are given in relative terms (early, mid, etc.) and in Britain can be translated as follows:

Flowering (start of)	Ripening
	Very early = late June
Early = first week of April	Early = late June to early July
Early-mid = second week of April	Early-mid = first week of July
Mid = third week of April	Mid = second week of July
Mid-late = fourth week of April	Mid-late = third week of July
Late = late April to early May	Late = late July to early August
Very late = early to mid May	Very late = mid August to early September

Early flowering cultivars need the least winter chilling hours, and late flowering the most.

Early flowering:
Brödtorp
Coronation
Cotswold Cross
Daniel's September
Malvern Cross
Matchless
Risager
Saunders
Strata
Swedish Black
Tsema

Early-mid flowering:
Baldwin
Baldwin Hilltop
Blackdown
Boskoop Giant
Coronet
Hatton Black
Laxton's Standard
Laxton's Tinker
Raven
Tenah
Topsy
Wellington XXX

Mid flowering:
Alagan
Davison's Eight
Eagle
Hatton Choice
Invincible Giant P
Kerry
Laleham Beauty
Laxton's Giant
Laxton's Grape
Mendip Cross
Perfection
Reliance
Schwarze Traube
Supreme
Tor Cross
Trinder's Long Bunch
Westwick Choice
Westwick Triumph

Mid-late flowering:
Black Tony
Climax
Consort
Defender
Hatton Giant
Ontario
Rosenthal's Black
Seabrook's Black
Seabrook's Seedling
Trail's Perfection

Late flowering:
Ben Alder
Ben Lomond
Ben Nevis
Ben Sarek
Ben Tirren
Black Naples
Black Reward
Blacksmith
Bogatyr
French Black
Goliath
Invigo
Merton Cottage
Noir de Bourgogne
Prince of Wales
Silvergieters Zwarte

Very late flowering:
Amos Black
Ben More
Kippen's Seedling
Jet
Mite Free

Very early ripening:
Boskoop Giant
Laxton's Giant
Trinder's Long Bunch
Tor Cross
Bourgogne

Early ripening:
Mendip Cross
Schwarze Traube
Laxton's Grape
Tsema

Early-mid ripening:
Bogatyr
Coronet
Noir de Bourgogne
Raven
Silvergieters Zwarte
Wellington XXX

Mid ripening:
Alagan
Blacksmith
Climax
Davison's Eight
Goliath
Hatton Black
Invigo
Kerry
Laxton's Tinker
Matchless
Öjebyn
Otelo
Saunders
Seabrook's Black
Seabrook's Seedling
Strata
Swedish Black

Mid-late ripening:
Ben Lomond
Ben More
Ben Nevis
Ben Sarek
Black Reward
Blackdown
Cotswold Cross
Hatton Giant
Invincible Giant P.
Wallace Seedling
Laxton's Standard
Malvern Cross
Mite Free
Westwick Choice
Westwick Triumph
Willoughby

Late ripening:
Baldwin
Baldwin Hilltop
Consort
Crusader
Daniel's September
Risager
Supreme
Tenah

Very late ripening:
Amos Black
Ben Tirran
Jet
Laleham Beauty

Blackcurrant cultivar list

Alagan	Mid flowering, mid ripening. Fruit: medium-large, good flavour, quite easy to harvest. Bushes are moderate in vigour, upright. Fruit yields: fair.
Amos Black	Very late flowering, very late ripening. Fruit: medium-large, somewhat acid, fairly juicy, borne in small clusters, quite easy to harvest. Bushes are moderate in vigour, very upright. Fruit yields: fair. Originated in UK. Unreliable cropping.
Baldwin	(Baldwin's Black, Carter's Champion) Early-mid flowering, late ripening. Fruit: medium-large, sub-acid, juicy, good flavour, borne in medium length clusters, quite easy to harvest. Bushes are moderate in vigour. Fruit yields: heavy. Originated in UK. Good in areas of high rainfall. Crops well on light soils. A greedy feeder.
Baldwin Hilltop	Early-mid flowering, late ripening. Fruit: medium-large, sub-acid, juicy, good flavour, borne in medium length clusters, quite easy to harvest. Bushes are vigorous. Fruit yields: heavy. Originated in UK. Good in areas of high rainfall. Crops well on light soils. A greedy feeder.
Barchatnaja	Very hardy Russian cultivar, early flowering, high yielding with large fruit. Flowers frost resistant. Self-sterile.
Ben Alder	Late flowering. Bushes are very vigorous. Originated in UK.
Ben Connan	Late flowering, mid-late ripening. Fruit large, good flavour. Compact bushes. Heavy yields.
Ben Gairn	Early season. Disease and reversion-resistant variety with high yields of large fruit, excellent flavour.
Ben Hope	Mid season, disease and gall mite-resistant variety. Very vigorous, upright, heavy cropper, fruit of excellent flavour.
Ben Lomond	Late flowering, mid-late ripening. Fruit: large, sub-acid, excellent flavour, borne in medium length clusters. Bushes are moderate in vigour, upright. Fruit yields: very heavy. Originated in UK. Leaves are resistant to pests.
Ben More	Very late flowering, mid-late ripening. Fruit: large, somewhat acid, good flavour. Bushes are vigorous, upright. Fruit yields: very heavy. Originated in UK.
Ben Nevis	Late flowering, mid-late ripening. Fruit: large, slightly sweet, fair flavour, borne in medium length clusters. Bushes are moderate in vigour, upright. Fruit yields: very heavy. Originated in UK.
Ben Sarek	Late flowering, mid-late ripening. Fruit: large, borne in small clusters. Bushes are quite low in vigour, spreading. Fruit yields: heavy. Originated in UK. Most appropriate for home gardens and small-scale commerce.
Ben Tirren	Late flowering, very late ripening. Heavy crops of very good flavour. Originated in UK.
Big Ben	Bears very large fruit with a sweet flavour. Disease resistant.
Black Boskoop	= Boskoop Giant
Black Reward	Late flowering, mid-late ripening. Fruit: medium-large, good flavour, borne in long clusters. Bushes are very vigorous, very upright. Fruit yields: good. Originated in Netherlands.

Black September	= Daniel's September
Black Tony	Mid ripening. Fruit: medium-large, acid. Bushes are vigorous, slightly spreading. Fruit yields: low. Originated in Netherlands.
Blackdown	Early-mid flowering, mid-late ripening. Fruit: large, sweet, good flavour. Bushes are moderate in vigour, spreading. Fruit yields: good. Originated in UK.
Blacksmith	(Laxton's Blacksmith) Late flowering, mid ripening. Fruit: medium-large, somewhat acid, juicy, good flavour, borne in long clusters, very easy to harvest. Bushes are very vigorous, spreading. Fruit yields: good. Originated in UK. Crops well on light soils.
Bogatyr	Late flowering, early-mid ripening. Fruit: medium sized. Bushes are low in vigour. Fruit yields: fair. Originated in USSR.
Boskoop Giant	(Dutch Black, Geant de Boskoop, Boscop Riesen, Black Boskoop) Early-mid flowering, very early ripening. Fruit: large, sweet, juicy, fair flavour, borne in long clusters, quite easy to harvest. Bushes are very vigorous, slightly spreading. Fruit yields: low. Originated in Netherlands. Good in areas of high rainfall. Intolerant of cold winds.
Brödtorp	Early ripening. Fruit: large, sweet. Bushes short, spreading. Yields: fair.
Byelorussian Sweet	Early season. Very hardy, large fruit, high yielding. Frost resistant flowers.
Carter's Champion	= Baldwin
Cassis Blanc	Old green-fruited selection from France, sweet pale green fruit on bushes of moderate vigour.
Climax	Mid ripening. Fruit large, somewhat acid, in long clusters. Bushes vigorous. Yields fair.
Consort	(Ottawa 396, Consort Black) Mid-late flowering, late ripening. Fruit: medium-large, sweet, good flavour, borne in medium length clusters. Vigorous, very upright. Heavy yields. Originated in Canada.
Coronet	(Ottawa 393, Coronet Black) Mid flowering, early-mid ripening. Fruit: medium sized, poor flavour, quite easy to harvest. Bushes very vigorous, upright. Yields fair. Originated in Canada.
Cotswold Cross	Early flowering, mid-late ripening. Fruit: medium sized, somewhat acid, good flavour, borne in medium length clusters, difficult to harvest. Bushes are vigorous, slightly spreading. Fruit yields: fair. Originated in UK.
Crusader	(Ottawa 381, Crusader Black) Mid flowering, late ripening. Fruit: large, poor flavour, quite easy to harvest. Bushes are very vigorous, very upright. Fruit yields: fair. Originated in Canada. Needs a pollinator.
Daniel's September	(Black September) Early flowering, late ripening. Fruit: medium-large, slightly sweet, fair flavour, borne in long clusters, quite easy to harvest. Bushes are vigorous, slightly spreading. Fruit yields: fair. Originated in UK. Some parts of bush may revert to Baldwin characteristics.
Davison's Eight	Mid ripening. Fruit: medium-large, sub-acid, juicy, difficult to harvest. Bushes are moderate in vigour, upright.

Dutch Black	= Boskoop Giant
Ebony	Early season. Fruit large, high yielding. Moderately vigorous bush.
Florence	Fruit: borne in long clusters. Bushes are quite low in vigour, very upright. Fruit yields: good.
French Black	= Seabrook's Black
Goliath	Mid ripening. Fruit: medium-large, slightly sweet, juicy. Bushes are vigorous, very upright. Fruit yields: low.
Golubka	Fruit yields: good. Originated in USSR.
Green's Black	= Hatton Black
Hatton Black	(Green's Black) Early-mid flowering, mid ripening. Fruit: medium-large, sub-acid, fair flavour, borne in small clusters, difficult to harvest. Bushes are moderate in vigour, very upright. Fruit yields: fair. Originated in England. Better if cross-pollinated.
Hatton Giant	Mid-late ripening. Fruit: medium-large, slightly sweet, juicy, good flavour, borne in small clusters. Bushes are moderate in vigour, very upright. Originated in UK.
Hystawneznaya	Very early season – mid June. Medium sized fruit on a hardy bush with frost resistant flowers. Russian.
Invigo	Late flowering, mid ripening. Fruit: medium sized, fair flavour, quite easy to harvest. Bushes are very vigorous. Fruit yields: good. Originated in Germany.
Invincible Giant Prolific	Mid flowering, mid-late ripening. Fruit: large, slightly sweet, fairly juicy, very easy to harvest. Bushes are vigorous, very upright. Needs cross-pollinating.
Jet	(Malling Jet) Very late flowering, very late ripening. Fruit: small-medium sized, sub-acid, juicy, fair flavour, borne in long clusters, very easy to harvest. Bushes are very vigorous, very upright. Fruit yields: heavy. Originated in UK.
Kerry	Mid flowering, mid ripening. Fruit: medium sized, fair flavour, quite easy to harvest. Bushes are very vigorous. Fruit yields: good. Originated in Canada.
Kosmichesnaya	Mid season. Medium sized fruit on hardy bush with frost resistant flowers. Russian.
Laleham Beauty	Mid flowering, very late ripening. Fruit: medium-large, sweet, juicy, borne in long clusters. Fruit yields: very heavy. Some branches may revert to earlier fruiting.
Laxton's Blacksmith	= Blacksmith
Laxton's Giant	Mid flowering, very early ripening. Fruit: very large, sweet, juicy, excellent flavour, very easy to harvest. Bushes are very vigorous, spreading. Fruit yields: heavy. Originated in UK. Brittle branches – tend to break in strong winds.
Laxton's Grape	Mid flowering, early-mid ripening. Fruit: large, acid, in long clusters, very easy to harvest. Bushes are vigorous. Fruit yields: heavy. Fruit tends to shrivel in strong sun.
Laxton's Standard	Early-mid flowering, mid-late ripening. Fruit: medium sized, sub-acid. Bushes are moderate in vigour, upright. Fruit yields: good. Originated in UK.
Laxton's Tinker	Early-mid flowering, mid ripening. Fruit: medium-large, sub-acid. Bushes are moderate in vigour, spreading. Fruit yields: fair. Originated in UK.
Malling Jet	= Jet
Malvern Cross	(Malvern) Early flowering, mid-late ripening. Fruit: medium sized, sub-acid, juicy, borne in medium length clusters, difficult to harvest. Bushes are vigorous, very upright. Fruit yields: good. Originated in UK. Resembles Baldwin.
Matchless	Early flowering, mid ripening. Fruit: medium-large, somewhat acid, juicy, borne in small clusters. Bushes are moderate in vigour, very upright. Fruit yields very heavy. Originated in UK.
Mendip Cross	Mid flowering, early ripening. Fruit: medium sized, slightly sweet, juicy, borne in long clusters, difficult to harvest. Bushes are vigorous, slightly spreading. Fruit yields: heavy. Originated in UK. Likes high rainfall and good drainage. Tolerates exposed positions.
Mite Free	Very late flowering, mid-late ripening. Fruit: small, acid, borne in long clusters. Bushes are moderate in vigour, upright. Originated in UK.
Mortti	Fruit: good flavour. Bushes very vigorous, upright. Yields very heavy. Originated in Finland.
Noir de Bourgogne	(Cassis de Dijon) Late flowering, early-mid ripening. Fruit: medium sized, quite easy to harvest. Bushes moderate in vigour, upright. Fruit yields: low. Originated in France.
Öjebyn	Mid ripening. Bushes are low in vigour. Fruit yields: very heavy. Originated in Sweden.
Otelo	Mid ripening. Fruit: large, borne in long clusters. Bushes are moderate in vigour, very upright. Originated in Czechoslovakia. 'Huge degree of tolerance for noxious factors.'
Polar	Early season. Large fruit of good flavour. Bushes compact.
Raven	Early-mid flowering, early-mid ripening. Fruit: medium-large, slightly sweet, juicy, good flavour, borne in long clusters. Bushes are vigorous, spreading. Fruit yields: very heavy. Originated in UK. Reliable cropping.
Risager	Early flowering, late ripening. Bushes low vigour. Good yields. Origin: Netherlands.
Roodknop	Late ripening. Bushes are moderate in vigour. Fruit yields: heavy.
Saunders	Early flowering, mid ripening. Fruit: small. Bushes low vigour. Fair yields. Origin: Canada.
Schwarze Traube	(Black Bunch) Early flowering, early ripening. Fruit: small-medium sized, sub-acid. Bushes are moderate in vigour, upright. Fruit yields: good. Originated in Germany.
Seabrook's Black	(French Black, Merveille de la Gironde) Mid-late flowering, mid ripening. Fruit: medium sized, acid, borne in small clusters. Bushes are very vigorous, slightly spreading. Fruit yields: fair. Originated in UK. Crops even in exposed positions.
Seabrook's Seedling	Mid-late flowering, mid ripening. Fruit: medium sized, slightly sweet, very easy to harvest. Bushes are very vigorous, spreading. Fruit yields: heavy.
Silvergieters Zwarte	(Silvergieter, Silvergieter's Schwarze) Late flowering, early-mid ripening. Fruit: large, sub-acid, juicy, borne in long clusters, very easy to harvest. Bushes are very vigorous, very upright. Fruit yields: good. Originated in Netherlands.

Strata	Early flowering, mid ripening. Fruit: very large, sweet, good flavour, quite easy to harvest. Bushes are very vigorous, spreading. Fruit yields: fair. Originated in Germany.
Supreme	Mid flowering, late ripening. Fruit: medium sized, sub-acid, borne in long clusters. Bushes are vigorous, upright. Fruit yields: good. Originated in UK.
Swedish Black	Early flowering, mid ripening. Fruit: large, fair flavour, quite easy to harvest. Bushes are moderate in vigour. Fruit yields: fair. Originated in Sweden.
Tenah	(Tena) Early-mid flowering, late ripening. Fruit: large, borne in long clusters. Bushes are moderate in vigour, spreading. Fruit yields: heavy. Originated in the Netherlands.
Topsy	Early-mid flowering, mid ripening. Fruit: medium-large, fair flavour, quite easy to harvest. Bushes are very vigorous, upright. Fruit yields: heavy. Originated in Canada.
Tor Cross	Mid flowering, early ripening. Fruit: medium-large, sub-acid. Bushes are vigorous. Fruit yields: good. Originated in UK.
Trinder's Long Bunch	Mid flowering, very early ripening. Fruit: medium sized, sub-acid, borne in long clusters, very easy to harvest. Bushes are moderate in vigour, slightly spreading. Fruit yields: good.
Tsema	Early flowering, early ripening. Fruit: medium sized, good flavour, borne in long clusters. Bushes are vigorous, spreading. Fruit yields: fair. Originated in the Netherlands.
Vertii	One of several Finnish green-fruited selections. Fruit sweet, green, good aromatic flavour.
Wallace Seedling	Late ripening. Fruit: sweet, good flavour, borne in long clusters. Bushes are moderate in vigour, very upright. Fruit yields: good. Indistinguishable from Baldwin.
Wellington XXX	Mid flowering, early-mid ripening. Fruit: medium-large, slightly sweet, borne in medium length clusters. Bushes are very vigorous, spreading. Fruit yields: heavy. Originated in UK.
Westwick Choice	Mid flowering, mid-late ripening. Fruit: medium-large, sub-acid, excellent flavour, borne in small clusters, quite difficult to harvest. Bushes are vigorous, slightly spreading. Fruit yields: heavy. Originated in UK. Prefers drier areas.
Westwick Triumph	Mid flowering, mid-late ripening. Fruit: medium sized, sub-acid, borne in medium length clusters, difficult to harvest. Bushes are vigorous, spreading. Fruit yields: fair. Originated in UK.
Willoughby	(Willoughby Black) Mid-late ripening. Fruit: medium-large, juicy, borne in long clusters. Bushes are quite low in vigour, slightly spreading. Originated in Canada.

Cultivation

Blackcurrants grow best in cool, moist climates (zones 4-7) such as Northern Europe, Canada and New Zealand; the high cold requirement to break winter dormancy (800-1500 hours of chilling) makes cultivation in warmer climates unpredictable. Even in cooler climates, flowers are susceptible to frost damage in the spring. Frost pockets should be avoided and for good crops, a mostly sunny position is required (part shade is tolerated, but fruiting will be less). It is essential to choose a position that is sheltered from cold winds, especially at flowering time because insects are partly responsible for pollination.

Blackcurrants are tolerant of many soils, but ideally prefer a well-drained but moist, deep loamy soil, with a high humus content, and with an ideal pH of 6.7-7 (near neutral).

Bushes should be planted 25mm (1ins) lower in the ground than they were in the nursery to encourage new shoots beneath soil level. Bushes are planted 1.2-1.8m (4-6ft) apart between plants and rows, depending on the vigour of the cultivar. Commercial growers have wider row widths and closer plants within rows, 60-90cm (2-3ft) apart.

Plants are usually grown as stooled bushes, the branches arising at ground level, though sometimes they are grown commercially on a short stem, with branches tied to wires, to facilitate easier machine harvesting: yields are usually lower this way.

Plants should be mulched if possible, preferably with organic materials. The soil around the bushes should never be disturbed, even by shallow hoeing, as this damages surface roots and reduces fruit yields. At planting, all shoots are cut back to a bud at 25-50mm (1-2ins) above the soil.

The best fruiting is on one-year-old shoots, while two and three-year-old shoots also produce well; on older shoots, fruiting quality quickly declines. Fruit buds are formed along the whole length of young shoots. Thus either every year or irregularly, old (almost black) wood is cut out at the base. In addition, low-lying and any diseased branches should be cut out.

The main feeding requirement is for nitrogen, to maintain the continual production of new shoots. The best way to apply this is by using organic mulches, composts etc.

Flowering is early (April in the UK) and flowers are very susceptible to frosts, even of only -1°C (30°F), although some new cultivars are more frost hardy. Most cultivars are self-fertile (pollinated by wind), but in some, cross-pollination is more successful. Bumblebees are one of the main pollinators.

Fruits are produced from June to September, depending on the cultivar; the main season is July. Annual yields of fruit reach 5kg (11lb) for traditional cultivars but can be as high as 15-20kg (33-44lb) for some of the new high yielding cultivars. Some cultivars ripen their fruit unevenly – some may be green on the 'strig' (bunch) while others are ripe; this may be an advantage for the small-scale grower. Fruits also hang on the bushes when ripe for a long time (3-5 weeks) on several cultivars, and gets sweeter although the vitamin content diminishes fairly rapidly after the fruit is fully ripe.

Harvest in dry weather. Like many small fruit on decent length stalks, using a berry picker (or harvesting comb) can speed up the work tremendously.

Propagation is usually from hardwood cuttings, and is very easy. One-year-old shoots, 15-25cm (6-10ins) long, are taken from healthy plants in autumn after leaf fall; any unripened shoot tips are removed, and the shoots planted in soil leaving two buds above soil level; all buds are left on, and underground buds will grow out to form shoots.

Pests and diseases

The main pest is the blackcurrant gall mite or big bud mite (*Cecidophyopsis ribis*) which destroys buds and (more seriously) transmits reversion disease. The tiny mites (0.25mm) feed and breed within the buds, which become round and swollen at any time of the year. In spring the mites move to the young buds, and it is now that control is possible. Before leafing out, bushes should be examined and any swollen buds picked off and removed. Badly infested bushes should be destroyed. Several cultivars have resistance.

Reversion is a serious disease which is spread by the blackcurrant gall mite, and causes a large reduction in the fruit crop, sometimes to almost zero. The size and shape of leaves is affected and this is the main method of identification. Leaves become bunched and nettle-like, sharply pointed and narrow with no basal cleft and four or fewer main leaf veins. There is no control; bushes must be dug up and destroyed.

Leaf spot (anthracnose) and American gooseberry mildew are occasional problems, and in North America, rust (white pine blister rust) can be a serious problem where white pines are nearby.

The green variety 'Vertii'

Related species

Redcurrant and whitecurrant (p.181), Other currants and gooseberries (p.76), Gooseberry (p.104).

BLUEBERRY, *Vaccinium* spp.

Zone 4-6, H6-7
Deciduous (most)
Edible fruit

Origin and history

There are several *Vaccinium* species called blueberries, but the fruit usually grown by home and commercial growers are highbush blueberries, derived mainly from the North American species *V. corymbosum* and *V. australe*.

Description

Highbush blueberries are deciduous shrubs, growing to 1.5-1.8m (5-6ft) high at maturity. They are made up of several woody branches or canes arising from buds in the crown. The branches, especially when young, are yellowish-green and warty.

The dense fibrous root system is relatively small, reaching depths of about 1m (3ft), though most feeder roots are in the top 25cm (10ins) of soil. It only extends about as far as the drip line of the bush.

Leaves are 3-8cm long, quite shiny green above. In cool wet springs, leaves often have a reddish tinge on opening. The leaves on most selections turn red and gold in the autumn, making bushes very ornamental.

Flower buds are set in late summer and autumn on new shoots and flower the following spring. Older wood bears no flower buds. The urn-shaped flowers are born in dense clusters in May, each flower 6-10mm (0.3-0.4ins) long, white or slightly reddish.

The berries, borne in clusters of 5-10, are blue-black when fully ripe, with a waxy white bloom, which makes them appear light blue. They are 8-15mm (0.3-0.6ins) across in the wild, but up to 20mm (0.8ins) across on cultivars selected for fruiting.

Uses

The fruits are edible and an important commercial crop in many parts of the world. They are sweet and juicy, occasionally bland when raw, but are excellent cooked and they freeze and bottle well. They are quite nutritious, are low in calories and sodium and are a good source of fibre and pectin; they are high in ascorbic acid (vitamin C). They also contain quantities of ellagic acid, a known anti-cancer agent.

Blueberries were highly regarded by Native Americans who ate them fresh and added them liberally to pudding and cakes. Some fruit was preserved by drying in the sun, then added to breads, stews and crushed with meat or fish to make a dried meat cake called pemmican.

Recent investigations have confirmed many useful medicinal properties of blueberries:

The juice from fruit contains a component that is useful in treating urinary tract infections, especially of *E.coli*. The component, an anti-adhesin, blocks the binding of the bacteria to the urinary tract wall.

Another component, comprising of proanthgocyanidins, has anti-carcinogenic properties.

The pigments found in blueberry fruit, and which make them blue, comprise of anthocyanins. These substances possess

Blueberry

interesting biological properties: they are antioxidants which play an important role in preventing disease. They decrease the fragility and permeability of capillaries. They can inhibit blood platelet aggregation and thus help prevent thrombosis and atherosclerosis.

Early American settlers used the strong, flexible wood or larger branches for tool handles.

The leaves and fruit can both be used for dyeing, giving a variety of colours.

Varieties/Cultivars

Much breeding work has been done and continues to be carried out in the USA, where recent developments include hybrids of *Vaccinium corymbosum* with the southern species *V. ashei* and *V. darrowi* to produce cultivars that require much less winter chilling (200-400 chilling hours below 7.2°C / 45°F as opposed to 900 hours or so for most) which can be grown in warmer parts of the world. These so-called 'southern highbush' types are sometimes evergreen and not particularly winter hardy and should not be planted in areas with severe winters, but they should be fine in Britain; they are hardy to about -20°C / -10°F (zone 6 / H6-7). Other developments include 'half-high' cultivars, which only grow about 1m (3ft) high and survive better in cold areas.

Early season cultivars need about 120 days from flowering to fruit ripening: mid season 140 days and late season 160 days. In Britain, flowering is usually from early May and fruits ripen in August, September and October. For most cultivars, fruit ripen over a period of 3-5 weeks.

The flowers of Berkeley, Dixi, Earliblue, Coville, Jersey and Stanley are relatively unattractive to bees and should certainly be planted with other cultivars so that bees are attracted nearby.

The fruit scar is the opening where the berry has been removed from the fruit stalk, and can be the point of entry for disease organisms. A small, dry, shallow scar is preferable to one that is large, deep and moist.

Cultivars resistant to fruit cracking

This can be a problem with some cultivars in wet weather. As well as spoiling fruit, it can also make the fruit and plant more susceptible to other diseases. The following are resistant to fruit cracking:

Atlantic	Coville	Meader
Berkeley	Croatan	Olympia
Bluecrop	Darrow	Pender
Bluejay	Earliblue	Stanley
Blueray	Elliott	Summit
Burlington	Herbert	
Collins	Ivanhoe	

KEY TO CULTIVAR TABLE

Type: S = southern highbush type, N = northern highbush type.

Ripening season: VE = very early, E = early, EM = early-med, M = mid, ML = mid-late, L = late, VL = very late.

Vigour: vigour of bush. low, mod = moderate, high.

Bush: bush characteristics. sm = small, spr = spreading, up = upright, se-up = semi-upright, cmp = compact.

Fruit size: small, medium, large, v.large; s-m = small-medium, m-l = medium-large.

Fruit flavour: acid, fair, mild, good, exc = excellent.

Fruit scar: small, med = medium, large. See above for details.

Fruit firmness: soft, q.firm = quite firm, firm, v.firm = very firm. Cultivars with firm fruit are more resistant to infection by grey mould.

Fruit yield: fair, mod = moderate, high, v.high = very high.

Cultivar	Type	VE	E	EM	M	ML	L	VL	Vigour	Bush	Size	Flavour	Scar	Firm	Yield
Atlantic	N						✓		high	spr	large	good		firm	high
Avonblue	S								low	sm, spr	m-l	good	small		
Berkeley	N				✓				high	up, spr	m-l	mild	large	firm	v. high
Biloxi	S		✓						high	up	med	good	small	firm	high
Bladen	S		✓						high	up	med	good	small	firm	high
Blue Gold	N						✓		high	low	med	good	small	firm	v. high
Blue Ridge	S			✓					high	up	l-vl	acid	wet	firm	high
Bluechip									high	up	v.large	good	small		
Bluecrisp	S		✓						mod	up		good	small	firm	
Bluecrop	N		✓						mod	up	large	fair	small	firm	high
Bluegold	N						✓		high	low		good	small	firm	v. high

Cultivar	Type	VE	E	EM	M	ML	L	VL	Vigour	Bush	Size	Flavour	Scar	Firm	Yield
Bluetta	N		✓						mod	cmp, spr	s-m		large	firm	high
Bluehaven	N		✓							up	large	good	small		
Bluejay	N		✓						high	up	m-l	mild	small		
Blueray	N			✓					v.high	up,spr	v.large	good	med	firm	high
Bounty	N				✓				mod	spr	v.large	exc	small		
Brigitta	N						✓		high	up	large	good	small	v.firm	high
Burlington	N						✓			sl spr	s-m		small	v.firm	
Cape Fear	S								high	se-up	l-vl	exc	small	firm	v. high
Chandler	N					✓			high	up	large	good	small	firm	high
Chanticleer	N	✓								up,small	med	mild	small	firm	
Chippewa	N				✓					up	large			firm	high
Collins	N			✓					high	up	m-l	good	small	firm	mod
Cooper	N	✓							mod	up	med	good	small	firm	mod
Coville	N	✓							high	up,spr	v.large	good	small		v. high
Croatan	N		✓						high	up	large	fair	small		
Darrow	N							✓	high	up	v.large	good	med	firm	
Dixi	N						✓			spr	v.large	good	large		high
Duke	N			✓					high	up	med	mild	small	firm	
Duplin	S			✓					high	se-up	large	good	small	firm	high
Earliblue	N		✓						high	up	large	good	med		high
Echota	N					✓			high	se-up	large	good	small	firm	high
Elliott	N							✓		up		good	small		
Elizabeth	N				✓					up,spr	v.large	fair		firm	fair
Emil	N									up,small	small	good		firm	high
Flordablue	S								mod		large	good	med	firm	
Friendship	N			✓						small		mild		q.firm	high
Georgiagem	S		✓						high	up,tall	med	good	small	firm	mod
Gulfcoast	S		✓						high	se-up	med	good	small		mod
Harrison	N			✓					high	se-up	large	good			
Herbert	N				✓				mod	spr	v.large	exc	large		
Ivanhoe	N				✓				high	up		good	small		
Jersey	N						✓			up,spr	s-m	exc	small		
Jubilee	S		✓						high	up	med	good	small	firm	high
Lateblue	N							✓	high	up	med	good	small		
Legacy	N					✓			high	up	med	good	small	firm	high
Little Giant	N				✓						small	good	small		mod
Magnolia	S		✓						high	spr	med	good	small	firm	high
Meader	N				✓				high	up,spr	m-l	fair	small	v. firm	v. high
Misty	S								high	up	large		small	firm	

Cultivar	Type	VE	E	EM	M	ML	L	VL	Vigour	Bush	Size	Flavour	Scar	Firm	Yield
Morrow	N								low	se-up	large	good			
Murphy	N		✓						high	spr	large	fair			
Nelson	N					✓			high		med		med	firm	v. high
Northblue	N		✓						high	v.small	large	good			v. high
Northcountry	N		✓						mod	small	med	mild	small	soft	high
Northland	N			✓						small	s-m	good	small		
Northsky	N				✓					v.small	med	good		soft	mod
Nui	N		✓								v.large	good			mod
O'Neal	S		✓						high	se-up	v.large	exc	small	v. firm	high
Olympia	N				✓				high	tall,spr	m-l	v.good			high
Ornablue	N								low	small,spr					v. high
Ozarkblue	N			✓					high	se-up	large	good	small	firm	high
Patriot	N		✓							small,spr	large	good	small		
Pemberton	N				✓						large		med		
Pender	N				✓				high	se-up	small	good	small	firm	high
Pioneer													med		
Polaris	N		✓							up	med	exc	s-med	v. firm	high
Puru	N		✓								v.large	good			
Putte	N				✓					small	s-m	mild	med		v. high
Rancocas	N				✓					up,spr	med	poor	med		high
Reka	N		✓								med				v. high
Reveille	S		✓						high	up	s-m	good	small	firm	high
Rubel	N						✓		high	up	small	good	med	firm	v. high
Sampson	S		✓						high	se-up	v.large	exc	small	firm	
Santa Fe	S		✓						high	up	m-l	good	small	firm	mod
Sharpblue	S		✓						high				small		
Sierra	N				✓				high	up	med	good	small	firm	high
Southmoon	S				✓				mod	up	large	good	small	firm	
Spartan	N			✓					high	up	med	exc	med	firm	high
St. Cloud	N		✓							small,up	large	good	small	firm	v. high
Stanley	N			✓					high	up	s-m	exc	large	firm	
Summit	N				✓				mod	se-up	v.large	exc	small	firm	high
Sunrise	N		✓						mod	up	s-m	good	small	firm	mod
Sunshine Blue	S									small	small	good		firm	
Tophat	N								low	dwarf	med	good		firm	
Toro	N			✓					high	up	med	good	small		v. high
Weymouth	N	✓											large		
Wolcott	N												small		

Blueberry cultivar list

Cultivar	Description
Atlantic	Late season. Bush vigorous, open, spreading, very productive. Fruit large, firm, good flavour, moderate quality, resistant to cracking.
Avonblue	Southern highbush type. Bush small, low vigour, spreading, requires heavy pruning after flowering. Fruit medium-large, light blue, small scar, very good quality. Introduced 1977.
Berkeley	Mid season. Bush vigorous, upright, open-spreading, very productive. Fruit medium-large, light blue, firm, mild sweet flavour, large scar, fair quality. Resistant to cracking. Fruit fall if harvest delayed; yields better on heavy soils. Introduced 1949.
Biloxi	Southern highbush type, early season. Bush vigorous, productive, upright. Fruit medium sized, firm, good flavour, small scar. Introduced 1998.
Bladen	Southern highbush type, early season. Bush upright, vigorous, good productivity. Fruit medium sized, dark blue, firm, good flavour, small scar. Introduced 1994.
Blue Gold	Late season. Bush vigorous, low growing, very productive. Fruit medium sized, with good flavour, colour and firmness; scar is small and dry. Requires good pruning. Introduced 1989.
Blue Ridge	Southern highbush type, early-mid season. Bush vigorous, very upright, productive. Fruit large to very large, very light blue, acid, firm, wet scar. Introduced 1987.
Bluechip	Bush vigorous, upright. Fruit very large, excellent colour and quality, small scar. Easy to prune. Introduced 1979.
Bluecrisp	(Crunchyblue) Southern highbush type, early season. Bush upright, moderately vigorous. Fruit very firm, good flavour, small scar. Introduced 1998.
Bluecrop	Early season. Bush upright, moderately vigorous, with good autumn colour. Fruit large, very light blue, firm, moderate quality, small scar; a good cropper. Resistant to drought and fruit cracking. Still the leading cultivar in the world despite its age. Introduced 1952.
Bluegold	Late season. Bush vigorous, low growing, highly productive. Fruit firm, good quality, small scar. Introduced 1988.
Bluetta	Early season. Bush compact-spreading, moderately vigorous, productive. Fruit small-medium sized, light blue, firm, broad scar, softens rapidly after ripening. Difficult to prune. Introduced 1968.
Bluehaven	Early season. Bush upright with good autumn colour. Fruit large, light blue, scar very small and dry, excellent quality, ripens over a short period. Introduced 1968.
Bluejay	Early season. Bush vigorous, upright, slightly spreading, flowers late. Fruit medium-large, light blue, mild flavour, small scar. Resistant to premature drop and cracking. Long fruit stems aid mechanical harvesting. Introduced 1978.
Blueray	Early-mid season. Bush upright, very vigorous, spreading, productive. Fruit very large, light blue, firm, excellent quality, medium scar. Resistant to cracking. Introduced 1955.
Bounty	Mid season. Bush moderately vigorous, spreading, needs extensive early training. Fruit very large, excellent flavour and colour, small scar. Likes soils high in organic matter. Introduced 1987.
Brigitta	Late season. Bush vigorous, upright, very productive, easily propagated. Fruit large, firm, small scar, good flavour, excellent quality. Bred in Australia.
Burlington	Late season. Bush slightly spreading with a wide crown. Fruit small-medium, very firm, very small dry scar, adapted to mechanical harvesting, resistant to cracking. Introduced 1939.
Cape Fear	Southern highbush type. Bush vigorous, semi-upright, very productive, precocious. Fruit large to very large, light blue, small scar, excellent flavour and firmness, needs a high removal force. Introduced 1987.
Chandler	Mid-late season. Bush vigorous, upright, well branched, high yielding. Fruit large, light blue, small dry scar, firm, good flavour; ripens over a long period. Introduced 1994.
Chanticleer	Very early season. Bush upright, moderate height. Fruit medium sized, firm, small scar, mild flavoured. Introduced 1997.
Chippewa	Mid season. Bush upright, productive. Fruit large, firm, light blue, sweet. Introduced 1996.
Collins	Early-mid season. Bush upright, vigorous, fairly productive. Fruit medium-large, light blue, firm, highly flavoured, small scar. Resistant to fruit cracking and premature drop. May not sucker freely. Introduced 1959.
Cooper	Very early season. Southern highbush type. Bush moderately vigorous, upright, moderately productive. Fruit medium sized, good flavour and colour, firm, small scar. Introduced 1987.
Coville	Very late season. Bush vigorous, upright-spreading, very productive. Fruit very large in open sprays, medium blue, hold well on bush, very good quality, small scar. Resistant to premature drop and cracking. Self-sterile. Introduced 1949.
Croatan	Early season. Bush upright, vigorous. Fruit large, dark blue, fair quality, small scar, resistant to cracking. Introduced 1954.
Darrow	Very late season. Bush upright, vigorous. Fruit very large, firm, light blue, very good quality, medium scar. Resistant to cracking. Introduced 1965.
Dixi	Late ripening. Bush open-spreading, productive. Fruit very large, medium blue, large scar, high quality, cracks easily. Introduced 1936.
Duke	Early-mid season. Bush vigorous, upright, numerous canes, fairly late flowering. Fruit medium sized, light blue, firm, mild flavour, small dry scar. Introduced 1985.
Duplin	Southern highbush type, early-mid season. Bush semi-upright, vigorous, high yielding. Fruit large, firm, good flavour, small scar. Introduced 1998.
Earliblue	Early season. Bush with strong upright growth and good autumn colour; productive but erratic. Fruit large, aromatic, light blue, good quality, medium scar. Resistant to cracking and premature drop. Introduced 1952.
Echota	Mid-late season. Bush vigorous, semi-upright, productive. Fruit large, very light blue, good flavour, firm, small scar, keeps well.
Elizabeth	Mid season. Bush upright-spreading. Fruit very large, mid blue, fair quality, firm. Productivity inconsistent. Introduced 1966.

Elliott	Very late season. Bush upright, very hardy. Fruit mid blue, good quality, very small scar, ripen over a short period, resistant to cracking. Introduced 1973.
Emil	Bush moderately upright, small, very hardy, productive. Fruit small, firm, good flavour. Introduced 1997, bred in Sweden.
Flordablue	Southern highbush type. Bush moderately vigorous. Fruit large, light blue, firm, medium scar, good quality. Poor shipper. Introduced 1976.
Friendship	Early-mid season. Bush small (80cm, 30ins), very productive, hardy. Fruit sky blue, mild flavour, moderately firm. Introduced 1990.
Georgiagem	Southern highbush type, early season. Bush upright, tall, vigorous, moderately productive. Fruit medium, small dry scar, firm, good flavour. Likes a well-drained soil. Introduced 1986.
Gulfcoast	Southern highbush type, early season. Bush vigorous, semi-upright, moderately productive. Fruit medium sized, small scar, good flavour, stem often remains attached after picking. Introduced 1987.
Harrison	Early-mid season. Bush semi-upright, vigorous. Fruit large, good quality. Introduced 1974.
Herbert	Mid season. Bush much branched, fairly open and spreading, moderately vigorous. Fruit very large, medium blue, in very heavy compact clusters, excellent flavour; large wet scar. Resistant to cracking. Introduced 1952.
Ivanhoe	Mid season. Bush strong with upright growth and good autumn colour. Fruit dark, in tight clusters, very good flavour, small scar, resistant to cracking.
Jersey	Late season. Bush upright, spreading. Fruit small-medium, excellent flavour, small scar. Suited to mechanical harvesting and widely grown for processing. Introduced 1928.
Jubilee	Southern highbush type, early season. Bush vigorous, upright, very productive. Fruit medium sized, firm, good flavour, small scar. Introduced 1994.
Lateblue	Very late ripening. Bush vigorous, erect. Fruit medium sized, light blue, good quality, small scar. Adapted to mechanical harvesting. Introduced 1967.
Legacy	Mid-late season. Bush vigorous, upright, high yielding. Fruit medium sized, good flavour, firm, small scar. Introduced 1993.
Little Giant	Mid season. Bush medium height and productivity. Fruit small, dark blue, good flavour, small scar; ripen over a short period. Intended for processing market. Introduced 1995.
Magnolia	Southern highbush type, early season. Bush vigorous, productive, spreading, medium height. Fruit medium sized, firm, good flavour, small scar. Introduced 1994.
Meader	Mid season. Bush upright, vigorous, open-spreading, very hardy. Fruit medium-large, mid blue, fair quality, very firm, small scar, ripens over a short period, easy to pick. Resistant to cracking. Prone to overbearing – requires heavy pruning. Suited to mechanical harvesting. Introduced 1971.
Misty	Southern highbush type. Bush tall, upright, vigorous, small crown. Fruit large, light blue, firm, small scar. Introduced 1990.

Morrow	Bush semi-upright, slow growing. Fruit large, light blue, high quality, ripens over a short season. Introduced 1964.
Murphy	Early season. Bush vigorous, spreading. Fruit large, dark blue, fair quality. Slow to start bearing. Introduced 1950.
Nelson	Mid-late season. Bush vigorous, medium tall, highly productive. Fruit medium sized, light blue, firm, dry medium scar. Introduced 1988.
Northblue	Early season. Bush very low (60cm, 2ft), vigorous, very hardy, non-rhizomatous, very productive. Fruit large, dark blue, good quality. Introduced 1983.
Northcountry	Early season. Bush short (under 1m, 40ins), moderately vigorous, very hardy, productive. Fruit medium sized, very light blue, mild flavour, soft, small scar.
Northland	Early-mid season. Bush small (120cm, 4ft), spreading, branches flexible, suckers freely, difficult to prune. Fruit small-medium, mid blue, good quality, small scar. Can be mechanically harvested. Introduced 1967.
Northsky	Mid season. Bush very low (25-45cm, 10-18ins), dense, moderately productive, extremely hardy. Fruit medium sized, light blue, good flavour, soft. Introduced 1983.
Nui	Early season. Bush moderate yielding. Fruit very large, good flavour. Introduced 1989 – bred in New Zealand.
O'Neal	Southern highbush type, early season. Bush vigorous, semi-upright, flowers early and for a long period, productive. Fruit very large, medium blue, very firm, excellent flavour, small scar. Introduced 1987.
Olympia	Mid season. Bush very tall, spreading, vigorous, very productive. Fruit medium-large, mid blue, thin skinned, flavour aromatic, very good. Resists cracking and holds well on bush.
Ornablue	Ornamental cultivar. Bush low (1m, 3ft tall), spreading, dense. Heavy bearer of dark blue fruit. Long-lasting red leaf colour in the autumn.
Ozarkblue	Early-mid season. Bush vigorous, semi-upright, high yielding. Fruit large, light blue, firm, good flavour, small scar. Introduced 1996.
Patriot	Early season. Bush small (120cm, 48ins), open-spreading, very hardy. Fruit large, light blue, very good quality, small scar.
Pemberton	Mid season. Bush hardy. Fruit thin skinned, large, juicy, medium scar. An old variety.
Pender	Mid season. Bush vigorous, semi-upright, productive, suited for mechanical harvesting. Fruit small, good flavour, small scar, firm, resistant to cracking, stores well. Introduced 1997.
Pioneer	Fruit with medium scar.
Polaris	Early season. Bush upright, moderate height and spread (1.3m, 4ft), productive. Fruit medium sized, light blue, scar small-medium, very firm, excellent flavour. Introduced 1996.
Puru	Early season. Bush medium yielding. Fruit very large, good flavour. Introduced 1989 – bred in New Zealand.
Putte	Mid season. Bush small, hardy, very productive. Fruit small-medium, black, medium scar, mild sweet flavour. Introduced 1986 – bred in Sweden.

Rancocas	Mid season. Bush upright-spreading, high yielding. Fruit medium sized, medium scar, cracks when ripe, poor quality. Grown for processing only. Introduced 1926.
Reka	Early season. Bush very high yielding. Fruit medium sized. Tolerates less acid soils. Introduced 1989 – bred in New Zealand.
Reveille	Southern highbush type, early season. Bush very upright, narrow, vigorous on light soils, precocious and productive. Fruit small-medium size, light blue, firm, good flavour, small scar. High yielding; adapted to mechanised harvesting. Introduced 1990.
Rubel	Late season. Bush vigorous, upright, very productive, good autumn colour. Fruit small, light blue, firm, good quality, medium scar, keep well. Adapted to mechanical harvesting, usually grown for processing. Introduced 1912.
Sampson	Southern highbush type, early season. Bush sturdy, vigorous, semi-upright. Fruit very large, firm, excellent flavour, small scar. Introduced 1998.
Santa Fe	Southern highbush type, early season. Bush vigorous, upright, medium-high yields. Fruit medium-large, firm, good flavour, small scar. Introduced 1998.
Sharpblue	Southern highbush type, early season. Bush vigorous. Fruit dark blue, small scar. Introduced 1976.
Sierra	Mid season. Bush vigorous, upright, productive. Fruit medium-sized, good flavour, firm, small dry scar, very good quality. Very productive. Introduced 1988.
Southmoon	Southern highbush type, mid season. Bush moderately vigorous and upright. Fruit large, mid blue, firm, good flavour, small scar. Introduced 1995.
Spartan	Early-mid season. Bush vigorous, upright, productive. Fruit medium sized, firm, light blue, excellent flavour, medium dry scar; good yields. Introduced 1978.
St. Cloud	Early season. Bush small (1.3m, 4ft), upright. Fruit large, slightly flattened, scar small and dry, firm, good flavour. Very productive. Self-sterile.
Stanley	Early-mid season. Bush upright, vigorous, few branches. Fruit small-medium, firm, very aromatic, excellent flavour, large scar. Resistant to cracking; easily pruned. Introduced 1930.
Summit	Mid season. Bush moderately vigorous, semi-upright, productive. Fruit very large, excellent flavour, firm, small scar, resistant to cracking. Introduced 1997.
Sunrise	Early season. Bush moderately vigorous, upright. Fruit small-medium, light blue, firm, small scar, good quality. Moderate yielding. Introduced 1988.
Sunshine Blue	Southern highbush type. Bush small (1.2m, 4ft), wide. Fruit small, firm, firm, stores well, good flavour. Tolerates soil up to pH 6 and drought.
Tophat	Ornamental dwarf cultivar, growing 50cm (20ins) high. Fruit medium sized, firm, good flavour.
Toro	Early-mid season. Bush vigorous, upright, highly productive. Fruit medium sized, good flavour, small dry scar; ripen over a short period. Introduced 1987.
Weymouth	Very early season. Fruit with large scar.
Wolcott	Fruit with small scar.

Cultivation

Blueberries need a very acid soil (pH between 4 and 5.5) with plenty of summer moisture. They like full sun or light shade and shelter from strong winds. Soils nearer neutral or alkaline pH are simply not worth considering for blueberries. In these cases, bushes can be grown in large containers (45cm / 18ins diameter) with an acid compost; water these generously throughout the growing season. They prefer well-drained soils with plenty of organic matter.

Plant young bushes between November and March with two or three-year-old plants spaced 1.2-1.5m (4-5ft) each way; in commercial plantings, wider alleys need to be allowed for mechanised access. Plant bushes deeper than usual to encourage new stool shoots. A mulch of leaves, leafmould, pine needles, grass clippings or straw is beneficial.

Blueberries have both surface-feeding roots and deeper roots and do not tolerate root disturbance. It is best to keep them permanently mulched with 7-12cm (3-5ins) of an acid organic mulch such as leafmould or shredded bark.

Blueberries are quite hungry feeders and require nutrients to maintain good annual growth. Recommendations in North America are to apply regular doses of nitrogen, potassium and phosphorus (15g of each per year per mature bush of the actual element), applied in two doses, one at the start of flowering and the other 5-6 weeks later. Of these, the nitrogen component is essential, to maintain production of new wood. Occasional applications of potassium will suffice, whilst phosphorus may not be needed at all. The cut leaves from one healthy comfrey plant, cut several times per year, and used as mulch under a blueberry bush, should provide enough nitrogen and phosphorus to maintain cropping. Compost or well-rotted manure can also be applied in early spring. Feed the plants in a wide band around the drip line.

In dry weather, bushes may need watering; use natural rain water or soft water.

Blueberries are grown as stooled bushes in exactly the same way as blackcurrants. Pruning is not necessary until the third or fourth year after planting; the best fruit is produced on two and three-year-old wood, so pruning should stimulate strong new growth from the base of the bush each year.

Prune in early March. Cut out the oldest, unproductive wood, removing about a quarter of the bush. Cut some branches back

Blueberry 'Chandler'

to the base and others to strong upright shoots. Remove low branches too near the ground and any weak growth.

Some cultivars, particularly 'Berkeley', do not produce much strong new replacement growth and they crop quite well on older branches. With such cultivars, or others where pruning is kept to a minimum, just remove weak and old wood as long as a good strong framework exists.

Blueberries are members of the Ericaceae and have urn-shaped flowers that are insect-pollinated; bumblebees are by far the best pollinators. Honey bees also love the flowers and commercial growers usually place 2-3 hives per acre (0.4 ha) to ensure good pollination. Cross-pollination gives better yields, although bushes are self-fertile, so that two or more cultivars should be grown if possible. Two rows of a main crop can be interspersed with one row of a secondary pollinating crop for adequate pollination. Different cultivars should be no farther than 6m (20ft) apart.

Flowering can extend for as long as a month with early and late flowering cultivars grown together. Generally, early season cultivars flower early and late ones late, and pollinating partners should be ripening at a similar time. Adequate pollination is indicated if you observe at least 15-20 bee entries into blueberry flowers on a bush within a 10 minute period.

Bushes start cropping after two years, yielding lightly at first but by the fifth year should yield 2.2kg (5lb) per bush per year, increasing to 4.5kg (10lb) when fully grown. Mature plants can continue cropping well for more than 50 years.

Commercial plantations with high yielding cultivars expect yields of 9-11t/ha/year.

Fruits are borne in clusters and do not ripen all at once. Ripe berries are soft and should leave the cluster easily. Immature fruits have an inferior flavour and berries should be left for a few days after they have turned blue before picking. Each cultivar should be picked once a week for the 3-4 weeks over which ripening continues. To reduce tearing and bruising of fruit, roll ripe berries from the cluster into the palm of the hand with the thumb.

Propagation is usually by cuttings: softwood cuttings are usually used in Britain, taken in late June or early July, when new shoots are 10-15cm (4-6ins); hardwood cuttings can be taken from dormant, pencil-thick shoots of the previous season's growth, 10-12cm (4-5ins) long, taken in the spring before bud growth begins. In addition, suckers can be dug up in winter, and layering can be undertaken by pegging stems to the ground.

Pests and diseases

There are various fungal diseases of blueberry in North America. Grey mould (*Botrytis cinerea*) can spread from fruit to branches and cause a dieback of bushes branch by branch. Dead wood should be cut out and bushes pruned to allow light and air into them. Cultivars with firm fruit are more resistant to infection and include Bluechip, Earliblue, Ivanhoe and Meader. Blueberries are resistant to honey fungus.

Birds are the main pest and netting may be essential to protect the crop if attacks are bad.

Yellow, stunted young leaves are a sign of iron deficiency, usually caused when the pH has become too high. Lowering the pH by use of acid mulches is the best long-term solution.

Related species

Cranberry (page 72), Lingonberry (page 137).

BOG MYRTLE, *Myrica gale*

Zone 1, H7
Deciduous
Nitrogen-fixation, Flavouring, Insect repellent, Wax plant

Origin and history

Bog myrtle, or sweet gale, originates from Northern and Western Europe, and from parts of North America. It has a long history of use by people, including as an insect repellent, to flavour beer, medicinally and for other uses.

Description

A deciduous upright shrub, growing to 2.5m (8ft) high, but sometimes (from grazing pressure or poor sites) only to 50cm (20ins) or less. It spreads by rhizomes to produce thickets. Alternate leaves are 3-5cm (1-2ins) long, deep green and smooth above, somewhat pubescent beneath. Although mostly dioecious (i.e. male and female flowers are on different plants), sometimes male and female flowers are formed on the same plant or even the same branch; flowers are brownish, cone-like catkins, 1.5cm (0.6ins) long in April-June, the females thicker than the males. Fruits are 3mm across, yellowish-brown, consisting of a single seed surrounded by a waxy covering.

Extremely hardy, bog myrtle is usually found on wet acid soils, also on neutral soils. The most striking feature of the plant is the pleasant smell of the volatile oil which is secreted from numerous glands on its leaves and catkins. The scent resembles that of sage or bay, but is more camphoraceous.

Bog myrtle belongs to the group of actinorhizal plants, that is temperate region plants that form associations with *Frankia* species of fungi in root nodules, which fix atmospheric nitrogen for the plant. Bog myrtle will also accept infection by many different *Frankia* strains from different species, including alders (*Alnus*), *Elaeagnus*, and sea buckthorn (*Hippophae rhamnoides*).

Uses

The wax which coats the small fruit can be used to make candles which are quite brittle, aromatic and don't smoke when put out. Other uses for the wax include soap, ointments, leather-polishes, etching, and medicinal mixtures. The wax melts in the high 40s °C (high 110s °F), so is easily melted off fruit in hot water, and skimmed off the surface. It is harder and more brittle than beeswax. The fruits are smaller than other *Myrica* species so making wax is more time consuming with bog myrtle.

The flowers (catkins) are attractive to bees, although pollination is mainly via wind.

All the *Myrica* species are green manure plants, increasing the amounts of nitrogen in the soil and making available significant amounts to other nearby plants. Dense stands of *M. gale* are estimated to fix at least 30kg/ha/year.

The shrub has been harvested from the wild and utilised in various ways for centuries.

The most widespread use in the past has been for flavouring beer, called gruit. Evidence stretches from Roman and Viking sites for its use in brewing as a flavouring and preserving agent. 'Gale beer' in Yorkshire was considered very efficacious for slaking thirst. It is also used to flavour mead. The beer-

Bog myrtle foliage

Bog myrtle flowering

preserving activity of *M. gale* is at least partly explained by the discovery of antibacterial flavonoids which are particularly active against gram-positive bacteria; these act in a similar way to the bitter compounds humulone and lupulone obtained from hops. The use of bog myrtle in commercial beer making, fell into disrepute 250 years ago because excessive consumption was believed to cause poisoning; but the present widespread consumption of *M. gale* flavoured drinks in Scandinavia (see below) is evidence against any severe toxic effects at the doses normally consumed. Bog myrtle beer is still made by home-brewers in Britain on occasion and also sometimes by small commercial brewers.

In Scandinavia, leaves are still gathered to flavour alcoholic drinks. In Denmark, Aalborg Pors Snaps is flavoured with an extract made by soaking freshly picked leaves in 35% aqueous alcohol; in Norway, dried and powdered leaves are sold to the public for flavouring spirits and homemade beer. Leaves are sometimes used to make a tea, and the fruit sometimes used as a condiment to season roast meat.

There is pharmacological evidence that some of the constituents from the leaves and fruit may have anti-cancer properties. There are also reports of *M. gale* having an abortifacient action, and pregnant women should avoid taking any plant parts of any of this species internally.

Recent pharmacological studies have focused on myrigalone B (MyB), a flavonoid extracted from the fruit. MyB is a potent antioxidant that may help to protect liver tissue from toxin-induced injury, and act as a preventative to atherosclerosis. A fresh extract of plant material in water has also demonstrated antiviral activity, which supports the Scandinavian folkloric use of *M. gale* extract to treat *Herpes zoster*, shingles.

The essential oil distilled from the leaves is sometimes used in perfumery, as well as medicinally for skin complaints.

The roots have been used to produce a yellow dye for wool, used in the Scottish Highlands within the last 80 years. The stem tips also yield a yellow dye.

Leaves yield a flavonoid and a volatile oil with antifungal activity against several species including *Fusarium* spp. and *Penicillium citrinum*.

There is plentiful historical evidence of the use of sweet gale as an insect (moth) and flea repellent in Scandinavian and British folklore, though the volatile oil was never produced for this purpose. A strong decoction of the leaves can be used as

a parasiticide to kill external body parasites (lice). Research in Scotland demonstrated that the steam-distilled volatile oil is an effective insect repellent (a 0.5% gel preparation of the oil repelled biting midges [*Culicoides impunctatus*] for up to three hours). The oil has also been shown to repel ants. The volatile oil is produced on catkins and fruit, but mainly in the leaves. Bog myrtle is now harvested commercially from the wild for use in commercial insect repellents.

Varieties/Cultivars

Nanas is low and spreading and makes a good ground cover; it is very shade tolerant.

Cultivation

Bog myrtle prefers an open position in sun or partial shade (including in the understorey of open forests), and an acid or neutral soil. Wet or boggy soils are tolerated but not essential as long as they stay moist in summer. It tolerates strong winds.

Propagation methods include:

- Seed: wash in warm soapy water to remove any wax, rinse, then cold stratify for three months before sowing on the surface of a fine seed compost. Expose to light for germination.
- Layering of low branches
- Root cuttings in spring.

Young plants in the nursery may naturally become inoculated with *Frankia* species, and if they do then nodules will be seen on the roots. Plants can also be inoculated on planting by mixing a little soil from an established stand of the species or a relative in the planting hole.

Pests and diseases

Readily grazed by hares, goat, sheep, cattle and deer.

Related species

Myrica pensylvanica, the northern bayberry, is described on page 152.

Myrica californica (Californian wax myrtle) and *M. cerifera* (wax myrtle) are larger species described in *Trees for Gardens, Orchards and Permaculture* (see Bibliography, p.234).

BROOMS, *Cytisus* species

Zones 5-9, H3-7 H1
Deciduous and evergreen H2
Nitrogen-fixing, Nurse shrubs, Bee plants H2

Origin and history

The broom family of some 50 species of shrubs (occasionally small trees) has long been used ornamentally, for the pretty yellow or white pea-like flowers borne over long periods. As nitrogen-fixing pioneer shrubs, their ecological role is to invade into disturbed areas (often disturbed by fire), colonise and cover the soil, and improve soil conditions for the trees that will succeed them. Hence they all have the potential to become weedy in some places and indeed, Scotch broom (*Cytisus scoparius*) is known for its weediness in warm climates. Nevertheless, if used in appropriate climates they can be very useful sources of nitrogen and bee fodder.

Included here is tagasaste (*Cytisus proliferus*), which much of the world counts as a broom, whilst the other half puts it in a different genus, *Chamaecytisus*. It can be a very useful plant in agroecological systems and is worth mentioning, whatever the naming convention.

Description

The brooms are evergreen or deciduous plants, spineless, often with ribbed branches. They rarely put out new growth from old wood, so with age tend to become leggy and susceptible to wind or snow damage. Having said that, like all pioneer plants, they are short-lived, often 10-15 years.

Pea-like flowers, yellow or white, are borne in spring and/or summer near or at the end of growing shoots. Some species flower on the previous year's wood (e.g. *C. scoparius*), others on the current year's wood.

Following flowerings, pods form that turn from green to brown as they ripen, containing small flat seeds. In dry weather when fully ripe, the pods will open explosively and scatter the seeds in the vicinity.

Uses

Mainly used for nitrogen-fixation and as nurse shrubs. In regions with very dry summers, the benefits of nitrogen fixed may be partly offset by competitive effects, especially competition for water.

Brooms are great bee plants.

Can be used for short-lived hedges (or hedge nurses).

Long leggy branches of *C. scoparius* were once used to make brooms – hence the name! Branches of several species have also been used for dyeing.

Using nurse shrubs

Nurse plants, often used in forestry, can be very useful when establishing ecological growing systems on more exposed sites.

The idea is that you make your planting much denser than the final plan envisaged, because then there is more shelter from wind for all the plants involved – remember, trees and shrubs like the company of other trees and shrubs; they do not like being stuck out on their own, on an exposed site.

To use nurse shrubs:

- Make a planting plan of the end planting with proper spacings between fruit trees etc. as you would normally.
- Mark out positions and plant the fruit trees and shrubs.
- Now infill some or all of the space between the planted species. How you do this depends on your initial management; it could be planting in wavy lines to allow for easy cutting of grasses; or it could be saturation planting where little ground control is envisaged in the early years.

Ideally choose short-lived and sun-demanding pioneer shrubs (this is why *Cytisus* can be ideal), then when they die they will have done their job and space becomes available for underplanting. If you use longer-lived shrubs or trees, or shade-tolerant species, then you may have to cut these out yourself some years down the line.

Scotch broom used as a nurse in a young forest garden

Scotch broom (*Cytisus scoparius*)

Flowers of *C. scoparius* have been used to make wine (you can still find broom flower wine recipes on the internet and in wine making books), however the flowers are toxic, with heart-stimulating properties similar to *Digitalis*, and should not be used. They were also smoked for their hallucinogenic effects!

Several species have traditional medicinal uses, and recent research has confirmed medicinally interesting compounds present, some of which can easily be toxic, so home use is not advised.

C. proliferus (tagasaste), is used as a fodder crop in warm-climate regions. Grazed directly, fresh cut, or dried as a hay crop, it has high levels of protein and fibre, and is used for feeding cattle and sheep in Australasia and Africa.

Varieties/Cultivars

Cytisus proliferus (*C. palmensis*) – Tagasaste

Evergreen shrub, 3-5m (10-16ft) high, from the Canary Isles. Has long pubescent stems, larger leaflets, white flowers early spring to summer. Hardy to zone 9 / H3. Leaves can be damaged and small plants killed by sub-zero temperatures.

Cytisus scoparius – Scotch broom, Common broom

European upright deciduous shrub growing to 2.5m (8ft) with many narrow green branches and small leaves. Rich yellow flowers borne late spring to summer. Hardy to zone 5 / H7. There are many named cultivars bred mainly for different flower characteristics.

Cultivation

All species need a well-drained soil and full sun. Plants resent root disturbance and should be pot grown, however they need good staking after planting on an exposed site.

Sandy, stony and clay soils are all suitable as long as drainage is good. Soils of poor fertility are also suitable (indeed, nitrogen-fixation will be greater on such soils).

Propagation is usually by seed. The seed benefits from scarification; soak in almost-boiling water overnight before sowing. Germination is then quite fast.

Pests and diseases

There are no pests or diseases of note.

Tagasaste in the Canary Isles

Tagasaste leaves

BUSH CHERRIES, *Prunus* species

Zone 2-3, H7
Deciduous
Edible fruit

Origin and history

Bush cherries have been bred over the last half century, mostly in Canada. The aim has been to hybridise cherry species to achieve hardy bush forms with good yields of sour and sweet cherries that can also be machine harvested.

Description

Rounded bushes 1-2.5m high and across.

Uses

Fruits are edible, mainly cooked.

Varieties/Cultivars

Athos	Spreading bush, medium sized fruit, fairly sweet. Ripens mid season. Origin Canada, *P. cerasus*.
Carmine Jewel	Grows about 2m (6ft) tall, fruit small, very dark, almost black. Very hardy. Ripens early. Origin Canada, *P. cerasus* x *P. fruticosa*.
Crimson Passion	Small, semi-upright bush to 1m high, large sweet fruit. Origin Canada, *P. fruticosa* x *P. cerasus*.
Cupid	Medium sized bush with very large sweet fruit. Ripens early-mid season. Origin Canada, *P. fruticosa* x *P. cerasus*.
d'Artagnan	Drooping habit, dark red medium sized fruit, fairly sour. Ripens mid season. Origin Canada, *P. cerasus*.
Juliet	Small to medium bush with medium sized sweet fruit. Origin Canada, *P. fruticosa* x *P. cerasus*.
Porthos	Upright bush with large fruit, fairly sweet. Ripens mid season. Origin Canada, *P. cerasus*.
Romeo	Semi-upright bush with large sweet fruit. Ripens early. Origin Canada, *P. fruticosa* x *P. cerasus*.
Saint Valentine	Medium sized, very sweet fruit. Ripens early. Origin Canada, *P. fruticosa* x *P. cerasus*.

Prunus tomentosa flowers

Cultivation

Tolerant of most soils, bush cherries require full sun and a well-drained soil. Most varieties are self-fertile.

Cropping starts 3-4 years from planting.

Pests and diseases

None of note. Like sour cherries (*P. cerasus*) these are hardy and disease resistant.

Related species

Nanking cherry, *Prunus tomentosa* (p.147).

BUSH CLOVERS, *Lespedeza* species

Zones 4-6, H6-7
Deciduous
Nitrogen-fixing, Bee plants

Lespedeza bicolor

Origin and history

Lespedeza is a family of shrubs, perennials and short-lived plants belonging to the legume family of nitrogen-fixing plants. The species used in agroforestry are usually the shrubs and perennials (in fact several species seem midway between perennials and woody shrubs) and those are the species described here.

Description

Shrubs and perennials from Asia and the USA, growing up to 4m (13ft) high, from sunny well-drained sites. They all have trifoliate leaves and small pea-like flowers borne over a long period in summer and autumn, on current season's growth. These are followed by small 'pods' containing a single seed. Hardy to zones 4-6 / H6-7, though some species turn from shrub to hardy perennial at lesser temperatures than the hardiness limit.

Uses

The main use is a nitrogen-fixing green manure shrub. Suitable for using in forest gardens in sunnier locations.

All species are valuable bee plants, flowering over a long period.

L. bicolor, *L. cyrtobotrya* and *L. sericea* are used as fodder (fresh or dried as a hay) for sheep, goats and cattle. They are also used in reforestation schemes and for soil conservation.

L. bicolor, *L. buergeri*, *L. cyrtobotrya*, *L. juncea* and *L. sericea* have a history of their young shoots being used medicinally and also eaten as a cooked vegetable. Like many legumes they contain a number of medicinally-active compounds and should probably be eaten only sparingly, if at all.

Compounds from *L. capitata* are used in medicine.

Several species' long whippy growth has traditionally been used for making brooms.

Varieties/Cultivars

Lespedeza bicolor – bush clover

From China and Japan, shrub to 3m (10ft) high, flowers purple-rose in late summer. Hardy to zone 5 / H7.

Lespedeza buergeri

From Japan and China, shrub 40-80cm (16-32ins) high, flowers white-purple in late summer. Hardy to zone 6 / H6-7.

Lespedeza capitate

From the USA, a perennial up to 1.5m (5ft) high, flowers white-yellow in late summer to early autumn. Hardy to zone 4 / H7.

Lespedeza cyrtobotrya

From Japan and Korea, a shrub or perennial to 1.2m (4ft) high, flowers rose-purple in late summer to early autumn. Hardy to zone 6 / H6-7.

Lespedeza juncea

From Japan, China, Korea, Siberia and Australia, an upright shrub or perennial to 1.2m (4ft) high, flowers yellow-white in autumn. Hardy to zone 5 / H7.

Lespedeza maximowiczii

From Japan, a shrub to 4m (13ft) high, flowers purple in summer. Hardy to zone 5 / H7.

Lespedeza sericea

From Japan and China, a perennial to 70cm (28ins) high. Hardy to zone 6 / H6-7.

Lespedeza thunbergii

From Japan and China, a shrub or perennial to 2m (6ft) high, flowers rose-purple in late summer. Hardy to zone 6 / H6-7.

Cultivation

Grow in a warm, sunny, well-drained location.

Shrubs regenerate well from old wood, so can be pruned back hard if necessary – or even right to the ground. Some dieback of new growth can occur in winter in cool temperate locations if the new growth has not hardened off sufficiently.

Propagate by seed (not dormant but responds well to scarification, e.g. hot water soak prior to sowing), or by semi-ripe cuttings of lateral shoots with a heel or root cuttings.

Pests and diseases

None of note.

Flowers of *Lespedeza bicolor*

CALIFORNIA LILACS, *Ceanothus* species

Zone 5-9, H6-7
Deciduous and evergreen
Nitrogen-fixing, Bee plants

Origin and history

A family of mainly shrubs, some deciduous and others evergreen, largely from western North America. They have long been widely used in ornamental plantings for their flowers and ground cover abilities.

Description

Deciduous or evergreen shrubs, from under 1m high to 9m or more in their native habitats, most growing 1-2m (3-6ft) high. Dark green leaves, and heads of flowers – white, blue, purple, lavender or pink. Species can hybridise freely with each other, which has led to many hybrid cultivars.

Uses

All species are nitrogen-fixing actinorhizal plants, fixing moderate amounts of nitrogen.

All species are good bee plants.

Some *Ceanothus* species are used for soil stabilisation.

In most species, the flowers can be used to dye green; they are rich in saponins, and when crushed and mixed with water they produce a good lather which is an effective and gentle soap.

Varieties/Cultivars

Ceanothus americanus – New Jersey tea

Small deciduous shrub from eastern North America, growing 1.2m high; hardy to zone 4 / H7. Fast growing.

Uses: A refreshing and stimulating tea is made from the dried leaves, which is a good substitute for Chinese tea though it does not contain caffeine; the leaves are gathered when the plant is in full bloom and are dried in the shade. Medicinally, the roots and bark are antispasmodic, antisyphilitic, astringent, expectorant, haemostatic, sedative. The roots are strongly astringent (they contain 8% tannin), expectorant and sedative; an alkaloid in the roots is mildly hypotensive; a tea has been used in the treatment of asthma, dysentery, sore throats etc. The powdered bark has been used to wash sores. A green dye is obtained from the flowers. A cinnamon coloured dye is obtained from the whole plant; a red dye is obtained from the root. The flowers are rich in saponins; when crushed and mixed with water they produce an excellent lather which is an effective and gentle soap. They can be used as a body wash (simply rub the wet blossoms over the body) or to clean clothes.

Ceanothus cuneatus – Buckbrush

Medium evergreen shrub from southwestern North America, growing 1.8m high; hardy to zone 7 / H6. Fast growing.

Uses: Edible seed. The leaves and flowers make an excellent tea when steeped in boiling water for about five minutes. Medicinally the plant is astringent, digestive, pectoral, tonic (used as a liver tonic). A green dye is obtained from the flowers; a red dye is obtained from the root. The flowers are rich in saponins; when crushed and mixed with water they produce a good lather which is an effective and gentle soap.

Ceanothus divergens – Cropleaf ceanothus

Small evergreen shrub from California, growing 1.5m high and spreading 2.5m; hardy to zone 8 / H6.

Uses: A green dye is obtained from the flowers. The flowers are rich in saponins; when crushed and mixed with water they produce a good lather which is an effective and gentle soap. A useful ground cover plant, especially on warm sunny slopes.

Ceanothus fendleri

Medium deciduous shrub from western North America, growing 2m high; hardy to zone 5 / H7.

Uses: Edible fruit (only 5mm wide), used for food in New Mexico. The leaves are used as a substitute for tea. Used medicinally as a sedative. A green dye is obtained from the flowers. The flowers are rich in saponins; when crushed and mixed with water they produce a good lather which is an effective and gentle soap.

Ceanothus integerrimus – Deer brush

Medium/large deciduous shrub from western North America, growing 4m high; hardy to zone 7 / H6.

Uses: Edible seed, used as piñole. A green dye is obtained from the flowers. The flowers are rich in saponins; when crushed and mixed with water they produce a good lather which is an effective and gentle soap.

Ceanothus megacarpus – Bigpod ceanothus

Large evergreen shrub from California, growing 4m high; hardy to zone 7 / H6.

Uses: the wood is hard and durable: used for fence posts and wedges.

Ceanothus thyrsiflorus

Ceanothus oliganthus

Medium evergreen shrub from California, growing 3m high; hardy to zone 8 / H6.

Uses: The wood is hard and durable: used for fence posts, awls and wedges.

Ceanothus ovatus – Smaller red-root

Dwarf deciduous shrub from eastern and central North America, growing 1m high; hardy to zone 5 / H7.

Uses: The young leaves and flowers are made into a tea, tasting similar to Oriental tea but milder and sweeter. A green dye is obtained from the flowers. The flowers are rich in saponins; when crushed and mixed with water they produce a good lather which is an effective and gentle soap.

Ceanothus prostratus – Squaw carpet

Prostrate evergreen shrub from western North America, growing 5cm high but spreading up to 2.5m; hardy to zone 7 / H6. This species is particularly susceptible to damage by frost when it is young, though it should become hardy as it grows older. The subspecies *C. prostratus occidentalis* is a form growing by the coast in north California, which may be a more suitable form for maritime areas. The branches are prostrate and often form roots where they touch the soil.

Uses: A green dye is obtained from the flowers. The flowers are rich in saponins; when crushed and mixed with water they produce a good lather which is an effective and gentle soap. A useful ground cover plant, especially on warm sunny slopes.

Ceanothus purpureus – Hollyleaf ceanothus

Medium evergreen shrub from California, growing 2m high; hardy to zone 8 / H6.

Uses: A green dye is obtained from the flowers. The flowers are rich in saponins; when crushed and mixed with water they produce a good lather which is an effective and gentle soap. The spreading forms of this species make a useful ground cover, especially on warm sunny slopes.

Ceanothus sanguineus – Oregon tea tree

Medium deciduous shrub from western North America, growing 2-3m high; hardy to zone 5 / H7.

Uses: A tea is made from the leaves. A green dye is obtained from the flowers. The flowers are rich in saponins; when crushed and mixed with water they produce a good lather which is an effective and gentle soap.

Ceanothus spinosus – Red heart

Large evergreen shrub from California, growing 6m high; hardy to zone 8 / H7.

Uses: The wood is hard and durable: used for fence posts, awls and wedges.

Ceanothus thyrsiflorus – Blue brush

Large evergreen shrub from southwestern North America, growing to 4.5m in height and spread; hardy to zone 7 / H6. Tolerant of maritime exposure. The subspecies *C. thyrsiflorus repens* is somewhat hardier.

Uses: A green dye is obtained from the flowers. The flowers are rich in saponins; when crushed and mixed with water they produce a good lather which is an effective and gentle soap. *C. thyrsiflorus repens* is a good ground cover plant for sunny positions, growing well on banks and reaching a height of 90cm. Plants can be grown as a hedge in exposed maritime areas though they can be slow to establish.

Ceanothus velutinus – Sticky laurel

Medium evergreen shrub from western North America, growing 2.5m high; hardy to zone 7 / H6. The leaves have a strong scent of balsam.

Uses: The leaves are used as a tea substitute. A green dye is obtained from the flowers. The flowers are rich in saponins; when crushed and mixed with water they produce a good lather which is an effective and gentle soap.

Cultivation

Ceanothus require full sun or light shade and a well-drained soil; they tolerate maritime climates and do well in the mild conditions of Britain. They dislike root disturbance and heavy pruning, and flower at a young age, often in their second year from seed.

Propagate by seed or summer cuttings.

Pests and diseases

Some species are prone to frost damage when young.

CAPER BUSH
Capparis spinosa

Zone 8/9, H4
Evergreen
Condiment (flower buds)

Caper bush

Origin and history

Caper plants are small evergreen shrubs, reaching 1m (3ft) high or more. However, wild caper plants are more often seen hanging, draped and sprawling as they scramble over soil and rocks. The caper's vegetative canopy covers soil surfaces that help to conserve soil water reserves. Leaf stipules may be formed into spines. Flowers, 5cm (2ins) across, white with purple stamens, are borne on first year branches.

There is a strong association between the caper bush and oceans and seas. *Capparis spinosa* is said to be native to the Mediterranean basin, but its range stretches from the Atlantic coasts of the Canary Islands and Morocco to the Black Sea to the Crimea and Armenia, and eastward to the Caspian Sea and into Iran. Capers probably originated from dry regions in west or central Asia. Known and used for millennia, capers were mentioned by Dioscoroides as being a marketable product of the ancient Greeks. Capers are also mentioned by the Roman scholar, Pliny the Elder.

Description

Dry heat and intense sunlight make the preferred environment for caper plants. Plants are productive in zones having 350mm annual precipitation (falling mostly in winter and spring months) and easily survive summertime temperatures higher than 40°C (105°F). However, caper is a cold tender plant and has a temperature hardiness range similar to the olive tree (-8°C, 18°F) i.e. zone 8/9 (H4).

Where native, plants grow spontaneously in cracks and crevices of rocks and stone walls. Plants grow well in nutrient poor, sharply-drained gravelly soils. Mature plants develop large extensive root systems that penetrate deeply into the earth. Capers are salt tolerant and flourish along shores within sea-spray zones.

Wild caper plants are harvested locally throughout their natural range. There is intensive caper cultivation in Spain and Italy, with some cultivation in Greece, Croatia, North Africa, Cyprus, and Iran.

Uses

Capers of commerce are immature flower buds which have been pickled in vinegar or preserved in granular salt. Semi-mature fruit (caperberries) and young shoots with small leaves may also be pickled for use as a condiment.

Capers have a sharp piquant flavour and add pungency, a peculiar aroma and saltiness to comestibles such as pasta sauces, pizza, fish, meats and salads. The flavour of caper may be described as being similar to that of mustard and black pepper. In fact, the caper's strong flavour comes from methyl isothiocyanate (the same compound as in mustard oil) arising from crushed buds.

Tender young shoots including immature small leaves may also be eaten as a vegetable, or pickled. More rarely, mature and semi-mature fruits are eaten as a cooked vegetable. Additionally, ash from burned caper roots has been used as a source of salt.

Medicinal uses

Recent research has shown that the plant has anti-inflammatory and antioxidant properties. Capers are said to reduce flatulence and to be anti-rheumatic in effect. In Ayurvedic medicine, capers are recorded as hepatic stimulants and protectors, improving liver function. Capers also have reported uses for arteriosclerosis, as diuretics, kidney disinfectants, vermifuges and tonics. Capers contain considerable amounts of the antioxidant bioflavonoid rutin.

Caper extracts and pulps have been used in cosmetics, but it has been connected with contact dermatitis and sensitivity from their use.

Caper flowers

Caper fruit and seeds

Varieties/Cultivars

Varieties have been selected for spinelessness, round firm buds, and flavour (not yield).

Aculeata	
Dolce di Filicudi e Alicudi	From the Aeolian Archipelago
Inermis	Without stipular spines
Josephine	One of the better Mediterranean selections
Nocellana	Spineless, with globose buds, mustard-green colour, and strong aroma
Nuciddara or Nucidda	
Senza Spina	Italian selection or form without stipular spines
Spinosa Comune	Italian form with stipular spines
Testa di Lucertola	
Tondino	Grown on the island of Pantelleria

Cultivation

Plants are transplanted during winter and spring, and in the Mediterranean region first year plants are mulched with stones. Full sun and a well-drained site are required.

In Italy, plants are spaced 2-2.5m (6-8ft). Flowering should begin in 1-4 years, with a full yield some three years after. Plants are pruned back in winter to remove dead wood and watersprouts. Pruning is crucial to high production. Heavy branch pruning is used to maximise yield, as flower buds arise on one-year-old branches. Three-year-old plants will yield 1-3kg (2-6lb) of caper flower buds per plant. Caper bushes can remain productive for 20-30 years.

Harvesting: the unopened flower buds should be picked on dry days. Harvesting is carried out regularly throughout the growing season. In southern Italy, caper flower buds are collected by hand about every 8-12 days, resulting in 9-12 harvest times per season.

Capers are preserved either in vinegar or under layers of salt in a jar. Raw capers are bland flavoured and need to be cured to develop their piquant flavour. In commercial production, capers are graded using screens to sort different sizes (generally 7-16mm). The larger capers are more commercially valuable. Capers in vinegar are traditionally packaged in tall narrow glass bottles.

Caper fruit (caperberry, capperone or taperone) may be used in making caper flavoured sauces, or sometimes pickled for eating like small gherkins.

Plants are grown from seed and by vegetative cuttings.

Caper seeds are small and are slow to grow into transplantable seedlings. Fresh caper seeds germinate readily but only in low percentages. Dried seeds become dormant and are notably difficult to germinate and therefore require extra measures to grow. Dried seeds should be initially immersed in warm water (40°C / 105°F) and then let to soak for one day. Seeds should be wrapped in a moist cloth, placed in a sealed glass jar and kept in the refrigerator for 2-3 months. After refrigeration, soak the seeds again in warm water overnight. Plant the seeds about 1cm (0.4ins) deep in a loose, well-drained soil medium. Young caper plants can be grown in a greenhouse (preferable minimum temperature of 10°C / 50°F).

Stem cuttings propagation: collect cuttings in February, March or April. Use stems from the basal portions, greater than 1cm (0.4ins) diameter and 8cm (3.2ins) in length with 6-10 buds. Use a loose, well-drained media with bottom heat. A dip in a rooting hormone solution is recommended.

Pests and diseases

A variety of fungal and insect pests can be occasional problems. In more temperate climates, grey mould (*Botrytis*) may be a problem in wet periods.

CHASTE TREE, *Vitex agnus-castus*

Zone 7, H4-5
Deciduous
Spice plant, Medicinal

Origin and history

The chaste tree is often grown as an ornamental for its fragrant leaves and flowers. It is native to the Mediterranean region and western Asia and naturalised in other warm areas. Its other main common name, agnus castus, is also applied to the medicinal parts commonly used.

Description

A deciduous large shrub growing up to 5m+ (16ft+) high and wide but often less, with light grey, aromatic branches and an open spreading form.

The leaves are aromatic, with elliptic leaflets up to 10 x 1.5cm (4 x 0.5ins). They are green above and grey and felted beneath.

Flowers are formed in spikes up to 15cm (6ins) long at the end of the branchlets; they are lilac or light blue, fragrant, in late summer and autumn. Although plants bear both sexes of flowers, they are not very self-fertile and cross-pollination is usually required for fruit to form.

Fruits are rounded, 3mm across, reddish-black, hard and aromatic. They look and smell similar to black pepper.

The wood is hard and close grained.

Chaste tree flowers

Uses

The fruit of the chaste tree have long been used medicinally and associated with chastity. Ground seeds were once used in monasteries as a peppery condiment to suppress libido, hence another common name, monk's pepper; it has been found they indeed inhibit the action of male sex hormones. The leaves too can be used as a spice. The leaves and seeds are still sometimes used as one of the ingredients of the Moroccan spice mix, ras el hanout, which is used in savoury dishes or stirred into rice or couscous.

The fruit contain volatile oils (the essential oil contains over 70 components, including sabinene and cineol), alkaloids (including viticine), flavonoids (including casticin) and iridoids (including aucubin, agnoside and eurostoside) and affects the hormonal balance in both men and women. The most important use is its ability to rectify hormonal imbalances caused by an excess of oestrogen and an insufficiency of progesterone. This is used in malfunctions of the feminine reproductive system and has been used with great effect in restoring absent menstruation, regulating heavy periods, restoring fertility when this is caused by hormonal imbalance, relieving pre-menstrual tension and easing the change of the menopause. They are also used to promote lactation. However, side effects can be significant and it should only be used under medical supervision.

Most agnus castus sold commercially are harvested from the wild in China. They are used medicinally as a powder incorporated into tablets, as a liquid extract or as a tincture. The leaves have similar medicinal properties to the fruit and are sometimes used instead. Note that excessive use can cause a nerve disorder of the skin.

Fruit of *Vitex agnus-castus*

Cultivation

A warm location in sun is needed in temperate climates with protection from cold drying winds. Good drainage is also required, with a light or medium well-drained soil preferred. It is drought tolerant. Growth is about 30cm (1ft) per year. It is wise to plant out young plants in the spring to allow them to establish before experiencing winter wet and cold.

In continental climates with hot summers and cold winters, the plant sometimes survives as a perennial, dying to the ground each winter.

For fruiting to occur, long hot summers are required. Fruits are usually harvested soon after the leaves have fallen, in dry conditions.

Flowers are produced at the ends of the current year's growth, hence any pruning is best carried out in the spring and should consist of cutting out dead wood and shortening the previous year's flowering branches.

There has been recent interest in the essential oil of agnus castus, distilled from the fruit. The yield is 0.1-2.8%, depending on the plant chemotype, climate and other factors. The oil shows moderate antibacterial activity. A leaf oil can also be distilled which contains similar components to the fruit oil. The oil is used in perfumery and medicine.

The young stems can be used in basketry.

A yellow dye can be obtained from the leaves, fruit and roots.

Bees like the flowers in September and October.

Varieties/Cultivars

V. agnus-castus f. latifolia, the broad-leaved chaste tree, is similar in most respects but is slightly hardier, to zone 6 / H4. It has purple flowers.

Agnus castus is usually grown from seed. Seeds have variable dormancy; some are not dormant at all while others are. If sown in spring, some seeds of each batch germinate quite quickly. Semi-ripe cuttings taken in summer can also succeed.

Pests and diseases

There are no significant pests or diseases in temperate climates.

CHILEAN HAZEL, *Gevuina avellana*

Zone 8-9, H4
Evergreen
Edible nuts

Origin and history

Gevuina avellana, known as the Chilean hazelnut, Chile nut, Gevuin or Gevuina, is an evergreen tree native to Chile between latitudes 35° and 44°S, from sea level to 700m altitude, mainly in the cool rainforests of Valdivia and Chiloe. It grows under the influence of a temperate oceanic climate in a wide range of temperatures and rainfall with a good frost resistance. Adapted to many well-drained soils, Gevuina has good potential as an edible nut-producing tree and is related to the Macadamia nut.

Description

The Gevuina is an evergreen tree of the Proteaceae family, growing 5-10m (16-33ft) high, with a large conical head and compact canopy. Branches are stout and pubescent, young shoots covered in dense reddish hair.

Leaves are shiny dark green, bipinnate and leathery, 15-40cm (6-16ins) long by 10-25cm (4-10ins) wide with leaflets of varying size.

Flowering occurs in summer to autumn, at the same time as fruits ripen from the previous year's flowers. Flowers are white, borne in racemes about 10cm (4ins) long on the outside of the tree canopy. Pollination is via bees. Cross-pollination between different trees is essential for a good fruit set, although the male and female parts are found in the same flowers.

Fruits become coral red when ripe and contain a single hard woody black seed between 15-25mm (0.6-1ins) in diameter.

Trees are intolerant of wet soils – it is vital that in winter their soils remain well drained and not waterlogged.

Uses

The nuts can be eaten raw, dried, or cooked (usually roasted). The nut is black with a thin, easy-to-peel, smooth shell which can be cut off with a knife. The kernel is creamy white with a crisp texture like coconut, a rich flavour reminiscent of hazel and macadamia.

The nuts are mainly used at present in breakfast cereals, and are also roasted and sold in small bags like peanuts. It is used in the food industry mixed with chocolate, in butter and pastries, in flours, pressed as a table oil etc. The whole nut can be processed into a 'Gevuina butter' paste of high nutritional value, similar to peanut butter. Nuts can also be dried and ground into a flour. Roasted seeds can be made into a coffee-like drink.

Nuts are high in protein, fats, vitamin E and energy content. The oil is similar to olive or canola oil in unsaturated fatty acids, except for one thing: palmitoleic acid, a fatty acid with special properties (it is easily absorbed by the skin and blocks UV radiation) which is present in large quantities. Per 100g portion, nuts on average contain:

Water	7.1g
Protein	12.6g
Fat	47.7g
Carbohydrates	20.5g
Fibre	4.9-10.2g
Calories	680

It is often planted ornamentally for its beauty. The cut foliage is very durable and is widely sold in the Chilean floristry trade. The nuts are used as an important stock feed in Chile, notably for poultry.

Gevuina nuts ripening on tree

Chilean hazel in Cornwall, England

Bees are fond of the nectar and perform pollination – honey production from Gevuina being important in Chile.

The wood has a distinctive grain pattern and is strong, flexible and light; it has been used in cabinet work, for making furniture, roof shingles, tools, oars and musical instruments.

The husks of Gevuina are rich in tannin and tannin extraction after nut processing is feasible.

Varieties/Cultivars

Breeding for superior selections has been going on in Chile since 1970 both for quality and yields of nuts (and nut composition for nutritional, cosmetic and pharmaceutical applications) as well as for superior 'plus trees' for forestry use. Six superior cultivars (called the VAX cultivars or clones) have been selected which are adapted to low summer rainfall, soils of low natural fertility and good drainage, with frost resistance. These cultivars start cropping between 3-5 years of age, reaching full cropping at 8-10 years (as opposed to unselected seedling trees which take 7-10 years to start cropping).

Cultivation

Plants are intolerant of root disturbance (the roots are somewhat fleshy and easily broken) and are best transplanted as young potted plants.

Chilean hazel is shade tolerant, but does not flower or fruit well there – full sun is optimum. Strong winds are also disliked because of the weak root system and high sail area of the foliage. Acid to neutral soils are preferred. Plants are apparently sensitive to chemical fertilisers, disliking too much nitrogen.

Most production until recently in Chile was from wild trees, which yield about 5kg (11lb) annually. But better performing selections are now increasingly grown. Yields per tree from some of the VAX cultivars reach about 24kg/tree (53lb/tree). Nut counts are 380-460 nuts/kg, with individual nut weights at 2.1-2.6g. Nut size is on average 17 x 20mm (0.6 x 0.8ins) long, with some over 25mm (1ins) across. The kernels form 36-44% of the nut weight, weigh 0.9-1.0g, and are about 12mm (0.5ins) diameter. Shells are about 2.5mm (0.1ins) thick. Tree vigour varies in the VAX cultivars from low (tree reaches 3.5-4m / 11-13ft canopy width) to medium/high (4.5-5.5m / 15-18ft canopy width).

Yields per hectare depend on planting density. The medium to high vigour cultivars can be planted at 4 x 6m = 416 trees/ha (13 x 20ft = 166 trees/acre), giving yields of 11.5 tonnes/ha (4.6 tonnes/acre) nuts (4.2 tonnes/ha / 1.7 tonnes/acre kernels). The lower vigour clones can be planted at 3 x 5m = 666 trees/ha (10 x 16ft = 266 trees/acre), giving yields of 10.8 tonnes/ha (4.3 tons/acre) nuts (4.2 tonnes/ha / 1.7 tonnes/acre kernels). These are comparable to very good yields of hazelnut (*Corylus avellana*). These yields are obtained from trees in orchards with minimum management – trees allowed to grow freely without pruning, fertilisation or pesticides; only a hay crop was taken between trees to allow for harvest.

Harvest is carried out in autumn each year in Chile (Feb-March there) over a period of about a month, after the nuts have turned from red to brownish-black, gathering from the ground 80% of the nuts in 15-20 days. To prepare nuts for roasting, the kernels are removed from the shells and blanched in boiling water to separate the seed coat (pellicle).

Established trees coppice well if necessary to rejuvenate them.

Cuttings are the easiest way to propagate good selections. Semi-ripe cuttings in July-August are recommended.

Trees can be grown from seed,which is not dormant.

Pests and diseases

Young seedlings are very susceptible to fungal diseases, with a survival rate of 30% or less not uncommon. Using a well-drained compost of medium fertility is recommended.

Seedlings and young plants are susceptible to a 'sudden death', when roots rot and suddenly the top growth wilts completely. The cause is not known; it may be a response to high nitrogen, a lack of mycorrhizal fungi, pathogenic *Phytophthora* fungi or a combination of these. Spreading a little soil from beneath an established tree around seedlings may help survival rates.

CHINESE DATE, *Ziziphus jujuba*

Zone 5-6, H4
Deciduous
Edible fruit

Origin and history

Cultivars of *Ziziphus jujuba* (synonyms *Z. sativa*, *Z. vulgaris*), known as jujube, Chinese jujube, red date or Chinese date, have long been grown for their excellent dessert fruit. Native to warm temperate and subtropical Asia, where there are many cultivars grown for fruit, it has become naturalised in many other regions; jujube plants were brought from Syria to the Mediterranean in ancient Roman times. In China it is considered one of the five principal fruit.

Description

The jujube is a deciduous shrub or tree growing up to 9m (30ft) high and 7m (23ft) wide with drooping branches, flexuous twigs and pairs of short curved and occasional long spines. The jujube is unusual in that it sheds many of the short lateral-bearing twigs, i.e. it has deciduous branches as well as leaves. This branchlet loss gives the tree a distinctive zig-zag appearance in winter. Trees often send up suckers many feet from the mother plant.

As the growing season commences, each node of a woody branch produces 1-10 branchlets. Leaves are 2.5-6cm (1-2.5ins) long, elliptic, leathery, shiny and on short stalks.

Flowers are small and yellow, about 5mm (0.2ins) across, in axillary clusters of 2-3 on the current season's growth from the small lateral branchlets. They appear in late spring or summer, depending on the climate; flowering can continue over an extended period, although each flower is receptive to pollen for a day only. Pollination is via insects including bees; although trees are usually self-fertile, fruits are bigger and more numerous with cross-pollination.

Fruits are between a cherry and plum in size, 1.5-4cm (0.6-1.5ins) long, roundish, egg shaped like small plums (sometimes round or pear shaped). The amount of flesh is very variable between selections. The skin is bright green and shiny when the fruit is mature – at this stage the flesh is crisp and sweet, with an apple flavour; if left on the tree, the skin begins to brown in a few spots, the brown areas coalesce to completely cover the surface, then the fruit begins to dry and wrinkle; by the time it is fully ripe the jujube is a rich red-bronze and most resembles a prune or dry date, hence the name Chinese date. The texture now is chewy and resembling a date, and the taste has improved.

The fruits contain a single, hard-shelled stone that encloses one or two seeds.

Under natural conditions, *Z. jujuba* forms a deep and substantial taproot, making it drought tolerant.

Although the tree is winter hardy to USDA zone 5-6, -20 to 25°C (-4 to -15°F), in oceanic temperate climates like Britain, the wood will often not ripen properly following a cool summer, and will get cut back by only moderately cold weather in winter. This explains the difference between the USDA and RHS hardiness ratings.

It has a short chilling requirement and tolerates extreme heat to 40°C (104°F) or more.

Uses

The fruits have a pleasant acid taste when fresh, but are usually allowed to dry on the tree, when they are chewy and more palatable. The rough and sharp-pointed seed shell is not very suitable for young children. They are used as a substitute for dates and used in savoury dishes, rice, fish, soup and in cakes. In Asia they are sometimes ground into flour and used for bread; they can be added to bread mixes. The fresh fruit pulp contains about 9% sugars, 1.7% pectin, 2.5% protein and 200-350mg vitamin C per 100g of pulp.

Fresh green fruits are sometimes used to make jams. The dried fruits contain 20-35% sugars (just under half that being sucrose, the rest fructose and glucose) and are rich in vitamin C. Oriental food shops often sell Chinese dates that have been boiled with sugar and honey, the most popular Chinese way of eating them. In Korea, jujube flour is used in the preparation of 'kochujang', a fermented hot pepper-soyabean paste that resembles miso.

An edible oil can be obtained from the seed, though presumably yields are low as the kernel is small.

The fruits are also medicinal and widely used in Chinese herbal medicine for arthritis and insomnia. They are often used in mixtures with other species' parts and such mixtures have been shown useful in treating hepatitis B. They are used in the Himalayas as an antidote to aconite poisoning and for nausea and vomiting; for abdominal pain during pregnancy; and externally in poultices for wounds.

The fruits were often formerly used (probably in the boiled-with-honey form) in Britain to alleviate coughs and sore throats, and were formerly imported into Britain in large quantities from southern France for this purpose.

Leaves and flowers of Chinese date

The seeds are used in Chinese medicine for insomnia, amnesia and vertigo; the root is used for dyspepsia, as a powder for wounds and as a febrifuge. The plant is widely used in China as a treatment for burns.

The leaves are also medicinal and are used in the Himalayas for scabies and throat troubles. A broth is made from the leaves in Tajikistan and used for treating liver, kidney and stomach problems, and to improve vital functions. In China they are used for fevers and are said to promote hair growth.

The wood of the tree is very hard and durable, and used to make agricultural implements and for turnery. It makes good fuel and charcoal.

The leaves are used as a fodder for sheep and goats in the Himalayas. They have also been used for silkworm fodder in China.

In China, jujube is widely used in shelterbelts, with over 200,000 ha (500,000 acres) planted, with optimum spacing of rows 3.7m (12ft) wide (two lines of trees) with alleys between rows of some 14m (45ft) width where cereals like wheat are grown.

Jujube is also used to stabilise mountainous slopes from erosion, and is regarded in Central Asia as one of the best crops for this.

The jujube is also an attractive ornamental tree.

Varieties/Cultivars

Most of these originated in China and arrived in the West via the USA in the early twentieth century. China currently has over 400 superior cultivars, although only a handful are obtainable in the West. Seedling trees come relatively true to their parent, although they take a few more years to bear fruit.

Chinese date fruit

Cultivar	Description
Admiral Wilkes	Fruit elongated, 50mm (2ins) long, very late to ripen.
Ant Admire	Fruit medium sized, narrow, elongated, very sweet; mid season ripening. From China.
Chico	Fruit small, round, often seedless (seed is round when present), good to eat green when crisp and acid; tree thorny, needs hot location. From California, USA.
Davis	Fruit of excellent flavour; productive tree. From the USA.
GA 866	Fruit elongated, 50mm (2ins) long, very sweet, mid-season ripening. Tree has few thorns. From California, USA.
Geant Sloboda	A selection from the former USSR.
Honey Jar	Fruit very small (under 25mm, 1ins across), round, extremely sweet both fresh and dried. From China.
Jin	Fruit very uniform, elongated, 50mm (2ins) or more in length, very small seeds. Dried fruit are very chewy and date-like. Ripens early; hangs on the tree well after drying.
Lang	Fruit large, up to 50 x 40mm (2 x 1.5ins), pear shaped, with a thin shiny skin and sweet, melting plentiful flesh with a hint of caramel flavour; tree large, upright, early bearing, generally has only a few thorns. Good fresh, excellent dried. Mid-season ripening. From China.
Li	Fruit very large, up to 50mm (2ins) in diameter, round, excellent flavour, good to eat green, flesh sweet and crisp, and with a small stone, early season ripening; will ripen if picked at the yellow-green stage. Tree large, spreading, suckering. From China.
Redlands 4	Fruit large, round, like Li but larger; excellent sweet flavour and crisp texture; mid-season ripening. From California.
Sherwood	Fruit very large, 40-50mm (1.5-2ins) long or more, flesh of excellent quality, dense; very late ripening. Will keep for six weeks in refrigeration. Tree with small or no thorns, very productive. From Louisiana, USA.
Shui Men	Fruit medium sized, elongated, sweet-acid flavour, good fresh or dried; ripens mid season. Tree a good bearer, with small thorns. From China.
Silverhill	(Silverhill Round, Tigers Tooth): Fruit large, 25mm (1ins) across by 40-50mm (1.5-2ins) long, elongated (plum shaped), with sweet solid flesh, good for drying, mid season ripening; tree large with few suckers or thorns, a prolific bearer. From Georgia, USA.
So	Fruit round, of excellent flavour. Tree branches grows in a zig-zag manner.
Sugar Cane	Fruit small-medium sized, oval, 25mm (1ins) long, very sweet and crunchy, very dense, small seeds. Tree thorny. From California, USA.
Sweet-Meaty	Fruit round, meaty; very late ripening. Tree with large thorns.
Tajanczao	A selection from the former USSR.
Texas Tart	A high acid jujube. From Texas, USA.
Yu	Fruit large, elongated, tapering at the bottom; flesh sweet, firm, good keeping qualities. Tree tall with few side branches and large leaves, and few thorns. From China.

Other cultivars grown in the former USSR (particularly Tajikistan, Uzbekistan, Azerbaijan) include 'Kitaiskij N' selections, 'Azerbaijanskij N22', 'Apsheronskij', 'Mardakyanskij N1', 'Tadjikskij N24' and 'Shirvanskij'.

Cultivation

Jujubes can be grown for fruit production in warm temperate or subtropical climates; hot dry weather is required for good fruiting. In areas where there are prolonged or severe frosts, the plants need the protection of a cool or intermediate glasshouse if fruiting is desired. In Britain, lack of summer heat can often prevent good fruiting; planting against a warm wall or in a greenhouse is recommended.

Grow in any well-drained soil, including alkaline and saline soils, in sun. Jujubes like low humidity during the growth season and a dry soil in winter. Pot-grown trees may need regular root pruning to prevent the formation of a dominant long tap root. Jujube orchards should be planted at 7-8 x 4-5m (23-27 x 13-16ft) – the larger spacing on more fertile soils and for more vigorous trees.

Pruning should be carried out during dormancy in winter. Fruit is borne on the current season's growth, hence there is no danger of pruning off fruiting wood; pruning should concentrate on removing dead or dying wood, and keeping the tree open and well ventilated. Initially it may be wise to select a framework of 3-4 branches in a pyramid form.

In China, girdling is commonly used to increase yields by up to 200%. A circular strip of bark is either removed or reversed on the main trunk of the tree. This procedure causes the tree to set fruit earlier (it can also be applied to fig trees).

Fruiting on grafted plants starts after 2-4 years; seedlings may take 3-7 years. The first few crops do not give a true indication of eventual fruit size. Although trees are usually self-fertile, fruits are bigger and more numerous with cross-pollination.

Harvesting can begin as soon as the green fruit develop a few brown spots on the skin – they will then fully ripen off the tree; if you have dry conditions, then leave them on the tree to ripen and harvest them as they fall to the ground. The fruits ripen gradually (over a month or more) and not all at once, and should be picked or shaken every few days over this period. In China, harvest normally takes place early in the morning before the dew dries; this is supposed to improve the flavour and texture of harvested fruit. Yields vary tremendously but can average 45kg (100lb) per tree or more for mature trees.

In humid climates, fruit should be picked when starting to turn brownish-red and dried at 45°C (115°F), stirring frequently. If not picked, rain and humid weather can cause the skin to crack, and then fungi can develop in the cracks.

Fresh ripe fruit will keep for 1-2 months at 10°C (50°F) or for 1-4 weeks at room temperature; dried ripe fruit will keep for a year at cool temperatures and 50% relative humidity. They should be kept in unsealed containers.

Seed propagation is fairly easy. Jujube seeds have a hard, rough, pointed outer shell which has a distinct suture line aligned from end to end. This shell needs to be removed to facilitate reliable germination; the best way is to carefully align the suture in the blades of a pair of secateurs and cut firmly; the seed usually comes out unscathed from this operation! The naked seeds are then not dormant and should be sown immediately in warmth; germination takes place over the next 2-5 weeks. First year growth can reach 20cm (8ins).

Cutting propagation is difficult but possible. Take greenwood cuttings in summer about 15cm (6ins) long, just as the base is starting to harden, and use mist and bottom heat. The success rate may be as low as 10%, but it may be worth it to get trees on their own roots, whose suckers will be identical to the mother tree.

Cultivars of *Z. jujuba* are usually propagated by grafting onto jujube seedlings or seedlings of the related *Ziziphus rotundifolia* – the latter limits top growth and is better suited to pot culture, but is not very hardy. A whip and tongue graft is used with the previous season's wood at least 7mm (2.75ins) thick.

Jujubes can sometimes be propagated by root cuttings; success depends on the cultivar and of course it must be on its own roots and not grafted.

Pests and diseases

There are few pests or diseases in Europe or North America.

Related species

There are a number of related species with edible fruit but all require a subtropical climate.

CHOCOLATE VINES, *Akebia* species

Zone 5-6, H7
Deciduous, semi-evergreen, evergreen
Edible pulp

Origin and history

Akebia species are vines which have a long history of usage in their native regions of China, Korea and Japan, where they occur in woods and thickets in mountainous areas. The name Akebia comes from the Japanese name for these plants, *Akebi*.

Description

The main two species in cultivation are *A. quinata* (five leaf Akebia) and *A. trifoliata* (synonym *A. lobata*, three leaf Akebia); and the hybrid between them (with intermediate characteristics and similar uses), *A. x pentaphylla*.

Deciduous, semi-evergreen or evergreen twining vines, growing to 9-12m (30-40ft) high (*A. quinata*), 6-9m (20-30ft) high (*A. trifoliata*). New shoots are shiny and purplish. *A. quinata* is slightly faster growing. In very mild areas they are evergreen, in mild areas semi-evergreen (most of the UK) and in colder areas they become deciduous.

Leaves are alternate and compound, tough and fleshy, 3-7cm (1.2-3ins) long. *A. quinata* has five leaflets, oval-elliptic, smooth-edged with long stalks, dark green above and blue-green beneath. *A. trifoliata* has three leaflets, with slightly wavy edges, dark green above and lighter beneath.

Flowers are borne on thin stalks in April-May (*A. trifoliata*) or May-June (*A. quinata*), with male and female flowers borne on the same flowering raceme; those of *A. quinata* have a spicy vanilla-like fragrance. Female flowers are violet-brown (*A. quinata*) or chestnut-brown (*A. trifoliata*) and 2-3.5cm (0.8-1.5ins) across. Male flowers are smaller (6mm/0.25ins across), pinkish-purple and numerous. Both sexes are borne on plants but individuals are not self-fertile, hence two different clones are required for fruiting to occur.

Fruits are pods like small light violet/purple cucumbers, 5-10cm (2-4ins) long (*A. quinata*), 7-15cm (3-6ins) long (*A. trifoliata*) by 3-6cm (1-2.5ins) wide. They contain a whitish, tasty sweet pulp and numerous small black seeds. If not picked they eventually split lengthways.

Akebia species are resistant to honey fungus (*Armillaria* spp.).

Uses

The delicately watermelon-flavoured sweet pulp from the fruit is eaten raw, or with lemon juice, or made into a drink. Fruits of *A. quinata* vary from 45-70g (1.5-2.5oz) each in weight.

Fruit on *Akebia quinata*

The bitter skins of the fruit can be fried. The soft young shoots can be eaten raw in salads or used for salt pickling. The dried young leaves can be used to make a tea.

The stems are strong and pliable and are prized for basket making in its native habitat. They can be used unprocessed or are sometimes peeled in the same way as willow is.

A. quinata and *A. trifoliata* are used interchangeably in Chinese medicine, regarded as a pungent bitter herb that controls bacterial and fungal infections, and stimulates the circulatory and urinary systems and female organs. It is used in Chinese medicine internally for urinary tract infections, rheumatoid arthritis, absence of menstruation and insufficient lactation. Stems are cut in autumn and dried for use in decoctions (teas) and powders.

All three are grown ornamentally for their elegant foliage, often up walls or fences. Plants also make good façade insulation, trained up wires or trellises on walls.

The Akebias can be used for ground cover; they are excellent for covering banks, providing good erosion control over large

Akebia quinata

Inside an *Akebia quinata* fruit

areas. As ground cover they only reach 15-30cm (6-12ins) high, but are only good companions to large-trunked trees (which they cannot wrap themselves around); they will overrun smaller trees and shrubs. They don't tolerate much foot traffic. Plants for ground cover can be spaced about 1m (3ft) apart.

Varieties/Cultivars

If you want fruit, one problem with buying plants is that they are likely to have been propagated vegetatively, and if they are genetically identical they will not cross-pollinate each other. You can check with a nursery how plants are propagated and if necessary try and obtain different species or cultivars or grow your own plants from seed.

Breeding work to produce good fruiting cultivars is taking place in China and Korea as well as the USA. At present, there are a few mostly ornamental cultivars of *A. quinata* available which should provide cross-pollination for each other:

Cultivar	Description
Alba	Flowers and fruit white
Cream form	Flowers creamy white
Rosea	Flowers pinkish-purple
Shirobana	Flowers white, highly fragrant
Variegata	Flowers pale pink, leaves with white variegation
#1	Flowers deep purple, fruit 7-10cm (3-4ins) long
#2	Flowers white-light pink, fruit 7-10cm (3-4ins) long

Cultivation

The Akebias are fast growing vines which climb readily on a trellis or into other plants. They need little training or tying, as the stems will readily fix themselves by twining round any wire, small branch etc. with which they make contact. Most growth occurs between mid-April and early July. They are good for training over hedges. They resent root disturbance once planted.

Their main requirement is for a moderate to highly fertile, well-drained but moisture retentive soil (a sandy loam is ideal) of any pH. They like sun or partial shade (and will tolerate deep shade but won't flower there), and grow well on the sunnier edges of a woodland. They tolerate moderate drought as well as strong drying winds.

Young plants may require some winter protection in cold areas. Plants of *A. trifoliata* may require a slightly more sheltered position because they flower earlier and are more susceptible to frost damage to the flowers.

Expected growth rates in Britain are about 80cm (32ins) per year for *A. quinata* and 30-50cm (12-20ins) per year for *A. trifoliata*. Nearly twice these rates have been recorded in warmer regions.

Because ornamental plants in Britain have nearly always been grown singly, there are few reports of good fruiting here; however, the plants have fruited, particularly in the south and south west of Britain, and there is no reason why good fruiting should not occur given two or more clones for cross-pollination. Cross-pollination can occur between *A. quinata* and *A. trifoliata* or between either of these and *A.* x *pentaphylla*. Different clones can be grown from seed or bought as plants.

Propagation can be via layering, cuttings or seed:

- Layering – as for other woody plants. Peg down a stem, cover with earth, and leave for 6-12 months before removing layered plant. Serpentine layering (i.e. repeatedly layering the same stem) works well.
- Cuttings – semi-ripe cuttings of wood just getting firm – use a rooting hormone and place in gentle heat in a very well-drained rooting medium. Root cuttings can also be taken in December and placed in warmth.
- Seed – fresh seed germinates quickly on sowing. Dry seed germinates best after about one month of cold stratification.

Fruits ripen in September-October.

The only management required is to trim back growth excess to requirements in early spring.

Pests and diseases

There are no serious pest or disease problems.

CHOKEBERRIES / ARONIA BERRIES, *Aronia* species

Zone 4, H7
Deciduous
Edible fruit

Origin and history

The name chokeberry does not exactly inspire confidence, but the chokeberries are a fine cooked fruit very popular in Russia and Eastern Europe. In fact, the name in Eastern Europe, where they are grown commercially, translates as 'Service Tree' and the Aronias are closely related to the mountain ash, *Sorbus aucuparia* (and sometimes hybridise with it). They are in fact native to eastern North America.

Description

Chokeberry bushes are slightly spreading, medium-growing suckering deciduous shrubs reaching 1-3m (3-10ft) high, which naturally grow wild in thickets and woods. There are three species, one possibly a naturally occurring hybrid of the two:

A. arbutifolia – red chokeberry
A. melanocarpa – black chokeberry
A. prunifolia – purple chokeberry

The leaves are elliptic, with toothed margins and paler undersides. They are 2.5-7cm (1-3ins) long, and turn to shades of red and orange in the autumn – one reason that chokeberries are often planted ornamentally.

Flowers are white or whitish-pink, borne in loose clusters of up to 6-20 and quite ornamental in spring (April to June, depending

Flowers on black chokeberry

on location). Bushes are insect-pollinated and self-fertile, so only one is needed for good fruiting.

The fruits, red or black, appear like clusters of small blueberries without the waxy bloom. They are 7-9mm (0.3-0.4ins) in diameter, rising to 12mm (0.5ins) in larger-fruited cultivars. The fruits have a small soft core, soft enough to be eaten unnoticed and remain firm even when ripe. They ripen from September onwards but are often hidden by the dark leaves until the leaves change colour.

Uses

Eaten raw, the fruit can be astringent, leaving the mouth feeling dry and, true to name, the throat nearly choking. However, they are sometimes lacking astringency, especially from the named cultivars, and there is some evidence that growing Aronia in long-season areas may lead to milder tasting fruit.

When chokeberries are made into jelly or preserves, however, they develop a unique, rich flavour. The taste is reminiscent of blackcurrant with added pine and other aromas. The jelly from *A. melanocarpa* has a bright blue to burgundy colour. The fruits contain more polyphenols than almost any other plant, which makes the juice desirable to add into commercial fruit juice mixes for colour and their antioxidant properties. They also contain significant quantities of vitamin C. Fruits are also processed into syrups, compotes etc. and are dried for future use (the native North Americans used to make pemmican from them with dried meat and melted fat). The fruits are grown commercially in Denmark, Poland, Russia and elsewhere. They are high in pectin and can be added to other fruit jams/jellies to help them set.

Medicinally, the fruits contain substances that lower arterial blood pressure and are used in Russia and former USSR countries for this. Ongoing studies in the USA suggest that they may also include compounds that are anti-cancer.

Aronia plants are sometimes used as a windbreak in North America.

Varieties/Cultivars

Named cultivars of *A. melanocarpa* are usually grown on their own roots but can be grafted to *Sorbus aucuparia* rootstocks, the latter making slightly larger bushes with improved yields. Fruiting starts in the second year and gradually increases to yields averaging 10kg (22lb) per bush for the fruiting cultivars. In addition to those listed below, there are some ornamental varieties selected for good autumn colour but not fruiting.

Cultivar	Species	Description
Aron	*A. prunifolia*	Danish fruiting selection growing 1.5-2m (5-6ft) high, producing numerous large fruit.
Galicjanka	*A.* spp.	Polish selection, upright bearing large fruit, recommended for commercial plantations.
Hugin	*A. melanocarpa*	Compact shrub to 1m (3ft) high, numerous black fruit. Fruiting selection from Sweden.
Nero	*A. prunifolia*	A good fruiting cultivar from the former USSR. Fruit shiny black, twice the weight of wild types, good flavour, borne in large clusters. Fast growing.
Rubina	*A. prunifolia*	Russian variety, a Viking cross, with good crops of large fruit.
Viking	*A. prunifolia*	A good fruiting cultivar from Sweden with slightly larger berries. Fruit bluish-black, very good flavour.

Cultivation

Chokeberries are very hardy and easy to grow. They do well on any reasonable soil other than shallow chalk or very boggy ground. They tolerate partial shade (they are naturally woodland edge plants) and air pollution. For just a few plants, space at 2m (6ft) apart to maximise cropping, and keep mulched. Larger and commercial plantings are usually spaced with rows of plants at 1m (3ft) apart and allowed to sucker to fill in the space like a hedgerow.

Plants tend to sucker, turning them into a stool much like blackcurrants, but they can be kept to a single stem if desired by removing sucker growths in the autumn. Plants could even be grown against a wall or on wires. Thinning of older shoots is recommended every few years, otherwise bushes grow too dense and the poor light levels reduce productivity.

The fruits ripen in September onwards, but the flavour improves and the fruit become sweet if left on the bush. This may necessitate keeping birds off if they show an interest. Fruits are usually hand harvested, but mechanical harvesting is possible

Aronia melanocarpa fruit

(using equipment designed for blueberries) and is sometimes practised in Eastern Europe.

Propagation of named cultivars is usually by cuttings (softwood in summer, semi-hardwood in July-August or hardwood in early autumn). Occasionally grafting onto rowan rootstock is used. Plants can also be divided if they have suckers, or layered in the normal way. Seeds require three months of cold stratification and then germination can take a few months.

Pests and diseases

The fruits are liked by birds (though commercial plantings are not too troubled), but there are no other significant pests or diseases. Chokeberries are notably resistant to honey fungus.

Chokeberry jelly

Wash the chokeberries and place in a pan (not aluminium) with just enough water to cover them. Simmer gently until the fruit is soft. Transfer the fruit mixture into a clean jelly bag and allow to hang and drip into a container for several hours or overnight. Do not squeeze or press the bag as this will produce sediment that clouds the jelly. For every three cups of juice, allow 4.5 cups sugar and 0.25 cups fresh lemon juice. Pour the juice into a clean pan and bring to the boil, stirring in the sugar. Add the lemon juice. Then boil rapidly until setting point is reached. Bottle into hot jars. Chokeberries contain sufficient pectin to set on their own, although complete setting may take a few days.

CRANBERRY, *Vaccinium macrocarpon*

Zone 2, H7
Evergreen
Edible fruit / juice

Origin and history

Cranberries are native to eastern North America and Northern Asia, found in marshlands with high soil acidity in the range pH 4.0-5.0.

The early settlers in eastern North America found the wild berries in the marshlands where other vegetation did not compete strongly. The trailing, woody, evergreen plants spread out through the moss carpet, usually *Sphagnum* sp., and pushed hair-like roots into the moss and above the water level in the marsh.

Cranberry cultivation is now an industry worth several hundred million dollars annually in the USA and Canada, and commercial cultivation is also present in Austria, Finland, Germany, Poland and former USSR countries.

Description

Cranberry is a creeping evergreen shrub which spreads over and forms a mass above the level of the soil/marsh, 30cm (1ft) high. The slender woody stems are 30-200cm (1-7ft) long, and these bear ascending shoots, 5-8cm (2-3ins) long which have horizontal leaves and bear flowers and fruit. The leaves are small, elliptic-oblong, flat, apically rounded, 5-18mm (0.2-0.7ins) long and half as wide, dark green above and whitish beneath.

Cranberry

The cranberry plant evolved in an environment with a plentiful water supply provided by the wicking action of the moss and surface peat layers. It evolved without root hairs, the minute root adaptations which provide great surface area for absorption for most land plants. It produces only a shallow fibrous root system that explores only small amounts of the surface 'soil' available for its use; the roots can only go a few centimetres into the soil. It is thus adapted to, and dependent upon, a moist root medium of shallow depths. It associates with various mycorrhizae which aid considerably in plant nutrition.

The flowers are borne singly or in groups of up to 10, on shoots or slender stems arising from leaf axils. They are light purple, just under 1cm (0.4ins) long, bell shaped. Pollination is via bees.

The fruits are botanically berries, deep pink to red in colour and 1-2.5cm (0.4-1ins) in diameter. Each berry is carried on a slender stalk bringing it well out from the leaves.

Cranberries are extremely hardy as long as they do not desiccate in cold winter conditions.

Uses

The fruits have a wide range of uses nowadays in cakes, preserves, jams, juices etc.

Native Americans used cranberries raw or dried and added them to pemmican (a dried meat product). The fruits contain large amounts of benzoic acid, a natural preservative. The berries are very acid; the juice is about pH 2.5, and astringent on the tongue when ripe.

Cranberries are especially high in sugars, vitamins and minerals, with average composition as follows (per 100g):

Water	88%
Vitamin A	40 IU
Calcium	14mg
Protein	0.4g
Vitamin B (thiamin)	0.03mg
Phosphorus	10mg
Fat	0.7g
Vitamin B (riboflavin)	0.02mg
Potassium	82mg
Carbohydrate	10.8g
Vitamin C	11.0g
Sodium	2mg
Pectin	0.3-0.6%

Fruit harvesting comb (being used for bilberries here)

Traditional uses of the fruits were to make cranberry sauce and jelly. Sauce is made by boiling 500ml water with 420g sugar and 500g cranberries for 10 minutes. Jelly is made by boiling berries with a little water, then filtering and boiling with sugar to setting point.

There are numerous other culinary uses, including cake fillings, salads, fruit pies and crumbles, chutneys and relishes, ice creams etc. Jams can be made (e.g. cranberry and carrot). The fruit can be frozen directly without any processing. They can be bottled like redcurrants. They can be used to make wine (but need extra nutrients to get the yeast working, e.g. rice).

The fruits keep for a long time and were taken on long sea voyages, stored in barrels full of plain water, as a remedy against scurvy.

The fruits contain various anthocyanins and benzoic acid, which have medicinal benefits. Anthocyanins are antioxidants which play an important role in preventing disease. The juice from fruit contains a component that is useful in treating urinary tract infections.

Native Americans used an infusion of branches as a medicine for pleurisy.

Cranberries are a bee plant in summer, particularly for bumblebees, although they supply only small quantities of nectar and pollen.

The fruits can be used as the source of a red dye.

Plants can be grown as a ground cover and spread rapidly when they are thriving but this necessitates ideal conditions. If the soil is not acid enough they are likely to be vigorously outcompeted by weeds.

Varieties/Cultivars

For juice production, cultivars with high anthocyanin levels (and hence dark red colour) are required e.g. Bergman, Black Veil, CN, Crowley, Early Black, Franklin. Cultivars with dark red juice usually have smaller fruit and lower yields.

Cultivar	Description
Beaver	Fruit very early ripening, large, keep well in cold storage. Moderately productive. Origin: an old Canadian variety from Nova Scotia.
Beckwith	Late season. Fruit large, oval-oblong, deep red, very high in flavour, makes excellent sauce. Productive vine. Resistant to false blossom disease. Origin: New Jersey.
Ben Lear	Early season. Fruit medium-large, deep red. Vine productive. Origin: USA.
Bergman	Mid season. Fruit medium sized, pear shaped, red, keeps very well. Moderate yielding. Juice dark red. Resistant to false blossom disease. Origin: USA.
Black Veil	Fruit small. Juice very dark red. Low yielding.
CN	Fruit large. Juice dark red. Moderate yielding.
Cropper	Mid season. Fruit large, deep red, firm, resists rots. Good for processing.
Crowley	Fruit very large. Juice medium red colour. Very high yielding.
Early black	Early season. Fruit dark red, of good firmness and quality. Low yielding. Vine slender, producing many uprights and few runners. An old variety from the USA.
Franklin	Fruit small-medium size, round, red to very dark red, resistant to rots, keeps well. Juice dark red. Low to medium yielding. Resistant to false blossom disease. Origin: USA.
Howes	Fruit medium sized, mid-red colour, excellent keeping qualities. Low yielding. Origin: An old variety from the USA.
McFarlin	Late season. Fruit large, dark red, round-oblong, variable shape and size, good flavour. Plants are very productive, frost resistant, and resistant to false blossom disease.
Norman Lemunyon	Fruit large. Juice light red. Moderate yielding.
Pilgrim	Late season. Fruit large, long-oval, purplish-red with a bloom, good keeping qualities. Juice light red. Moderate to high yielding. Upright growth is moderately vigorous. Resistant to false blossom disease.
Red Star	Vigorous plant with large bright red fruit.
Searles Jumbo	Mid season. Fruit large, olive shaped, red, moderate keeper, fair quality. Very productive.
Stevens	Mid-late season. Fruit very large, round, dark red, glossy, firm, good keeping qualities. Juice light red. Vines vigorous, low to moderate yielding. Resistant to false blossom disease. Origin: USA.
Wilcox	Very early ripening. Fruit medium sized, oval, deep red, firm, good keeping quality. Vines very vigorous, productive, resistant to false blossom disease. Origin: USA.

Cultivation

In terms of soil, cranberries will tolerate pH 3.5 and grows fine in soils up to pH 6.5, but when the soil approaches pH 7.0 the plant begins to show iron chlorosis. Thus the plant does not demand highly acid sites, but it is able to thrive in such sites where the competition is limited.

Cranberries need constantly moist, very to slightly acid, peaty conditions and sun or light shade. Sites can be made on the edge of a river or pond by building up a layer of stones covered with peaty soil. The plants need to stand above the water for most of the time.

If you do not have acid soil, you can make an acid planting bed by digging a hole and filling with acid soil or ericaceous compost (or doing the same in a container, which only needs to be 15-20cm / 6-8ins deep). Plant into this and remember to water during dry spells and any other time to keep the soil moist near the surface.

Put plants at a spacing of 30-40cm (12-16ins). Any long trailing stems should be held down with sand or small pegs to stop them blowing around; they will usually root and layer naturally there.

Wetness and acidity are the best controls for weeds. Other weed control without chemicals necessitates some hand weeding. Cranberries are difficult to mulch with the usual materials because the stems (vines) trail over the ground and don't really appreciate being buried. A sand mulch of 5-7cm (2-3ins) depth helps to keep the rooting medium moist and allows for easy pulling out of weeds.

No pruning is usually required; if growth is poor, then some runners and uprights can be thinned after harvest or in early spring to promote growth. Similarly, if uprights are too dense (i.e. over 32m^2) then these should be thinned.

During winter, plants may die due to drying winds if the soil around the roots is frozen, hence the commercial practice of winter flooding. On a small scale, try and locate plants in a protected site.

Cranberries are unusual in not being able to utilise the nitrate form of nitrogen, but only the ammonium form. Very often they will grow perfectly well without any additional nitrogen for many years. Excessive nitrogen reduces yields and increases fruit rot. If growth and fruiting are poor, fertilise with urine in spring before the uprights have grown 5cm (2ins). The requirements for potassium and phosphorus are very low and are met from the planting medium without any extra needed.

Full production takes 3-5 years and then plants can crop well for 60-100 years. Fruits crop on the previous year's uprights (i.e. not the current year's new uprights). The optimum number of uprights is 20-32m^2.

Flowering takes place over a period of about a month within the period mid-June to mid-August. Cranberries are self-fertile, but larger and more fruit occur with cross-pollination. The flowers are pollinated by bees, bumblebees are particularly valuable pollinators.

Harvest takes place when the berries enlarge and redden; when 75% of the surface of individual berries turn pink or red, the berries can be picked in a single picking. Ripening occurs from early September to mid-October, depending on cultivar, and the berries then become only loosely attached to the stems. Hand picking is slow; for reasonable quantities it may be worth trying to make a scoop, as formerly used in North America – a person could harvest 160-540kg of berries per day by this method. A small scoop can be made from a plastic dustpan by cutting the edge so it has teeth like a comb. Scooping every year in the same direction decreases damage and speeds harvesting. A fruit harvesting comb (as used for bilberries) can also work.

After harvest, the berries can be stored in cool conditions for several weeks (3-4 months at 2-4°C with 90-95% humidity). They continue to develop red pigment when exposed to light. Yields from commercial plantations are in the range 0.5-1.5kg/m^2 or 5-15 tonnes/ha (2-6 tonnes/acre). Berry weights vary from 1-1.5g/berry and berry count/volume varies from 300-460/litre.

Propagation is normally via cuttings. Hardwood cuttings can be taken in spring, before growth starts, of 13-15cm (5-10ins) lengths of two-year-old woody stems; root in a well-drained but constantly moist medium. Softwood cuttings can be taken in late spring or early summer, and semi-ripe cuttings in mid to late summer; they require rooting hormone and mist, and success rates are high.

Layering is easy; in spring or autumn simply peg down a stem or cover it with a pile of sand. Remove the rooted layer after 1-2 years.

Pests and diseases

There are no major pest or disease problems outside of North America. There, disease problems are primarily problems of fruit rot either in the field or in storage. Cranberries are resistant to honey fungus.

False blossom disease is caused by a virus (mycoplasma) transmitted by a leafhopper native to North America and causes malformed vines; several cultivars are resistant.

Related species

The European cranberry, *Vaccinium oxycoccos*, is a similar plant from Northern Europe and North America, with smaller fruit only reaching 12mm (0.5ins) across. The fruit can be used similarly.

The American cranberry industry

The initial development of cranberry culture was to build ditches and dykes in marshes to gain some control of the water supply. It was discovered that flooding in spring and autumn could prevent frosts and not kill the cranberries; that flooding in summer could facilitate harvesting; and then that the plants could be submerged for several months over the winter, thus preventing winter desiccation. It was found that in warm weather, plants could only tolerate submersion for a matter of hours.

Later, flooding was largely replaced by use of sprinklers but flooding is still used to facilitate harvest and for winter protection in colder areas.

Cranberries are not very competitive with other plants and invasion by wetland sedges, grasses and shrubby pioneers is a major hurdle. Hand weeding was the norm before chemical herbicides were developed and now most commercial growers use a whole selection of herbicides.

Hand picking was soon superseded by small hand scoops that allow berries to be combed or raked off the vines; larger rakes allowed the harvester to stand and swing the rake through the vines to collect the berries. The observation that the berries rose to the surface during flooding led to water raking 'on the flood' which is now the norm, using floating harvesting machines.

The market for cranberry products has shifted from jelly and sauces to pure and blended juice products which have a red colour from naturally occurring pigment in the fruit.

Large-scale cranberry harvest

90% of the cranberries grown in North America are marketed by a growers' co-operative, enabling a focussed international marketing campaign.

CURRANTS and GOOSEBERRIES (other)

Ribes species

Zones 2-9, H4-H7
Most deciduous, some evergreen
Edible fruit

Origin and history

There are several hundred species of *Ribes*, the family having a world wide distribution, with most temperate and continental climate regions having species of use, notably for edible fruit.

Description

Mainly deciduous shrubs from many parts of the world.

Uses

Edible fruit. The quality obviously varies from species to species, and edibility raw also depends partly on the individual palate. Those too acid to be enjoyed raw can still be cooked in pies, puddings etc. and make great jams and jellies. There is a long tradition for many species of drying the fruit to preserve them as a food for the winter. Others were made into wine.

All species are good bee plants, particularly for wild and bumblebees.

Varieties/Cultivars

The commonly grown blackcurrant (*R. nigrum*, page 28), redcurrant (*R. rubrum*, page 181) and gooseberry (*R. uva-crispa*, page 104) have long been bred and many named cultivars selected. They are not included in the list adjacent. All the species opposite have edible fruits unless noted; there are many more which probably have too.

Buffalo currant fruit (*Ribes odoratum*)

Species	Common name	Origin	Z/H	Height	Comments
Ribes aciculare	Needle-spined gooseberry	Siberia	Z3/H7	1m	Fruits are large, red, green or yellow, sweet and tasty.
Ribes alpestris	Hedge gooseberry	Himalayas and China	Z3/H7	3m	Fruits are oval, 16mm long, purplish-red.
Ribes alpinum	Alpine currant, Mountain currant	Europe	Z2/H7	1.2m	Fruit are sweet, 5mm in diameter, scarlet, freely borne when male and female plants are grown (unusually, this species is dioecious). Suckering widely. The cultivar 'Green Mound' makes a good dwarf hedge.
Ribes altissimum		Siberia	Z6/H6-7	3m	Fruits are small with a thick skin and a pleasant acid taste.
Ribes amarum	Bitter gooseberry	North America			Fruits were eaten to quench the thirst.
Ribes ambiguum		China, Japan	Z6/H6-7	0.6m	Fruit are to 12mm in diameter, translucent green, acid flavour.
Ribes americanum	American blackcurrant	Eastern North America	Z2/H7	1.8m	Fruits are black, to 10mm in diameter, fair flavour. Roots have been used medicinally. Shoots and leaves used for dyeing.
Ribes aureum	Golden currant	Western North America	Z2/H7	2.4m	Fruit are purplish-black, 5mm in diameter, good flavour. The flowers are also eaten raw – very sweet. The inner bark has been used medicinally. Plant sometimes used as a rootstock for currants and gooseberries.
Ribes bracteosum	Stink currant, Californian blackcurrant	Southwestern North America	Z7/H5-6	2.5m	Fruits are black with a white bloom, about 5-8mm in diameter, poor flavour. The fruit, roots and shoots have all been used medicinally.
Ribes burejense		Northern North America and Northern Asia	Z5/H7	1m	Fruits are green, about 10mm in diameter, acid but palatable, a gooseberry which can hang on the bush until November when it develops a good blackcurrant flavour.
Ribes californicum	Hillside gooseberry	Southwestern North America	Z7/H5-6	2m	
Ribes cereum	Wax currant, Squaw currant	Western North America	Z5/H7	1.8m	Fruits are scarlet, 6m in diameter, poorly flavoured. The young leaves are used in teas, and the flowers also eaten raw (sweet). The fruits and inner bark have been used medicinally. Straight stems were used as arrow shafts.
Ribes cruentum	Shinyleaf currant	North America			
Ribes curvatum		Southeastern North America	Z7/H5-6	1m	Fruits are purplish gooseberries about 7.5mm in diameter.
Ribes cynosbati	Dogberry, American wild gooseberry	Eastern North America	Z2/H7	1.5m	Fruits are dark red, about 10-12mm in diameter, covered with short weak bristles; good sub-acid flavour. The roots have been used medicinally.
Ribes diacanthum		Siberia to Manchuria	Z2/H7	1.8m	Fruit are green-scarlet, about 5mm in diameter with a good sweetish-acid flavour. Dioecious shrub.
Ribes distans		China, Korea, Manchuria	Z5/H7	0.6m	Scarlet fruit have a poor flavour.
Ribes divaricatum	Worcesterberry	Western North America	Z4/H7	2.7m	Fruit are reddish-black, about 10mm in diameter with a sweet-acid flavour. Bush is very spiny, making an animal-proof hedge plant. A parent of several mildew resistant gooseberries. The inner bark and roots have been used medicinally. The roots were also used to make fishing nets.
Ribes emodense		Himalayas and China	Z6/H6-7		Fruits are reddish-black, large with large seeds (synonym *R. himalayense*).
Ribes fasciculatum		China, Japan, Korea	Z5/H7	1.5m	Fruits are reddish, about 5mm in diameter, containing a lot of fairly large seeds. Flavour unpalatable. Young leaves are eaten cooked.
Ribes fragrans		Mongolia, Siberia	Z3/H7	0.6m	Fruits are brown gooseberries about 8mm in diameter with a sweet and pleasant flavour.
Ribes gayanum		Chile	Z8/Z4-5	1.5m	Fruits are black, 7-8mm across with a good flavour. Evergreen.
Ribes glaciale		China to the Himalayas			Fruits are scarlet, very acid.

Species	Common name	Origin	Z/H	Height	Comments
Ribes glandulosum	Skunk currant	North America	Z2/H7	0.4m	Fruits are red, about 6-8mm in diameter, with a blackcurrant flavour but the odour of a skunk! Can be used as a ground cover plant. The stems and roots have been used medicinally.
Ribes griffithii		Nepal, Tibet			Fruits are acid in flavour.
Ribes hirtellum	Currant-gooseberry	Northern North America	Z4/H7	1m	Fruits are purplish-black, about 8 - 25mm in diameter, a smooth-skinned gooseberry with a pleasant taste. Parent of several gooseberry cultivars.
Ribes horridum		China, Japan		1.5m	Fruits are acid but succulent.
Ribes x houghtonianum		Europe	Z5/H7	2m	Red fruit – similar to redcurrants. Hybrid of *R. silvestre* and *R. spicatum*.
Ribes hudsonianum	Hudson Bay currant, Northern blackcurrant	Northern North America	Z2/H7	1m	Fruits are black, about 5-10mm in diameter, acid. The stems, roots and bark have all been used medicinally.
Ribes indecorum	Whiteflower currant	California	Z8/Z4-5	2.5m	Fruit not recorded as edible; roots used medicinally for toothaches.
Ribes inebrians		Western North America	Z4/H7	2m	Fruits are pale red, about 5mm in diameter.
Ribes inerme	Whitestem gooseberry	Western North America	Z6/H6-7	2m	Fruits are purplish-red gooseberry about 8mm in diameter.
Ribes irriguum		Northwestern North America		3m	Fruits are black gooseberry 7-13mm in diameter. Roots have been used medicinally.
Ribes janczewskii		Central Asia			Fruits are large, aromatic blackcurrants.
Ribes japonicum		Japan	Z7/H5-6		Fruits are black.
Ribes lacustre	Prickly blackcurrant, Swamp gooseberry	North America	Z4/H7	1.5m	Fruits are black, acid and very juicy with a strange odour; about 5mm in diameter. The leaves, bark and shoots have all been used medicinally. The roots were also used to make fishing nets.
Ribes latifolium		Japan, Siberia			
Ribes laurifolium		Western China	Z9/H3-4	1m	Fruits are reddish-black, a type of blackcurrant. Evergreen.
Ribes laxiflorum	Trailing black currant	Western North America	Z5/H7	0.3m	The roots and shoots have been used medicinally.
Ribes leptanthum	Trumpet gooseberry	Southwestern North America	Z6/H6-7	1m	Fruits are black, about 6-8mm in diameter.
Ribes lobbii	Gummy gooseberry	Western North America	Z7/H5-6	1.8m	Purple fruit. Roots have been used medicinally and were also used to make fishing nets.
Ribes longeracemosum		Western China	Z6/H6-7	3.5m	Fruits are black, 10mm in diameter with a good flavour.
Ribes luridum		Tibet, Sikkim and Nepal	Z5/H7	1m	Fruits are black, acid.
Ribes magellanicum		Chile, Tierra del Fuego		4m	Fruits have a pleasant flavour.
Ribes malvaceum	Chaparral currant	California	Z7/H5-6	2m	Roots used medicinally.
Ribes mandschuricum		Korea, Manchuria	Z6/H6-7		Fruits are red, about 10mm in diameter.
Ribes mescalerium	Mescalero currant	Southern North America			
Ribes maximowiczii		Western China	Z6/H6-7	2.7m	Fruits are red, yellow or green redcurrants, good flavour, about 1cm in diameter. Subspecies *floribundum* a good cropper.
Ribes menziesii	Canyon gooseberry	Western North America	Z7/H5-6	1.8m	Fruits are black gooseberries.

Flowers of golden currant (*Ribes aureum*)

Species	Common name	Origin	Z/H	Height	Comments
Ribes meyeri		Central and Eastern Asia	Z7/H5-6	1m	Black fruit, with a pleasant flavour.
Ribes missouriense	Missouri gooseberry	Central North America	Z5/H7	2m	Fruits are smooth-skinned purplish-brown gooseberries 10-14mm in diameter, with a good rich sub-acid vinous flavour.
Ribes montigenum	Gooseberry-currant	Western North America	Z6/H6-7	0.75m	Fruits are dark red, about 10mm in diameter.
Ribes multiflorum		Balkans	Z6/H6-7	2m	Fruits are dark red, about 7mm in diameter. A parent of several redcurrant varieties.
Ribes nevadense	Sierra currant	California	Z7/H5-6	1.5m	
Ribes x nidigrolaria	Jostaberry	Hybrid	Z6/H6-7	1.8m	Fruit reddish-black, 12-15mm in diameter, good flavour. Hybrid of blackcurrant and gooseberry, thornless, resistant to white pine blister rust and gooseberry mildew. Some named cultivars available.
Ribes niveum	Slender branched gooseberry	Western North America	Z6/H6-7	2.7m	Fruits are blue-black, about 8mm in diameter.
Ribes odoratum (sometimes included in *R. aureum*)	Buffalo currant, Clove currant	Central North America	Z5/H7	2.5m	Fruit are black, 10-15mm in diameter, good sweet aromatic flavour. The flowers are also eaten raw (sweet). The leaves can be used to make a tea or as a flavouring in foods. The straight stems were used to make arrows. The cultivar 'Crandall' has large fruit, 15mm across.

Species	Common name	Origin	Z/H	Height	Comments
Ribes oxyacanthoides	American mountain gooseberry	North America	Z2/H7	1.5m	Fruit are purplish-red gooseberries about 10-12mm in diameter with a sweet and pleasant flavour. The leaves are sometimes eaten raw. The roots, bark and stems have been used medicinally.
Ribes palczewskii		Central and Eastern Asia		1.5m	
Ribes pauciflorum		Siberia to Manchuria		1.5m	Fruits are large and tasty blackcurrants.
Ribes petiolare		Northern Europe, Northern Asia, Western Northern America	Z3/H7	1.5m	Fruit are blue-black blackcurrants about 10mm in diameter, abundant, not aromatic.
Ribes petraeum	Rock red currant	Western and Central Europe	Z6/H6-7	1.8m	Fruits are acid red or reddish-black redcurrants; one of the parents of cultivated redcurrants.
Ribes pinetorum		Arizona, New Mexico	Z6/H6-7		Fruits are purplish-black, up to 15mm in diameter with a good gooseberry taste; densely covered with spines. The stems were used to make arrow shafts, and the thorns arrow points.
Ribes procumbens		North Korea, Manchuria	Z3/H7	0.2m	Fruits are brownish with a very good flavour.
Ribes punctatum		Chile			
Ribes quercetorum	Rock gooseberry	California	Z8/Z4-5	1.5m	Fruit black, 6mm in diameter.
Ribes x robustum			Z6/H6-7		Fruit black, acid. Hybrid of *R. niveum* and *R. inerme*.
Ribes roezlii	Sierra gooseberry	California	Z7/H5-6	1.5m	Fruits are reddish-purple, up to 15mm in diameter.
Ribes rotundifolium	Eastern wild gooseberry	Eastern North America	Z6/H6-7	1m	Fruits are smooth-skinned purple gooseberries 6-8mm in diameter with a very good flavour. Leaves and bark have been used medicinally.
Ribes sachalinense		Northern Japan		1m	Fruits have an acid pleasant taste.
Ribes sanguineum	Flowering currant	Western North America	Z6/H6-7	2.5m	Fruits are about 10mm in diameter, fair flavour. Tolerates maritime exposure and can be grown as an informal hedge, though it is rather bare in winter. Occasionally naturalised in Britain.
Ribes setosum	Missouri gooseberry	Northwestern North America	Z2/H7	1m	Fruits are red or black, up to 10mm in diameter with a pleasant sub-acid flavour.
Ribes sinanense		Japan			
Ribes speciosum	Fuchsia-flowered gooseberry	California	Z7/H5-6	4m	Red fruit, bristly. Evergreen.
Ribes spicatum	Nordic currant	Europe	Z3/H7	2m	Fruit translucent red.
Ribes stenocarpum		Northwestern China	Z6/H6-7	2m	Fruits are green or red gooseberries about 25mm long with a pleasant but quite strongly acid flavour and a hairy skin.
Ribes triste	American red currant, Swamp red currant	Northern Europe to Northern North America	Z2/H7	0.5m	Fruits are red, acid, 6mm in diameter, similar to cultivated redcurrants. Stems, leaves and roots have all been used medicinally.
Ribes ussuriense		Korea, Manchuria	Z5/H7	1m	Fruits are blue-black blackcurrants about 8mm in diameter.
Ribes valdivianum		Chile, Argentina		3.5m	
Ribes velutinum	Desert gooseberry	Southern North America			
Ribes viburnifolium		Southern California	Z9/H3-4	2m	Fruits are red, about 8mm in diameter. Evergreen.
Ribes viscosissimum	Sticky currant	British Columbia to California	Z7/H5-6	1m	Fruits are black, about 10mm in diameter.
Ribes warszewiczii		Eastern Siberia	Z3/H7	1.5m	Fruits are reddish-black redcurrants with a good acid flavour, up to 10mm in diameter.
Ribes wolfii	Wolf's currant	Southwestern USA	Z6/H6-7	3m	Black fruit, bloomy.

Jostaberry (*Ribes* x *nidigrolaria*)

Cultivation

Most *Ribes* species are easily grown, preferring a moisture retentive but well-drained loamy soil of at least moderate quality. They are quite tolerant of shade though not fruiting so well there.

Pests and diseases

Many species can harbour a stage of white pine blister rust, so they should not be grown in the vicinity of certain pine trees, particularly in North America. Plants in this genus are also notably susceptible to honey fungus.

Related species

Blackcurrant (*R. nigrum*, page 28), Redcurrant (*R. rubrum*, page 181), Gooseberry (*R. uva-crispa*, page 104).

DAISY BUSH, *Brachyglottis greyi* and hybrids

Zone 7, H5
Evergreen
Beneficial insect attractant

Origin and history

Originating from New Zealand, and long used ornamentally in milder climates as ornamental plants for their pale leaves and bright yellow flowers.

Description

Rounded shrubs to 1.5m (5ft) high and a little more across, with whitish branches and light grey leaves (furry white beneath). Produces bright yellow flowers in summer and sometimes again in autumn.

Uses

Particularly good at attracting hoverflies, so this is an excellent plant to use for aphid protection and control. We use hedges of it in our nursery for aphid control. Very wind tolerant in milder climates.

Varieties/Cultivars

The Dunedin hybrids (e.g. 'Sunshine') are the most common forms grown.

Cultivation

Position in full sun and in a well-drained soil. Can be pruned back after flowering if they get leggy.

Propagate by seed or semi-ripe cuttings.

Pests and diseases

None; cold damage is a possibility in cooler climates.

Brachyglottis 'Sunshine' (a Dunedin hybrid)

DRIMYS, *Drimys species*

Zone 8, H4
Evergreen
Spice bushes

Mountain pepper

Origin and history

Evergreen subtropical shrubs, the hardier ones from Australia and the far south of South America. There is a long history of use as spices.

Description

Evergreen shrubs with shiny aromatic green leaves. Dioecious – male and female forms must be grown for fruiting to occur. Sweet-scented flowers in spring are followed on female plants by aromatic black berries in autumn.

Varieties/Cultivars

Drimys lanceolata (*Tasmannia lanceolata*) – pepper tree, mountain pepper

A conical shrub or small tree to 3m (10ft) high. Purplish-red branches. Origin: Australia, Tasmania.

Uses: The berries and leaves are used as a pepper/allspice condiment.

Drimys winterii – Winter's bark

Large tree or shrub up to 20m high in warm locations, with aromatic bark. Origin: Chile, Argentina.

Uses: Leaves and bark are used as a pepper/allspice condiment. The bark is high in vitamin C (formerly used to prevent scurvy).

Cultivation

Plant in semi-shade, on light, acid to neutral soils that are well-drained but moisture retentive.

Propagate by summer cuttings or seed.

Pests and diseases

None of note but cold damage is more common.

Winter's bark (*Drimys winterii*)

ELAEAGNUS, *Elaeagnus* species

Zones 2-9, H3-7
Deciduous and evergreen
Nitrogen-fixers, Edible fruit, Hedging, Bee plants

Origin and history

The genus Elaeagnus consists of 30-40 deciduous and evergreen shrubs and small trees, often with prickly branches, from Southern Europe, Asia and North America.

In most temperate areas, including Britain, only the hardier shrubby species are recommended for hedging and interplanting: *E. commutata*, *E.* x *ebbingei*, *E. multiflora*, *E. pungens* and *E.* x *reflexa* (the larger species *E. umbellata* is also suitable, but is covered in *Trees for Gardens, Orchards and Permaculture*).

Elaeagnus have a long history of being used for edible fruit and for hedging, and more recently for their nitrogen-fixing abilities.

Description

All species have distinctive young branches and leaves covered with silvery or brownish scales. Evergreens have very dark green leaves, with paler undersides; deciduous species have mid-green leaves, also with paler undersides. The flowers are white, usually fragrant, borne in clusters from the leaf axils, and are attractive to insects and bees, particularly wild bumblebees etc. Reddish fruit, round or oval, contain a single seed and attract several species of wildlife.

As pioneer species, Elaeagnus are fast growing and excellent wind-resisters, tolerating maritime exposure. They also effectively suppress grass competition.

Elaeagnus form a symbiotic relationship with *Frankia* bacteria in root nodules, much in the same way as legumes do with Rhizobium bacteria. Species that do this with *Frankia* bacteria are called actinorhizal; they are found primarily in the temperate zone (whereas most legumes are tropical) and are especially important in high-latitude countries like Britain, where conditions are generally unfavourable for most legumes.

Frankia nodules form on all ***Elaeagnus*** species, and the strains of *Frankia* which infect Elaeagnus are generally also compatible with other members of the Elaeagnaceae family (***Hippophae*** and ***Shepherdia***) as well as *Myrica* species.

Via this symbiosis, ***Elaeagnus*** species fix large amounts of nitrogen, with nitrogen accumulation rates (i.e. amounts made available to other plants via leaf fall, root and nodule turnover) recorded of up to 240kg/ha/year (100kg/acre/year, or 24g/m^2/year).

Uses

The fruits are edible – always astringent before completely ripe, and very attractive to birds. The fruit of many members of this genus is a very rich source of vitamins and minerals, especially in vitamins A, C and E, flavanoids and other bioactive compounds. They are also a fairly good source of essential fatty acids, which is fairly unusual for fruit. Research is underway into their capability as a food to reduce the incidence of cancer and also as a means of halting or reversing the growth of cancers.

Kernels of the single seed inside each fruit are also edible (peanut flavoured), but the hulls are fibrous and the kernels not easy to extract, making it hardly worth it.

All Elaeagnus can be used in hedges and windbreaks; they are very tolerant of pruning – evergreens should be pruned in spring after they have fruited. They tolerate maritime exposure, so can be used near the sea.

Because they are excellent nitrogen-fixers, Elaeagnus are good companion plants; when grown in orchards, they can increase yields significantly. They can also be used as the major source of nitrogen for other crops, by interplanting a proportion of the crop area.

As well as being of great use in fruiting and forest gardens, Elaeagnus are widely used in forestry as ecosystem improvers (e.g. as a nitrogen-fixing understorey beneath crop trees, to reclaim degraded soils and as soil-improving nurse trees). They are often planted in alternate rows with a tree species, and don't usually compete for light due to their shrubby form.

All species are excellent bee plants. The deciduous species flower in spring, the evergreen species in autumn.

Varieties/Cultivars

Elaeagnus angustifolia – Oleaster, Russian olive

A deciduous large shrub or small tree from Europe and Western Asia, growing 7m (23ft) high and in spread, sometimes more. Hardy to zone 2 / H7; tolerates part shade, salt and air pollution. It has silvery branches, often thorny, with silvery scales when young, silvery willow-like leaves, silvery fragrant flowers in June and yellowish-silvery fruit, 1cm (0.4ins) long, ripening in October. Plants prefer a continental climate and are apt to be cut back in severe winters in cool temperate climates because the summers are often not warm enough to fully ripen the wood.

Silver leaves of *Elaeagnus commutata*

This species is cultivated in Europe and Asia for its edible fruit; there are named varieties and some of these are thornless. 'King Red' is virtually thornless and has very large fruit. Very tolerant of pruning, even right back into old wood. Considered weedy in some parts of the world.

The subspecies *orientalis* (synonym *E. orientalis*) is known as the 'Trebizond date'. This is more tree-like with larger fruit, and requires hotter summers to succeed, when yields of 7-9kg (16-20lb) per plant are possible. The fruit used to be commonly sold in the markets of Iran and Turkey but is rarely found there nowadays.

Other uses: The seed oil, flowers and leaves have been used medicinally. An essential oil obtained from the flowers is used in perfumery. A gum from the plant is used in the textile industry in calico printing. Leaves are used as goat and sheep fodder. The wood is hard, fine grained: used for posts, beams, carving, domestic items, makes a good fuel. This species is now sometimes grown as a biomass crop on a three-year rotation; in Pakistan it is valued as a pollarded fuel and fodder crop.

Elaeagnus commutata (synonym *E. argentea*) – Silverberry, Wolfberry

A medium deciduous shrub from North America, typically growing 3m (10ft) high and 1.5m (5ft) in spread, but sometimes almost double that; hardy to zone 2 / H0. Branches are thornless and reddish-brown, leaves are silvery on both sides. A profusion of fragrant silvery flowers appear in May-June, followed by round silvery fruit, 1cm (0.4ins) across, ripening in September. Plants produce suckers quite freely, often sending them up at some distance from the plant.

Fruit on *Elaeagnus x ebbingei*

Tolerates very alkaline soils and should grow well on chalk. Plants prefer a continental climate and are liable to be cut back in severe winters in cool temperate climates mainly because the wood is not fully ripened in the cooler summers.

It can regenerate from very old wood and so can be cut back severely if required. Resents root disturbance. Plants start fruiting at a young age, often after two years.

Other uses: The fibrous bark has been used in weaving and rope making.

Elaeagnus x ebbingei (E. x submacrophylla)

A large evergreen shrub (semi-deciduous in colder areas): a hybrid of *E. macrophylla* and *E. pungens*. Grows to 3.5m (12ft) in height and spread (sometimes a little more); hardy to zone 6 / H5. White fragrant flowers appear in October-November, followed by fruit, 2cm x 1cm (0.8 x 0.4ins), ripening in April-May; leaves are silvery beneath. Tolerates deep shade and can be grown under trees.

The cultivar 'Salcombe seedling' is said to flower more abundantly than the type. The cultivar 'Limelight' produces a good crop of fruit even on small bushes. Because fruitlets have to go through the winter, fruiting is greater the milder the winter, so in Britain fruiting is best in the southwest of the country, while across Europe plants do increasingly well towards the southwest (Spain and Portugal).

Elaeagnus formosana

An evergreen shrub from Taiwan, hardy to zone 9 / H3. Tolerates very alkaline soils and quite deep shade.

Elaeagnus fragrans

A medium deciduous shrub from central and southern Japan, hardy to zone 9 / H3. Tolerates part shade.

Elaeagnus glabra

A large, vigorous, evergreen shrub from China and Japan, growing 6m (20ft) high; hardy to zone 8 / H4. Branches are thornless; bears white fragrant flowers in October-November, followed by orange and silver fruit, 15mm (0.6ins) long in spring. Very shade tolerant, it can be planted under other trees and will eventually climb up into them. Closely related to *E. pungens*, differing in its unarmed branches and thinner more glossy leaves.

Other uses: The substance epigallocatechin from this species is antibacterial in action and used in traditional Japanese medicine.

Elaeagnus gonuanthes

A medium deciduous shrub from China, hardy to zone 9 / H3. Tolerates part shade.

Elaeagnus latifolia – Bastard oleaster

A deciduous shrub from India, hardy to zone 9 / H3 (-5°C). Needs full sun.

Elaeagnus macrophylla

A medium sized, rounded, evergreen shrub from Japan and Korea, growing to 3m (10ft) in height and spread; hardy to zone 8 / H4. Branches are erect, thornless and silvery; leaves are silvery both sides, becoming green over the season; very fragrant silvery flowers appear in September-November, followed by reddish fruit, 16mm (0.6ins) long, ripening the following May. Tolerates deep shade. Thicket-forming but slow growing in Britain.

Elaeagnus maritima

An evergreen shrub from Japan and Korea, hardy to zone 9 / H3. Tolerates deep shade. This species is probably a hybrid, *E. glabra* x *E. macrophylla*.

Elaeagnus montana

A medium deciduous shrub from central and southern Japan, hardy to zone 9 / H3. Tolerates part shade.

Elaeagnus multiflora – Goumi, Gumi, Cherry elaeagnus

A medium sized, spreading, deciduous (sometimes semi-evergreen) shrub from China and Japan, growing 3m (10ft) high and 2m (7ft) in spread; hardy to zone 6 / H6; tolerates part shade. Branches are scaly, leaves are silvery beneath; pale yellow flowers that appear in April-May are followed by dark reddish-brown fruit, 2cm (0.8ins) long, ripening in July. An easily cultivated plant that tolerates atmospheric pollution.

Cultivated for its edible fruit in Japan, there are some named varieties: 'Sweet Scarlet' is best known, and is self-fertile. Ideally, fruit should be allowed to hang until completely ripe before picking, however at this time of year birds tend to be more troublesome fruit scavengers, and you might find one day that the fruits have all vanished (the same happens with cherries); some protection of bushes may be required.

The fruits are tangy, juicy and pleasantly acid when ripe; they are usually made into pies, preserves etc. In Japan, whole branches are cut off with their ripe fruit and sold in markets as such.

Other uses: In Japan, the leaves, fruit and roots are all used in traditional medicine. Sometimes used as a rootstock for evergreen species that are hard to grow from cuttings, but it frequently sprouts from the base and can out compete the scion.

Elaeagnus oldhamii

An evergreen shrub from southern China, hardy to zone 9 / H3. Tolerates part shade.

Elaeagnus pungens – Thorny elaeagnus

A medium to large, dense, vigorous spreading evergreen shrub from Japan, growing up to 4m (13ft) in height and spread, though often less; hardy to zone 7 / H5. Branches are brown and thorny; silvery white fragrant flowers appear in October-November, followed by fruit, brown ripening to red, 12-15mm (0.5-0.6ins) long, the following May. Tolerates deep shade. The foliage can be damaged in severe wind-chill conditions. Closely related to *E. glabra*. Succeeds when planted under trees that have become bare at the base; in time it scrambles up into the tree and fills out the bottom. Several cultivars exist, some of which are thornless or with few thorns. 'Variegata' is the most vigorous of the named cultivars.

Other uses: The leaves, stems and roots are used in Japanese traditional medicine.

Elaeagnus pyriformis

A deciduous shrub from the Himalayas (Assam), hardy to zone 9 / H3.

Elaeagnus pungens fruit

Elaeagnus x *ebbingei* flowers in autumn

Elaeagnus x *reflexa*

A large, vigorous evergreen shrub, a hybrid of *E. pungens* and *E. glabra*. Grows to 4.5m (15ft) high; hardy to zone 7 / H5; tolerates deep shade. Branches have few thorns. Fruits ripen in April and May. It will climb into trees if planted under them. It can also be planted in windy gaps under trees in shelterbelts and will in time fill in the gaps and climb into the trees.

Elaeagnus thunbergii

An evergreen shrub from southern China, hardy to zone 9 / H3. Tolerates part shade.

Elaeagnus yoshinoi

A deciduous shrub from central Japan, hardy to zone 9 / H3. Tolerates part shade.

Cultivation

The deciduous species like full sun but tolerate part shade; the evergreens tolerate quite deep shade, and have excellent potential as understorey crops and green manure shrubs. All are good in any soil apart from waterlogged soils, and are drought tolerant. They are fast growing and resistant to honey fungus. They are very resistant to damage by salt winds and tolerant of regular trimming.

The evergreen species can be planted in the line of an old shelterbelt of trees that is becoming bare at the base and it will in time fill up the empty spaces and climb into the bottom parts of the trees.

All species appear to be self-sterile, so to achieve fruiting crops, make sure you plant at least two different selections. Pollination is mostly via bees so plant pollination partners relatively close.

Fruiting starts 3-4 years from planting young plants. Ripe fruit can be picked by hand or beaten from the branches onto sheets below. Fruits ripening in spring or early summer are more liable to be attractive to birds, so bushes may need protection.

Propagation is normally by seed or cuttings.

Seeds of the hardier species can either be sown in autumn and allowed to overwinter in cold temperatures, or stratified in storage, giving 2-3 months of cold stratification. Seeds from the evergreen species are not dormant and should be sown immediately in spring.

Semi-ripe cuttings can be taken July-September. They should be 7-10cm (3-4ins) long terminal shoots, with or without a heel. Give hormone rooting powder/dip treatment and keep in a humid atmosphere.

Hardwood cuttings can be taken in October-November. They should be 10-12cm (4-5ins) long terminal shoots, with or without a heel. For evergreen species, give hormone rooting powder/dip treatment, bottom heat of 15-20°C (59-68°F) and keep in a humid environment for 1-2 months. Deciduous species can be placed directly in the ground with no further treatment. Allow to grow on for 12 months before transplanting.

All species may be layered in September-October. Leave for 12 months before transplanting.

Pests and diseases

There are none of importance.

Elaeagnus sucker or psyllid is a sap sucking insect (psyllids are a group of sap-feeding insects related to aphids) causing distorted leaves, honeydew and sooty mould. Elaeagnus sucker originates from eastern Asia and was first detected in Britain in 2002, spreading rapidly, but has natural controls so is rarely a problem.

Related species

E. umbellata, autumn olive, a large shrub to small tree, is described in *Trees for Gardens, Orchards and Permaculture*.

FALSE INDIGO, *Amorpha fruticosa*

Zone 4, H7
Deciduous
Nitrogen-fixer, Bee plant

Origin and history

A shrub from the USA, of the legume family, found in scrub, on riverbanks and in light woodland.

Description

Upright shrub growing 2-4m (6-13ft) high and across. Has typical legume-like leaves and spikes of dark purple flowers.

Uses

A good nitrogen-fixing and bee plant.

The plant contains insecticidal compounds. Seed has been used as a condiment in the past but should probably not be eaten.

Cultivation

Grow in any well-drained soil in sun or light shade.

Propagate by seed.

Pests and diseases

None of note. In cool summer regions, some shoot dieback can occur when new wood does not properly harden off.

False indigo bush

FLOWERING QUINCES, *Chaenomeles* species

Zone 5, H7
Deciduous
Edible fruit (cooked / processed), Bee plants

Origin and history

Chaenomeles comprises of four species and many hybrids of deciduous shrubs and small trees originating in China and Japan and belonging to the family Rosaceae (which includes apples, pears etc.). They all bear ornamental flowers in spring (hence one of their common names, flowering quinces) followed by large, aromatic acid fruits, which are used cooked or processed. The oriental quinces are sometimes confused with true quince (*Cydonia oblonga*), with which they are closely related, and Chinese quince (*Pseudocydonia sinensis*).

Description

Plants often have spiny branches, and have alternate, simple leaves.

Flowers are borne at an early age, singly or in leafless clusters, usually with five large petals. They range from orange and salmon pink to red and white.

Fruits are apple-like, five-celled, with many seeds in the hollow cells. Fruit size varies from 3-6cm (1.2-2.4ins). The seeds are brown and shiny when fresh.

The white flowered 'Nivalis' in early spring

Uses

The fruits are hard with a great number of stone cells, acid, sometimes astringent and fragrant – citrus-like. The characteristic pleasant aroma is due to enathic-ethyl and pelargonic-ethyl ethers. The fruits are high in dietary fibre and vitamin C, and are moderately high in vitamins B1 and B2; the composition of *C. japonica* fruit is:

Dry matter	14-17%
Vitamin C	18-145mg/100g
Sugars	1.2-4.5%
Vitamin B1 (thiamin)	106-122mg/100g
Pectins	0.7-1.3%
Vitamin B2 (riboflavin)	78-330mg/100g
Titrated acids	3.6-7.2%

Fruits are used like those of the common quince, i.e. are cooked with other fruits for desserts, jams, jellies, syrups, sauces, juice, soft drinks, wines and liqueurs, candied fruit etc. The fruits are aromatic and impart a pleasant lemony flavour. Slices of fruit can be used as a lemon substitute in drinks. The fruits are also used in the confectionery industry and in perfumery. The vitamin C and phenolics are antioxidant and prevent browning of the fruit during processing. Fruit stores well for at least two months in cool conditions.

The juice is quite easily extracted from crushed fruit, with a juice yield of 60%. The raw juice can be used as a substitute for vinegar or lemon (as an acidifying agent with antioxidant properties it is ten times stronger than apple juice). A sweetened juice extract is now used to flavour ice cream and yoghurt in the Baltics.

The raw fruit contains tannins (830-2300mg/100g) and can be used for tanning and dyeing.

Plants are widely used as ornamentals in gardens; the cut flowering shoots last well if cut and brought indoors. In sunny sites, ornamental cultivars may produce up to 60 flowers on shoots 40cm (16ins) long. The larger species can be used as informal hedges, several making wide-spreading, thorny mounds.

Chaenomeles are good bee plants, flowering early in the year and providing pollen and nectar.

Some species are used medicinally in their native range.

Varieties/Cultivars

Many ornamental cultivars of *Chaenomeles* have been selected for their flowers (colour and abundance). Only those that are known to have good fruiting characteristics (large size or good cropping) are listed below.

C. x *californica*

A hybrid of all three species. An erect spiny shrub of stiff habit to 2m (7ft) high, with thorny short branches. Flowers are to 5cm (2ins) diameter, pink or rose red. Fruits are apple, orange or egg shaped, to 6 x 6m (2.5 x 2.5ins). Seeds are ovoid, pointed at one end, 9 x 5mm (0.4 x 0.2ins).

Enchantress – compact shrub, flowers dark rose-pink, fruit large, yellow.

Masterpiece – flowers pink-red, early; fruit large, ovate.

C. x *clarkiana* (*C. cathayensis* x *C. japonica*)

Low shrub with erect to spreading branches, densely covered with short thorny side branches. Flowers large, pink; fruit medium sized, apple or orange shaped.

C. japonica – Japonica, Japanese quince, Maules quince

A dense, spreading, thorny, small shrub to 1m (3ft) high and 1.8m (6ft) wide. Bears many flowers, orange-red, scarlet or crimson, 3-4cm (1-1.5ins) in diameter in clusters of 2-4, appearing from April to June. Fruits are usually abundant, apple shaped, 4-5cm (1.5-2ins) across, weighing 20-50g, usually with several deep furrows, yellow, red stained, aromatic; ripening in September and October. Each fruit contains 50-80 brown glossy seeds. Fruiting begins from the age of 2-3 years and five year-old bushes can yield 4-5kg of fruit. *C. alba* bears white flowers. var. *alpina* is lower, makes a good ground cover, but does not fruit as well. Native to Japan, found on hillsides, riverbanks and lake shores; synonym *C. maulei*.

Lower forms are sometimes useful as ground cover.

Fruiting selections of this species have been made and it has been grown commercially in several regions. In the Baltic countries of Latvia and Lithuania, breeding programmes began in 1951, and by 1993 there were 400ha (1000 acres) of plantations. Baltic-Swedish breeding programmes are ongoing at present.

Large crop of 'Cido' quinces

Inside a fruit of *Chaenomeles speciosa*

Cido is a thornless form selected for fruit production in the Baltic region of the USSR in the cold war years, where it is known as the northern lemon. Fruits are yellow to yellowish-orange, much larger (up to 80g) and ripen early, in August or September. They have a strong pleasant aroma and are very high in vitamin C (up to 150mg/100g – more than lemons) and pectin (twice as much as in apples). Bushes grow up to 1.5m (5ft) high with few branching main shoots; flowers are orange-red; it is grown on a commercial scale with fruit yields averaging 12-15 tonnes/ha (5-6 tonnes/acre) but sometimes double that in Latvia.

Cido Red is a red-fleshed sport of Cido.

C. speciosa (*C. lagenaria*) – Japanese quince

Vigorous shrub of wide spreading habit, growing to 2.4m (8ft) high and 4.6m (15ft) wide, with spiny shiny branches. Flowers 3-4.5cm (1.5-2ins) diameter borne on older wood, scarlet to crimson, usually in clusters of 2-4, borne from February to June. Fruits are apple or pear shaped, to 4-6.5cm (1.5-2ins) long, greenish-yellow, sometimes with a reddish flush, speckled with small dots, and are aromatic. Each fruit contains up to 100 seeds. Native to China, synonym *C. lagenaria*. Many cultivars have been selected for their flowering habit; those below are also noted for their fruit.

Lower forms (e.g. 'Jet Trail') are sometimes useful as ground cover. Others can be used for hedging.

The fruits are used in Chinese medicine, as an analgesic, anti-inflammatory, antispasmodic and astringent that acts mainly as a circulatory and digestive stimulant. It is used for rheumatism, arthritis, cramps etc.

Aurora – tall growing, flowers pink with yellow overtones. Fruit large, orange.

Falconnet Charlet – vigorous, flowers light and dark pink, fruit large, apple shaped.

Grandiflora – strong sprawling grower, flowers white, pink and yellowish; fruit ovate, large.

Nivalis – to 2.5m high, white flowers followed by greenish-yellow fruit.

C. x *superba* (*C. speciosa* x *C. japonica*)

Shrub to 1.5m (5ft) high with many erect to spreading branches with slender spines. Flowers are white, pink, crimson to orange and orange-scarlet. Fruit are usually apple shaped, to 6 x 6cm (2.5 x 2.5ins). Seeds 8 x 5mm (0.3 x 0.2ins), ovoid, glossy red-brown.

A good hedging plant, it can be clipped and will still flower and fruit.

Boule de Fer – to 2m (6ft) high, very thorny; flowers early, carmine-red; a heavy cropper.

Crimson and Gold – only 1m (3ft) high, becoming very wide, dense foliage, suckering. Flowers are dark red, early, with golden-yellow anthers. Fruits are apple shaped, borne abundantly. Makes a good ground cover.

Fusion – bred for heavy fruit production with large green fruit.

Nicoline – to 1.8m (6ft) high with abundant scarlet flowers and followed by large rounded fruit, deep yellow.

Ruby Glow – vigorous and upright with few thorns; flower red, fruit large, ovate.

Flowers on *Chaenomeles japonica*

C. thibetica – Tibetan quince

Shrub growing 1.5-3m (5-10ft) high, only recently 'discovered'. Fruits are oblong or pear shaped, 6-11cm (2.5-4.5ins) long by 5-9cm (2-3.5ins) across. Native to Tibet, growing at high altitudes up to 3760m – should be extremely hardy.

C. x vilmoriana (*C. speciosa* x *C. cathayensis*)

Shrub up to 2.5m (8ft) high with stiff branches and short side branches with large thorns. Flowers are large, white, pink-flushed. Fruit 8cm (3ins) long, but not borne abundantly, ripening in October.

Cultivation

Chaenomeles can be grown on walls, banks or normal garden locations. They are quite shade tolerant and do well in conditions of zero full sun as long as there is plenty of light, though flowering is delayed and reduced without sun.

All species are tolerant of atmospheric pollution and of a wide range of soil types (they can become chlorotic on very alkaline soils though). They are fairly drought tolerant once established.

Grow in any moderately fertile, well-drained soil. Plants resent root disturbance. In general, plants only need pruning to thin out overcrowded branches.

Propagation is by seed, cuttings or layering.

Fresh seed can be removed from fruit and sown in autumn, allowing winter cold to stratify the seeds. Dry seed must be pre-stratified for three months. Seed-grown plants take 3-5 years to flower and fruit; cultivars will not come true from seed.

Take semi-ripe heel cuttings in summer (June-July), using bottom heat of 16°C (60°F). Large cuttings (over 20cm, 8ins) are most successful.

Hardwood cuttings sometimes succeed. Take cuttings of mature wood of the current year's growth in November and place in a cold frame.

Layer plants in February or March. Detach the new rooted plant the following winter.

Pests and diseases

Plants are susceptible to fireblight (*Erwinia amylovora*). Plants in this genus are notably resistant to honey fungus.

Insect pests of note are aphids, brown scale (*Parthenolecanium corni*); wipe off with a soft rag; and sawfly larvae of the pear and cherry slugworm (*Caliroa cerasi*), which can skeletonise the upper surface of leaves. None of these are very significant and control is not usually necessary.

Related species

The Cathay quince, *C. cathayensis*, is the largest species and is described in *Trees for Gardens, Orchards and Permaculture*.

FUCHSIA, *Fuchsia magellanica*

Zone 6-7, H5-6
Evergreen
Edible fruit, Bee plant

Origin and history

The fuchsia family contains many species but this is by far the hardiest; most are hardy only to zone 9 or 10. Brought into cultivation a long time ago from South America (Chile and Argentina), it has been hybridised with other species to create the numerous hardy cultivars available today.

Description

An erect or scrambling evergreen shrub growing 0.6-3m (2-10ft) high. Young branches reddish-brown; on older branches the bark becomes flaky. Flowers of the true species are hermaphrodite but not all cultivars appear to be self-fertile, and some hybrid cultivars are dioecious, so self-sterile. Fruits are 1.5-2cm long, black.

Uses

The fruits are edible, with a plum flavour and peppery aftertaste.

Bees love the flowers.

Hedging in mild areas.

Varieties/Cultivars

Only a limited number of cultivars have been observed to set fruit outside of South America. These include Globosa, Gracilis, Riccartonii and Vielebachen.

Cultivation

Grow in any fairly fertile, well-drained soil, in sun or part shade.

In colder areas, fuchsias may die down to the ground in winter but regrow and flower each year.

Pruning can be undertaken in spring as growth starts, to shape bushes and cut out any dead wood.

Pests and diseases

Fuchsia gall mite (*Aculops fuchsiae*) causes swollen or distorted growth of shoots and flowers. Cut out affected shoots.

Related species

Most other ***Fuchsia*** species also have edible fruit but can only be grown in warm areas or greenhouses.

Fuchsia 'Riccartonii' flower

GAULTHERIA, *Gaultheria* species

Zones 3-9, H3-7
Evergreen
Edible / medicinal fruit, Bee plants, Ground cover

Origin and history

There are some 200 species in the genus *Gaultheria*, originating from North and South America, Japan to India, Australia and New Zealand. Many of these evergreen shrubs have potential uses: many (if not all) have edible fruit; some have medicinal uses and are a source of oil of wintergreen; and many are excellent ground cover plants.

Description

The genus *Gaultheria* belongs to the acid-loving family Ericaceae. *Gaultheria* species are evergreen, glabrous to hairy, generally with rhizomes, upright or prostrate shrubs. Hardiness varies from species to species, from zone 3-4 (e.g. *Gaultheria procumbens*) to zone 10 (only to zone 9 are included here).

Gaultherias are very similar in outward appearance to *Vaccinium* (the blueberry family), especially in leaf.

Winter buds are ovoid with several outer scales. Leaves are tough and leathery, alternate (occasionally opposite) on stems, short-stalked and minutely toothed.

Flowers are solitary or in racemes and bell shaped; there are five fused sepals and five petals, often white or pink. Pollination is mainly via bees. Spent flowers enlarge and become fleshy, surrounding or enclosing the fruit capsule (which is then berry-like in appearance).

Fruits are five-chambered capsules surrounded by the fleshy calyx; they are often highly coloured. Within fruit there are numerous, very tiny seeds.

Uses

All the species below have edible fruit, either used directly, in preserves or for flavouring. Fruit quality varies widely, and a number of species (usually called 'wintergreen') have fruits that are more medicinal than edible, with a strong wintergreen flavour which reminds most people of antiseptic and hospitals! Others have very pleasant sweet fruit with no wintergreen flavour at all.

Several suckering species make good ground cover plants.

Varieties/Cultivars

Gaultheria adenothrix

A prostrate shrub, 30cm (1ft) high from Japanese conifer forests, hardy to zone 9 / H3-4. Cylindrical, wavy, ascending, reddish-brown stems which spread via underground runners and are clothed with glandular hairs; leaves are ovate, 10-30mm (0.5-1.25ins) long, smooth and leathery, edged with a few glandular hairs; flowers are solitary, nodding from the leaf axils near the end of branches, white-pink in colour; fruits are bright red, 6mm (0.25ins) thick. Fruits are sometimes used to make wine. Ground cover in very mild regions.

Gaultheria antarctica

A prostrate shrub to 10cm (4ins) high, from Patagonia and the Falkland Islands, hardy to zone 9 / H3-4. A wide-spreading shrub with hairy branches; leaves are ovate, 6mm (0.25ins) long, hairy and leathery; white flowers in spring, solitary, in the axils of the upper leaves; fruits are round or pear shaped, white to pink, 6-8mm (0.25ins) thick with a fleshy calyx.

Gaultheria antipoda – Tasmanian Gaultheria, Takapo taupuka

A shrub, variable in height: 10cm (4ins) in mountainous, exposed locations, and 50-100cm (20-39ins) or more in sheltered places. From New Zealand and Tasmania, hardy to zone 9 / H3-4. Young branches are bristly; leaves are oblong, 8-15mm (0.3-0.6ins) long, thick, smooth and leathery, deep green and distinctly veined; fragrant white flowers in June-July, solitary in the upper leaf axils; fruits are fleshy, white or red, to 12mm (0.5ins) thick, of good flavour.

Gaultheria cuneata

A prostrate shrub from western China, grows to 30cm (1ft) high, hardy to zone 6 / H6. A bushy shrub, with young branches very downy; leaves scattered, oblong, leathery, tapering to both ends, 1-3cm (0.5-1.25ins) long and 6-12mm (0.25-0.5ins) wide, dark glossy green above, paler beneath; white flowers in June, in short racemes in the upper leaf axils; fruits from August onwards are white, round, 6-10mm (0.25-0.4ins) containing numerous shining brown seeds. Also used as a ground cover.

Gaultheria forrestii

A rounded shrub from western China, grows to 1m (3ft) high or more, hardy to zone 6. Young branches are bristly; leaves are narrowly elliptic, 5-9cm (2-3.25ins) long, bristly, dark green above and lighter beneath; white, conspicuous, fragrant flowers in May-June in racemes along the entire length of the previous year's shoots; dark blue, round fruit, 6-10mm (0.25-0.4ins), only sparsely produced.

Gaultheria fragrantissima Indian wintergreen

A large Indian shrub or small tree, hardy to zone 8-9 / H4. Young branches are smooth and angular; leaves tough and leathery, ovate, 3-10cm long by 2-5cm wide, bright green above, spotted brown beneath; nodding, greenish-yellow to white, very fragrant nodding flowers produced in April in 3-7cm (1.2-2.8ins) long racemes from leaf axils on the previous year's wood; fruit dark or light blue, 8mm (0.3ins) across.

Fruits are used for flavouring, with a medicinal wintergreen flavour; leaves used to make a tea. Leaves and the oil from leaves (oil of wintergreen) used medicinally (see *G. procumbens* below); oil from leaves also used in perfumery and is reported to have insecticidal properties.

Gaultheria hispida – Tasmanian waxberry, Waxberry

A Tasmanian shrub to 50cm (20ins) or more, hardy to zone 8 / H4-5. Erect and spreading, with all parts bristly; leaves oblong, 25-50mm (1-2ins) long with short tips, leathery; white flowers in short, compact, terminal racemes 3-7cm (1.2-2.8ins) long containing 6-10 flowers; fruit white, round, 10-12mm (0.5ins) thick, sometimes bitter. Ground cover in mild areas.

Gaultheria hispidula – Moxie plum, Creeping snowberry, Maidenhair berry

Prostrate shrub from North America and Japan, growing to 30cm (1ft), hardy to zone 6 / H6. A fast growing, creeping and matted shrub with rough hairy branches; leaves oval-rounded, 4-10mm (0.2-0.4ins) long, bristly beneath; white flowers in May-June, solitary in leaf axils; fruit white, rough, hairy, 6mm (0.25ins) thick. Fruits used for flavouring, with a medicinal wintergreen aroma; leaves used to make a tea. Ground cover.

Gaultheria hookeri

A Himalayan shrub to 1.5m (5ft) high, hardy to zone 6 / H6. A broadly upright, clumped shrub, spreading by underground stems and with bristly young branches; leaves 5-10cm (2-4ins) long, ovate, smooth above and bristly beneath, tough and leathery; pink flowers are densely packed in terminal racemes 2-5cm (1-2ins) long in March-April; fruit round, violet, 5-6mm (0.2-0.25ins). Used for hedging.

Gaultheria humifusa – Alpine wintergreen, Western wintergreen

Prostrate shrub from western North America, grows to 10cm (4ins) high, hardy to zone 5 / H7. A bushy, creeping, matted shrub with wavy branches; leaves elliptic to rounded, 1-2cm (0.4-0.8ins) long, glossy above with bristly edges; flowers in July, solitary, white-pink; fruit red or scarlet, roundish, 6-7mm (0.25ins) thick.

Fruits are used for flavouring and in preserves: they are aromatic with a medicinal wintergreen flavour; leaves used to make a tea, and eaten cooked. Reportedly difficult to cultivate.

Gaultheria lanceolata

A Tasmanian shrub up to 1.5m (5ft) high, hardy to zone 7 / H5-6. Upright branches; smooth narrow leaves, 10-25mm (0.5-1ins) long; white flowers.

Gaultheria minima

A small Chilean shrub up to 1m (3ft) high, hardy to zone 7 / H5-6. Leaves are smooth, oblong, 3-4mm long; flowers are upright, borne on short stalks.

Gaultheria miqueliana – Miquel berry

Japanese prostrate shrub to 30cm (1ft) high, hardy to zone 6 / H6-7. Young branches hairy, becoming smooth with age; leaves ovate, 2-4cm (0.8-1.6ins) long, smooth and dark green above and spotted brown beneath, crowded at the ends of branches; nodding white flowers in May-June in small racemes 2-6cm (0.8-2.4ins) long near the tips of branches; fruits are round, white to light pink, 10mm (0.4ins) thick.

Gaultheria nummularioides

Himalayan prostrate shrub to 30cm (1ft) high, hardy to zone 9 / H3-4. Spreading by underground runners; branches are long, thin and bristly; bristly leaves are leathery, in two rows, rounded, 6-15mm (0.25-0.6ins) long, dull green above and lighter beneath; flowers are solitary, hidden under the foliage, white-pink or brown, in July-August; fruits are blue-black, 8mm (0.3ins) long. A shy bearer of fruit, may be dioecious. Used as a ground cover.

Gaultheria ovatifolia – Mountain checkerberry, Oregon wintergreen

Prostrate shrub from western North American fir forests, grows to 30cm (1ft) high, hardy to zone 6 / H6-7. A wide-spreading shrub with hairy, partly erect branches; leaves nearly circular, 15-25mm (0.6-1ins) long, hard and leathery, dark green above, with smooth surfaces but with bristly edges; white-pink flowers solitary, in June; fruit scarlet-red, roundish, 6-9mm (0.25-0.4ins) thick, 'spicy and delicious'. Reputedly difficult to cultivate.

Salal (*Gaultheria shallon*)

Gaultheria procumbens – Creeping wintergreen

Prostrate shrub from eastern North America, grows to 15cm (6ins) high, hardy to zone 3 / H7. An aromatic, creeping, stoloniferous shrub with short branches rising up; leaves elliptic, clustered at the branch tips, 1-5cm (0.5-2ins) long, glossy dark green above, strongly aromatic and turning red in autumn; white-light pink flowers in June-August are solitary (or occasionally in small racemes) at the top of the stems and nodding; fruits are round, 8-18mm (0.3-0.7ins) thick, red-scarlet and very aromatic when rubbed. Fruits persist all through the winter, often hidden beneath the foliage.

Uses: Fruits have been used in preserves, beers and desserts: a strong, medicinal, wintergreen flavour. Fruit can be picked throughout the winter. Young leaves are edible in salads; leaves and bark can be made into a tea ('mountain tea'), and the leaves and oil from the fruit can be used as a wintergreen flavouring (e.g. in chewing gums). All parts should not be used in excess.

This is the original source of 'Oil of Wintergreen', which is now mainly produced from the cherry birch (*Betula lenta*) or synthetically; the aroma is due to the chemical methyl salicylate. Oil of Wintergreen and methyl salicylate, like other salicylates (aspirin-like compounds), have long been used as a treatment for rheumatism and arthritis, acting as an anti-inflammatory/counterirritant. The oil also has antibiotic and antiseptic properties. Leaves can be used as a febrifuge (for fevers), amongst other things. Note that methyl salicylate can be poisonous if consumed in large quantities.

The oil is also used in perfumery; and has potential uses as a fungicide and insecticide.

Gaultheria pumila

A prostrate spreading shrub from southern South America, growing to 30cm (1ft) high, hardy to zone 7 / H5-6. A rapidly spreading shrub; leaves very dense, glossy on both sides, elliptic, 6-15mm (0.2-0.6ins) long by 1.5mm wide, leathery; white flowers in April-May, solitary; fruits are round, white to reddish, 6-20mm (0.2-0.8ins) thick. Possibly dioecious.

Gaultheria pyroloides

Himalayan prostrate shrub to 15cm (6ins) high, hardy to zone 6 / H6-7. Spreading shrub with slightly hairy branches; leaves are clustered at the branch tips, rounded, 15-35mm (0.6-1.4ins) long; white-pink flowers in May-June in loose racemes; fruits are roundish-oval, smooth, blue-black and 8mm (0.3ins) thick. Used as ground cover.

Gaultheria rupestris – Rock snowberry

A variable New Zealand shrub, 30-100cm (1-3ft) high, hardy to zone 7 / H5-6. Plants may be erect or prostrate and are much branched; leaves are oblong, hairy along edges, 15-25mm (0.6-1ins) long, leathery; white flowers in June-July in terminal racemes at the branch tips; fruits are brown, to 12mm (0.5ins) across, dry.

Gaultheria shallon – Salal, Shallon

Shrub from the forests of western North America, grows to 0.6-1.8m (2-6ft) high, hardy to zone 5-6 / H7. A dense, vigorous, spreading shrub which develops into thickets; branches are reddish and erect with glandular hairs, becoming rough with age; leaves are oval-rounded, 5-10cm (2-4ins) long with hairy edges; reddish-white flowers in May-June, in drooping terminal racemes at the end of the previous year's shoots; fruits are juicy, round, red-black with some glandular hairs, 10mm (0.4ins) across with many tiny seeds.

Creeping wintergreen (*Gaultheria procumbens*)

Sometimes regarded as an invasive plant on acid sites.

Fruits, abundantly produced, have a pleasant mild flavour like sweet blueberries, often being made into preserves and pies; they can also be dried and stored. Leaves have medicinal properties.

The plant is a rampant ground cover, though it takes a year or two to settle after transplanting; it is also good as a low hedging species, and is a bee plant. Also cultivated for the foliage for floristry, the foliage is sold as 'lemonleaf' in florists.

Gaultheria tetramera

A low shrub from China and Tibet, grows to 50cm (20ins) high or more, hardy to zone 8 / Z4-5. Erect, spreading bush with bristly stems; leaves elliptic, 3-7cm (1-3ins) long, glossy above with bristly edges; fragrant flowers in May are greenish-white, in small racemes; fruit are round, fleshy, blue, 6mm (0.25ins) thick.

Gaultheria trichophylla

Himalayan prostrate shrub to 30cm (1ft) high, hardy to zone

8 / Z4-5. Carpet-like spreading growth with very thin, bristly branches; leaves narrowly oblong, in clusters, 5-10mm (0.2-0.4ins) long, smooth with bristly edges; flowers in May are red, pink or white, solitary in leaf axils; fruits are light blue, 10-12mm (0.4-0.5ins) long and 6mm (0.25ins) across. Fruits not abundant; may be dioecious.

Gaultheria wardii

A low Tibetan shrub, 70-100cm (2-3ft) high, hardy to zone 6 / Z6-7. Wide-spreading, bristly branches; leaves hard and leathery, oblong, 3-8cm (1-3ins) long, bristly all over; racemes of 6-10 white flowers in May-June, from the axils of the terminal leaves of the previous season's growth; fruit dryish, blue with a white bloom, 5mm (0.2ins) thick.

The best species to grow for fruit production in Britain are: *G. cuneata*, *G. humifusa*, *G. miqueliana*, *G. procumbens*, *G. pumila*, and *G. shallon*. The best quality fruit for eating is from *G. shallon*. The best species for an evergreen ground cover are: *G. cuneata*, *G. hispidula*, *G. procumbens*, *G. pyroloides*, and *G. shallon*.

Cultivation

All species require acid soil (pH under 6.0); light soils are preferred but many species grow fine on heavier soils. Most prefer partial shade; most tolerate both sun (as long as the soil is moist) and full shade. Most species need a moist location and the ideal location is in the understorey of an open forest, forest garden or orchard.

Propagation can be by one of several methods:

Seeds are very small (e.g. 1,000,000/kg for *G. procumbens*, 200,000/kg for *G. shallon*) and are best sown either immediately in the autumn or in spring after being given a short stratification. Sow on the surface of an acid compost and keep moist (with mist or a polythene cover) and in the light. Take special care when transplanting seedlings, which are at risk from drying out.

Other methods of propagation include layering in the spring; suckers removed in autumn; division in the autumn; and cuttings of semi-ripened wood taken in July or August.

Pests and diseases

Nothing much of note. Birds can be interested in the fruit, particularly the less medicinal ones.

Related species

Related to the blueberries and cranberries, but the *Gaultheria* family is more shade tolerant than them.

GENISTA, *Genista* species

Zone 4-8, H4-7
Deciduous and evergreen
Nitrogen-fixers, Bee plants

Origin and history

Some 80 species of shrubs, deciduous or evergreen and sometimes spiny. Found in temperate regions of Europe, North Africa, the Mediterranean region and western Asia, often on scrub and dry lands. Most species are very drought resistant and useful in preventing sand dune erosion. Most species contain poisonous alkaloids and are not suitable fodder.

Description

Closely allied to the broom family (*Cytisus*), these are shrubs often with yellow flowers in open sunny positions.

Uses

As legumes, the family are all good nitrogen-fixers and bee plants.

Varieties/Cultivars

Genista aetnensis – Mount Etna broom

Large deciduous shrub from Sardinia and Sicily, growing 6m high; hardy to zone 8 / H4-5.

Uses: Bee plant.

Genista germanica – German broom

Dwarf deciduous shrub from Central and Western Europe, growing 60cm high; hardy to zone 5 / H7. Tolerates poor, very acid and very alkaline soils. Resents root disturbance.

Uses: A yellow dye is obtained from the branches. Bee plant.

Genista hispanica – Spanish gorse, Spanish broom

Dwarf deciduous shrub from France and Spain, growing 75cm high and spreading 1.5m; hardy to zone 6 / H6-7. Resents root disturbance and should be planted into its permanent position whilst small.

Uses: Good ground cover for a sunny position. Bee plant.

Genista lydia

Dwarf deciduous shrub from the Balkans, growing 30cm high; hardy to zone 7 / H5-6.

Uses: Good ground cover for a sunny position. Bee plant.

Genista pilosa

Prostrate deciduous shrub from Central and Western Europe, growing 50cm high; hardy to zone 6 / H6-7.

Uses: Good ground cover for a sunny position.

Dyers greenweed (*Genista tinctoria*)

Genista sagittalis

Prostrate deciduous shrub from Central and Southern Europe, growing 30cm high; hardy to zone 4 / H7.

Uses: Good ground cover for a sunny position.

Genista tinctoria – Dyer's greenweed

Dwarf deciduous shrub from Europe and Britain, growing 60cm high and 1m in spread; hardy to zone 2 / H7. Sometimes cultivated as a dye plant, it is usually treated as a biennial for this purpose, the whole plant being harvested in the second year. Resents root disturbance and should only be transplanted whilst young.

Uses: The seed has been suggested as a possible coffee substitute; the flower buds are a substitute for capers. (N.B. The plant contains toxins and caution should not be taken.) Medicinally, used (with caution) as a cathartic, diuretic, emetic, stimulant, and vasoconstrictor.

A yellow dye is obtained from the flowers and shoots (one of the constituents, along with woad, of the dye Kendal Green). A fibre obtained from the stems is used for coarse cloth and cordage.

Plants can be used as a ground cover (the cultivar 'Flore Pleno' is always dwarf and is more reliable than the species). Rabbit fodder. Bee plant.

Genista villarsii

Prostrate shrub from Southern Europe, growing 25cm high; hardy to zone 6.

Uses: A yellow dye is obtained from the flowers.

Cultivation

Need full sun and a well-drained soil. Tolerates acid and alkaline soils.

This family does not recover well from heavy pruning.

Pests and diseases

None of note – cold damage is sometimes a problem on less hardy species.

Related species

The brooms – *Cytisus* (p.46).

GOJI BERRY, *Lycium barbarum*

Zone 5, H7
Deciduous
Edible fruit / leaves

Origin and history

Lycium barbarum has long been cultivated in ornamental gardens, under the common names 'box thorn', of 'Duke or Argyll's tea tree' (he introduced it to Britain in the 1730s) and until recent years the fruit was not even considered edible. However, this same species has long been cultivated in China and Nepal and valued for its edible/medicinal fruit as well as the edible young shoots and leaves. Other common names used include 'wolfberry' and 'matrimony vine'.

Goji berry bush

Description

Goji berry plants are hardy deciduous shrubs growing 2-3m (6-10ft) high and spreading widely as they grow. Wild plants are spiny, with thorns – hence the name box thorn – however named varieties are often selected with few or no thorns. Leaves are greyish-green, often arranged in bundles of two or three along stems.

Flowers appear from June to August, followed by fruits that ripen from August to October. The flowers are light purple or lavender in colour and closely resemble flowers in related species, e.g. potato. Plants are self-fertile and pollinated mainly by bees. The fruits are ellipsoid, 1-2.5cm (0.75-1ins) long and red when ripe. They contain 10-60 tiny yellow seeds.

Uses

Edible fruit. There has been an enormous amount of hype about goji fruit over the past few years. Undoubtedly they do contain large amounts of beneficial phytochemicals, but so do most fruit especially those red and purple in colour. What little mainstream medical research has been undertaken on goji fruit has so far failed to show any particular health benefits.

Dried goji berries are chewy and similar in texture to raisins, with a slight bitterness. They can also be quite palatable and add nutrition when added to other foods such as yoghurt, breakfast cereals, cooked grains, chilli, stuffing, biscuits/cookies, trail mix, etc.

The fruits are used commercially in various foods including wines and beers. The fruits are also attractive to birds once ripe.

Edible leaves. The leaves can be somewhat cress-like, and are used with young shoots as a steamed vegetable – they only need 3-4 minutes steaming – or in teas. In China they are often added to soups or stir-fries or are eaten with rice.

The plant has a very long history of use in Chinese medicine, including the fruit, and the leaves made into a tonic tea.

The root bark is medicinal and has been used to treat

Leaf production

In commercial plantations for leaf production, plants are kept coppiced to a height of 60cm (2ft) to maximise shoot production.

Leaves and young stems can be harvested throughout the growing season. Heavy spring and summer pruning will promote new leaf and stem growth. Stems for vegetable use should still be totally green and show no woodiness. Stems 15cm (6ins) or less in length are the most tender.

Leaves can be left on stems and the entire stem can be used as a vegetable or dried for later use. Leaves and stems are dried in a dehydrator at 40°C (105°F) and take less than 12 hours to dry. Dried product should be stored in an airtight container in a cool, dry place. Dried stems and leaves can also be powdered in a blender.

If growing plants for both fruit and leaves, the best time to harvest the leaves is late autumn, after the majority of the fruit season is over. You can strip all leaves from the vines before the first really hard frost and dry them for tea. Older leaves may be dried and powdered for vegetable use, but are not tender enough to use as fresh vegetables. Leaves are easily stripped off the stems by starting at the base and pulling toward the tip. Wear leather gloves to avoid the occasional thorn.

Leaves may be used fresh, dried, powdered or frozen. Leaves for fresh use should not be washed before placing in the refrigerator. Wash the leaves when ready to use in a recipe. Leaves for drying should be washed and spread on drying racks. The liquid in other recipe components usually rehydrates dried leaves used for vegetables.

hypertension, diabetes, and as an aid in lowering blood pressure. Root bark is best harvested in early spring. Bark is peeled off the roots and is then dried.

Goji is used as a soil stabiliser in areas of sandy soil. It is also happy in a hedge with other plants.

Varieties/Cultivars

In China, many varieties have been selected as fruiting plants, and others for leaf and stem production (these latter may fruit poorly). In Europe, only fruiting varieties have made the journey so far, although these can also be used for leaf production, and most have high leaf nutrient levels. The following have all been selected for good fruit yields:

Amber Sweet	Fruit amber coloured, large, sweet.
Big Lifeberry	Fruit very large, 2cm or more in length.
Crimson Star	
New Big	Another large fruited variety.
Number One Lifeberry	Fruit are larger, 2cm or more long, and very sweet.
Phoenix Tears	
Sweet Lifeberry	Fruit are medium sized, but significantly sweeter.
Vermillion Sunset	A heavy bearing variety with large fruit.

Goji flowers

Cultivation

Gojis are easy to grow. They fruit best in full sun (though they tolerate some shade), and are very hardy. They tolerate exposure (including salt-laden winds near the sea) and drought. Indeed they are naturalised around the coast of Britain in several places.

Plant in any fairly fertile, well-drained soil, spacing plants 2-3m (6-10ft) apart.

Goji plants grow with an open lax habit, often putting on huge amounts of shoot growth that can sprawl over the ground and self-layer. To ensure good sun for ripening fruit, some summer pruning is advisable (removing some of the excess growth), and plants can be trained against a wall or fence.

Flowers and fruits are formed mainly on previous year's stems. Any regular pruning should ensure that a plentiful supply of recent wood is present. If plants get too large or out of control, they can always be coppiced back and allowed to regrow.

Plants start flowering at 2-3 years of age. The fruits ripen from late summer through the autumn, turning from green to orange to bright red when ripe. Fruits can turn black when handled so if all fruits are fairly ripe on a branch it might be suitable to shake the berries off onto a sheet placed below. Commercial harvests are washed before drying. Fresh fruit will keep in a fridge for a week or more, but are usually dried or frozen for later use.

Propagation is by seed or cuttings taken in summer or winter. Stems can also self-layer.

Pests and diseases

None of note in Europe. This plant is in the same family as potatoes and tomatoes.

Related species

L. chinense and *L. barbarum* are used interchangeably in China and most authorities regard them as the same species.

Goji fruit

GOOSEBERRY, *Ribes uva-crispa*

Zone 3, H7
Deciduous
Edible fruit

Origin and history

Gooseberries (*Ribes uva-crispa*, formerly *R. grossularia*) are native to Eastern and Central Europe and Western Asia, but were already in cultivation in the UK since 1276. Until a hundred years ago it was an important soft fruit; in 1929 over 19,000 acres were grown in the UK, but their popularity has steadily declined since. It is also a popular fruit in Germany and several parts of the former USSR; the major commercial producing countries (mainly for processing) are Germany and Poland, followed by Belgium, England, France, Holland and Hungary.

The American gooseberry, *Ribes hirtellum*, is also cultivated and many cultivars are hybrids of this and the European species. Others are derived from the natural variety *R. uva-crispa reclinatum*, native to Europe, North Africa and the Caucasus.

Gooseberry cultivation in America has been profoundly affected by white pine blister rust. This disease requires both host plants, white pine and a susceptible *Ribes* species, to survive, and in the early 20th century, restrictions were placed on growing *Ribes* as a protective measure. In fact gooseberries are generally relatively resistant to the disease and not very effective agents in its spread.

Description

The gooseberry is a bush, 60-120cm (2-4ft) high (which can also be grown as a taller cordon with support), with an upright or spreading/drooping habit. Stems are generally spiny. The leaves are usually three-lobed (sometimes five-lobed), mid-green in colour.

Inconspicuous reddish-green flowers are borne in late March or April in England, laterally on one-year-old wood and on short spurs of older wood. Flowers are wind and/or insect-pollinated. Floral initiation for the next year starts in late summer.

These are followed by smooth or hairy fruit that can be white, yellow, green or reddish; ripening in June, July and August. Fruits of wild plants are sometimes only 1cm across; however, this rises to 3cm with many cultivars.

Uses

The fruits are delicious raw when fully ripe, and excellent cooked in pies, tarts etc. They can also be used unripe, cooked and sweetened or bottled.

The fruits are still used commercially, for canning, freezing, and fresh fruit for culinary purposes; the jam industry uses a small quantity and a small area is still devoted to the commercial production of dessert berries.

The average composition of gooseberry fruit is (per 100g):

Protein 0.8g
Fat 0.2g
Carbohydrate 9.7g
Vitamin A 290 IU
Vitamin C 33mg
Calcium 18mg
Phosphorus 15mg
Iron 0.5mg
Sodium 1mg
Potassium 155mg

In the past, in addition to its value as a soft fruit, the gooseberry was used as a major source of pectin by the confectionery and jam industries (particularly for strawberry jam); other sources of pectin are now used commercially.

A slightly acid but very pleasant light wine can be made with the juice from the fruit. The fruit pulp is used cosmetically in face masks for its cleansing effect on greasy skin.

The bushes are used in forestry windbreaks in Eastern Europe as a low shrubby layer.

Varieties/Cultivars

Other species apart from *Ribes uva-crispa* have been used to breed gooseberry cultivars, including the native American gooseberry *R. hirtellum*, and Worcesterberry, *R. divaricatum*, which are sources of mildew resistance; and the species *R. leptanthum*, *R. missouriense*, *R. oxycanthoides*, *R. sanguineum* and *R. watsonianum*. The European species are generally considered superior in both fruit size and flavour; American hybrids can tolerate more of a continental climate (cold winters, hot summers) than the European. The yellow-fruited varieties are valued the most highly for eating as dessert fruit.

In the last century there were hundreds of varieties of gooseberries listed, and a great interest in them particularly in the Midlands and north of the UK where gardeners competed in gooseberry clubs to produce new varieties which bore prize-winning large individual fruit. As a consequence, over 110 cultivars are still commercially available in the UK – a huge selection for a bush fruit species; and the National Fruit Collection at Brogdale holds over 150 cultivars.

Gooseberry

The main gooseberry cultivars

Cultivar	Description
Annelii	Vigorous bushes bearing red fruit of good flavour. Late season, resistant to mildew.
Black Velvet	A Worcesterberry-gooseberry cross, very vigorous, upright, very resistant to mildew. Fruit are small-medium size, dark reddish-black, oval, and of very good flavour. Heavy cropping, resistant to mildew. Mid season.
Captivator	Late season, late flowering. Moderately vigorous, spreading habit; almost thornless; cropping moderate. Fruit medium to large, pear-shaped, sweet, dark red. Resistant to mildew and leaf spot. Tolerant of hot summers.
Careless	Early-mid season, mid flowering. Moderately vigorous, upright then spreading, crops well. Fruit smooth, large, oval, green (lightening on ripening), flavour fair to good. Often used for pick-your-own enterprises. Sulphur-shy. Not good under trees. Susceptible to mildew.
Early Sulphur	Early season; early flowering. Vigorous, upright then spreading bush, cropping well. Fruit medium sized, golden-yellow, roundish-oblong, hairy; flavour quite good; ripens over a long period. Sulphur-shy.
Gold Ball	Fruit yellow, borne heavily. Late season.
Golden Drop	Early to mid season, mid flowering. Compact, upright bush. Fruit greenish-yellow, small to medium, round, very good flavour; thin skinned. Susceptible to mildew.
Greenfinch	Mid season. Vigorous, upright, crops well; a recent release, resistant to mildew and leaf spot. Fruit green, fair flavour.
Hamamekii	Vigorous bushes, fruit red, good flavour. Mid season. Resistant to mildew.
Hino Green	(Hinnonmaki Green) Vigorous bushes, fruit yellowish-green, sweet, good. Resistant to mildew. Late season.
Hino Red	(Hinnonmaki Red) Fruit dark red, very good flavour. Resistant to mildew. Mid season.
Hino Yellow	(Hinnonmaki Yellow) Compact bushes, fruit yellowish-green, medium-large, good flavour. Resistant to mildew. Mid season.
Howard's Lancer	Late season, late flowering. Vigorous, upright then spreading; heavy cropping. Fruit medium sized, smooth, roundish-oval, pale greenish-yellow, thin skinned, transparent, very good flavour. Susceptible to mildew.
Invicta	Mid season. Vigorous, spreading, thorny; crops heavily, fruit green, medium sized, good flavour. One of the recent mildew resistant releases.
Jubilee	A virus-tested selection of 'Careless', cropping more heavily.

Keepsake	Mid season, mid flowering, often picked early for cooking. Vigorous, spreading bush, very heavy cropping. Susceptible to frost damage and mildew. Fruit medium to large, oval, green (lightening when ripening), slightly hairy, very good flavour.
Kim	Thornless bush of moderate cropping, vigorous. Fruit green, sweet, good flavour.
Lancashire Lad	Mid to late season, mid flowering. Moderate cropping. Vigorous, upright then spreading, good cropper, some mildew resistance, needs good soil. Fruit large, oval, deep red, hairy, fair flavour.
Langley Gage	Mid season, early flowering. Vigorous, upright; cropping good. Fruit large, roundish-oval, few hairs, silvery white, transparent, exceptional flavour. Some resistance to mildew. Sulphur-shy.
Larell	Thornless bush, medium vigorous, fruit red, sweet, delicious. Mid-late season.
Leveller	Mid season, mid flowering. Moderately vigorous and spreading, weak on poor soils; needs good drainage. Cropping very good. Fruit very large, yellowish-green, oval, smooth, good flavour. Sulphur-shy. Very susceptible to mildew.
Lord Derby	Late season, late flowering. Small, pendulous habit, cropping moderate. Fruit very large, dark red almost black, round, smooth, fair to good flavour.
May Duke	Early season, early flowering. Moderately vigorous, upright, good cropper. Fruit medium to large, deep red, smooth, slightly downy, roundish-oblong, fair-good flavour; picked green for cooking.
Mucurines	Vigorous bushes with large sweet aromatic green fruit of good flavour. Mid-late season.
Pax	Early season. Bearing few thorns, this is a very recent mildew-resistant release. Fruits are round, dark red, of excellent flavour.
Redeva	Vigorous bushes, virtually thornless, bearing large purplish-red sweet aromatic fruit. Very late season.
Spinefree	Bushes of moderate vigorous. Medium size red fruit, good flavour. Late season.
Whinham's Industry	Mid season, mid flowering. Very vigorous, upright, heavy cropper; tolerant of poor soils but very mildew-susceptible. Fruit medium to large, oval, dark red, hairy, very good flavour.
Whitesmith	Mid season, early flowering. Vigorous, upright then spreading; heavy cropping. Fruit medium to large, oval, whitish-green, few hairs, very good flavour. Shows some mildew resistance, and resistant to leaf spot.

Extremely hardy cultivars: Downing, Houghton, Poorman, Sylvia; Scandinavian cultivars like Annelii, Hamamekii, Hankkijan Herkku, Hankkijas Delikatess, Hinnonmaki Gold/Red, Lepaa Red, Matkakoski, Pellervo, Sunderbyn II; and Russian cultivars e.g. Malahit, Manzherok, Oroktoi, Pjatiletka, Plodorodnyj, Rekord, Russkij, Smena. Keepsake is noted as being frost-susceptible.

Cultivars tolerant of hot summers: Captivator, Glendale, Josselyn, Oregon Champion, Pixwell, Poorman, Welcome.

Cultivars whose fruit hang well/ripen over a long period: Early Sulphur, Hönings Früheste, Jumbo, Pitmaston Green Gage.

Cultivation

Gooseberries are long-lived, fruiting well after 20-30 years or more. They are usually grown as open-centred bushes on a short stem, but can also be grown as cordons, fans or even standards. These latter forms all make harvesting the fruit considerably easier. Upright varieties can be planted closer and are most suited to a small garden.

Shelter is essential, because gooseberries flower very early in the spring, and because the young shoots are quite brittle and susceptible to wind damage. Fruiting is best in a sunny location, but gooseberries are quite shade tolerant, and can be grown on north-facing walls or fences where there is no direct sunlight at all (note that in these situations, yields will be lower and fruit will ripen later).

A well-drained, slightly acid, loamy soil is ideal, but a wide range of soil types is tolerated as long as they are not waterlogged. Sites should be chosen that are not susceptible to late spring frosts; gooseberries are slightly more frost hardy than blackcurrants, but flower earlier. Gooseberries have a high potash requirement; interplanting them with comfrey (or having a good supply nearby), which is cut regularly and used as mulch around them, may be a good idea. Placing bushes in a hot dry position increases the likelihood of mildew.

Plant bushes at 1.5-1.8m (5-6ft) apart on fertile soils, or 1.2-1.5m (4-5ft) on light soils. Single cordons should be 30cm (1ft) apart, with 1.5m (5ft) between the rows; double cordons are planted 60cm (2ft) apart, allowing one stem per 30cm (1ft) run. Give bushes a little more space if interplanting them beneath fruit trees or in a forest garden. After planting, mulch with organic materials. Commercial plantations are planted at a wider row spacing to allow tractor access, usually 2.4-2.7m (8-9ft), with bushes 0.9-1.2m (3-4ft) apart in the row.

Gooseberries are traditionally grown a short stem or leg of 10-15cm (4-6ins), to allow for hand weeding around the spiny bushes. They can also be grown as a stooled bush like a blackcurrant, which may live longer but will be more difficult to pick and weed.

Standards are forms grafted onto a long stem (1-1.2m, 3-4ft) of the related *R. aureum* or *R. divaricatum* (Worcesterberry). They need very good staking, but then are treated like bushes on a longer stem.

Weeds should be kept under control by mulching; gooseberries are shallow rooting and digging or hoeing may damage the roots.

Any formation pruning for bushes aims to achieve an open-centred, goblet or cup-shaped bush with 6-8 main branches. Established bushes can be pruned in winter to keep the centre open to allow for good air penetration.

Potash is the most critical mineral needed by gooseberries, which are very susceptible to a deficiency (which appears as a marginal scorching on the leaves). Use of comfrey, wood ash, compost or urine in sustainable growing systems will suffice.

Gooseberries are self-fertile, and are mainly pollinated by insects including bees, usually wild bumblebees because they flower so early; some wind pollination can also occur. Flowering of an individual bush lasts on average for 17-18 days, with full flowering halfway through this period. The date of full flower varies with the cultivar, over a range of about three weeks from early to late April in the UK. The vast majority of cultivars in fact fall into the mid-flowering season, with their peak flowering in the third week of April.

The true colour of the fruit does not develop until it has ripened; for dessert fruit, wait until the colour changes and the taste is sweet. Changes from green to red are easiest to see, those to lighter green or yellow are more difficult; when ripe, fruit will easily part from the bush and be significantly softer.

Bushes yield a little fruit within a year or two of planting, but maximum yields are not usually obtained until about the fifth or sixth year. Well grown mature bushes should yield at least 3.5-4.5kg (8-10lb) fruit each year, and a single cordon about 0.5-1kg (1-2lb) per year. Commercial plantations can regularly yield 5-6 tonnes/acre (12-15 tonnes/ha).

Green and red gooseberries

American gooseberry mildew

Propagation is usually by cuttings. Hardwood cuttings should be 30cm (12ins) long after preparation, with all their buds left intact, taken from strong healthy shoots of the summer's growth. The unripe shoot tip is cut off just above a bud, and the base trimmed just below a bud. Place the cuttings, with 15cm (6ins) out of the ground to allow for a good stem or leg at the base. The rooted cuttings can be transplanted after one or two years.

Cuttings can also be taken of half-ripe wood, in July and August. They should be 10-15cm (4-6ins) long, preferably with a heel, and will need warm sheltered conditions to strike.

Gooseberries are very shade tolerant and are very suitable for growing as part of the understorey in a forest garden. Intercropping by growing under fruit trees is a traditional technique (one of the few agroforestry techniques used for a long time in the UK), using apple or plum trees above the gooseberries. As the trees mature, the gooseberry yield naturally falls, but the bushes will continue to yield even in the shade of established plums or apples provided the soil is reasonably good and that weed competition is not severe.

Pests and diseases

Birds, especially bullfinches, may attack the buds throughout the winter. If attacks are bad, netting will be the only sure method of protection. 'Leveller' is particularly susceptible. Birds may also attack and eat the ripe fruit (especially the red varieties); netting may again be needed.

Gooseberry sawfly or currantworm (*Nematus ribesii*, formerly *Pteronidea ribesii*) caterpillars feed on the leaves, reducing them to a skeletal state within a few days, and can have three generations over the summer. The caterpillars are pale green with dark heads and black spots on their bodies, which are up to 4cm (1.6ins) long. Adults appear in April and May depositing eggs on the underside of leaves, especially low down in the centre of bushes. Each adult lays 20-30 white eggs per leaf in rows close to the midrib. Look out for the first signs of them from May onwards; with just a few bushes, hand-pick and destroy eggs and caterpillars, which otherwise eventually pupate in the soil. Some will drop from the bushes if disturbed, so lay down a sheet or tarp to collect them. The second generation lays its eggs in June, and the third in September. The caterpillars are attacked by various predators, e.g. birds, beetles, spiders and social wasps.

Mildew, American gooseberry mildew (*Sphaerotheca mors-uvae*) especially, is often a problem. This American disease appeared in Europe around 1900. It is a fungal disease affecting leaves, shoots and fruit, producing a white powdery coating. First signs are seen as white powdery patches on the young leaves soon after they unfold in spring, and under favourable conditions (soft sappy growth from high nitrogen levels and high humidity) the disease soon spreads to fruit and shoots. Diseased shoots distort at the tips, and can be cut out. If fruits are affected, the whole crop may be ruined. Excess nitrogen increases susceptibility, as does a hot, dry location. Cordon-grown fruits are less susceptible because of better aeration. Better still, grow cultivars that are resistant, of which there are an increasing number from several breeding programmes around the world.

Related species

Blackcurrant (p.28), Redcurrant (p.181), Other currants and gooseberries (p.76).

GRAPE VINES, *Vitis* species

Zone 6, H6-7
Deciduous
Edible fruit, leaves

Origin and history

Grapes are one of the earliest temperate fruits to have been cultivated; vineyards were planted in Egypt some 4,200 years ago. They are the most important and most widely grown deciduous fruit and a major crop in all continents, with some 65 million tonnes produced per year, two-thirds in Europe.

Very commonly grown in the temperate and Mediterranean regions of the world for its edible fruit, there are numerous named varieties, some of which have been developed for their use as a dried fruit, others for dessert use and others for wine.

Cultivated grape vines are derived mostly from *Vitis vinifera*, although many hybrid cultivars have been bred using other *Vitis* species (notably *V. labrusca* and *V. rotundifolia* from North America). *V. vinifera* is native to the Caucasus where it grows along riversides and in damp woods.

Description

The grape vine is a vigorous deciduous climber, reaching 15-20m (50-70ft) high if allowed, with clinging tendrils. It has brown bark which shreds in long strips.

After bud break, a shoot and leaf appear first, then 2-3 flower clusters per shoot appear opposite the leaves. Leaves are rounded to heart shaped with 3-5 lobes, 7-15cm (3-6ins) wide on stalks 4-10cm (1.5-4ins) long.

Grape vine

Flowers emerge in June or July in Britain, and fruits ripen from August to November, depending on the selection. The flower clusters are produced from a complex bud or 'eye'. Each eye, borne on the previous year's growth, contains a number of buds but only the central bud usually develops.

Fruits are blue, green or red, often with a bloom. Each fruit contains 2-4 seeds.

Uses

Grapes are edible, eaten raw or dried for later use. The dried fruits are the raisins, sultanas and currants of commerce, different varieties producing the different types of dried fruit. The nutritional composition of grapes (per 100g) is approximately:

Water	81.4%	Vitamin B2	0.03mg
Vitamin A	100 IU	Iron	0.4mg
Calcium	12mg	Carbohydrate	17.3g
Protein	0.6g	Vitamin B	0.3mg
Vitamin B1	0.05mg	Sodium	3mg
Phosphorus	20mg	Vitamin C	4mg
Fat	0.3g	Potassium	173mg

The fruit juice is widely produced and drunk as it is; it can also be concentrated and used as a sweetener.

The fruits are widely used in making wine in many parts of the world.

The leaves are edible when cooked. Usually the young leaves are wrapped around other foods and then baked, imparting a pleasant flavour. Also edible, but rarely used as they are small, are the young tendrils (raw or cooked) and the flower clusters (cooked).

An edible oil similar to sunflower oil is obtained from the seed; it needs refining before it can be eaten. The oil is polyunsaturated and is suitable for mayonnaise and cooking, especially frying. The oil can also be used for illumination, and in soaps, paints etc.

The sap is edible raw, with a sweet taste.

The roasted seed is edible, used as a coffee substitute.

Cream of tartar, also known as potassium bitartrate, a crystalline salt, is extracted from the residue of pressed grapes, and from the sediment of wine barrels. It is used in making baking powder. It is also used in fluxes for soldering.

Rootstocks

Grapes are very susceptible to attacks by *Phylloxera*, a root louse which is especially prevalent in some areas of Europe and which almost destroyed the grape industry there after its introduction from North America around 1860. The response of grape growers was to experiment with Euro-American hybrid grapes, and to develop rootstocks. American species of grapes that are resistant to *Phylloxera* are used as rootstocks and this allows grapes to be grown in areas where the disease is common. Grafted vines yield slightly lower than those on their own roots, and have a useful life of only 25 years or so (as opposed to 70 years or more for ungrafted vines) and start to decline after 15-20 years. Britain is relatively free of the disease at present and grapes are often grown on their own roots.

Rootstocks were initially bred for *Phylloxera* resistance and graft compatibility, but selection has also taken place for resistance to root rots and nematodes and for tolerance for drought, high lime and high soil salts. Rootstocks have been derived mainly from hybrids of following species:

Vitis riparia, the riverbank grape. It is cold hardy and resistant to *Phylloxera*, downy mildew and black rot, but is susceptible to lime-induced chlorosis and drought. It roots readily and prefers moist, sandy soil. The root system is shallow and spreading. Bud burst is very early in spring. It encourages early ripening.

Vitis rupestris, the sand grape. It is hardy and resistant to *Phylloxera*, mildew and black rot. It is easily rooted and grows well in sandy soil. It is moderately tolerant to lime and slightly more drought tolerant than *riparia*. Roots are less fibrous and go deeper than *riparia*. Bud burst is early. It encourages early ripening.

Vitis berlandieri, little mountain grape. It is moderately hardy and resistant to *Phylloxera*, mildew, black rot and drought stress. It does not root easily, but the roots grow deep in the soil and are tolerant of high lime. Bud burst is late. It prolongs maturing dates.

Vitis champini, the adobe land grape. It is resistant to *Phylloxera*, black rot and limy soils, and is moderately resistant to downy mildew. It is only moderately hardy but is very drought tolerant. It does not root easily, but it grows well in both sandy and clay soils, and its hard roots penetrate deeply into the soil.

KEY TO ROOTSTOCK TABLE

Species: rip = riparia, rup = rupestris, ber = berlandieri, vin = vinifera, cor = cordifolia, cha = champini, lab = labrusca.

P: resistance to phylloxera, 5 = very resistant, 1 = very susceptible.

N: resistance to nematodes, 5 = very resistant, 1 = very susceptible.

D: resistance to drought, 5 = very resistant, 1 = very susceptible.

L: tolerance of Calcium as a % of soil level.

S: tolerance of NaCl in g/l of soil.

Comments: GC = graft compatibility, EER = encourages early ripening.

Rootstock	Species	P	N	D	L	S	Vigour	Soil types	Comments
101-14 Mgt	rip x rup	4	2	1	9	0	moderate	moist	Inconsistent GC; EER
110 Richter	rup x ber	4	2	4	17		v.vigorous	most, including dry	Good GC
1103 Paulson	rup x ber	4	2	3	17	0.6	vigorous	dry, sandy/alkaline	Good GC
1202 Couderc	rip x vin	2	1	2	13	0.8	v.vigorous	poor sandy	Good GC; very fertile
125 AA							vigorous	most	Encourages good set
140 Ruggeri	rup x ber	4	3	4	20		v.vigorous	shallow, dry	Good GC
1613 Couderc	Solonis x (lab x rip x vin)	2	4	2	low		moderate	fertile moist	
161-49 Couderc	rip x ber	4	1		25	0			Poor GC
1616 Couderc	rip x Solonis	3	1	1	11	0.8	moderate	fertile, moist/wet	Fertile, EER
3306 Couderc	rip x rup	4	1	1	11	0.4	moderate	fertile well-drained	Good GC
3309 Couderc	rip x rup	4	1	1	11	0.4	vigorous	fertile well-drained	Very EER; good GC
333 EM	ber x vin	2	1	2	40	v.sen		alkaline	Gives good crops, high sugar
41 B Mgt	ber x vin	4	1	3	40	v.sen	vigorous	poor alkaline	Gives good crops; good GC
420 A Mgt	rip x ber	4	2	2	20		moderate	deep fertile heavy	Retards maturity; not easily grafted
44-53 Malegue	rip x rup x cor	4	4	2	10		moderate	acid, sandy	Good GC; fertile
5 BB Teleki	rip x ber	4	3	1	20		v.vigorous	moist clay/alkaline	inconsistent GC
5 C	rip x ber	4	4	1	17		moderate	clay, loam	
8B	ber x rip	4	4	3	17	0	v.vigorous		
99 Richter	rup x ber	4	3	2	17	0	v.vigorous	moist deep fertile	Good GC
AXR #1	rip x vin	2	1	2	13	0.8			
Dogridge	cha	2	4	2			v.vigorous	light sandy	Poor GC
Freedom	1613c x Dogridge	2	4	2					
Harmony	1613c x Dogridge	2	4	2			moderate		Good GC
Riparia Gloire	V.rip	5	2	1	6	0.7	low	deep fertile	Good GC; EER; scion res to coulure
Rupestris St.George	V.rup	4	2	2	15	0.7	v.vigorous	deep	Good GC; scion has low fertility
Salt Creek	cha	2	4	2			v.vigorous	deep sandy	Poor GC
SO 4	rip x ber	4	4	1	17	0.4	moderate	moist clay/loam	Fairly good GC; EER

Grape 'Regent'

Varieties/Cultivars

There are some three thousand grape cultivars, bred in all grape-growing regions. Climate is of great importance in influencing the quality and production of individual cultivars, and great care must be taken to choose appropriate cultivars for a particular site. It would take a whole (large) book to describe all grape cultivars, so here I concentrate on the hardy cultivars in cooler areas.

Hybrid vines crop more heavily than pure *vinifera*, and wines made from the grapes mature faster, store for less time in the bottle, lack high-quality taste and are regarded as of inferior denomination. In some parts of Europe they are not allowed in commercial plantings. They are, however, often bred from classic vines (e.g. Chardonnay, Pinot Noir).

It is vital for commercial plantings of vines for wine to produce a viable crop every year, even after bad summers, and thus it is tempting for such growers in northern areas to plant early ripening varieties. The drawback with this strategy is that in very good summers, there might be significant wasp damage to the fruit. With summers warming due to climate change, the case for planting later ripening varieties is becoming stronger.

The main desirable attributes when choosing a cultivar for northern areas are:

- The ability to ripen its replacement wood really well before the onset of winter frosts. Without this, the vine is susceptible to debilitating mildew and botrytis attack in winter and subsequent dieback. When replacement canes are not ripened adequately, the vine has to be pruned back so hard that there will be insufficient wood to bear much fruit in the following season.
- Thick, dark, glossy leaves – less susceptible to mildew and botrytis than a downy dull leaf, and less susceptible to extremes of heat and sun or cold.
- The ability to produce adequate pollen and to set the flowers quickly and well, particularly in cool damp conditions. Flowers are reluctant to pollinate if the temperature is under 10°C (50°F). Some vines manage well in poor conditions, others fail to set any grapes at all.
- Adequate vigour. Excessive vigour in a vineyard causes a lot of extra work.
- The ability to produce viable yields with reliable consistency. Fruit buds are laid down in July of the current year, and this is reliant on the weather and temperature in July.
- The quality of the grapes reflects the parentage of the vine. For wine, a good sugar-acid balance is necessary along with sufficient bouquet and flavour, and the ability to give a good extract from the pulp.

White *vinifera* cultivars

Cultivar	Description
Auxerrois	Widely grown in Alsace and Luxembourg, used for wine. Moderately vigorous and productive, prefers alkaline sites. Mid season. The wood ripens well. Leaves are dark and glossy, not susceptible to mildew. The grapes are loose in the bunch and make a good wine. Of French origin.
Bacchus	Similar in habit to Muller Thurgau, but more reliable in flowering and better quality. Early ripening, medium sized fruit. Vigorous grower. Makes a good wine.
Chardonnay	One of the great wine grapes, but needs a very favoured site to ripen its grapes in England. Likes an alkaline site. A healthy vine, slow growing in spring. The wood ripens well. Of French origin.
Chasselas	For wall culture in England, late ripening. Widely grown in France as an eating grape – low in acidity. A vigorous vine. The wood ripens moderately well. Of French origin.
Forta 100	A German bred vine which is very winter hardy but needs a good site. Yields 5-7.5 tonnes/ha (2-3 tonnes/acre) and produces a good wine.
Freisamer	German bred vine which likes a good site and soil, is frost hardy, early ripening with grapes of good quality which make a good wine.
Gewurztraminer	Grown extensively in Alsace and Germany for wine, producing a fruity, full-bodied wine. The vine is vigorous and mid to late ripening in Britain – requires a good site and soil. The wood ripens well. Should be trained by the double Guyot method with each replacement cane highly arched rather than flat to encourage buds nearer the stem to be fruitful. Of French origin. Makes an excellent juice with a flowery flavour.
Gutenborner	A Muller Thurgau cross, with grapes of similar behaviour.
Huxelrebe	Thrives in a warm, well-drained soil and a good site. This German vine is very vigorous and fertile, producing large crops (can become biennial if not thinned). The grapes are early ripening, with high sugar and acidity, making a strong wine, good when aged. The wood ripens well.
Kerner	A German vine with good frost resistance, moderate vigour and excellent wood ripening. It carries moderate yields of mid-ripening grapes which make an outstanding wine. Sets fruit well in a poor year. Moderately vigorous, late to drop its leaves.
Madeleine Angevine	Grown as an eating grape in France, it has gained a good reputation in Britain due to early ripening, consistent cropping and making a good wine. The fruit sets well even in poor weather and yields are heavy (7.5-10 tonnes/ha, 3-4 tonnes/acre). The vine is vigorous, quite healthy and sets a good crop (often three bunches per lateral); the wood ripens well. Of French origin.
Madeleine Sylvaner	Another old French vine, vigorous, early flowering, sets well and produces a moderate crop of very early ripening grapes for dessert or wine. Produces a good wine. The wood ripens well.
Mireille	Produces early fruit of Muscat flavour. Needs a wall to ripen outdoors in Britain.
Muller Thurgau	A German vine, widely grown there. Mid ripening. It adapts to most soils and situations, but is extremely vigorous, needing constant summer pruning; the wood ripens poorly and flower set is poor in poor summers. Produces a pleasant wine.
Muscat de Saumur	An early ripening golden Muscat grape, with high quality fruit. Quite low yielding, but can be used in mixtures to improve wines. It ripens its wood well. Crops on six-bud spurs.
Noblessa	German bred vine, early ripening and moderate yielding. Has good potential for wine making.
Optima	German vine, producing moderate yields of very early ripening grapes. Healthy, moderately vigorous vine. Produces a good wine. The wood ripens well.
Osiris	German bred vine, early to mid season ripening, yielding good crops of grapes which make a fine wine. Ripens its wood well.
Perle	A German vine, adaptable to most soils and sites, frost resistant and ripens its wood well. Produces mild wines. Moderately vigorous vine, and a reliable moderate cropper of early ripening grapes.
Perlette	An old French variety, vigorous and producing a low acid wine. The grapes are seedless and plentiful. Early ripening.
Perle de Czaba	A very old French variety, early ripening and moderately vigorous. Produces a good wine. Very often vines only crop on long six-bud spurs. The wood ripens well.
Pinot Gris	(Tokay) Mid-ripening, moderately vigorous and a fairly light cropper, bearing small bunches of greyish-mauve grapes. Used in mixtures for wine. The wood ripens well. Of French origin.
Precoce de Malingre	An old French vine of somewhat shrubby habit, responding best to long six-bud spurs. Berries small, pale amber, sweet and juicy – dual use. Extremely early ripening grapes make a good wine. The wood ripens well.
Regner	A German vine which likes a good site and well-drained soil. Moderately vigorous, mid ripening, setting well in poor summers, and makes a good wine. The wood ripens well.
Reichensteiner	A German vine which likes a good well-drained site and fairly rich soil. Early ripening, small-medium sized grapes. The wood ripens late and poorly and is somewhat disease-prone. Growth is moderate to strong and flower set is good even in poor years. Produces a good wine.
Schonburger	(Rosa Muskat) A German vine which adapts to all soils and conditions (prefers fertile, well-drained), sets well in poor weather and produces a good wine from mid-ripening grapes. Needs a hot south-facing slope. The wood ripens well.
Septimer	A German vine, early ripening, moderately vigorous, adaptable to soil and site, ripens wood well. Produces moderate yields of quality grapes that make a good wine.
Siegerrebe	A German vine which dislikes alkaline conditions. Moderately vigorous, and doesn't set too well in poor weather, but otherwise produces good yields of very early ripening grapes for dessert or wine. Makes a good wine. The wood ripens well and leaves are dark and thick.
Wurzer	A German vine, moderately vigorous, liking a neutral fertile, well-drained soil and good site. It produces heavy crops of early ripening grapes, making a good wine. It ripens its wood well.

White hybrid cultivars

Concord	A leading American vine, with an unmistakable 'foxy' flavour from its *labrusca* origins. Used for dessert and wine. Needs a wall in Britain. Has ornamental autumn foliage.
Emerald	An American vine, which ripens its grapes well in the open vineyard in Britain. Produces a large crop of round green grapes that make a fair wine.
Faber	Tolerant of most soils and frost hardy, this vine needs a good site and ripens mid season. Heavy cropping, of good vigour, sets well in a poor year and bears grapes with a good sugar-acid balance, making a very good wine. Wood ripening is only fair, poor in a cool year.
Himrod Seedless	An American vine producing seedless grapes of good flavour. Needs a wall in Britain.
Seibel 5279	(Aurora) A very vigorous, healthy vine with drooping growth which demands spur pruning. The grapes are mid-ripening, small, grey-yellow with an attractive spicy flavour, produces a good wine. The wood ripens well. Widely grown in New York state.
Seyval Blanc	(Seyve-Villard 5276) A very popular vine in Britain, very suited to the climate. Produces a clean wine, also very suitable for blending. Heavy cropping, mid ripening, can suffer from poor fruit set, and ripens its wood very well.

Red *vinifera* cultivars

Dunkelfelder	A German vine, moderately vigorous and early ripening. Ripens wood well, but susceptible to botrytis. Makes a reasonable wine. The wood ripens well. The vine has good autumn colour. The grapes have blood-red juice, useful for colouring wine red (usually this is achieved by fermenting the wine of the skins of red grapes).
Noir Hatif de Marseilles	An old French cultivar, low in vigour, producing low to moderate yields of early ripening grapes of good quality for wine. Susceptible to mildew.
Pinot Noir	A classic French grape, mid ripening and can be used for white wine production in Britain. Vine of low vigour, moderately cropping, needs a good site and alkaline soil. The wood ripens well.
Wrotham Pinot	(Meunier) A hardy French vine which buds late and does not need an alkaline soil. It has white down on its leaves and is one of the Champagne grapes. Best on a wall in Britain, but may be satisfactory outside.
Zweigeltrebe	An Austrian vine of extreme vigour and large leaves. Produces heavy crops of large loose bunches of late ripening grapes that make an acceptable wine. The wood ripens well. Only suited to the best sites in southern England.

Red hybrid cultivars

Baco	(Baco No.1) A French hybrid of great vigour (plant vines 2-3m apart); practically immune from mildew and botrytis. A fairly heavy cropper of mid-ripening intensely black grapes which make a clean, slightly spicy wine. It ripens its wood well.
Brandt	Of Canadian origin, a very vigorous healthy vine which produces good crops of black grapes that make a fair red wine if allowed to mature for a year or two. Has good autumn colour and ripens its wood well. Widely grown in Britain as a wall vine.
Foch	Bred in Alsace, it is vigorous and healthy. The small berries make a mediocre Burgundy-style wine.
Fragole	(Strawberry grape) Fruit mauve with a strawberry flavour. Vigorous dual use vine.
Gagarin Blue	A Russian dual purpose hybrid from Pinot Noir and *V. amurensis*. Crops freely, early to mid season ripening, with large bunches of grapes which are very open and thus less liable to mildew and botrytis attack.
Glory of Boskoop	Hardy variety bred in Holland producing black sweet grapes.
Joffre	(Marshall Joffre) Bred in Alsace, the grapes ripen early and are borne in light crops. They make an ordinary wine. The wood ripens well.
Kuibishevski	A Russian hybrid from Pinot Noir and *V. amurensis*. Crops freely, mid season ripening, with open bunches of grapes which are very open and thus less liable to mildew and botrytis attack.
Leon Millot	Very vigorous, mid season ripening and bearing heavy crops. Vines respond well to arched cane pruning. Grapes are dual use. The wood ripens well. The wine is good, improving with a year in bulk followed by a year in bottle. Resistant to mildew and botrytis; not attractive to birds. Juice rich with an intense cherry flavour.
Oberlin 595	Bred in Alsace, this is a vigorous healthy vine, giving a moderate to good crop of small tight black bunches. Very early ripening, with good wood ripening.
Pirovano 14	A vine suited to wall growing, where it produces masses of large black eating or wine grapes. Late ripening, with good wood ripening.
Ravat 262	A Pinot Noir hybrid, this ripens its grapes early to mid-season, but it can have flower set problems. Makes a quality wine.
Schuyler	An American vine, mid season ripening, producing moderate to good crops of black grapes with a pleasant flavour which make a very fair wine. Moderately vigorous.
Seibel 13053	(Cascade) An early ripening, hardy prolific vine, grown quite a lot in Britain as a rosé or red wine grape. Mildew resistant; ornamental autumn foliage. The wine needs a year in bulk before bottling. It ripens its wood well.
Tereshkova	A Russian dual purpose hybrid from Pinot Noir and *V. amurensis*. Crops freely, mid season ripening, with open bunches of round grapes which are very open and thus less liable to mildew and botrytis attack.
Triomphe d'Alsace	A vigorous and disease resistant vine, which needs good weather at flowering time and can bear a very heavy crop of intensely-flavoured black grapes. The wine needs keeping in bulk for two years followed by a year in bottle, when it is quite good. Early to mid ripening and ripens its wood well. Resistant to mildew and botrytis; not attractive to birds.

Cultivation

Grape vines grow in most soils but prefer a deep, rich, moist, well-drained, moderately fertile loam. They grow in sun or partial shade though a warm sunny sheltered position is required for the fruit to ripen. Sites should be chosen avoiding frost pockets, as late frosts can damage young shoots. Grapes grow well in the company of hyssop, chives, and basil.

Grapes grow with very little winter chilling, but grow much faster after long chilling similar to most temperate fruit. Relatively long hot summers are required to mature the fruit.

The planting site should be weed-free and have compost or manure applied before planting.

Commercial vineyards

If vines are to be planted on a reasonable scale, then they should be planted in rows, ideally 1.3-1.5m (4-5ft) apart. When rows are over 2m (6ft) apart, the vineyard loses its microclimate and no heat is retained between rows: this is particularly important when the grapes are ripening and air temperatures are declining.

Row placement depends on wind speed and direction, slope, and the need for maximum light. North-south rows intercept more light than east-west ones. On sites with high winds, rows should be parallel to the wind direction.

If post and wire pruning systems are to be used, these should be set out before planting. End posts need to be really substantial: 2.4-3m (8-10ft) long and 10cm (4ins) in diameter, sunk 1m (3ft) into the ground. Intermediate posts should be 7.5cm (3ins) in diameter and positioned at least one per five vines for the Guyot system to prevent wind damage when the vines are in full leaf. Double wires are useful at each wire height, so that fruiting laterals can be tucked between the wires rather than tied.

The planting distance within rows depends on the fertility of the soil and vigour of the vine. On very poor soils, spacing of 60cm (2ft) is adequate, on moderately fertile soils 1.2m (4ft) may suffice, while on very rich soils or with very vigorous vines, 2m (6ft) may be necessary. In general 1.2m (4ft) is a good norm.

Vines can be planted at any time in the dormant season from November to late April or early May. Cut all vine roots back to 7.5cm (3ins), top growth back to 2-3 buds and soak the plants in water for several hours prior to planting. Plant them deep

Grape 'Rondo'

enough so that only 7.5cm (3ins) is above soil level, and if grafted so the graft is just above soil level. Each vine requires a bamboo or similar support about 1.5m (5ft) long.

It is common practice now to mulch new vine rows to a width of 60cm (2ft) ideally with a loose organic mulch. This ensures that young vines grow away strongly with no weed competition or drought stress.

Pruning systems

Pruning can be undertaken at any time between January and April. Vines should not be pruned during frosts, or the vine can suffer dieback from the pruning wound; branches are also apt to snap if bent when frosted. Some of the most common pruning systems are described below, though there are numerous others in different parts of the world.

Guyot system

The most common system used in cooler and borderline areas, requiring posts and wires. Cropping begins in the third year; vines allowed to crop in their second year may be set back, and the fruit will be of poor quality. The bottom wire is at a height of 50cm (20ins), then pairs of wires are attached at 80cm (2ft 8ins) and 130cm (4ft 4ins); strong end posts are needed. This system has the huge advantage in borderline areas of bearing the crop 30-40cm (12-16ins) from the ground, taking advantage of heat radiation from the ground; it is also sturdy in windy and stormy conditions.

Year 1: Allow just one shoot to grow, tying it to the cane every 15cm (6ins). Keep the ground between vines clean.

Winter: In the winter, cut this down to two or three buds.

Year 2: Allow two shoots to grow into strong pencil-thick rods of 1.2m (4ft) or more in length. Some feed in the spring will encourage such growth if necessary. Tie these to the bamboo shoot again. During the season, side shoots (sub-laterals) will grow from the leaf axils; these should be pinched out after one leaf, and vines should be checked every 2-4 weeks for axils. (This practice should be undertaken every year, as sub-laterals do little for the ripening of grapes or wood.) Keep the ground between vines clean.

Winter: If no shoots are pencil thick, repeat from winter of year 1. Otherwise, bend the stronger rod down and tie to the bottom wire and cut after the 7-8th upward-facing bud (less with weaker vines), cutting the second rod out, leaving a 2-3 bud spur. This spur will form the two fruiting rods and spur for the next year.

Year 3: Allow 6-8 fruiting shoots to grow from upward-facing buds on the rod, rubbing out other buds and shoots soon after bud burst. Tuck these growing fruiting laterals between the wires until they reach above the top wire, when they should be nipped out. Pinch out side shoots as for year 2. Each fruiting lateral may bear 1-2 bunches of grapes. In autumn, removal of the bottom leaves is sometimes practised to improve fruit ripening and reduce the risk of botrytis.

Winter: Cut away the horizontal two-year wood and fruiting laterals, leaving 3-4 young rods on or near the head of the vine from which to choose the new fruiting wood and spur. Choose the rod best placed to provide a spur, and cut this to three buds; then choose one (single Guyot) or two (double Guyot, the normal system) rods and tie these to the bottom wire. Trim off all sub-laterals and tendrils as these tend to harbour mildew and botrytis.

Note, most of the ancient French vines fail to fruit when Guyot trained. This is because the vines are unfruitful on the first five buds and the sixth bud is the first to be fertile. For these, prune the fruiting laterals down to leave eight buds. Rub off the middle buds after bud burst, and leave the first and sixth to develop.

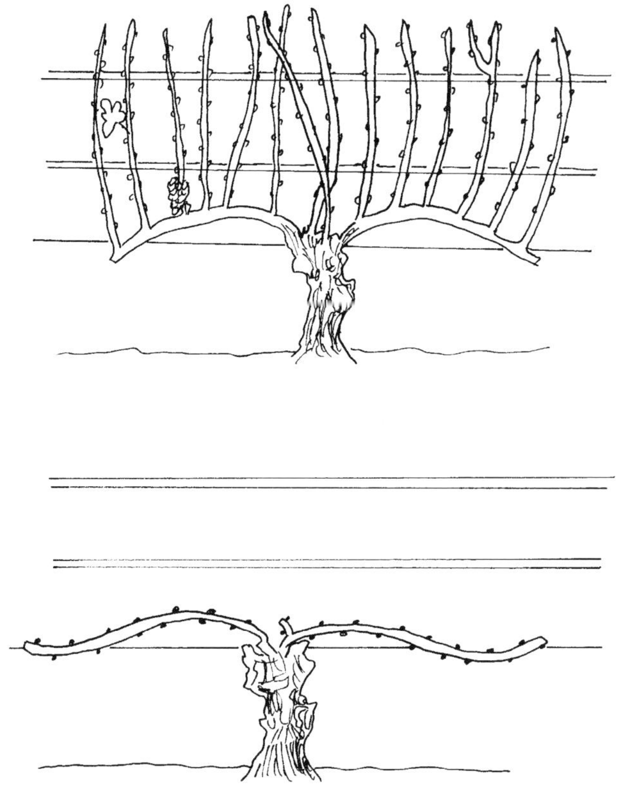

Guyot training system

Year 4: Allow 6-8 fruiting shoots to grow from upward-facing buds on each rod, rubbing out other buds and shoots soon after bud burst. Avoid overcrowding by spacing the shoots about 7.5cm (3ins) apart. Tuck these growing fruiting laterals between the wires until they reach above the top wire, when they should be nipped out. Pinch out side shoots as for year 2. Each fruiting lateral may bear 1-2 bunches of grapes: it is French practice to pinch out the third, weakest flower cluster from each fruiting lateral before flowering to improve the quality and overall yield. In Germany they prefer to allow three bunches per lateral, with the drawback of lower quality and a reduced life for the vine. In autumn, removal of the bottom leaves is sometimes practised to improve fruit ripening and reduce the risk of botrytis.

Winter: As for year 3. Then continue with year 4 procedures.

Variations on the Guyot system

For lighter-cropping small-clustered hybrid vines, the replacement canes can be arched to increase the number of

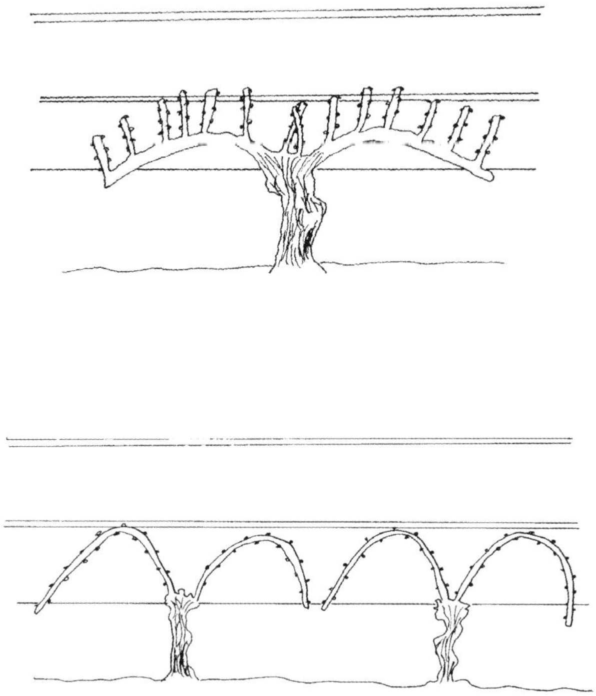

Goblet pruning

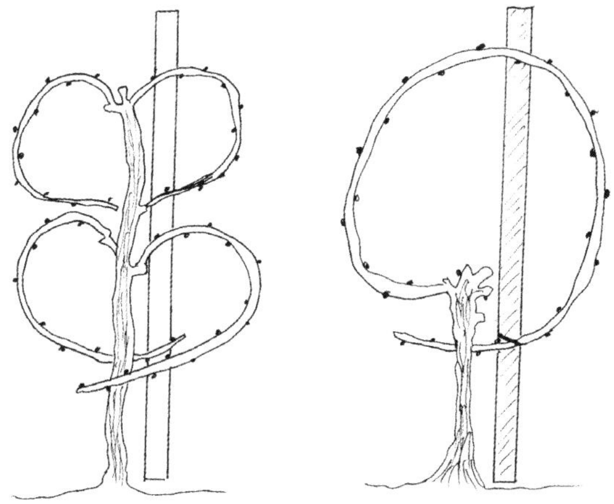

Guyot variations

Mosel system

fruiting laterals. Space vines at 1.5-1.8m (5-6ft).

Head or goblet pruning

This is practised in France and other areas, sometimes with a single low wire as support, more often with no wire at all. The vine is formed as a short-stemmed, low free-standing bush, spur-pruned back to the head or crown each winter.

Year 1 and winter 1: Train as for Guyot system.

Year 2: Allow new growth to extend to 30cm (1ft), then pinch out. On remaining stem, rub out all but top two buds, which will develop and grow, pinching them out after two leaves but leaving sub-laterals; tie these to a bamboo cane.

Winter: Cut back each shoot to leave six buds (for old French varieties) / 2-3 buds (other varieties) on mature, well-ripened cane. As the vine ages, more fruiting spurs can be left to the head of the vine, until a maximum of 12 is reached, which will in turn produce 12 fruiting laterals.

Year 3: In spring after bud burst, keep only the strongest and most fertile shoot on each spur. When summer growth is at its maximum, the rods can be gathered together and tied, so they support each other. Nip out the tops of each fruiting lateral after the 12th leaf.

Winter onwards: As for year 2 winter onwards.

Mosel system

This is used on steep and undulating sites in Germany where post and wire trellis is unfeasible. It is really a variation of the Guyot system, in that two replacement canes are grown each year, which replace the two of the previous year when pruning takes place in winter. No wires are used, each vine being supported by its own 2m (6ft) stake. The stem or leg of the vine is grown to a height of 1m (3ft) or more and instead of tying the replacement rods sideways onto wires, they are bent in a complete arc downwards and tied back to the stem of the vine.

This method is as productive as the Guyot system, but of course is less expensive to set up. Access to vines is much easier, as one can walk between vines in any direction.

Flowering takes place over 10-21 days, depending on the temperature and humidity, in late June or (more commonly) early July in Britain. Grapes are wind-pollinated and self-fertile, although fruit size can be doubled when cross-pollination occurs; thus two or more cultivars are a good idea. Warm, dry, windy conditions are perfect; in cold wet seasons, pollination is often poor.

Grapes are voracious feeders, but any additions needed will largely depend on the soil; on some soils, very little is ever needed, while on poor soils, annual feeds are required. Vine leaves of a yellowish colour indicate a mineral deficiency of some kind. Vines need little nitrogen (certainly don't add any except on the poorest of soils when little growth is made), but require plentiful magnesium, potash, zinc and boron.

Fruit maturity is best indicated by the balances between sugars and acids. Picking too early results in very high acidity and reduced yield; picking too late results in high sugars and low acids. The optimum sugar: acid ratios are different for juice, fresh, wine and different cultivars. Taste is an invaluable test for ripeness; before they are fully ripe, grapes are very acid. Any serious grower, especially for wine, will test the sugar content by using a hydrometer or refractometer.

Grapes are often machine harvested for processing but not for fresh use; clusters tend to break up and berries get damaged, necessitating immediate processing. Manual harvesters should use a sharp pruning knife or secateurs to cleanly cut off the bunches.

Yields vary depending on region, variety and climate, but are on average 7.5-15 tonnes/ha (3-6 tonnes/acre.) Harvested fruit can be stored at 0-1°C (32-33.8°F) for several months; store in shallow layers in slatted wooden boxes for good air circulation. The stems eventually become brittle and the berries may shrivel a little, but the fruit flavour and character remain good for some time. The best storing varieties tend to be those with tight clusters, where the berries don't crack easily, and which have fairly tough skins.

Grapes can be frozen for storage: wash the clusters, remove the berries from the stems and freeze in containers. When thawed, they can be used on cereal, in cooking, or by themselves (when still partly frozen, some varieties rival a good sorbet). Avoid using varieties with acid or bitter skins unless they are destined for cooking; the acid/bitterness will permeate through the flesh when frozen.

Grapes from all grape cultivars can be made into juice. Wine grapes press mechanically much better than dessert grapes as the latter have thicker flesh; wine grapes also have a better sugar to acid ratio for juice. If using a press, use a nylon bag to stop seeds passing through the gaps in the staves; remember to chop/cut the grapes first, after removing them from the stems. On a small scale, with seedless grapes, it is often easier to use an electric juicer; don't use it for grapes with seeds though, as the seeds too will be ground, releasing tannins and gritty bits into the juice. On a small scale, the best way to preserve juice is by freezing it.

The processing of fruit into wine is both an art and a science on which numerous books have been written.

Propagation is usually by cuttings (where Phylloxera is not a serious problem) or grafting. Hardwood cuttings of mature wood of the current seasons' growth are taken in winter. Grafting onto rootstocks is commonly done in late winter using grafting pliers which cut a Ω shape in stock and scion. Manually, any grafting method can be used.

Agroforestry potential for grapes

Grapes can be grown up trees; they are supposed to do particularly well with elm and mulberry. Until three centuries ago, many European landscapes were still agroforests and fruit trees of the Rosaceae family (apples, pears, plums, apricots, peaches, almonds) were left scattered across fields, not hindering manual cultivation techniques; these often provided living trellises for grape vines. One of the Roman agroforestry systems involved using poplar trees as trellises for grapes, which were tended by slaves.

However, this technique of using trees as live vine trellises can cause a lot of extra work for little benefit. The grapes, if any, will be borne high in the trees necessitating ladders for harvest. Pruning is a nightmare and summer pruning is more or less impossible, although winter pruning may be possible, e.g. treat the limbs of the tree like the wires in a Geneva double curtain system, and train permanent rods along each limb; each of these rods can then be spur-pruned each winter. The fruiting laterals will trail down (ish) from the rods each year. Only attempt this on a small scale, and with trees that have a thin canopy: shading will drastically reduce fruiting and delay ripening.

Windbreaks are commonly used in windy areas for vineyards, particularly in Britain. The force of a strong wind on Guyot or other system trained vines on wires is tremendous and protection is vital although this has to be weighed up against good air flow to reduce diseases. Alley cropping of vines is certainly feasible, with fairly wide-spaced rows of trees or shrubs and alleys of vine rows. The trees used in such systems should have thin canopies and not be nitrogen-fixers unless the soil is very poor.

Alley cropping is also feasible using the space between vine rows; in China, grapes are intercropped with vegetables and medicinal herbs. Such intercropping is uncommon in Europe, where occasionally vineyards are grassed between vine rows but the grass is mown regularly and not utilised otherwise.

For sensible intercropping, vine rows need to be wider than normally spaced: 3m (10ft) or more. The central part can be cultivated and planted with vegetables or herbs, allowing enough of a gap at each side for manual access to the vines for summer pruning, harvest etc. The vines will cast significant shade in summer, so the most appropriate interplant crops are likely to be overwintered crops, fast growing spring crops or shade tolerant crops.

In China, grape vines are sometimes trained over streams and irrigation canals on sturdy post and wire systems, giving potential for grape production in areas not usually used for plants.

Pests and diseases

Powdery mildew (*Uncinula necator*) can be a major fungal disease. It forms a fine grey, powdery skin on the leaves, young shoots and grapes. It is favoured by warm, humid conditions and often appears in autumn. Good air flow around vines helps prevent it. It can be treated with powdered sulphur. Biodynamic growers use sprays made from horsetail (*Equisetum*) to minimise mildew diseases.

Downy mildew (*Plasmopara viticola*) is another major disease which also occurs on *Parthenocissus* species. This forms pale translucent or yellow-greenish spreading patches on the upper side of the leaves; as it develops, a thick white down forms on the leaf undersides and sometimes the grapes. The mould disappears when conditions become drier. Young shoots, leaf stalks, tendrils and flowers may turn brown and mature fruit may rot. This fungus can be controlled with Bordeaux mixture; it overwinters as spores on dead leaves beneath vines.

Botrytis (*Botrytis cinerea*) is the third of the three major fungal diseases. It attacks all parts of the vine including the fruit. Try and improve air flow to reduce susceptibility.

Phylloxera (*Daktulosphaira vitifoliae*) is a North American species introduced into Europe around 1863. It ravaged European vineyards in the second half of the nineteenth century and was eventually checked only by grafting all commercial European vines onto resistant rootstocks derived from North American vine species. It is still present in Europe but is no longer a serious pest; it is not established in Britain but is occasionally accidentally introduced, when vines must be destroyed by law.

This root louse attacks and eats vine roots of *V. vinifera* cultivars. The roots stop growing, leaves turn reddish and vines rapidly collapse and die. Leaf galls may develop on some vines during attacks.

Vine weevil (*Otiorhynchus sulcatus*) lays grubs that eat vine roots. Signs of attack are indicated by chunks taken out of the edges of leaves. Ground beetles are good predators of vine weevil; encourage these if possible. A good biological control is available which is watered onto the soil surface around the affected vine.

Birds can be a major problem in some areas, attacking the ripening grapes. Deterrents sometimes work, like hanging long strips of yellow plastic above the vineyard. Others net the whole vineyard against both birds and wasps; one way of doing this is, about three weeks before harvest, to attach netting to the second wire up (Guyot system) and moor it to the ground with stones. Repeat this on the other side of the vines as well, and the fruiting sections will be completely covered. Lift the nets immediately before harvest.

Wasps can be another potential major problem. Not only might they attack ripening fruit, but they might then sting pickers during harvest. Options are to destroy nearby nests, to hang traps (narrow-necked containers half-full of beer) near where the wasps are likely to live, or netting as for birds. Wasps are repelled by lavender; vines can be interplanted with lavender in the rows. Later ripening cultivars (October-November) may ripen after the wasps hibernate and so may escape the problem.

Coulure is the abortion of fruit embryos prior to flowering; the embryo flower shoot suddenly browns and shrivels. It is caused by potash, zinc, boron or calcium deficiency. Prevent by spraying seaweed solution at least twice before flowering.

Millerandage is symptomatic of very poor pollination or fruit set, resulting in a few berries in each bunch setting and swelling normally, the remainder staying tiny. It is caused by mineral deficiencies and/or poor weather. Seaweed solution used for coulure (above) should help prevent the problem.

Crown gall (*Agrobacterium tumefaciens*) can attack vines especially after the bark splits after very cold temperatures (-20°C / -4°F or lower). It is more common in a grassed down vineyard, particularly where lush clover is present. Vines affected display a spongy mass emanating from the damaged area at ground level, lose vigour and slowly die.

Honey fungus: grapes are also notably susceptible to honey fungus (*Armillaria* spp.).

HIGHBUSH CRANBERRY

Viburnum trilobum (V. opulus var. americanum)

Zone 2, H7
Deciduous
Edible fruit

Origin and history

Long used in North America as an edible and medicinal plant, this is sometimes grown commercially for its fruit used in preserves.

Description

Closely related to the European guelder rose (*Viburnum opulus*) and treated as a subspecies of that by some botanists. A rounded shrub growing 3m (10ft) high and round, with shiny young branches.

Heads of white flowers are followed by bunches of red fruit, each 9mm across. Plants are self-fertile.

Uses

Fruits are edible, though bitter. Traditionally used like cranberries in North America and made into bitter preserves particularly used with meat.

Varieties/Cultivars

Improved fruiting cultivars from North America include:

Cultivar	Description
Alfredo	Smaller bush to 1.8m (6ft) high.
Andrews	Compact, dense habit.
Bailey Compact	Smaller bush, average cropping.
Compactum	Smaller bush, fruit well.
Hahs	Bush to 2.4m (8ft) high, with larger fruit.
Phillips	Bears fruit less bitter, produced in large clusters.
Wentworth	Bears large fruit in very large clusters.

Cultivation

Grow in any moisture retentive soil in sun or semi-shade. Ideally harvest fruit late, after a frost, when the flavour may be less bitter.

Propagate by hardwood cuttings.

Pests and diseases

None of note. Even birds leave the fruit until late into winter before being interested.

Related species

The European guelder rose (*Viburnum opulus*) is very closely related, with some botanists putting highbush cranberry as part of *V. opulus*.

American highbush cranberry is closely related to the European Guelder rose

Ripening fruit of highbush cranberry

HONEYBERRY / HASKAP, *Lonicera caerulea*

Zone 2, H7
Deciduous
Edible fruit, Bee plant

Origin and history

Also called 'blue honeysuckle' and 'mayberry', this fruiting shrub is rapidly becoming popular in Europe and North America, but it has been well known for a long time in other parts of the world from where it originates. There are different subspecies in different regions: in Siberia (mainly subspecies *edulis*, *kamtschatica*, *boczkarnikovae*, *altai*, *turczaninowii*); northern China (subspecies *edulis*) and Hokkaido; the northern island of Japan (subspecies *emphyllocalyx*). Almost any garden in the Russian north contains some of these tough fruiting plants. It is noted especially for its early fruit ripening, usually in May or June.

Traditionally, and into present times, large amounts of fruit have been collected from wild plants. Research into selection and cultivation began in Russia around 1914. More extensive breeding work started at the Vavilov Research Institute in St Petersburg and at the Siberian Horticultural Institute in the 1950s. Dozens of cultivars have been released for home and commercial production in Russia. In the 1980s Japan began a research programme to identify superior forms of their local subspecies, and several selections have since been released. Since the 1990s, breeding programmes in Eastern Europe and North America have concentrated on the Japanese subspecies *emphyllocalyx* and many cultivars have been released, with big improvements in fruit size, yields and sweetness. Commercial plantations, long established in Western Siberia, now exist in many European countries, Canada and the USA.

Description

Honeyberries are long-lived, dense, multi-branched shrubs that reach 1-2m (3-6ft) tall and rather more in width, with a rounded crown. They are usually found growing wild in forest glades and hedgerows.

Flowers are bright yellow, borne in early spring (March and April in Britain). Pollination is by bees, mainly wild/bumblebees. Cross-pollination is essential for a good fruit set and size.

Leaves are greyish-green and elliptical, 4-10cm (1.5-4ins) long. They turn yellow in autumn, making the shrub quite ornamental.

The fruits (berries) are dark blue, with a white waxy bloom. Fruit shape is very variable, from round, oval, ovate, pear shaped, jug shaped, to long and thin. The fruits ripen in late spring, usually May or June.

Shrubs are extremely cold hardy and have a short chilling requirement; in a cool maritime climate they start to bud out and flower in late winter (February or March). The young growth is also very hardy (to -18°C / -27°F) and undamaged by frosts. The flowers too are hardy, tolerating -8 to -10°C (-22 to -23°F) without damage.

Most of the cultivars originating from Russia require very cold winters and do not perform well in more mild climates; in milder areas haskaps (the subspecies from Japan) do better. These flower later than the hardier blue honeysuckles and crop better in milder climates.

Uses

Fruits have long been eaten where they are native, appreciated especially for their earliness (two weeks before the earliest strawberries). The colour and taste is similar to that of blueberries, often with a hint of honey (hence the name). The fruits contain 6-8% sugars, 2-3% acids, 0.3-0.7% pectin, exceptionally high amounts of vitamin C (40-170mg per 100g fresh weight); they are also high in anthocyanins and phenolic compounds which provide health benefits due to antioxidant properties. Due to the high stability of the dark red pigments on processing, the fruits are very suitable for making juice as well as providing a source of food colouring for other products.

Fruits are eaten fresh and are processed in a number of ways. The Japanese have developed products such as assorted sweets, jam, jelly, gelatine, ice cream, yoghurt, fruit cake, tarts, juice, juice concentrate, sparkling drinks, wine, berry bars, baby foods, canned fruit, frozen fruit, chewing gum, tea and even berry-flavoured noodles. The dark red pigment colouring is used in caramel and marmalade production.

Medicinally, the fruits are known for their therapeutic effect on cardiovascular diseases – they are known to reduce blood pressure and there are claims of curative effects for malaria and gastrointestinal diseases.

Varieties/Cultivars

Many cultivars have been released in recent years and continue to be released, particularly from Canadian research programmes. Fruits vary in size and shape, and by sweetness more than anything else.

Harvesting groups of recent varieties

Early: week 1 Cooler climate	Berry Moose Blue Moose Happy Giant Honey Delight Indigo Gem
Mid: +2 weeks Cooler/warmer	Aurora Blue Angus Blue Banana Blue Palm Blue Stuart Honey Gin Wojtek Zojka
Late: + 3 weeks Cooler/warmer	Boreal Blizzard Bunny Blue Giants Heart
Very late: +4 weeks Cooler/warmer	Blue Treasure Blue Velvet Boreal Beauty Strawberry Sensation

Flavour comparison of recent varieties

Flavour	Cultivars
Tart	Blue Belle Blue Pinwheel Blue Velvet
Tart/sweet	Berry Blue Blue Horn Blue Palm Happy Giant Wojtek
Sweet/tart	Balalaika Blue Cloud Borealis Eisbar Kalinka Strawberry Sensation Tundra
Sweet	Aurora Blue Angus Blue Moose Blue Stuart Blue Treasure Boreal Beauty Boreal Blizzard Bunny Blue Honey Bee Indigo Gem Indigo Yum
Sweet plus	Blue Banana Giants Heart Honey Delight Honey Gin Zojka

Honeyberry flowering in early spring

Cultivation

Plants are not demanding and will grow well in sandy soils, loams and clay soils; they are adapted to acid to neutral soils (pH 5-7) with high humus levels and require good soil moisture throughout the growing season for optimum growth. Highest yields are in full sun, although partial shade is tolerated.

Commercial orchards (in Canada, Scotland etc.) use rows at 1.2m (4ft) apart and a total of about 2,500 plants/ha (1,000 plants per acre). Expected yields are 9-13 tonnes/ha (8,000-12,000 lb/acre). Ideal conditions for commercial growing are organic matter levels of 4-10%, soil pH of 6.3, and good levels of the main nutrients.

Pruning is not required on young plants. After 8-10 years of fruiting, branches can be thinned out. Good fruit yields require an annual supply of new wood, and if growth is poor then applications of nitrogen and potassium should be made. The soil around plants is best mulched with organic matter.

Honeyberry flowers are hermaphrodite and are mostly self-incompatible. To obtain a good harvest, it is generally accepted two or more cultivars must be planted together for cross-pollination. Ideal honeyberry pollinators include bumblebees, hive or honeybees (one or two hives per acre) and other native or local bees. For commercial growing a mix of cultivars (up to

Honeyberry fruit

4-6 types) is recommended. Sugar levels tend to be higher in a mixed variety planting.

The seeds are very small and quite acceptable to eat. The flavour from different selections varies, with the best being pleasantly sweet-acid.

Fruits ripen around the same time as strawberries, late May to late June usually, depending on variety. Yields from recent cultivars are around 5kg (11lb) per bush.

Shrubs are precocious in bearing, with many plants producing some fruit in their first year, and most in their second. Growth of plants during the first few years is slow, but yields of 300-500g of berries per bush can be obtained 2-3 years from planting. Maximum yields of 2-5kg per bush are obtained from plants 7-15 years old. The bushes can remain productive for 25-30 years.

Ripe berries detach easily and are easy to harvest manually or by machine.

Birds can sometimes be a pest to the fruit, but bushes are easy to net if necessary. Aphids and the botrytis fungus are two problems sometimes encountered in Russia and Japan.

Seeds, cuttings and layers are all possible. Seeds are soft and mechanical extraction methods from berries are not suitable. The seeds are not dormant and can be sown immediately. Softwood cuttings are relatively easy to take; hardwood cuttings are more difficult. Layering is easy, as is the division of established plants.

Pests and diseases

Birds may be interested in the ripe fruit.

JAPANESE WINEBERRY, *Rubus phoenicolasius*

Zone 5, H7
Deciduous
Edible fruit

Origin and history

This is a shrub native to Japan, Korea and China, where the fruits are widely used. It is naturalised in the UK, Europe and parts of North America.

Description

The Japanese wineberry is a deciduous long-lived shrub growing to 3m (10ft) high, with spreading, reddish bristly and prickly stems. It has characteristics of both blackberry and raspberry: like blackberry, the long stems tip-layer if they touch the ground for long enough; like raspberry, each new stem lives for two years, growing vigorously the first, and flowering the second year, then dying. New stems arise each year close to the centre of the plant (it does not sucker widely like raspberries).

Leaves are trifoliate, to 18cm (6ins) across, with bright green ovate leaflets which have a white down beneath.

Flowers are borne in June and July in terminal racemes on second year wood. They are pale pink and up to 4cm (1.5ins) across. Plants are self-fertile, with pollination mainly by bees.

After flowering, the developing fruit remain wrapped up within the calyx until they ripen.

Japanese wineberry fruit are beautiful and delicious

Closed flowers on Japanese wineberry

Fruits are conical, amber to bright red, raspberry-like, sweet and juicy, 15-20mm (0.6-0.8ins) long, slightly sticky to the touch, ripening in late July and August. An excellent flavour (why somebody called them 'wineberry', implying only good enough for wine, is a mystery) but they do not travel or keep well so should be used quickly.

Uses

The fruits are great eaten raw (best going straight from bush to mouth!), or can be cooked or made into jelly or jam. They are especially valued in Asia for desserts; good with cream or ice cream.

Varieties/Cultivars

There are no named cultivars.

Cultivation

Requirements are similar to raspberries, they require a moist soil throughout summer, and a good supply of nutrients, especially nitrogen. Wineberries tolerate moderate shade, though fruiting will be improved in sun; they do not like too much wind exposure.

Laterals can be encouraged in spring by pinching out the growing tips of canes. Otherwise, canes may need to be tied to any support as they grow during spring and summer. They are easy to grow as bushes (without support) as long as the growing tips of canes are regularly pinched out to avoid self-layering (when you'll end up with a thicket). Stems can also be trained against wires or walls in the same way as raspberries. New stems (canes) are produced each year and live for two seasons before dying back. Old canes can thus be cut out/broken off each year in late winter or after fruiting.

Because fruits are wrapped within the calyx until they ripen, they do not suffer from maggots at all. Fruits are easily picked, leaving a dry centre receptacle and hollow fruit.

There are no named fruiting cultivars, but seedling plants crop well.

Rubus phoenicolasius can be propagated from seed. (Squash fresh fruit and sow immediately, allowing to overwinter in cold conditions. Germination should occur in early spring.) The tips can also be layered very easily in late summer and early autumn.

Pests and diseases

They do not suffer from any major diseases or pests.

Related species

Part of the *Rubus* family which includes Blackberry and hybrid berries (p.22), Raspberry (p.166) etc.

JUNIPER, *Juniperus communis*

Zone 3, H7 H1
Evergreen H2
Fruit for flavouring H2

Origin and history

The junipers, *Juniperus* spp., are a group of about 60 evergreen coniferous shrubs, small and large trees originating in the Northern Hemisphere from the Polar Regions to the mountains of the tropics.

Common juniper (*Juniperus communis*) is a very variable species, native to many parts of the Northern Hemisphere from the mountains of northern Africa to the Arctic, in Europe, North America and Asia. In Britain it is found mainly in Scotland and northern England (in birch and pine woods) and in south eastern England. It is mostly found in the wild in areas of chalk and limestone, and also on acid soils in mountainous areas.

Description

Juniper is an erect or spreading plant: in its single stemmed tree-like forms it can reach 11m (35ft) high; alternatively it can form a wide-spreading shrub only 30-60cm (1-2ft) high. Most commonly it is found as a sprawling shrub growing 2-4m (6-13ft) high. Juniper is very drought tolerant.
The species is dioecious, with male and female flowers on different plants.

Shoots, which start extending in May and June, are slender and three-cornered; growth is very slow, usually only a few centimetres per year.
The bark is reddish-brown, thin and shredding.

The aromatic, stiff leathery leaves are alternate and occur in whorls of three; they are narrow, awl shaped, spine tipped, 8-30mm (0.3-1.2ins) long by 1mm (0.04ins) wide.

Flowers are small and open between April and June; male flowers are catkin-like. Female flowers are wind-pollinated and plants of both sexes are needed for pollination to occur and fruit to form.

The fruits are in fact small cones, being the interlacing of three fleshy cone scales – they are false berries. They are fleshy, globular, 6-9mm (0.2-0.4ins) across, green at first becoming blue-black with a dull bloom during their second or third year after pollination (thus both immature and mature fruit exist on female plants at the same time). The fruits have a thin leathery skin but are soft and porous inside, and contain 1-3 seeds which are ovate, light brown, extremely hard and stone-like. The oil-holding cells are located on the surface of the seeds.

The aromatic ripe fruits are sweet, with a slightly bitter resinous aftertaste; they are readily eaten by birds and grazing animals.

Uses

The fruit is edible either raw or cooked; usually dried. The fruit is most often used as a flavouring to flavour gin, genever, genievre, brandies, liqueurs and alcoholic bitters; in non-alcoholic beverages, dairy desserts, sweets, gelatins, puddings and meat products. The fruits are used in cooking to season meats, stuffings, vegetable pâtés, in sauces and in sauerkraut; when using them in the kitchen about half a teaspoon of berries per person is used. Other uses for the fruit include the

Juniper

making of beer and jam. Fruits contain 0.2-3.4% of an aromatic, complex, volatile, essential oil, 30% invert sugar, 9% resin and small amounts of vitamin C (which degrades during drying and storage).

Warning: large doses of the fruit can cause renal damage. Juniper should not be used internally in any quantities by pregnant women.

The roasted dried fruit has been used as a coffee substitute. A tea is made by boiling the leaves and stems. A tea made from the berries has a spicy gin-like flavour. The berries are also used with beech wood in the smoking of Westphalian hams.

Medicine: Juniper fruit is commonly used in herbal medicine, as a household remedy, in herb teas and also in some commercial preparations. They are harvested from wild plants. The fully ripe fruits and used in the treatment of digestive disorders plus kidney and bladder problems, and are used in diuretic and laxative preparations. Other parts of the plant have also been used medicinally including the branches, leaves, roots and bark (the latter crushed and the paste applied to relieve rheumatic pains). Juniper tar, extracted by heating woody parts of the plant, has been used in dermatology.

An essential oil (Juniperi fructus) is sometimes steam distilled from the fruits and twigs; the oil is pale yellow with a sweet, fresh, woody-balsamic odour, and contains over 60 constituents. It is used as a flavouring in foods, drinks (notably gin) and liqueurs, in aromatherapy, soaps, detergents, cosmetics and in perfumes with spicy fragrances. Average yields are around 1% but vary from 0.2 to 3.4% of dry fruit; yields from fresh fruit are about 6-12kg of oil per tonne.

The wood is used for fencing in some European countries. The timber has blue-brown heartwood and paler sapwood, both with a pungent aroma. Timber is straight, fine grained, quite light, hard, durable and easily worked; it is traditionally used for decorative cabinet work (inlays, veneers), tool handles, turnery, buckets etc. The stringy fibrous bark has been used as cordage, and has also been used to make mats.

It is a good nurse shrub for other species, tolerating exposed conditions and protecting other species from browsing and also a soil stabiliser for erosion control – excellent on dry soils. Spreading and prostrate forms make a good ground cover in sun; good cultivars to use include var. *depressa*, var. *jackii*, and the forms listed next. Note that ground covering forms used singly will almost certainly not bear fruit because they are of one sex only.

Wildlife use: Fruits are a source of insect and bird food; plants are used for nesting cover, and as a source of deer browse.

The foliage is dry and resinous, and burns freely; along with the bark, it is used as kindling, and to smoke ham, bacon and cheeses.

Varieties/Cultivars

var. *depressa* has a procumbent habit, growing to 1m (3ft) high.

ssp. *hemisphaerica* is an alpine variety, a low dense rounded shrub to 2.5m (8ft) high and wide but usually less.

var. *jackii* is procumbent with branches to 1m (3ft) long.

ssp. *nana* (mountain juniper = Nana) is procumbent and mat-forming, 20-30cm (8-12ins) high with rounded fruit.

Female cultivar

Suecica (synonym *J. suecica*, Swedish juniper) – broadly columnar to 10m (33ft) high, leaves bluish-green, fruit oblong.

Ground cover cultivars

Brien – has soft needles.

Corielagan – dark green, 15cm (6ins) high by 2m (6ft) wide.

Dumosa – form of var. *depressa*, to 1m (3ft) high, silver-banded leaves.

Effusa – procumbent, to 60cm (2ft) high with silver-banded leaves.

Green Carpet – bright green prickly foliage.

Hornibrookii – procumbent, 50cm (20ins) high by 1.5-2m (5-6ft) wide or more. Leaves golden then light green.

Prostrata – procumbent, 20-30cm (8-12ins) high by 1.5-2m (5-6ft) wide.

Repanda – creeping dwarf form, 30-40cm (12-16ins) high by 1.5m (5ft) wide.

Cultivation

Juniper is easily cultivated, requiring a moist but well-drained soil – it does not tolerate waterlogged soils. It is tolerant of both acid and alkaline soils in the pH range 4.5-7.5. It prefers full sun, and tolerates only light shade. It is extremely tolerant of wind

Ripe juniper fruit

exposure, and is unaffected by salt-laden winds near the sea. Juniper does not regenerate well after cutting.

In a garden setting, several plants should be planted in a cluster, so that both male and female plants are present; after flowering has begun and plants can be sexed, some male plants can be removed to make way for the productive females. Commercial plantations (for example in Hungary) are planted with rows 1-1.5m (3-5ft) apart and plants 0.6m (2ft) in the rows.

Plants begin fruiting a year or two after planting, and ripe fruit is available within three or four years of planting. The ripe fruits are harvested from September to November in their second year – usually by carefully knocking branches and letting ripe fruit fall into baskets or onto canvas sheets. Commercially, the fruits are harvested from both wild and cultivated plants, mostly in Southern and Central Europe (Italy, Hungary, Spain etc.).

Leaves and other debris are removed prior to drying. Fruit should be dried slowly in an airy place out of direct sunlight. They can be spread in layers 20-50mm (0.8-2ins) deep and left to dry for 4-6 weeks: they are sufficiently dry when the weight of fruit has reduced by half. Dry fruit is strongly hygroscopic and should be stored in airtight containers.

The yield of essential oil, distilled from fruit, is 0.6-1.2% (by weight) for fresh fruit and 0.9-1.3% (by weight) for dry fruit.

Propagation is by seed or cuttings. Seed requires pretreatment but germination is erratic with all treatments. Alternatives are: macerate and sow immediately; cold stratify for 16 months; warm stratify for three months followed by cold stratification for three months. Named cultivars are propagated by cuttings, which can be taken of current season's growth with a heel in late summer/early autumn and placed in cold frames; alternatively, softwood cuttings can be taken in July and August, and given bottom heat (20°C / 68°F) and mist.

Pests and diseases

Juniper has no significant pests, and few diseases. Young plants may suffer from the fungal diseases grey mould (*Botrytis cinerea*), black snow mould (*Herpotrichia juniperi*), *Phomopsis juniperovora* (causing shoot blight and canker) and *Coniothyrium fuckelii* (causing leaf and shoot death – causes cane blight of raspberries) but usually only in a nursery situation with a high density of plants. Established trees may suffer from several minor fungal diseases.

KIWI FRUITS, *Actinidia* species

Zone 4-8, H4-7
Deciduous/Evergreen
Edible fruit

Origin and history

A family of vigorous vines from Asia. The hardy species originate from China, Siberia and Japan.

Description

The kiwi family are all vigorous deciduous, twining climbing vines, reaching the tops of large trees in their native ranges, able to climb 15m (50ft) into trees. They are long-lived and shallow rooting, with shoot growth in the region of 2-4m (6-12ft) per year.

Leaves are alternate, heart shaped, bright green, glossy and smooth in the hardier species, hairy/fuzzy in the main commercial kiwi fruit. Kiwi leaves open relatively early, because no species, even the hardier ones, need a lot of winter cold, and as soon as the first warm weather arrives in spring they will emerge. Leaves drop soon after the first frosts of autumn.

Flowers are produced in July, in clusters of three from the leaf axils, each flower 20mm (0.8ins) across, creamy white and fragrant; the flowers aren't conspicuous. All species in the family are dioecious so that male and female flowers are produced on different plants, and male and female plants are both needed for fruit to form (although there are a few self-fertile cultivars available). Pollination is by a mixture of wind and insects.

Fruits are oval, sweet and high in vitamin C with many very small embedded seeds. The hardier species have thin-skinned, smooth fruit, green, red or purple, 25-44mm (1-1.75ins) long. *A. chinensis/ deliciosa* fruits are larger, usually with hairs on the skin.

Fruits of hardier species ripen between late August and early October, and tend to ripen over a long period – ideal for the small-scale grower. When fully ripe they fall from the vine. Fruit composition is as follows:

Glucose	33% (dry matter)/ 9% (fresh)
Starch	25% (dry matter)
Cellulose	15% (dry matter)
Pectin	5% (dry matter)
Protein	under 3% (dry matter)
Vitamin C	400mg/100g (dry matter)
Vitamin PP	55mg/100g; 80mg/100g (fresh)
Provitamin A (Carotin)	0.28mg/100g
Vitamin B1 & B2	
3-Oxy 2-pyranol	
Actinidin	

Bush trained *Actinidia arguta*

Uses

Edible uses: Fruit, excellent raw, can be dried or made into jam, jellies, wine etc.

The vine is rich in sap, which is drinkable.

Medicinal uses: The leaves are used medicinally, reducing fevers, stimulating blood circulation and lactation in nursing mothers.

In China, *Actinidia* fruits are well known as medicines against cancer. The substances actinidin and 3-Oxy 2-pyranol are believed to be responsible. Fruits are used both as curative medicines and as prophylactics.

Other uses: The plant makes a good shade vine and façade insulation; it is easily trained around windows etc.

Leaves are high in starch and protein, and make good pig fodder.

Roots can be processed to give an insecticide.

A glue is extracted from the stalks by soaking in water, and used in papermaking, construction materials, printing, dyeing, and for manufacturing plastics and chemicals.

Male flowers on *Actinidia arguta*

Actinidia kolomikta 'Dr Szymanowski'

Varieties/Cultivars

Hardy kiwi species – *A. arguta* / *A. kolomikta*

Self-fertile cultivars

Dr Szymanowski	Self-fertile kolomikta variety. Fruit early ripening in August, good flavour.
Issai	Less hardy than some; bears fruit one year after planting. Fruit is small-medium in size, cylindrical, with a good flavour; seedless when not pollinated. Vine has low vigour. Increased fruiting when other male(s) nearby.
Kokuwa	Japanese self-fertile form with delicious lemon-flavoured fruit.
Meader	Productive. Sweet, medium sized fruit with a good flavour. Early ripening. Good pollinator too.
119-40	Vigorous, large-leaved plant; a good pollinator for other females. Fruit is medium sized with a good, pineapple-like flavour.

Male cultivars

Adam	Kolomikta variety to pollinate Sentyabraskaya.
Belfast	Less hardy, to zone 6.
Longwood	
Pacific	Flowers over a long period.
Weiki male	A good pollinator for all *arguta* females.
Woodenville	
1971	Used to pollinated the Geneva selections.
74-32	Very hardy. Pollinator for 74 series.
74-46	Pollinator for 74 series. Very large numbers of flowers over a long period.
74-52	Pollinator for 74 series. Early flowering.
127-40	Pollinator for 124-40 and 125-40.
40537-C	Precocious, flowers in second year.

Actinidia arguta 'Weiki'

Female cultivars

Akin #3	Large round fruit.
Ananasnaja	(Anna) probably a *A. arguta* x *kolomikta* cross. Very hardy and vigorous; large oval fruit, 30-40mm x 25mm, dark green flushed burgundy in sun, excellent flavour.
Belfast bay	Large fruit with a fine flavour. Crops late September.
Bingo	Polish selection with large red fruit, pineapple flavour.
Collett	Heavy producer of fine flavoured fruit.
Dumbarton Oaks	Very sweet medium-large fruit.
Frenchmans Bay	Medium-large fruit, ripening mid September.
Geneva #1	Vigorous, large-leaved vine; very hardy. Fruit medium sized. Late ripening.
Geneva #2	Vigorous, large-leaved vine; very hardy. Fruit medium sized, good flavour. Late ripening.
Geneva HH1	Medium sized fruit with excellent flavour. Vigorous, hardy vine. Pollinated by '1971'.
Geneva HH2	Vigorous, hardy vine. Pollinated by '1971'.
Hardy Red	From the subspecies *Purpurea*, ripens early September, cherry red fruit.
Jumbo	Italian variety, large fruit, yellowish-green, sweet, hang well.
Jumbo Verde	Large fruit.
Keeper Berry	Small fruit with a very good flavour. Very heavy cropping.
Ken's Red	Fruit medium sized, red, fine flavour.
Langer	(Hood River) Vigorous plant with long leaves; medium sized fruit.
Longwood	Hardy plant.
Michigan State	(MSU) Hardy to zone 4. Large fruit, with a good flavour. Vigorous, partly self-fertile vine; may be a *arguta* x *kolomikta* cross.
Nat. Arb. #8	Vigorous vine with large thick leaves.
Nest vine	Hardy vine with large fruit, excellent flavour.
Noel	A New Zealand-bred cultivar.
Purpurna Sadowa	Polish selection, bears masses of purple fruit of excellent flavour.

Red Beauty	Red fruit, medium sized.
Rogow	Polish selection, prolific fruiter with large fruit of good flavour.
Scarlet September	Polish selection, sweet red fruit, excellent flavour, early ripening.
Sentyabraskaya	Kolomikta selection, prolific bearer of good quality fruit.
Turrets	Heavy crops of medium sized fruit.
Vikakola	Czech kolomikta selection bearing exceptionally long green fruit.
Vitikiwi	Sets fruit without pollination, prolific small green seedless fruit.
Weiki Female	Bears greenish-brown fruit in abundance, hang well on vine.
Woodenville	Hardy to zone 4. Early season – suited to short season areas.
74-8	Hardy to zone 4, productive vine; fruit large, elliptical, firm with a good flavour. Late ripening.
74-49	Large, round, sweet, aromatic fruit. Mid season cropping. Vigorous and productive.
74-55	Medium-large round fruit, sweet, early-mid season. Vigorous, productive vine.
74-62	Productive; long cylindrical fruit with good flavour.
124-40	Large, vigorous hardy plant.
125-40	Vigorous plant with large fruit.

Actinidia arguta 'Ken's Red'

Young fruit on *Actinidia kolomikta*

Tender kiwi fruit (*A. chinensis / deliciosa*)

Gold3	(SunGold) *A. chinensis* selection from New Zealand, more disease resistant than Hort16A but with somewhat less sweet fruit.
Hayward	The standard commercial variety for many years, with large fruit and good flavour.
Hort16A	(Zespri) The first *A. chinensis* cultivars selected outside of China. Smooth hairless fruit with yellow flesh of excellent flavour.
Koryoku	Japanese selection, a Hayward seedling, earlier ripening and with sweeter fruit.
Tomua	A Hayward cross from New Zealand. Early flowering and ripening with large fruit of good, sweet flavour but of limited storage life.
Top Star	A Hayward sport which has smooth, essentially hairless fruit, and is a less vigorous vine.

Male pollinating cultivars include Autari, King, Ranger and Tomuri

A. chinensis fruit

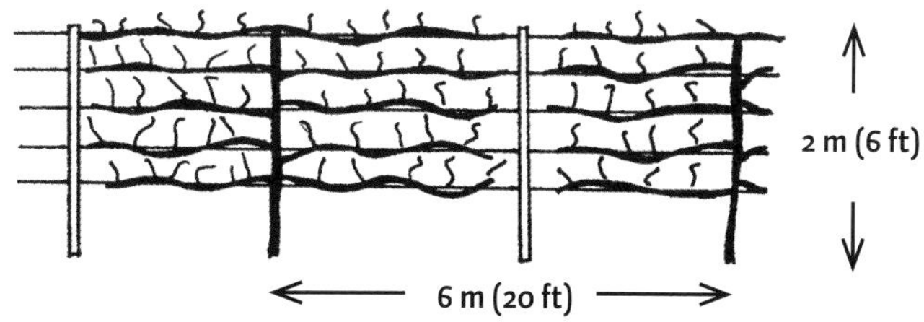

Vertical trellis system

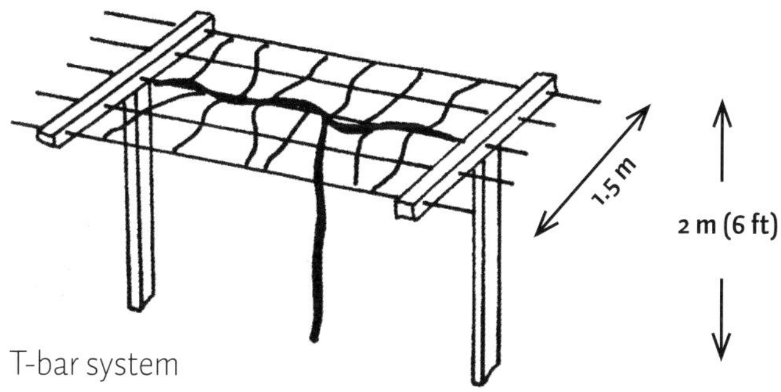

T-bar system

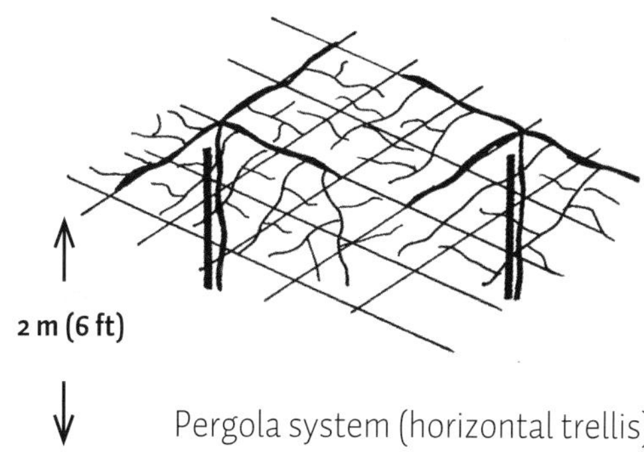

Pergola system (horizontal trellis)

Cultivation

Kiwis are forest edge, shallow-rooting plants; they enjoy forest conditions, where a moist, humus-rich soil provides perfect conditions.

Hardy kiwis are most reliably grown for fruit in zones 6-9, needing only a moderate amount of winter chilling. They like a moist climate and a rich, fertile, moist but well-drained soil, preferring acid conditions with a pH between 5.0 and 6.5. Full sun is preferred, though part shade is tolerated, and they will quickly climb up and over trees and shrubs to get to the light. Protection from strong winds is essential. Once in growth, frosts of -1.5°C (29°F) will damage the young branches and flowers, so frost pockets should be avoided. They are susceptible to late spring frosts, especially in zones 4-7; vines caught by frosts will not crop in that year but will usually recover. Once established, they also tolerate a grass ground cover.

It is best to plant out well-established plants – if in doubt, grow on young plants for a further year in protected conditions. Young plants are particularly susceptible to slug and snail damage and to damage from cats, who find certain chemicals in the plant irresistible. If there are cats around, plants should be protected with tree shelters or wire guards. Planting should take place in late winter or early spring, taking care not to plant the roots too deeply.

In continental climates (including eastern England) with hot, dry summers, and where rainfall is under around 800mm per year, irrigation will be necessary. Drip irrigation systems are normally used since sprinkler systems can lead to water staining of the fruit.

All kiwi species need support of some kind to climb up (although vigorous, well-established vines will even sprawl over the ground). The methods normally recommended are the same for all species, growing on vertical or horizontal trellises, growing on horizontal pergolas or arbours, or growing over arches or against walls. These are all designed to maximise fruit production but have many disadvantages: they are very labour-intensive needing frequent pruning, and they need expensive structures to begin with; they also usually necessitate extra windbreaks, irrigation systems etc. Some commonly used systems are shown below.

In low-input growing systems like food forests, it is possible to grow plants in a more natural way, allowing them to climb up other trees and ramble over hedges; fruit yields will be less, and where the vines are high, fruit must be left to fall, but the plants are likely to be given frost protection by the trees, and are well out of reach of slugs and snails which can decimate a trellised orchard in a wet year. Vines should be trained through trees which aren't being grown themselves for a fruit crop, unless the trees are vigorous and heavy croppers, as the hardy kiwis will climb to the tops of the trees and somewhat shade them. Another possibility is to train kiwi vines into trees that are pollarded (either for the wood or as a tree vegetable), and pollard both tree and vine at the same time to keep them both manageable.

A compromise between intensive and extensive systems could be to grow female, fruiting plants intensively to maximise fruit production, and to grow male pollinators on nearby trees/hedges.

Whether using an intensive system or not, for the first year or two the young plants must be trained with a single stem growing up until the level of the trellis or the tree/shrub is reached: all other growth and side shoots are pinched out to

A trellised orchard of *Actinidia deliciosa*

concentrate energy into the leader. The following year in trellis systems, a framework of stems (called cordons) is created over the trellis which is retained for many years.

In trained systems, prune in late winter/early spring, removing the oldest third of branches growing from the main trunk/ framework; also remove wood that has fruited for two seasons, and any damaged wood or tortuous twisted growth. Intensive growing systems require pruning in the summer too, removing basal suckers and unwanted shoots. Prunings can be left on the ground to add to the mulch.

A few cultivars are self-fertile, but most are not and males must be planted as well as females for fruiting to occur. Self-fertile cultivars fruit better with extra males as well.

One male will pollinate 6-8 females within about 15m (50ft). Flowering takes place in summer so there should be plentiful insects about, and fruit set shouldn't be a problem.

Fruit is usually borne 2-4 years after planting; mature vines are quite capable of yielding 50kg (110lb) of fruit per vine. Fruit of hardy species ripen over a long period and are usually picked when they are just starting to soften (i.e. the firm-ripe stage); they drop from the plant when fully ripe. Less hardy kiwi fruits are harvested in late autumn before the first frosts. Fruits picked at the firm-ripe stage can be stored refrigerated for 2-3 months, but at room temperature fruit ripens fully very quickly.

Propagation of named cultivars is usually by softwood cuttings. 10-15cm (4-6ins) cuttings from semi-mature shoots are taken in June and July, dipped in hormone rooting substance and given high humidity/mist and gentle heat (20°C/ 68°F). Use any well-drained rooting medium.

Pests and diseases

The only disease of any note is *Phytophthora* root rots in wet soils. As long as soils are well-drained and loose mulches are kept away from stems, this shouldn't be a problem.

The leaves of young (and in wet years even older) plants are very susceptible to slug and snail damage and try to plant out large, well-established plants if this is likely to be a problem, and take other measures with small plants.

Young plants are also susceptible to damage from cats – plants contain a substance irresistible to cats, who are likely to rub, chew and claw plants to pieces if they can. Plants should be protected with tree or wire guards. If moles are a problem, line planting holes with wire mesh to deter them from undermining young plants.

LINGONBERRY, *Vaccinium vitis-idaea*

Zone 2, H7
Evergreen
Edible fruit

Origin and history

Lingonberry (also known, less invitingly, as Cowberry) grows widely across the colder parts of North America, Europe and Asia. The habitats where it is found vary from quite dense woods, to heath, grass moorland, raised bogs, rocky exposed cliffs and even mountain summits. It is sometimes known as the 'dry cranberry' because it prefers drier conditions than most of its relatives.

Description

A low growing, semi-woody evergreen shrub. Leaves are bright green, oval, 5-20mm (0.2-0.8ins) long by 5mm (0.2ins) wide, glossy above and dull below. Plants gradually spread outwards for 90cm (3ft) or more via runners or stolons, forming mats with uprights reaching 20-30cm (8-12ins) high. Flowers are white or pale pink in late spring/early summer, with pollination by bees, mainly wild bumblebees. The fruits are bright glossy

Lingonberry is common in the far north

Lingonberry flowers

red, 5-12mm (0.2-0.5ins) in diameter, ripening in autumn and hanging long through the winter on the bushes.

Uses

Lingonberry fruit has been of great importance in human diets wherever it is found and is still widely gathered from wild plants, as well as being grown commercially. They are best picked after a sharp frost, and store well (at least two months in a fridge, several years in a freezer). If unpicked they will remain a long time on the plants through the winter.

The berries have a richer, aromatic, less astringent flavour than commercial cranberries. They are rich in magnesium and vitamins A and C, and are well known for their use to treat blood disorders and urinary tract infections.

The berries have traditionally been made into a tart jelly with a high vitamin C content, often eaten with meat. The jelly is excellent for relieving symptoms of sore throats and colds. Other products made from the fruits are juices, syrups, wine and liqueur, pickles and sauces, candy and ice cream. Lingonberries are undergoing a revival and are being increasingly grown commercially in Europe. The harvest from Sweden alone is estimated at 200,000 tonne in a good year. Mature plants can yield 1kg (2.2lb) of berries (13.5-25 tonne/ha).

The leaves are used in a medicinal herb tea which is used in the treatment of arthritis, rheumatism, diarrhoea and other conditions. The leaves are gathered in early summer and dried for later use. The mature fruits are eaten fresh or dried as a home remedy for diarrhoea.

A yellow dye is obtained from the leaves and stems; a purple dye is obtained from the fruit.

Can be grown as a ground cover plant, spreading by underground runners. Plants are best spaced about 30cm apart.

Varieties/Cultivars

Most of these originate in Scandinavia, where there are ongoing breeding programmes.

Erntedank	Tolerates exposed conditions.
Ida	Swedish introduction with very large berries up to 50g (2oz) each. Growth vigorous, upright.
Koralle	Dutch selection, the main cultivar used in commercial production. Light red fruit of moderate size, borne young, heavy cropper. Bushy upright growth, doesn't spread fast.
Linnea	Swedish introduction, a heavy cropper. Fruit quite large, very aromatic; growth vigorous, upright.
Red Pearl	Dutch selection, fast growing, compact, uprights to 34cm (13ins) high. Less fussy about soil conditions than other cultivars. Flowers twice and produces berries in summer and autumn; fruit 8mm (0.3ins) across, dark red, excellent quality.
Regal	American selection, vigorous, moderately spreading, 20cm (8ins) high. Fruit 8mm (0.3ins) across. Flowers twice, main crop in autumn.
Sanna	Swedish introduction, spreads moderately, 30cm (12 ins) high, very heavy cropper with excellent quality fruit.
Splendor	American selection, vigorous, moderate spread, 20cm (8ins) high. Carmine-red fruit, 8mm (0.3ins) across, heavy cropper. Flowers twice, main crop in autumn.
Sussi	Swedish introduction, spreads readily, 18cm (6ins) high. Heavy yields or medium-large berries, excellent quality.

Lingonberry fruit

Cultivation

Cultivated lingonberries require well-drained acidic soil (pH 4.0-5.0) and a low level of nutrients – poor sandy soils are ideal. Like all *Vacciniums*, they will only grow healthily if they are growing in association with mycorrhizal fungi of the right kind (not the same as most trees and shrubs), so it may be worth inoculating young plants or transplants with the correct fungi. A position in full sun or light partial shade is required.

They are usually grown in beds or rows, with plants 30-45cm apart. Mulching with shredded pine bark or sawdust is beneficial. As they are shallow rooting, irrigation in dry summer months is often required, using drip irrigation. Cross-pollination produces a better fruit set and larger fruit, so two or more varieties should be planted. A mechanical aid is useful for harvesting, even just a hand-held scoop or harvesting comb (as used for cranberries). Propagation is by stem cuttings taken in late summer. Weed control needs special attention.

Pests and diseases

Lingonberries are notably resistant to honey fungus.

Related species

Blueberry (page 35), Cranberry (page 72).

MAGNOLIA VINES, *Schisandra* species

Zone 4-8, H4-7
Deciduous
Edible fruit

Origin and history

Some 25 species of deciduous or evergreen, aromatic climbing shrubs with twining stems, bearing fruit comprising a number of brightly coloured berries, some of which are edible and medicinal. They are found naturally as twining climbers of forest and woodland. Only some of the hardier species are covered here.

Description

Schisandra are attractive vines which are sometimes grown ornamentally for their showy (though short-lived) flowers, followed on female plants by drooping spikes of red (occasionally black) fruit. Note that the flowering (except for some cultivars below) is dioecious, so male and female plants are normally required for fruiting.

Uses

The species described here all have edible fruit. Some have other uses as detailed below.

Varieties/Cultivars

S. chinensis – Magnolia vine

Originates from Russia and China. Climbs to 8m (27ft) or more, with glossy deep green leaves; fragrant flowers to 1.2cm (0.5ins) across, pale rose to bright pink, in April to May; fruiting spikes to 10cm (4ins) long, densely covered with scarlet berries 6mm (0.25ins) long. Plants can produce 250-3000g fruit each, ripening September-October. All parts of the plant – berries, leaves and bark – have a lemon aroma.

Although often referred to as dioecious, it appears that most selections are actually monoecious (bear both male and female flowers) although there are also male and female dioecious forms. Hardy to zone 4 / H7.

Eastern Prince – a Russian selection with male and female flowers, very productive with large fruit.

Sadova No.1 – Ukranian selection, self-fertile, heavy cropper.

Schisandra chinensis, one of a family of climbing vines

Uses

The fruits are edible raw or cooked, being sweet and rich in flavour. Traditionally dried and used as a snack food, they are high in vitamin C. The fruits are very delicate, thin skinned with juicy flesh, and contain one or two hard seeds. Fruit harvest often begins 5-7 days before full ripeness, when they are still hard and easier to pick; they quickly ripen after harvest.

In Russia, the pasteurised juice is used to make wines and soft drinks and the juice and flesh are used in confectionery. The young leaves are traditionally eaten as a cooked vegetable.

This is one of the 50 fundamental herbs in Chinese medicine – the fruit is considered to be a substitute for ginseng. The fruit is harvested after the first frosts and dried for later use. Used for many ailments but best known for its use as a tonic especially to improve liver function.

S. grandiflora – Strawberry vine

Originates from Bhutan, Nepal and Northern India. Climbs to 7m (23ft). Bears fragrant flowers 2.5cm (1ins) across, white, cream or

Schisandra chinensis fruit

pale rose, in April to May. Male and female plants are needed for fruiting to occur. Fruiting spikes on female plants to 12cm (5ins) long, berries round, 6mm (0.25ins) across, red. Hardy to zone 8 or 9 / H3-5. Var. *rubriflora* from western China, Burma and India is similar but with scarlet to red flowers.

Apricot Blush – female form, heavy fruiting.

Jamu – male selection.

Lahlu – female selection.

Valentine – male selection.

Uses
The fruits are edible raw or cooked being pleasantly sweet-acid. They ripen September-October.

S. henryi

Originates from central and southern China. Climbs to 6m (20ft) high. White flowers in April-May are followed on female plants by scarlet fruit. Male and female plants are need for fruiting to occur. Hardy to zone 8 / H4-5.

Uses
The fruits are edible raw or cooked.

S. repanda

Originates from Japan and Korea. Climbs to 6m (20ft) high. Creamy-white flowers in May-June are followed on female plants by blue-black fruit. Male and female plants are needed for fruiting to occur. Hardy to zone 7 / H5-6.

Uses
The fruits are edible raw or cooked. Common in Japanese woods, the fruits are often made into preserves.

S. sphenanthera

Originates from southern and western China. Climbs to 7m (23ft) high. Orange flowers in April-June are followed on female plants by red fruit. Male and female plants are needed for fruiting to occur. Hardy to zone 7 / H5-6.

Uses
This species is used similarly to *S. chinensis* in China: the fruits are edible raw or cooked.

Medicinal uses similar to those for *S. chinensis*.

Cultivation

Plant in any fertile, well-drained but moisture retentive site in partial shade. Slightly acid soils rich in humus are preferred. Keep mulched with organic matter – plants are not drought tolerant.

Plants will happily scramble over rocks, walls etc. and into trees or shrubs, or can be trained up a framework of some kind. Prune in late winter or spring to remove dead wood and train/limit the plant for the space available.

Propagate by seed, cuttings or layering. Seed germinates best after 13 weeks' cold stratification. Take semi-ripe cuttings in summer. Long shoots can be layered during the autumn and removed the following year.

Pests and diseases

None of note.

MYRTLES, *Myrtus* and related species

Zones 7-9, H4-5
Evergreen
Edible fruit, Bee plants

Origin and history

The myrtles are a group of related evergreen aromatic plants, covered here as a whole and once all placed in the genus *Myrtus* but now split into:

- *Amomyrtus* (two species), *Luma* (four species) and *Ugni* (5-15 species), from temperate rainforests of Chile and Argentina
- *Austromyrtus*, from Australia – some eight species
- *Lophomyrtus*, from New Zealand – two species and their hybrid
- *Myrteola*, from Chile and the Falkland Islands
- *Myrtus* – the original Eurasian myrtle.

Description

Evergreen shrubs, 0.1-7m (4ins-23ft) high, with white flowers and small, often black fruit with an intense flavour. Plants are self-fertile, with flowers pollinated by bees. For milder regions only.

Uses

The small fruits are edible, raw or cooked. In some species they are mediocre (e.g. *Amomyrtus luma*) whilst in others they are excellent (e.g. *Ugni molinae*). Only the Mediterranean myrtle (*Myrtus communis*) appears to have had fruiting selections made, although some of the others have ornamental forms selected (some of which happen to be good fruit producers).

The essential oil extracted from leaves, shoots and fruit is used in food and medicine. *Myrtus communis* is the only species grown for commercial fruit and essential oil production, and its many uses are listed in the species description below.

All species are very good bee plants.

Varieties/Cultivars

Amomyrtus luma (synonym *Myrtus lechleriana*) – Luma

An evergreen shrub from Chile and Argentina growing to 7.5m high in its native habitat. Has strongly aromatic leaves. Very fragrant flowers in May (self-fertile) are followed by black fruit in autumn, 5-10mm in diameter, containing a few hard seeds. Probably hardy to -5°C (23°F) or so (zone 9 / H4) – will grow outdoors in mild maritime areas of Britain.

The fruits are very aromatic but rather seedy.

Luma in full flower

Austromyrtus dulcis (synonym *Myrtus dulcis*) – Midgen Berry

An evergreen shrub from Eastern Australia (New South Wales northwards to Queensland). Grows to about 2m (6ft) tall and wide. Has dark, glossy green aromatic leaves. Flowers in summer are followed by fruit 10mm across, white with blue spots. Hardy to about -5°C (23°F) (zone 9 / H4).

The fruits have an excellent sweet aniseed flavour.

Lophomyrtus bullata (synonym *L. aotearoana, Myrtus bullata*) – Ramarama

Large evergreen shrub from New Zealand, growing there to 5m (16ft) high and 3m (10ft) in width. Flowers in May-June are followed by fruit in autumn, 10mm across. Hardy to around -8°C (17°F) or so (zone 8-9 / H4), succeeding in mild areas of Britain. 'Matai Bay' is one of several ornamental varieties.

The fruits have a guava flavour when ripe. The plant has been used medicinally (same uses as *L. obcordata* below).

Lophomyrtus obcordata (synonym *Myrtus obcordata*) – Rohutu

An evergreen large shrub or small tree from New Zealand, growing there to 5m (16ft) tall. Flowers are followed by red to black fruit, 6-7mm (0.25ins) across. Hardy to around -8°C (17°F) (zone 8-9 / H4).

Mediterranean myrtle (*Myrtus communis*)

The plant has been used medicinally – the bark and berries used for dysmenorrhoea. The essential oil has been found to have some antibiotic properties.

Lophomyrtus x ralphii

Evergreen large shrubs (a naturally occurring hybrid of *L. bullata* x *L. obcordata*) from New Zealand growing up to 5m (16ft) high and 3m (10ft) wide. Flowers in May-June are followed by dark red fruit 7mm (0.25ins) across in late autumn through to spring. Hardy to around -8°C (17°F) (zone 8-9 / H4). There are a number of ornamental forms – 'Sundae' fruits well in mild areas of Britain.

The fruits are sweet, aromatic and pleasant. The plant probably has the same medicinal uses as its parents.

Luma apiculata (synonym *Myrtus apiculata*, *Myrtus luma*) – Arrayan

A large evergreen shrub from Argentina and Chile, growing there to 6m (20ft) high and 4m (13ft) wide. Has cinnamon-like bark. Flowers from July onwards (self-fertile) are followed by bluish-black fruit that ripens in October and November, 10mm (0.4ins) in diameter. Hardy to about -10°C (14°F) (zone 8 / H4). Grows in any reasonable soil with shelter and succeeds (fruiting well) in mild parts of Britain. 'Glanleam Gold' and 'Variegata' are ornamental variegated forms.

The best fruits are aromatic, sweet and succulent (though there is much variability).

Luma chequen (synonym *Myrtus chequen*) – Chequen, Arrayan blanco

A large evergreen shrub or small tree from Chile. Bears numerous bluish-black fruit, 6-10mm (0.25-0.4ins) in diameter. Hardy to -10°C (14°F) (zone 8 / H4).

The bark and leaves are used medicinally, the bark as an astringent; the leaves are highly aromatic, containing an essential oil consisting largely of pinene and cineol.

Recent analyses have shown the essential oil obtained from the leaves to be fungicidal and antifeedant against certain species.

Myrteola nummularia (synonym *Myrtus nummularia*)

A prostrate evergreen shrub from Southern Chile and the Falkland Islands, growing only 10cm (4ins) high and 50cm+ (20ins+) in spread. Flowers in May-June (self-fertile) are followed by fruit in autumn. Hardy to about -10°C (14°F) (zone 8 / H4) – grows well to the south and west of London in England.

The fruits have a sweet and pleasant flavour. Leaves are used to make a tea.

Ground cover plant in a well-drained site. Space plants about 45cm (18ins) apart.

Myrtus communis – myrtle

A very variable evergreen shrub from Southern Europe and Asia, typically found in maquis and scrub communities, growing up to several metres tall and wide, but usually less in Britain. White self-fertile flowers in July-August are followed by fruit ripening in October, usually bluish-black, 8-10mm (0.3-0.4ins) in diameter.

Hardy to between -10 and -15°C (zone 7-8 / H4-5) as long as the plant is sheltered from cold drying winds. It is very tolerant of mild winds and maritime exposure though. Grows well in large containers.

Fairly fast growing when young, slowing with age. There are a number of ornamental forms, including 'Tarentina' which has small narrow leaves and is hardier than the type (to zone 7 / H4) with small white fruit, and especially wind-resistant.

Selection and breeding work in Sardinia has now named several forms suitable for fruit and/or biomass production.

Commercial plantation of *Myrtus communis* in Sardinia

Angela	Heavy fruit production (whitish-green, non-pigmented), fruit moderately large, and high vigour – suited for biomass production.
Barbara	Selected for fruiting ability. A shrub of low vigour, 50cm (20ins) high and 80cm (2ft 8ins) wide. Fruit yields are about 800g per plant on 3-4 year old plants. The fruits are oval shaped, medium sized (about 1cm / 0.4ins), with a dark blue skin and white flesh. It contains a fairly low number of seeds (average eight). The fruit contains, on average, 785mg/100g anthocyanin pigments, 45g/100g tannins, 0.06% malonic acid. Flowering is early (April-May in Italy) and the fruits mature early (October) and uniformly. Propagation by cuttings is highly effective.
Daniella	Selected for fruiting ability and for vegetation production for essential oil extraction. A shrub of moderate vigour, growing to 130cm (4ft 4ins) high and 150cm (5ft) wide. Fruit yields are about 1000g per plant on 3-4 year old plants. The fruits are round, medium sized (about 1cm / 0.4ins) with bluish-black skin and white flesh. They contain many seeds (average 13). The fruits contain, on average, 583mg/100g of anthocyanin pigments, 121mg/100g tannins and 0.11% malonic acid. Flowering is late (May-June in Italy), though leaf growth starts early and continues late into autumn. Fruits mature early (early October) over several weeks. Propagation by cuttings is moderately effective.
Giovanna	Heavy fruit production (light purple and large), and medium high vigour – also suited for biomass production.
Grazia	Heavy fruit production (fruit whitish-yellow, non-pigmented, very large), and high vigour – suited for biomass production.
Ilaria	Quite vigorous, medium fruit production (dark blue, medium sized); a useful dual purpose cultivar.
Maria Antonietta	Quite vigorous, medium fruit production (large, dark blue); a useful dual purpose cultivar.
Maria Rita	Heavy fruit production (medium size, dark blue), moderate vigour – suited for fruit production.

Myrtle is mainly used for its medicinal and aromatic properties – the foliage is strongly aromatic. Its essential oil, obtained mainly from the leaves and shoots but also from the fruit, is utilised in cosmetics (perfumery, soaps) and the pharmaceutical industry (skin care products). Yield is low, 10g of oil from 100kg of leaves. It is harvested commercially, mainly in North Africa.

The fruit is often used as an aromatic food flavouring, especially in the Middle East, and can also be made into an acid drink. The leaves are used as a flavouring in cooked savoury dishes.

The dried fruit and flower buds are used to flavour sauces, syrups, jams etc. An essential oil from the leaves and twigs is used as a condiment, especially when mixed with other spices (caution advised). In Italy the flower buds are eaten.

In Sardinia, a commercial myrtle liqueur is made by infusion of the pigmented berries in alcohol. The success of this industry has been the main spur in efforts to breed heavily fruiting cultivars with dark fruit like 'Barbara' and 'Daniella'.

Myrtle has an important ecological role in the Mediterranean maquis, and is often used as an ornamental. The plant is very tolerant of regular clipping and can be grown as a hedge in the milder parts of Britain. In the Mediterranean the plant is regarded as a symbol of love and peace and is much prized for use in wedding bouquets; in the past, it has been held as the emblem of honour and authority, and was worn by the Athenian judges in the exercise of their functions, and it constituted the wreaths of the Grecian and Roman victors, in the Olympian and other festivities.

Chilean guava

The leaves are antibiotic, anticatarrhal, antiseptic (urinary, pulmonary), aromatic, astringent, balsamic, bactericidal, expectorant, haemostatic, regulator, slightly sedative and tonic. The leaves are harvested from wild plants from late spring to early autumn and usually distilled immediately or dried.

An essential oil is obtained by steam distillation of the leaves and twigs, is pale yellow or orange with a fresh, clear, camphoraceous scent similar to eucalyptus. It is antiseptic. It contains the compound myrtol. The oil is used in perfumery, soaps and skin care products, as a food flavouring in meat sauces and seasonings and in alcoholic drinks. Oil yields are about 0.5-1.1% from fresh leaves and twigs; or 5-11kg per ha of crop. The fruit is carminative.

The wood is hard, elastic and very fine grained – used traditionally for walking sticks, tool handles, furniture etc. and it makes a high quality charcoal.

Ugni molinae (synonym *Myrtus ugni*) – Chilean guava, Ugni

An evergreen shrub from Argentina and Chile, reaching to 2m (6ft) high and 1m (3ft) wide, with a fibrous root system. Leaves are glossy green, 12-25mm (1/2-1ins) long. Flowers in May-July (self-fertile) are followed by fruit that ripens August-October, 15mm (0.6ins) in diameter, containing small seeds. Flowers and fruits are borne freely on quite young plants. Hardy to about -10°C (14°F) (zone 8 / H4-5); good in containers.

Tolerates a wider range of soils than many other myrtles, succeeding in any reasonably good soil. Fairly tolerant of maritime exposure. 'Flambeau' is a variegated form which is hardier than the type.

Fruit of Chilean guava

The fruits are edible, raw or cooked, with a delicious aromatic strawberry/guava flavour and crisp texture. They are commonly seen in the markets of Chile, where they are mostly used in pies and jellies. In the past this was cultivated commercially in Cornwall – it was made into one of Queen Victoria's favourite jams. Leaves are used to make a tea. The roasted seeds are used to make a coffee-like drink.

Plants are tolerant of trimming and can be used to make a low hedge in mild areas.

Elite is an improved fruiting form.

Flambeau is a variegated leaf form.

Cultivation

The evergreen myrtles like most well-drained or dry soils; wet and frozen winter soils can kill plants. They also need sunny conditions in the UK, though in hotter climates they can tolerate some shade. They are best planted in spring, after the last spring frosts. Any pruning is best carried out in the spring.

Propagation is by seed, cuttings or layering:

Seed: Pre-soak 24 hours in warm water and sow in early spring with heat. Grow plants on under cover for at least their first winter. Plant out in late spring or early summer, after the last expected frosts.

Semi-ripe cuttings: 7-10cm / 3-4ins long with a heel, taken in July/August and given mist or a moist environment often succeed. Overwinter under cover.

Hardwood cuttings: Can be taken of the current season's growth, 7-12cm (3-5ins) long with a heel, in November in a shaded warm environment. Plant out in late spring or early autumn.

Layering can often succeed.

Pests and diseases

Plants are notably resistant to honey fungus.

NANKING CHERRY, *Prunus tomentosa*

Zone 2, H7
Deciduous
Edible fruit

Origin and history

A bush cherry from China, long used for its edible fruit.

Description

An upright shrub growing 2.4m (8ft) high and rather less in width. White flowers are produced quite early in spring and are followed by round red fruit, 10-15mm in diameter. Plants are self-fertile.

Uses

Edible fruit – good quality, sweeter than sour cherries.

Bee plant.

Cultivation

Grow in any reasonable soil in sun or light shade.

Pests and diseases

None of note.

Related species

Bush cherries (p.49).

Nanking cherry

NEW ZEALAND FLAX, *Phormium tenax*

Zone 7, H5
Evergreen
Leaves for tying and fibre, Edible seeds, Bee plant

Origin and history

New Zealand flax is quite unrelated to true flax, being part of the agave family, but can supply a fibre of great versatility and value, hence its name and the alternative, New Zealand hemp (the Maori name is Harakeke). It is native to New Zealand and other nearby islands, but is quite at home in Britain and Ireland, particularly in coastal areas, where it has naturalised in places.

The Maori used fibres from the sword shaped leaves to make mats, clothes, baskets and other domestic items as well as ropes and fishing nets. They had selected strains, including two they knew as 'Taiore' and 'Kohunga' that provided the long supple fibres needed to weave aprons and other clothes. European settlers in the nineteenth century sent flax samples to Dundee in Scotland (then the centre of the linen industry) to be processed and woven into shirts; the reports were favourable; clothing was particularly appreciated for its soft flexible wearing qualities and the way it absorbed sweat without becoming clammy and uncomfortable. Also in the nineteenth century, trials in Portsmouth (England) of sheets and sails made from flax fibres had been so promising that the British Government negotiated a contract for the supply of 800 tonnes of flax leaves to produce sails for naval trials.

Flax leaves became one of New Zealand's major exports during the nineteenth century, but unpredictability continued to be a problem and the fibres failed to achieve the hopes once raised. The main problem turned out to be the presence in the leaves of a plant gum which formed small hard granules as the leaves dried (it was dried leaves which were exported) that were difficult to dissolve, and these granules abraded the fibres and led to failure. The Maori wove their cloaks, fishing nets and other items from fibres extracted from fresh leaves in which these granules had not formed. So it was the use of dried leaves which caused the decline in commercial interest. Now, in the 21st century, there is once again renewed interest in the commercial possibilities of New Zealand flax.

Description

A large evergreen perennial, usually treated as a shrub although it is not strictly woody, slowly spreading by stout fleshy rhizomes.

Mature plants reach 2-3m (16-10ft) high, with flower stalks rising up to 4.5m (15ft) high; spread is 1-2m (3-6ft). Each plant consists of 8-12 shoots rising from a central base, each shoot quickly dividing into 5-6 leaves.

Leaves are dark green above (often bluish beneath), hard and stiff, long and narrow, sword shaped, in cross section V shaped in the central portion but flattening out towards the apex. The pointed end becomes slit and tattered on old leaves. They grow 1-3m (3-10ft) long by 5-12cm (2-5ins) wide, and 1-1.5mm thick. They are keeled beneath, the midrib and margins often with a red or orange line. Longer leaves often fold over lengthwise.

Flowers are bisexual and numerous, borne in erect panicles on a long leafless reddish-green stem (1.5-4.5m / 5-15ft high]), tubular in shape, dull red to reddish-brown, 25-50mm (1-2ins) long. The flowers open over a long period in summer (June to August in Britain) and contain large amounts of nectar which is very attractive to bees.

Fruits are brown leathery pods (a bit like brown broad beans), triangular in cross section and pointed at the ends, 5-10cm (2-4ins) long by 12mm (0.5ins) wide. A single flower stalk may produce up to 100 seed pods, each pod containing 60-100 black, shining, flattish seeds each about 5 x 10mm (0.2 x 0.4ins).

Uses

Leaves can also be used fresh (not processed apart from splitting down the length) for thatching, mats, nets, bags, cloaks, sieves, sandals, straps and garden twine (ties without breaking).

Flowers of New Zealand flax

New Zealand flax

The latter may be of most use to gardeners – simply split leaves into widths (5-25mm / 0.2-1ins depending on what strength you need) and use as twine immediately. Dressed and dyed strips of leaf were made into decorative patterned panels, a craft now flourishing again in New Zealand.

Several minor edible uses have been noted:

The seeds are edible and aromatic. They can be roasted and used as a coffee substitute, or can be used whole or chopped in bread, biscuits, cakes or other cooked dishes.

The seed oil is rich in linoleic acid and could be a premium vegetable oil, comparable to sunflower oil and superior to rape seed and soya bean oil. Seeds can yield up to 29% oil, with potential yields of 218kg/ha (87kg/acre). The seed residue would be very suitable for stock feed.

The sweet nectar from the flowers can be drunk. The flowers produce large amounts of nectar and Maori children use hollow grass stalks to suck it out as a treat – something which most people find irresistible once they have tried it.

The gum from the leaf bases was eaten.

The leaf pulp remaining after the fibre is removed and can be fermented to make alcohol (ethanol) for industrial uses – in Brazil it is used as a motor fuel, and the residue used as cattle feed.

A gum/gel is found in the leaf butt (the base of leaves discarded in fibre processing), which comprises mostly of sugars with a long polysaccharide structure. Flax gel ('pia harakeke') is an excellent glue, and is already being used commercially, with the potential to be used in cosmetics.

Flowers are rich in nectar and when open (June to August), are attractive to bees, especially wild bumblebees etc. Flax honey is a product in New Zealand.

The seedpods stain fingers when they are picked; they are also highly perfumed.

Several parts of the plant have been used medicinally by the Maori in New Zealand, most of which have been confirmed recently:

Roots have been used to treat abscesses and tumours (they contain well-known anti-tumour cucurbitacin compounds),

Fibre production

The Maoris extracted fibre by hand for many centuries. In the nineteenth century, a commercial industry grew in New Zealand, which at its peak produced 20,000 tons of fibre per year between 1900 and 1930. The industry was killed off by problems with dry leaves (see p.148), increasing labour costs, and the fibres abaca and sisal replacing it.

Plantations of New Zealand flax for fibre production still exist in many parts of the world, including South America (Argentina, Brazil, Chile), Africa (South Africa, the Congo, Kenya, Tanzania), Mexico, California, Japan, Italy and the Azores. It is an important crop on the island of St Helena – 70% of production there is exported to Britain. Attempts were made to grow New Zealand flax as a commercial crop in Ireland last century, but no industry resulted (however, it is used extensively in the south and west as a windbreak).

In these plantations, plants are spaced at 2m (6.5ft) apart. The first harvest can be made some 4-6 years after planting, with regular harvests each 3-4 years thereafter. The fibre is not the easiest to extract, the midrib on leaves being a particular problem.

The suitability of leaves for cutting is judged by the texture and firmness of each leaf. Leaves are cut in late spring or summer, using a semi-circular tool similar to a reaping hook; the outer 3-4 leaves of each plant are cut 15-20cm (6-8ins) above the ground.

Each harvest yields approx 30-40 tonnes of green leaf per acre, i.e. the overall yield is 3-4 tonnes/ha/year (7.5-10 tons/acre/year). The yield of fibre is about 10% of leaf matter, i.e. 300-400kg/ha/year (0.75-1 ton/acre/year).

Various machines have been constructed for cleaning (scutching) the fibres. Leaves are first crushed, then the pulp is scraped away from the tougher fibre strands. Prior to washing, the fibre strands are cleaned by revolving brushes which remove any remaining pulp. Then they are thoroughly soaked and hung to dry. After sorting and grading they can then be twisted into hanks and pressed into bales. The ultimate fibres are very delicate (12 micron), finer than hemp and longer than wood fibres.

When extracted, the fibre resembles abaca (manila hemp which comes from Musa textiles). It is 1-2m (3-7ft) long, white with a reddish-yellow tinge, soft, flexible and highly lustrous. Fibre filaments are of unequal thickness and are remarkable for their slight adherence; because of this the fibres can be separated into finer strands by friction. Fibres were traditionally bleached by being hung over long lengths of fences, although chemical methods were devised in the 1930s.

When hand cleaned, the fibres are so fine that they can be woven into delicate fabrics; machine-cleaned fibres are coarser and suitable for paper (cream-coloured), towelling and sacking. The fibre is only 60% as strong as abaca, which limits its use in ropes and cordage; it can be mixed with sisal or abaca for use in ropes and binder twine. Recent large-scale trials in New Zealand proved that the fibre makes a good paper, which will become an increasingly economically viable prospect as the strains on wood resources increase. It is already in demand as a handmade speciality paper.

New Zealand flax carpets, mats and underfelt are renowned for their hardwearing qualities and leading carpet manufacturers are interested in the fibre to develop more sustainable, recyclable alternatives to nylon. There is also interest in developing flax/wool carpet blends. South Africa has experimented with flax-blend curtain materials.

In the clothing area, most recent developments have been with mixed fibres (e.g. flax with possum or merino wool), non-woven fabrics, and performance fabrics for sporting and outdoor markets. Lack of carding/spinning machinery is currently holding up progress in this area.

Research is ongoing in New Zealand on flax fibre reinforced composites as alternatives to petroleum-based materials, as well as the utilisation of flax fibre as reinforcement in earth-cement construction.

and for their antifungal properties (they contain the antifungal compound musizin). Root extracts are sold as health products.

The gel/gum from leaf bases has been used as a styptic (i.e. to stop bleeding) and antiseptic, long used for burns and skin conditions including eczema.

Leaves have been used as emergency splints.

Both flowers and seedpods can be used for dyeing, being rich in tannins, producing a range of browns: coffee brown with no mordant or alum as a mordant; brownish-grey with copper/chrome mordants; and greyish-brown with an iron mordant. The leaves can also be used, producing coffee brown with no mordant; dark coffee with alum; dark grey-brown with copper; dark brown with iron; and brown with chromium mordant.

Used as part of riparian-zoned plantings, flax slows water runoff, helps absorb sediment and nutrients before they get to waterways (both at surface and subsurface levels) and increases water quality. The plant makes an excellent hedging and windbreak plant in mild and coastal areas, although the leaves are quite noisy in high winds. They do not require pruning. Roadside plantings absorb sound well. Flax is a successful nurse crop for other trees/shrubs.

Fodder value: the superior health of cows that graze on flax has been noted, and it has been claimed (but not substantiated yet) to provide some worm control.

Whole leaves are used in floristry and are made into a decorative woven textile ('hapene').

Varieties/Cultivars

Many ornamental varieties (with coloured or striped leaves) have been selected. Many of these are smaller than the species and some are hybrids with *Phormium colensoi* (mountain flax), a slightly less hardy and smaller species. Some of the coloured leaf forms have noticeably thinned, more flexible but less strong leaves. The Maoris selected many different cultivars for different uses.

Cultivation

New Zealand flax prefers a rich, well-drained loamy soil but will grow on most soils and sites, including peaty and wet sites, though waterlogged sites in winter can lead to plant death. It is also tolerant of some exposure (very cold winter winds may scorch leaves), salt winds, drought and industrial pollution.

In New Zealand the native Tui relishes the nectar from flowers

It tolerates light shade but much prefers full sun. If minimum winter temperatures are expected near or below the lower limit (around -14°C / 6°F), protect rhizomes with a deep mulch; if the tops are then killed, the rhizomes will survive and send up new shoots the following spring.

If plants are spaced at 2m (6ft) apart, then when fully grown they will fill the space between. Growth is quite fast, 30-60cm (1-2ft) per year, with maximum height reached in 5-10 years.

Propagation is easy by one of two methods, seed and division:

Seeds are not dormant and should be sown in the spring. Germination is slow, taking 1-4 months; plants grow to 30-50cm (12-20ins) in their first year and are then large enough to plant out. Plants set seed readily in Britain.

Large plants can be divided in spring. Alternatively, parts of rhizomes can be planted – one plant yields 20-30 rhizomes suitable for transplanting.

Pests and diseases

If growing plants from seed, watch out for slug and snail damage when plants are very small.

After transplanting, young plants are sometimes damaged by voles or mice, who are attracted by sugars in the leaf bases in winter – it might be worth protecting for the first year or two with a short tree or vole guard.

Related species

Phormium colensoi (mountain flax) is slightly less hardy (to zone 8 / H4) and smaller than New Zealand flax, typically 1.2m (4ft) high. The leaves have all the same uses.

NORTHERN BAYBERRY

Myrica pensylvanica (Morella pensylvanica)

Zone 2, H7
Deciduous
Source of wax, Flavouring, Nitrogen-fixation

Northern bayberry

Origin and history

Northern bayberry originates from eastern North America and has a very long history of human use dating from before European settlement. Indeed, at that time there was a significant malaria problem and European settlers discovered that burning bayberry candles helped repel the insects.

Description

A deciduous or semi-evergreen dense shrub growing 1-3m (3-10ft) high. Leaves 4-10cm (1.5-4ins) long, pubescent especially beneath, with glands beneath which make them aromatic when crushed. Fruits are to 4mm across, greyish-white, waxy, and persist long into winter.

Northern bayberry is a nitrogen-fixing plant, with roots associating with *Frankia* species of bacteria that also associate with alders (*Alnus*), Elaeagnus, and sea buckthorn (*Hippophae*).

Uses

Wax source. The fruits are gathered – a fast process as a handful can be gathered at a time from branches – then warmed in a pot of near-boiling water. The wax melts off the fruit and rises to the surface where it can be skimmed off. Bayberry candles were the main product widely made and still are on a small scale.

Leaves and fruits are used in cooking as a flavouring/condiment (best avoided by pregnant women). The flavour resembles bay leaves. The leaves, wax and candles have similar insect repellent properties to other *Myrica* species including bog myrtle (*M. gale*). Leaves and root bark have traditionally been used medicinally in North America.

The waxy fruit of Northern bayberry

A green dye is obtained from the leaves.

As a nitrogen-fixing plant it can be used as a living green manure plant, making some nitrogen available to other plants in the vicinity. Used for erosion control in North America.

Cultivation

Prefers an open position in sun or partial shade (including in the understorey of open forests), and an acid or neutral soil. Tolerates very acid, saline and light sandy soils.

Propagation methods include:

- Seed: wash in warm soapy water to remove any wax, rinse, then cold stratify for 2-3 months before sowing,
- Layering of low branches,
- Root cuttings in spring.

Young plants in the nursery may naturally become inoculated with *Frankia* species, and if they do then nodules will be seen on the roots. Plants can also be inoculated when planting by mixing a little soil from an established stand of the species or a relative in the planting hole.

Pests and diseases

Readily grazed by hares and goats, also by sheep, cattle and deer.

Related species

Myrica gale (bog myrtle), is described on page 43.

Myrica californica (Californian wax myrtle) and *M. cerifera* (wax myrtle) are larger species described in *Trees for Gardens, Orchards and Permaculture*.

OREGON GRAPES, *Mahonia* spp.

Zone 5-6, H6-7
Evergreen
Edible fruit, Ground cover

Origin and history

The name 'Oregon grape' is used for three species of *Mahonia*, *M. aquifolium*, *M. nervosa* and *M. repens*. They all originate from western North America, where they are found in mixed woodland.

Description

Evergreen shrubs. *M. aquifolium* (also known as mountain grape, holly mahonia, holly barberry and blue barberry) grows 1-2m (3-6ft) high, *M. nervosa* to 1m (3ft) high and *M. repens* to 0.5m (20ins) high.

The golden-yellow flowers are produced in groups on erect racemes from February to May (mostly April-May).

The abundant fruit, dark purple berries, 7-10mm (0.3-0.4ins) across, are covered with a fine violet bloom, and ripen July to September.

These thornless shrubs (though with slightly prickly, holly-like leaves) can all spread by underground suckers.

Flowers on *Mahonia repens*

Uses

The abundant fruits are edible, tart but tasty, and can be eaten raw or cooked, in jams or used to make a palatable wine. The bright yellow flowers are also edible and can be made into a lemonade-like drink.

In addition, the roots have medicinal properties. They contain berberine and are used in the same ways as *Berberis* species.

A variety of brown and beige dyes can be obtained from berries, roots and shoot tips.

They all make a good ground cover. *M. repens* (also known as creeping mahonia, creeping Oregon grape, creeping barberry) is the best.

Cultivation

These species tolerate shade and drought. They are not particular as to soil requirements. In hot dry climates they require shade.

Propagation is by seed, which requires 16 weeks of stratification, or plants can be divided in the spring. Note that all three species described here readily hybridize with each other.

Pests and diseases

Birds sometimes like the fruit.

Related species

Closely related to the *Berberis* species (p.13).

Fruit of *Mahonia aquifolium*

PASSION FRUITS, *Passiflora* species

Zones 7-9, H3-5
Evergreen
Edible fruit pulp

Origin and history

Passion fruit has been grown in South America for thousands of years as a fruit crop. The most widely grown there and elsewhere in the world today are the hard-shelled *P. edulis* varieties.

Some 10-12 species of the total number of *Passiflora* species (about 500-600) have been used commercially for their fruit, although most have edible fruit (not always good quality). In particular the subgenus *Tacsonia* contains over 40 species with edible fruit; these originate from the cool, mid to high altitude regions of the Andes and are better suited to oceanic-influenced climates.

Description

Passiflora species are woody or herbaceous vines with tendrils in the leaf axils, which prefer to climb over a structure – they do poorly sprawling on the ground. Leaves can be very variable in size. The flowers, located in the leaf axils, are extremely colourful and elaborate in most species – there are hundreds of ornamental varieties. Pollination is by hummingbirds, bats, bees, moths and other insects. Some species are self-fertile, others need cross pollinating with a different plant, and sometimes species can hybridise.

Blue passion flower with fruit (*Passiflora caerulea*)

Uses

The fruit pulp is used as flavouring.

Commercial passion fruit juice is made almost entirely from *P. edulis* (purple form) and *P. edulis f. flavicarpa* (yellow form). The juice and fresh pulp (with or without seeds) are used in tropical drinks, cordials, liqueurs, chocolates, sauces, ice creams, sorbets etc. Nutritional information is not available for most species but *P. edulis* fruit contain, per 100g portion of pulp:

Protein	2.90g
Thiamin	0.03mg
Sodium	28mg
Fat	0.50g
Riboflavin	0.10mg
Potassium	350mg
Carbohydrate	7.39g
Niacin	1.50mg
Magnesium	39mg
Water	84.70g
Vitamin C	20.0mg
Calcium	16mg
Fibre	3.30g
Vitamin E	3.0mg
Phosphorus	54mg
Sugars (total)	7.39g
Iron	1.1mg
Glucose	2.90g
Fructose	2.20g
Sucrose	2.29g

P. edulis leaves have a long history of medicinal uses in South America. Young leaves of some species, including *P. edulis*, are edible raw or cooked.

Varieties/Cultivars

Of the 500 species of *Passiflora*, only a small number are tolerant of sub-zero conditions. The following can all tolerate winter temperatures below 0°C (32°F) and represent the species best able to survive in temperate climates. These all have edible fruit pulp.

Species / hybrid	Origin or parentage	Cold tolerance	Fruit description
P. actinia	Orgãos mountains, Brazil	-8°C (18°F)	Small, yellow, slightly acid, grape flavour, very fragrant.
P. ampullacea	Ecuador, high altitude	Reportedly hardy	Large, thick rind. Very good.
P. antioquiensis	Columbia, high altitude	-2°C (28°F)	To 12cm long, ovoid, yellow, excellent flavour. Tolerates shade.
P. caerulea	Brazil	-8°C (18°F)	Bright orange, 60mm long, slight blackberry flavour.
P. caerulea 'Constance Eliott'		-10°C (14°F)	Bright orange, 60mm long, slight blackberry flavour.
P. x *colvillii*	*P. caerulea* x *P. incarnata*	-2°C or less (28°F)	Yellow, 50-60mm long.
P. cumbalensis	South America, high altitude	Reportedly hardy	Red, banana shaped, 100 x 35mm. Very good.
P. edulis		-2°C (28°F)	Purple, ovoid or round, 50-60mm, excellent flavour.
P. edulis 'Black Beauty'		-2°C (28°F)	Deep purple-black, excellent flavour.
P. edulis 'Black Knight'		-4°C (24°F)	Dark purple-black, large, excellent flavour.
P. edulis f. flavicarpa		-2°C (28°F)	Yellow, ovoid or round, 50-60mm, more acid than *P. edulis*.
P. edulis 'Frederick'		-2°C (28°F)	Red, very large, good flavoured.
P. edulis 'Nancy Garrison'		-3 to -5°C (24-27°F)	Excellent.
P. 'Elizabeth'	*P. phoenicea* x *P. incarnata*	Reportedly hardy	Large, very sweet, good flavoured.
P. x *exoniensis*	*P. antiqyuiensis* x *P. mollissima*	-4°C (24°F)	Banana shaped, 75-90mm long, yellow, very good flavour.
P. herbertiana	Australia	-3°C (27°F) or less	Ellipsoidal, green with white fragrant pulp.
P. incarnata	USA	-15°C (5°F)	Ovoid, yellow or lime green, 60mm long, slightly acid, good.
P. 'Incense'	*P. cincinnata* x *P. incarnata*	-4°C or less (24°F)	Egg shaped, 50 x 40mm, olive-green, lightening when ripe. Pulp with rose aroma, sweet and slightly acid.
P. 'Justine Lyons'	*P. caerulea* and *P. amethystina*	-8°C or less (17°F)	
P. manicata	Andes, mid-high altitude	Reportedly hardy	Small, 25 x 50mm, good flavour.
P. membranacea	Mexico	-7°C (20°F)	Green, ovoid, 40-90 x 30-40mm, very sweet, delicious.
P. mixta	Columbia, high altitude	-7°C (20°F)	Ovoid, yellow, to 100 x 25mm, good flavour, raspberry hint.
P. mollissima	Andes, high altitude = *P. tripartita* var. *mollissima*	-4 to -5°C (24-23°F)	Yellow, to 150 x 35mm, very good flavour, good for juice.
P. 'Paulo'	*P. edulis f. flavicarpa* x *P. caerulea*	-3°C (27°F)	
P. 'Pink Panther'	*P. mollissima*	-4°C (24°F)	
P. pinnatistipula	Andes, high altitude	Reportedly hardy	Egg shaped, 4-5cm long, good flavour.
P. schlimiana	Columbia, high altitude	Reportedly hardy	Yellow, to 12cm long, juice blackberry flavour.
P. 'Smythiana'	*P. manicata* x *P. mollissima*	-1°C (30°F)	Yellow, to 75 x 35mm, very good flavour.
P. trifoliata	Peru, high altitude	Reportedly hardy	Egg shaped, 35 x 50mm. Good flavour.
P. tripartita		-5°C (23°F)	Yellow, to 150 x 35mm, tart flavour.
P. 'White Queen'	*P. caerulea* x *P. eichleriana*	-4°C (24°F)	

Passion fruit (*Passiflora edulis*)

There are many other species and cultivars of similar hardiness but with unknown fruit edibility, including *P.* 'Amethyst', *P. capsularis* 'Vanilla Cream', *P.* 'Floral Fountain', *P. gracilis*, *P. hahnii*, *P. jamesonii*, *P. loefgrenii*, *P. lutea*, *P. parritae*, *P.* 'Pretty Ballerina', *P.* 'Purple Rain', *P. rosea*, *P. rubra*, *P. schlimiana*, *P.* 'Silvie', *P.* 'Sonia', *P. suberosa*, *P. tarminiana*, *P. tucumanensis*, and *P. umbilicata*.

Cultivation

Passiflora need well-drained soil – add sharp sand if necessary to improve drainage, and/or plant on a mound. All *Passiflora* hate having wet, cold roots in winter. They can also be grown in large pots.

In warm climes, passion fruit vines can be planted at a spacing of 3 x 1.8m and trellised. Each vine can be expected to produce 50-120 fruit, giving potential yields of 16-23 tonnes/ha.

In Britain, plant *Passiflora* close to a south-facing wall or fence to maximise the warmth. There is no prospect of growing commercial fruit here but they make an interesting and ornamental addition to a home garden. Even the hardier species which tolerate light frosts cannot tolerate frozen soil. In many parts of the UK they can be grown best by being in containers, and placing outdoors in summer and autumn, but kept in a cool greenhouse or similar conditions over winter and spring. The easiest to grow are *P. actinia*, *P. caerulea* and *P. caerulea* 'Constance Eliott' – these are all free flowering and usually set fruit easily. In a forest garden greenhouse, most of the hardier species can be grown.

Hand pollination can increase fruit set and fruit size. In Britain, bees, moths etc. often pollinate flowers. Some species are self-sterile so two clones are required.

Heavily fruiting plants should be fed similarly to tomatoes (i.e. high potassium feed), e.g. use a comfrey feed or seaweed extract feed. With too much nitrogen they may not flower. Once established, they should not require watering in summer.

Fruits can be harvested underripe and they will continue to ripen off the vine – indeed, even with ripe fruit, the flavour can improve by keeping for some days after harvest. Normally, let ripe fruit drop before harvesting. Although most *Passiflora* fruit are edible, some, like *P. caerulea* and its hybrids, are bland, some are delicious and a few taste awful.

Propagation:

- Seed is not dormant and should be sown in spring or fresh in autumn,
- Cuttings from young, newly mature wood can be rooted with mist of a humid environment and heat.

Pests and diseases

Various pests and diseases can attack plants in Britain; slugs and snails are sometimes partial to nibbling leaves. Ants climbing up plants should be regarded as a healthy sign for they are attracted by the nectar and have a protective role, disposing of other insects' eggs etc.

Related species

The maypop (*P. incarnata*) is a herbaceous perennial vine from North America, with edible fruit pulp and also a long tradition of medicinal uses. Recently, analysis of the leaves of maypop have revealed various compounds that act as a sedative (one of its traditional uses), also as an antispasmodic and analgesic.

PEA SHRUB / PEATREE, *Caragana arborescens*

Zone 2, H7
Deciduous/Evergreen
Nitrogen-fixer, Edible seeds/pods, Bee plant

Origin and history

Caragana species are a group of shrubs belonging to the legume family, mostly originating from Central Asia, of which *Caragana arborescens* (from Siberia and Mongolia) is one of the largest. The Latin name comes from the Mongolian name for *C. arborescens*, 'caragan'. This species is the most common of the *Caragana* found in gardens.

Description

C. arborescens is a deciduous shrub (of occasional tree-like habit) growing to 5-6m (16-20ft) high and 4m (13ft) width, with an upright habit. It is vigorous and free growing, with long, sparsely branched shoots which carry small stiff spines at each joint.

Leaves are alternate and pinnate, 4-7cm (1.5-3ins) long, consisting of 4-6 pairs of leaflets (more on young or vigorous shoots); individual leaflets are oval, 8-25mm (0.3-1ins) long, with a small prickly tip.

Flowers are borne from buds on the previous year's wood, and are typical of legumes, being yellow, cup shaped and 18mm (0.75ins) long. Flowering occurs in May. Pollination is via bees, usually wild bumblebees.

Pods develop from flowers, looking like small pea pods (hence the common name); they are 4-5cm (1.5-2ins) long, borne on slender stalks of a similar length, and are smooth, cylindrical and enclose 3-6 roundish or oblong seeds, each 2.5-4mm in diameter. The pods ripen to amber or brown from June or July onwards and seeds fall by August. The seeds ripen well in Britain.

Siberian pea shrub

Uses

The young pods are eaten as a vegetable, lightly cooked. The pods become tough later in the season.

The seeds are rich in fats and protein (12% and 36% respectively), about the size of lentils and can be cooked and used in any way that beans are used (the cooked flavour is somewhat bland, so best used in spicy dishes). The young raw seeds have a pea-like flavour. Dried seeds can be soaked and cooked in the same way as with other beans.

C. arborescens is widely used in windbreaks in North America and the former USSR, particularly on open prairies for farm shelter and outdoor screening in towns and cities. Some use has been made in wildlife-erosion control plantings in North America;

Yellow flowers are loved by bees

An azure blue dye can be obtained from the leaves.

It is a source of nectar and pollen, particularly for bumblebees.

Cultivation

Caragana species prefer a continental climate with hot dry summers and cold winters, but they grow reasonably well in Britain (especially in the east), given a good sunny site. They do not need a rich soil but need good drainage and tolerate sandy alkaline soils. They tolerate drought, full exposure to wind, and industrial air pollution. No pruning is normally required.

Growth in Britain is about 40cm (16ins) per year for the first 10 years. Shrubs take 3-5 years to reach commercial seed-bearing age, and good crops occur nearly every year.

Young pods of *C. arborescens* can be harvested as a vegetable, in June and July.

it is a good soil stabiliser with an extensive root system.

The seeds have great wildlife value in its native range; and the species is used as a supplementary reindeer food in the far north. Siberian pea tree is recommended as a self-forage species for chickens – the seeds will fall and be avidly consumed where chickens have access.

Because it is a nitrogen-fixing plant, it enriches the soil nearby and inputs nitrogen into the system. The rhizobium with which it nodulates is the clover and lupin group, and these are usually freely circulating, so addition of inoculant is rarely necessary. It can be used in polyculture systems, and is sometimes grown with black walnut (*Juglans nigra*) where it increases the growth of the walnut crop for several years until it is shaded out. In Britain, where it requires maximum sunlight, it is really only feasible to combine with smaller species than itself.

A fibre is obtained from the bark and used for rope.

For seed harvest, the pods should be collected in July or early August as they begin to open (the window for harvest is less than two weeks). The pods should be spread out to dry in a protected area until they pop open; the seeds are then easily extracted by light sifting, beating and fanning. Seed yield is 13-20% by weight of fresh pod yield. The seeds can be stored in the dry for many years at room temperature.

Seed propagation is the norm; seeds germinate better after a short period of stratification and/or soaking in warm water prior to planting.

Softwood or semi-ripe cuttings can be taken from May-July and rooted in a well-drained medium with bottom heat. Rooting hormone may not be necessary, but sometimes helps.

Ornamental cultivars are grafted onto seedling rootstocks and there is potential for good fruiting selections to be propagated this way.

The pods contain edible 5mm seeds

Pests and diseases

Slugs and snails can be a problem on young trees, eating the leaves.

Pea trees are resistant to honey fungus.

PINEAPPLE GUAVA, *Acca sellowiana*

Zones 6-8, H5-6
Evergreen
Edible fruit

Origin and history

The Feijoa or pineapple guava (*Acca* or *Feijoa sellowiana*) is a relative of the tropical guava, and is native to extreme southern Brazil, northern Argentina, western Paraguay and Uruguay where it grows wild in the mountains. It is cultivated in the highlands of Chile and other southern American countries, in Southern and Western Europe, in India in home gardens at temperate elevations, in New Zealand (producing several hundred tonnes per year) and California (where some 400 hectares/1000 acres are planted); also in Georgia (former USSR) where over 1000 hectares (2500 acres) are cultivated.

Description

The plant is a bushy evergreen shrub, 0.9-6m (3-20ft) in height, usually 2-4m (6-13ft) high, much branched, with pale grey bark. Spreading forms can spread as wide as they are high.

Leaves are opposite, short-stalked, bluntly elliptical, thick and leathery, smooth and glossy dark green on the upper surface and silvery-hairy beneath.

The flowers are conspicuous, 4cm (1.5ins) across, borne singly or in clusters from leaf axils of the previous year's growth, with four fleshy oval petals which are white outside and purplish-red inside. Within are a cluster of erect purple stamens with golden-yellow anthers. Some selections are self-fertile, others require cross-pollination.

The fruit is oblong or slightly pear shaped, 4-7cm (1.5-3ins) long and 2.5-5cm (1-2ins) wide, with a waxy skin about 7mm (0.25ins) thick. The fruit remains a dull green or yellowish-green until maturity, with a 'bloom' of fine whitish hairs and sometimes with a red or orange blush. The fruit emits a strong long-lasting perfume, even before it is fully ripe. When cut open the fruit has an edible creamy flesh and gelatinous pulp.

French orchard of pineapple guava with fruit ready to harvest

Within the fruits are 20-40, sometimes more, very small oblong seeds.

Uses

Fruits are aromatic and those from the named cultivars are delicious. The fruit flesh is thick, white, granular and juicy – translucent in the middle where it surrounds the seeds – and is sweet or sub-acid with a pineapple and strawberry flavour. The small seeds are hardly noticeable when the fruit is eaten. When cut, the flesh rapidly discolours from oxidation and turns brown – to prevent this, fruit can be dipped in a weak salt or lemon juice solution.

Flowers are unmissable, with excellent edible petals

The flesh and pulp (with seeds) are eaten raw as dessert or in salads, or are cooked in puddings, pastries, cakes, pies or tarts. They are also used as flavouring for ice cream and soft drinks. Surplus fruit can be peeled, halved and preserved in jars, or made into chutney, jam, jelly, sauces or sparkling wine.

Fresh fruit contains (per 100g portion):

Protein	0.9%
Potassium	166mg
Fat	0.2%
Sodium	5mg
Carbohydrate	10%
Calcium	4mg
Niacin	high
Phosphorus	10mg
Vitamin C	28-35mg (high)
Iron	0.05mg

Fruits are high in pectin (up to 20%), and those grown near the sea are also rich in water-soluble iodine compounds.

The thick petals are spicy and are eaten fresh. They can be picked without interfering with fruit set. In fact the petals are so delicious that it can be worth growing just for them in regions too cool for fruit to ripen.

The leaves, fruit (primarily seeds) and stems all have antibacterial properties. The fruit also show antioxidant properties.

In New Zealand, growers sometimes use the plant as a windbreak around other wind-sensitive crops. The wood is hard, dense and brittle.

Varieties/Cultivars

Andre	Fruit medium-large, oblong to round, rough, light green; thick flesh with few seeds, rich flavour and very aromatic. Self-fertile, heavy cropper.
Apollo	Fruit medium-large, oval, light green, smooth thin skin, susceptible to bruising; flesh slightly gritty, very pleasant flavour, good quality. Ripens mid-late season. Plant upright, spreading, to 2.5m (8ft) tall, vigorous, productive, self-fertile. Originates from New Zealand.
Beechwood	Fruit medium sized, elliptical, skin fairly smooth, dark green; good flavour. Tree self-fertile. Originates from California.
Besson	Fruit small-medium, oval, smooth, with red or maroon cheek, thin skinned; flesh medium-thick, fine grained, very juicy, numerous seeds, rich aromatic flavour.
Bliss	Plant is partly self-fertile.
Choiceana	Fruit round-oval, fairly smooth, small-medium, of good flavour. Ripens mid season. Spreading plant of moderate vigour; partly self-fertile.
Coolidge	Fruit oblong or pyriform, medium size, crinkled skin; flesh of average flavour, poor keeper. Plant upright, strong growing, heavy bearer, highly self-fertile; widely grown in California.
David	Fruit medium-large, round or oval, skin has sweet and agreeable flavour; flesh of good flavour and fair texture. Ripens mid season. Grown in Europe.
Duffy	Fruit large, round, thin skinned; pulp sweet, low acid; ripens late. Bush medium sized, erect and vigorous. An Australian selection.
Edenvale Improved Coolidge	Fruit large, oblong, very good flavour and quality. Tree slow growing, self-fertile, precocious and productive; early ripening. Originates from California.
Edenvale Late	Fruit medium sized, oblong, very good flavour and quality. Ripens late over a long period. Tree slow growing, self-fertile, very productive. Originates from California.
Edenvale Supreme	Fruit medium sized, oblong, very good flavour and quality. Ripens mid season; fruit doesn't store for long. Tree slow growing, self-fertile, precocious, and productive. Originates from California.
Gemini	Fruit small-medium sized, egg shaped, skin very smooth, thin, dark green with a heavy bloom. Flavour and texture excellent. Ripens early. Tree moderately vigorous, to 2.5m (8ft) tall, part self-fertile, high yielding. Originates from New Zealand.
Hehre	Fruit large, slender-pyriform, yellowish-green, thin skinned; flesh finely granular, very juicy, sweet, not aromatic, numerous large seeds. Seedlings erect, compact, vigorous, with lush foliage but only moderately productive.

Hirschvogel	Plant is highly self-fertile.
Jackson	Fruit medium sized, thick skinned; flesh dry, strong flavour, nearly seedless. Originates from California.
Lickver's Pride	Fruit large, round; very sweet, rich flavour. Tree rounded, self-fertile. Originates from California.
Magnifica	Fruit very large but of inferior quality.
Mammouth	Fruit large, round to oval, somewhat wrinkled, thick skin; flesh somewhat gritty, quality and flavour very good, poor keeper. Early-mid season. Plant of upright habit, vigorous, to 3m (10ft) tall; part self-fertile. A seedling of Choiceana widely grown in New Zealand.
Moore	Fruit large, of good flavour, ripens mid season. Plant very vigorous. Grown in California.
Nazemetz	Fruit large, pear shaped, side walls moderately thin. Flavour and quality excellent. Ripens mid to late season over a long period. Unusually, the pulp does not darken after being cut or as it ripens. Tree part self-fertile. Originates from California.
Pineapple Gem	Fruit small, round, good quality; mid to late season. Tree part self-fertile, dislikes coastal conditions.
Robert	Fruit medium sized, oval; flesh very juicy, somewhat gritty, mild flavour. Ripens very early. Leaves brownish. Needs cross-pollination.
Roundjon	Fruit oval or rounded, somewhat rough-skinned and red blushed. Good flavour. Grown in Europe.
Smilax	Fruit small-medium, round; flesh sweet, fine flavour – clear pulp extends almost to skin. Tree short, bushy, self-fertile. Originates from California.
Superba	Fruit small-medium, round to oval, quite smooth, of good flavour. Plant spreading, straggly habit, medium vigour; partly self-fertile.
Trask	A bud sport of Coolidge. Fruit medium to large, skin dark green and rough, flavour and quality very good. Ripens early. Tree part self-fertile, precocious. Originates from California.
Triumph	Fruit medium-large, short, oval, plump, smooth; skin firm, uneven; flesh somewhat gritty with an excellent sharp flavour; good keeper. Plant upright, of medium vigour, mid season ripening, part self-fertile. A seedling of Choiceana widely grown in New Zealand.
Unique	Fruit large, oval, smooth skinned, light green; pulp very smooth, good flavour. Early ripening. Tree to 2.5m (8ft) tall, vigorous, self-fertile, precocious; a regular, heavy bearer. Originates from New Zealand.

Cultivation

The Feijoa likes a warm temperate or subtropical climate with a cool season. It tolerates some drought and high humidity. Shelter is desirable as wind can cause fruit bruising and brittle wood to break. The flavour of the fruit is much better in cool rather than warm regions. Sudden autumn frosts can damage ripening fruit, so avoid frost pockets. A flush of new growth occurs in the spring. Winter temperatures below about -15°C (5°F) can lead to some leaves and/or stem tips becoming scorched, while at about -20°C (-4°F), bushes are cut to the ground but can regenerate well the following spring; both these are likely to adversely affect fruiting.

The shrub prefers a rich, organic, well-drained soil and prefers acid soils. It is drought resistant but needs adequate water for fruit production. The optimum annual rainfall is 760-1500mm (30-60ins). It tolerates partial shade (though fruiting will be reduced) and some exposure to salt spray.

In England, pineapple guava only flowers profusely in sunny locations and ripens fruit outdoors in favoured locations, for example grown as a wall shrub. It can fruit well given a position in a polytunnel or greenhouse.

Plants should be spaced at 4-5.5m (13-18ft) apart to allow for spread and good fruit production, unless upright selections are used when the spacing can be reduced; a typical commercial plantation may have 5-6m (16-20ft) between rows and plants 3-3.5m (10-12ft) in the row. Fruit is borne on the young wood, so pruning reduces the crop and is kept to a minimum; light pruning after harvest can encourage new growth if necessary, and thinning of dense plants makes for easier harvesting. An open tree (central leader or goblet shaped) can aid easy harvest. Shoots within 30cm (12ins) of the ground should be removed; the best fruiting branches are those at 20-30° to the horizontal, and these should be 30cm (1ft) apart. The plants have a shallow, fibrous root system and soil cultivation around them after establishment is inadvisable.

Barrier hedges have plants spaced at 1.5-2m (5-6ft) apart, but fruiting capacity in these will be much reduced especially if/when hedges are trimmed (plants respond well to trimming).

Flowering occurs from May to July, depending on the climate. Bees are the main pollinators, although birds which are attracted to eat the petals can also aid pollination. Most flowers pollinated with compatible pollen show 60-90% fruit set;

hand pollination is nearly 100% effective. Poor bearing is usually the result of inadequate pollination and two cultivars should be grown together unless you are sure of self-fertility. Good pollination produces many seeds, which in turn leads to larger and better-shaped fruit and a higher proportion of pulp.

For fruit production, any fertiliser used on a fertile soil should be low in nitrogen so as not to stimulate too much vegetative growth. Potassium is likely to be the main nutrient required, similar requirements as for other heavy fruiting trees. In hot dry spells and dry soil, plants carrying fruit should be watered and mulched.

With some varieties, e.g. Apollo, fruit thinning may be useful to achieve larger fruit. Thin in summer when the fruits approach grape size, 100-120 fruit on a tree 1.8m (6ft) high is sufficient. Take off damaged or misshapen fruit, then reduce to 2-3 fruit per cluster and remove any that will rub against a branch.

Fruits mature 18-26 weeks after flowering (depending on the cultivar), and ripen over several weeks. The fruits fall when mature and are usually collected daily from the ground and kept cool until slightly soft to the touch. A straw mulch, large cloths/tarpaulins, or suspended nets are often used beneath the plants to help avoid bruising, to which fruits are susceptible. Alternatively, mature fruit can be picked from the tree: a slight colour change (to a lighter green), softening, and easily detached fruits are ready to pick – although if picked from the tree before they are ready to fall, or if eaten before fully ripe, they won't have their full richness of flavour. In Europe, fruit usually matures in November.

In New Zealand test plantings, yields have averaged:

3rd year	6kg/plant (13.2lb/plant)	4 tonnes/ha (1.6 tonnes/acre)
4th year	12kg/plant (16.5lb/plant)	8 tonnes/ha (3.2 tonnes/acre)
5th year	18kg/plant (40lb/plant)	12 tonnes/ha (4.8 tonnes/acre)
projected full crop (10 years)	30kg/plant (66lb/plant)	25 tonnes/ha (10 tonnes/acre)

Trees remain productive for at least 30-40 years, and then can be rejuvenated by drastic pruning.

'Triumph' fruit

In a warm atmosphere, the interior of fruit turns brown and decays in 3-4 days. In cold humid storage, undamaged fruit remains in good condition for 4-5 weeks at 3-5°C (37-41°F) and 2-3 weeks at 10°C (50°F).

Propagation

Pineapple guava is often grown from seed but does not reproduce absolutely true to type. Germination takes place in around three weeks; seedlings are prone to damping off diseases. Seed-grown plants fruit in 3-5 years from sowing.

Cultivars are propagated vegetatively by one of several means. Vegetatively propagated plants can start to flower and fruit in two years.

For a few plants, or where there are already many cultivars planted, ground layering is used, with rooting occurring in three months.

Cuttings can be taken: young wood from branch tips or side shoots with a heel in summer will root in 1-2 months with bottom heat and a hormone rooting agent, given a moist humid atmosphere.

Grafting is not used much, but sometimes air layering and stool layering can succeed.

Pests and diseases

There are few pests or diseases of note. Various scale insects can attack the plant, and fruit flies can attack ripe fruit.

RASPBERRY, *Rubus* spp.

Zone 4-5, H7
Deciduous
Edible fruit

Origin and history

Raspberries are frequently cultivated in temperate regions of the world for their edible fruit. They were first cultivated in medieval monasteries, and over many years have been highly bred, mainly from the following species:

- *Rubus idaeus* – European red raspberry
- *Rubus idaeus* ssp. *strigosus* – North American red raspberry
- *Rubus occidentalis* – Black or blackcap raspberry.

Description

Raspberries are suckering shrubs growing to 2m (7ft) high, with a perennial root system, so that new canes are produced each year and live for just two years before dying. In summer fruiting cultivars, the new canes produce fruit in the following year (i.e. they are kept for two years), whereas in autumn fruiting cultivars, the new canes fruit in the same year and are only kept for a season. Plants produce both deep roots and masses of fibrous surface roots. Most raspberries are hardy, tolerating winter temperatures of -20 to -25°C / -4 to -13°F (zone 4-5 / H7).

Raspberries

Uses

The fruits are eaten raw or cooked in desserts, in salads, compotes, jams, syrups and juices. Wine and liqueur can also be made from them.

Raspberries contain up to 13% fruit sugars (fructose, glucose and saccharose), up to 6% pectins, citric acid, salicylic acid (the fever-reducing compound also found in willows and the basis of aspirin); also up to 20mg vitamin C per 100g, provitamin A, vitamins B1 and B2, iron, potassium, phosphorus, calcium and high levels of copper.

Other parts of the plant that have been eaten in times of shortage are the root (cooked for a long time); and the young shoots, peeled and eaten raw or cooked like asparagus. Neither of these are very palatable and are not recommended.

The fruit, roots and leaves have long been used for their medicinal properties.

The flowers, produced between May and July depending on the cultivar, are a good nectar source for bees.

Varieties/Cultivars

Black raspberries derive from *Rubus occidentalis*, and are widely grown in North America, but in Britain are susceptible to *Phytophthora* root rots; these include the cultivars Allen, Black Hawk, Bristol, Cumberland, Dundee, Haut, Huron, Jewel, John Robertson, Lowden, Mac Black, Morrison, Munger, New Logan, Plum Farmer and Wyoming.

KEY TO CULTIVAR TABLES

Cane characteristics
Cane vigour: mod = moderate, vig = vigorous, v.vig = very vigorous.
Type: ↗ means semi-erect/semi-upright, ↑ means erect/upright.
Spines: no means canes are spineless.

Ripening times are average for the UK. In regions with hotter summers, these dates will be brought forward to early June or even May. E = early, M = mid, L = late. Many autumn fruiting cultivars will cease fruiting at the first frosts which may be before or after mid/late October in some areas.

Fruit characteristics
Colour
Flavour: exc = excellent, v.gd = very good etc.
Size: x.lge = extremely large, v.lge = very large, lge = large, m-l = medium-large, med = medium, s-m = small to medium, small
Yields: v.high = very high, High, m-h = moderate to high, mod = moderate, l-m = low to moderate.

Summer fruiting cultivars

Season of ripeness corresponds approximately in southern England to the following (and in Scotland to about two weeks later):

Early: late June to mid or late July
Mid-late: mid July to early August
Early-mid: early July to mid or late July
Late: mid July to mid August
Mid: early July to late July
Very late: mid-late July to late August

Spineless (or very nearly so) cultivars: Anelma, Clutha, Festival, Framita, Glencoe, Glen Ample, Glen Coe, Glen Garry, Glen Lyon, Glen Magna, Glen Moy, Glen Rosa, Glen Shee, Glen Yarra, Malling Juno, Mammouth Red Thornless, OAC Regal, OAC Regency, Rusilva, Souris, Titan, Tulameen.

				June	July			August						
Cultivar	Vigour	Type	Spines	L	E	M	L	E	M	L	Colour	Flavour	Size	Yield
Algonquin		↑									bright red			
Allen	vig				✓	✓	✓				black			m-h
Amber	vig				✓	✓	✓				yellow	good	lge	high
Amethyst					✓	✓	✓				purple		lge	m-h
Anelma	v.vig		no		✓	✓	✓						med	
Anita	mod			✓	✓	✓					light red		m-l	m-h
Augusta	vig							✓	✓	✓	red	good	med	high
Balder	vig	↑		✓	✓	✓					dark red		med	high
Beskid	vig					✓	✓	✓	✓	✓	red		m-l	
Black	vig			✓	✓	✓					black			high
Black Hawk	v.vig					✓	✓	✓			black	good	lge	high
Boyne	mod				✓	✓	✓				dark red	good	med	high
Brandywine	v.vig	↑									red/purple		lge	high
Bristol	vig	↑			✓	✓	✓				black	mild	lge	m-h
Canby	vig				✓	✓	✓				red	exc	lge	high
Centennial	vig	↑			✓	✓	✓				red	mild	lge	
Chief	vig			✓	✓	✓					red	good	s-m	
Chilcotin	mod			✓	✓	✓	✓				red	v.good	lge	mod
Chilliwack	vig	↑			✓	✓	✓				red	v.good	lge	mod
Citadel	v.vig					✓	✓	✓			dark red	good	lge	
Clutha	mod	↗	no			✓	✓	✓			red		med	
Comet					✓	✓	✓					good	m-l	
Comox	vig	↑			✓	✓	✓				red	good	v.lge	high
Cumberland	vig	↑			✓	✓	✓				black	exc	lge	high
Cuthbert	vig					✓	✓	✓	✓		dark red	good	m-l	mod
Dorman Red	vig						✓	✓	✓	✓	dark red	mild	lge	high
Dundee	vig				✓	✓	✓				black	mild	lge	high
Early Black					✓	✓	✓				black		lge	high
Earlysweet	vig	↗		✓	✓	✓					black		med	m-h
Elida	vig			✓	✓	✓					red	fair	med	
Estate	vig	↑				✓	✓	✓	✓		purple		lge	

				June	July			August						
Cultivar	Vigour	Type	Spines	L	E	M	L	E	M	L	Colour	Flavour	Size	Yield
Fertodi Zamatos						✓	✓	✓			red	good	m-l	
Festival	vig		no		✓	✓	✓				red	fair	m-l	high
Framita	mod		no								dark red	exc	med	
Gaia	vig	↑				✓	✓	✓			dark red	good	lge	m-h
Gatineau				✓	✓	✓						good		
Gina	mod			✓	✓	✓					red		m-l	
Glencoe	vig	↗	no		✓	✓	✓				purple	exc	med	
Glen Ample	vig	↑	no		✓	✓	✓				red	exc	m-l	high
Glen Clova	vig	↑			✓	✓	✓				red	good	m-l	high
Glen Coe	vig	↗	no	✓	✓	✓	✓	✓			purple	exc	med	lge
Glen Garry	mod		no		✓	✓	✓				red	exc	v.lge	
Glen Lyon	mod		no		✓	✓	✓				red	acid	m-l	
Glen Magna	vig	↑	no			✓	✓	✓	✓		dark red	exc	v.lge	high
Glen Moy	vig	↑	no	✓	✓	✓						good	lge	m-h
Glen Prosen	mod				✓	✓	✓					good	med	m-h
Glen Rosa	mod	↑	no		✓	✓	✓				red	q.good	med	m-h
Glen Shee	vig	↑	no									fair		
Glen Yarra	vig	↑	no		✓	✓	✓				red		m-l	
Golden Everest	mod				✓	✓	✓				yellow	mild	med	m-h
Golden Queen											yellow		med	
Golden West	vig				✓	✓	✓				yellow		med	
Haida						✓	✓	✓			red	good	lge	high
Haut	vig					✓	✓	✓			black		med	high
Hilton	vig	↑			✓	✓	✓				red	good	lge	m-h
Himbo Queen	vig										red	exc	v.lge	high
Himbo Star	mod											q.good	lge	
Honey Queen	vig										yellow	mild	med	
Huron	vig			✓	✓	✓							lge	m-h
Jatsi												good	lge	
Jenkka											red			
Jewel	v.vig				✓	✓	✓				black	good	lge	
John Robertson											black	good	lge	
Julia	vig	↑			✓	✓	✓				red	good	lge	high
Keriberry														
Killarney					✓	✓	✓				dark red	good	lge	high
Kiwi Gold		↑						✓	✓	✓	yellow	good	sm	
Latham	vig	↑			✓	✓	✓	✓	✓		dark red	good	lge	high
Lawrence	vig												m-l	

				June	July			August						
Cultivar	Vigour	Type	Spines	L	E	M	L	E	M	L	Colour	Flavour	Size	Yield
Leo	v.vig	↑					✓	✓	✓	✓	orange	good	lge	mod
Lloyd George	vig				✓	✓	✓				dark red	exc	lge	m-h
Lowden	vig	↑				✓	✓	✓	✓		black	good	m-l	m-h
Mac Black	vig					✓	✓	✓	✓			v.good	m-l	
Madawaska Red				✓	✓	✓					red	fair	m-l	m-h
Malahat	vig	↑		✓	✓	✓					red	good	lge	high
Malling Admiral	vig	↑				✓	✓	✓			red	good	lge	high
Malling Augusta											dark red	acid	m-l	mod
Malling Delight	vig				✓	✓	✓				red	exc	v.lge	high
Malling Enterprise	mod					✓	✓	✓			red	good	lge	mod
Malling Exploit				✓	✓	✓					red	good	lge	high
Malling Jewel					✓	✓	✓				red	good	lge	high
Malling Joy					✓	✓	✓	✓	✓			good	lge	v.high
Malling Juno			no	✓	✓	✓	✓	✓			red	good	lge	
Malling Notable	mod				✓	✓	✓				red	v.good	lge	fair
Malling Orion	vig	↗			✓	✓	✓	✓			red		med	m-h
Malling Promise	vig			✓	✓	✓					red	good	lge	high
Mammoth Red Th'	vig		no		✓	✓	✓				red	good	v.lge	high
Marve	vig					✓	✓	✓	✓		red	good	lge	high
Matsqui												good		high
Meco												good	med	high
Meeker	vig				✓	✓	✓				dark red	good	lge	high
Milton	vig				✓	✓	✓				light red	exc	lge	high
Munger	vig	↑				✓	✓	✓			black		med	mod
Newburgh	vig				✓	✓	✓				light red	mild	lge	
Nootka														
Norfolk Giant	vig					✓	✓	✓	✓		red	fair	lge	high
Norna	v.vig				✓	✓	✓				dark red	mild	lge	
Nova	vig				✓	✓	✓				dark red	good	m-l	m-h
OAC Regal	vig	↑	no		✓	✓	✓				red		med	high
OAC Regency	vig		no		✓	✓	✓						med	high
Octavia						✓	✓	✓			red	good	lge	
Phylis King	vig	↗			✓	✓	✓				red	q.acid	lge	m-h
Prestige				✓	✓	✓					red		lge	v.high
Purple	mod					✓	✓	✓	✓		purple	exc	med	fair
Pyne's Royal	vig	↗			✓	✓	✓				dark red		lge	mod
Qualicum	vig	↑			✓	✓	✓				red	fair		

				June	July			August						
Cultivar	Vigour	Type	Spines	L	E	M	L	E	M	L	Colour	Flavour	Size	Yield
Rakaia	mod	↗			✓	✓	✓				dark red		lge	mod
Redbrook											red		lge	
Redsetter	mod				✓	✓	✓					good	lge	m-h
Red Cross	vig	↗		✓	✓	✓					light red	v.good	med	high
Resa				✓	✓	✓					red	good	m-l	low
Reveille	vig	↑		✓	✓	✓					red	good	lge	
Reward	vig	↗		✓	✓	✓					red		med	m-h
Rival	vig	↑			✓	✓	✓				red	sl.acid	lge	high
Royalty	vig					✓	✓	✓	✓		purple	good	lge	
Royal Scot	vig	↑		✓	✓	✓	✓				red	good	lge	high
Rubaca	mod					✓	✓	✓			red	good	med	
Ruby Beauty	low			✓	✓	✓								
Rucami	vig				✓	✓	✓				red	acid	lge	mod
Rumiloba	v.vig	↑				✓	✓	✓	✓		red		lge	m-h
Rusilva	mod		no		✓	✓	✓				light red	acid		high
Rutrago	vig	↑				✓	✓	✓	✓		red	good	med	high
Saint Walfried	vig					✓	✓	✓			red	good	lge	m-h
San Diego												good	med	
Schonemann						✓	✓	✓	✓				lge	
Selwyn		↑		✓	✓	✓					red		med	
Sentry	vig				✓	✓	✓				red	good	m-l	
Skeena		↑									red	good	m-l	high
Sodus	vig	↑			✓	✓	✓				purple	fair	lge	high
Souris			no		✓	✓	✓						sm	
Success		↑			✓	✓	✓				purple		m-l	
Sunrise				✓	✓	✓					red	good	lge	high
Taylor	vig					✓	✓	✓			red	v.good	lge	m-h
Titan	mod		no	✓	✓	✓					red	mild	v.lge	v.high
Tulameen	vig	↑	no		✓	✓	✓	✓	✓		red	good	v.lge	high
Vene				✓	✓	✓					dark red		sm	
Veten	mod	↑			✓	✓	✓				dark red	acid	lge	high
Waiau		↗				✓	✓	✓			red		lge	
Wawi												good	s-m	high
Willamette	vig			✓	✓	✓					dark red	acid	lge	high
Wyoming	vig										purple	mild		m-h
Yellow Antwerp	mod				✓	✓	✓				yellow	v.good	sm	high
Zenith		↑				✓	✓	✓	✓	✓	red		med	

Algonquin	Canes upright, compact, few thorns. Fruits bright red, medium firm. Hardy.
Allen	Mid season. Canes vigorous, productive. Fruits large, firm, juicy, very sweet, black.
Amber	Mid season. Canes vigorous, productive. Fruits large, somewhat soft and conical, yellowish-amber, very sweet, good flavour. Heavy bearer; fairly hardy.
Amethyst	Mid season. Canes very hardy, productive. Fruits large, glossy purple, easy to pick.
Anelma	Mid season. Canes very large and vigorous, very hardy, nearly spineless. Fruits medium size, round, very firm, very sweet.
Anita	Very early season. Canes moderately vigorous. Fruits medium-large, conic, medium firm, light red. Good cropper that needs a mild winter climate.
Balder	Early season. Canes vigorous, erect, numerous with large leaves hiding fruit. Fruits medium sized, dark dull red, soft, sweet-acid. Very heavy cropper; very hardy.
Beskid	Late ripening, over a long period. Canes vigorous, slightly spreading. Fruits medium-large, conic, firm, red.
Black	Early season. Canes vigorous. Fruits black, good quality. Heavy cropper. Very hardy commercial cropper from USA.
Black Hawk	Ripen mid-late season. Canes extremely vigorous and heavy yielding; don't sucker. Fruits large, roundish, glossy black, sweet rich flavour; easily picked. Drought resistant.
Boyne	Early-mid season. Canes moderately vigorous, sturdy. Fruits medium size, soft, dark red, aromatic, good quality, easily picked. Heavy bearer.
Brandywine	Canes extremely vigorous, erect, thorny, do not sucker. Fruits large, conic, firm, reddish-purple, tart aromatic flavour. Very hardy, heavy bearer.
Bristol	Mid season. Canes vigorous, upright, compact, sturdy. Fruits large, conical, firm, glossy black, mild flavour. Good cropper.
Canby	Mid season. Canes thornless, vigorous, tall. Fruits red, large, firm, excellent flavour. Heavy bearer, very hardy.
Centennial	Mid season. Canes upright, long, vigorous, soft prickles. Fruits large, long conic, bright red, mild flavour, medium firm.
Chief	Early season. Canes vigorous. Fruits small-medium, cherry red, very firm, good flavour. Very winter hardy.
Chilcotin	Early and mid season. Canes moderately vigorous. Fruits large, conic, red, moderately firm, very good flavour. Moderately productive.
Chilliwack	Mid season. Canes upright, long, vigorous. Fruits large, very sweet, firm, bright red, very good flavour. Tolerant of wet sites; moderate bearer.
Citadel	Mid-late season. Canes very vigorous. Fruits large dark red, very firm, good flavour.
Clutha	Mid-late season. Canes medium strong, semi-upright, few spines. Fruits red, medium sized. Good in fairly warm winter regions.
Comet	Mid season. Canes tall, spiny. Fruits medium-large, very sweet, good quality.

Comox	Mid season. Canes vigorous, fairly upright. Fruits very large, conic, red, good quality. Very heavy yielder.
Cumberland	Early-mid season. Canes vigorous, upright, strong. Fruits black, large, round, firm, excellent flavour and quality. Very heavy cropper. Grows well in shade.
Cuthbert	Late season. Canes vigorous, tall. Fruits medium-large, conical, dark red, good flavour. Moderate yielding.
Dorman Red	Very late season. Canes vigorous, non-suckering. Fruits large, round, firm, dark red, mild flavour. Very productive, drought resistant. Needs a warm climate.
Dundee	Mid season. Canes vigorous, tall. Fruits large, black, moderately firm, mild flavour. Heavy cropper.
Early Black	Fruits large, black, sweet; ripens mid season. Very heavy yielding.
Earlysweet	Early season, over a short period. Canes vigorous, semi-erect, productive. Fruits medium size, black, firm, sweet. Good cropper.
Elida	Very early season. Canes vigorous, abundant. Fruits medium size, firm, bright red, conic, fairly good flavour.
Estate	Late season. Canes vigorous, hardy, strong, upright. Fruit purple, large, round, sweet.
Fertodi Zamatos	Mid-late season. Canes very tall, hardy, productive. Fruits medium-large, bright red, firm, good flavour.
Festival	Mid season. Canes vigorous, short, nearly spineless, sucker freely. Fruits medium-large, firm, red, fair flavour. Heavy cropper, very hardy.
Framita	Canes moderately vigorous, strong, spineless. Fruits medium size, firm, dark red, round, excellent flavour.

Gaia	Canes vigorous, tall, erect, not too spiny. Fruits large, firm, dark red, round-conic, good flavour; easily picked. Good cropper.
Gatineau	Early season. Fruits of good flavour. Very hardy.
Gina	Very early season. Canes moderately vigorous, high yielding. Fruits medium-large, red, medium firm, conic. For warm winter areas.
Glen Ample	Mid season. Canes vigorous, upright, spineless. Fruits medium-large, bright red, round-conic, firm, excellent flavour but crumbly in cool climates; easily picked. Crops heavily.
Glen Clova	Early-mid season. Canes erect, strong. Fruits of good flavour, medium-large, round, bright red, ripens over a long period. Heavy cropper.
Glen Coe	Mid season. Fruit deep purple, rich flavour. Canes semi-erect, spineless.
Glen Garry	Early-mid season. Canes heavy yielding, spineless, moderately vigorous. Fruits very large, conic, firm, pale red, excellent flavour.
Glen Lyon	Early-mid season. Canes establish quickly, spineless, moderately vigorous. Fruits medium-large, bright red, firm, easily picked, acid flavour, keep well.
Glen Magna	Late season. Canes erect, vigorous, moderately numerous, few spines. Fruits very large, deep red, long conic, excellent flavour, moderately firm. Crops very heavily.
Glen Moy	Early season. Canes erect, vigorous, spine free. Fruits large, firm, good flavour. Crops well. Occasionally produces autumn fruits on the young canes.
Glen Prosen	Mid season. Canes moderately vigorous. Fruits firm, medium sized, good flavour. Crops well.
Glen Rosa	Mid season. Canes moderately vigorous and upright, spineless. Fruits medium sized, red, firm, fairly good flavour, good quality, easily picked. Moderate cropper, good in cool climates.
Glen Shee	Canes vigorous, quite upright, spineless. Fruits slightly pale, firm, fleshy, soft skin, fair flavour.
Glen Yarra	Mid season. Canes strong, erect, spineless. Fruits medium-large, firm, red. Adapted to warm winter regions.
Glencoe	Mid season. Canes vigorous, semi-erect, spineless. Fruits medium sized, round-conic, dull purple, very firm, intense flavour, easily picked. Not cold hardy.
Golden Everest	Mid season. Canes moderately vigorous. Fruits yellow, medium sized, round, good flavour; produced both on old and new canes, over a long season. Cropping quite good.
Golden Queen	Fruits medium sized, golden, soft, with a sugary flavour.
Golden West	Mid season. Canes vigorous, tall. Fruits medium sized, firm, yellow.
Haida	Mid-late season. Canes stout, self-supporting. Fruits red, large, firm, good flavour, good for freezing. A heavy cropper from Canada.
Haut	Mid-late season. Canes vigorous, freely branching. Fruits medium sized, round, firm, very sweet, black, ripen over a long period. Heavy yielding.
Hilton	Mid season. Canes vigorous, compact, erect, self-supporting. Fruits large, long, red, firm, good quality. Good cropper, hardy.
Himbo Queen	Canes vigorous, sturdy, very long laterals. Fruits very large, conic, bright red, firm, excellent aromatic flavour, easily picked. Very productive.
Himbo Star	Canes moderately vigorous, very long laterals. Fruits large, firm, fairly good flavour, easily picked, keep well.
Honey Queen	Canes vigorous, high yielding. Fruits medium sized, golden-yellow, sweet, mild flavour, few seeds. Hardy.
Huron	Very early season. Canes vigorous, productive. Fruits large. Hardy.
Jatsi	Canes thick, sturdy, small spines. Fruits large, firm, long, good flavour, difficult to pick. Hardy.
Jenkka	Canes thin, flexible. Fruits round, red, firm. Very cold hardy; a reliable yielder.
Jewel	Early-mid season. Canes very vigorous, heavy cropper. Fruits large, firm, black, slightly downy, rich flavour. Hardy.
John Robertson	Canes extremely hardy, productive. Fruits black, large, medium firm, good quality.
Julia	Mid season. Canes erect, vigorous, moderately numerous (plant closely). Fruits large, well flavoured, dull red, moderately firm, easily picked. Crops heavily.
Keriberry	Unusual evergreen black raspberry from New Zealand. Lush foliage, needs semi-shady conditions.
Killarney	Mid season. Canes very sturdy, medium size. Fruits large, deep red, firm, good quality. Vary hardy and productive.
Latham	Ripens mid and late season. Canes strong, vigorous, upright, medium tall. Fruits large, round, deep red, firm, good flavour, often crumbly. Heavy cropper.
Lawrence	Canes vigorous. Fruits medium-large, sweet, easily picked. Also fruits on primocanes.
Leo	Very late season – until late August. Canes upright, very vigorous but slow to multiply in early years, long laterals. Fruits large, round, pubescent, bright orange-red, firm, slightly acid, good flavour. A moderate cropper. Tolerant of poor soils.
Lloyd George	Mid season, though often fruits again in the autumn. Canes vigorous, may need thinning. Fruits large, dark red, firm, excellent flavour. A good cropper.
Lowden	Late season. Canes vigorous, upright. Fruits medium-large, black, good flavour. Productive, very hardy.
Mac Black	Late season. Canes vigorous, productive, hardy. Fruits medium-large, very good flavour.
Madawaska Red	Very early season. Fruits medium-large, firm, red, sweet, fair quality. Hardy and productive.
Malahat	Early season. Canes vigorous, fairly upright. Fruits large, firm, conic, red, good flavour, easily harvested, keep well. High yielder.
Malling Admiral	Mid-late season. Canes vigorous, fairly erect. Fruits large, red, firm, good flavour, pull easily off plug. Crops very well.
Malling Augusta	Canes moderate in number, tall, spreading. Fruits medium-large, firm, oval-conic, dark red, moderately acid, easily picked. Moderate yields.
Malling Delight	Early-mid season. Canes strong. Fruits very large, pale red, excellent flavour, soft (not good frozen), pull easily off plug. Crops very well.

Malling Enterprise	Mid-late season. Canes moderately vigorous. Fruits large, red, firm, good flavour. Crops quite well. Late flowering.
Malling Exploit	Early season. Canes vigorous. Fruits large, red, good flavour, pull easily off plug; heavy cropping.
Malling Jewel	Mid season. Canes sturdy. Fruits large, red, good flavour, pulls easily off plug, hang well on canes. Heavy cropper, frost resistant. Late flowering, easily picked.
Malling Joy	Mid and late season. Canes are tall, spreading, produce a large number of laterals and should be spaced wider than normal. Fruits large, blunt conic, very firm, slightly pubescent, good slightly acid flavour, pull easily off plug; very heavy cropper.
Malling Juno	Early season. Large fruit of good sweet flavour. Thornless canes with good disease resistance.
Malling Notable	Mid season. Canes moderately vigorous. Fruits large, red, very good flavour. Cropping fair.
Malling Orion	Mid season over a long period. Canes vigorous, semi-erect. Fruits bright red, firm, medium size. A good cropper.
Malling Promise	Early season – June. Canes vigorous – slow to multiply at first. Fruits good flavour, large, bright red, soft, crumbly, pull easily off plug; heavy yielding & frost resistant.
Mammouth Red Thornless	Early-mid season. Canes vigorous, tall, spineless. Fruits very large, conic, sweet, red, soft, good flavour. Hardy and very productive.
Marve	Late season. Canes vigorous, strong. Fruits large, red, firm, conic, good flavour, fairly easily picked. High yielding.
Matsqui	Fruits of good flavour. A hardy, heavy cropper from Canada.
Meco	Fruits medium sized, soft, good flavour. Very high yielding.
Meeker	Mid season. Canes vigorous, tall. Fruits large, firm, deep red, very sweet, good quality, ripen over a long period. Very productive. Requires mild winters.
Milton	Mid season. Canes vigorous. Fruits large, light red, very firm, hang well, excellent flavour. Cropping very good; does well in wet seasons.
Munger	Mid-late season. Canes stout, vigorous, upright. Fruits medium sized, firm, glossy black, sweet flavour. Very hardy, moderate cropper.
Newburgh	Mid season. Canes vigorous, tolerant of heavy and wet soils. Fruits large, firm, very sweet, light red, mild flavour. Very hardy, productive. Good on heavy soils.
Nootka	Canes stout, self-supporting. Very hardy selection from Canada.
Norfolk Giant	Late season. Canes tall and vigorous. Fruits large, bright red, acid, of fair flavour. A tough variety which flowers late. Heavy cropper, does well on light soils.
Norna	Early-mid ripening. Canes erect, very vigorous, moderate in number. Fruits large, round, dark red, medium firm, mild flavour; easily picked.
Nova	Mid season. Canes vigorous, of medium height. Fruits medium-large, dark red, firm, good flavour. Hardy and productive.
OAC Regal	Mid season. Canes vigorous, upright, numerous, few spines. Fruits medium size, red, firm, conic, easily picked. High yielding, very hardy.
OAC Regency	Early-mid season. Canes vigorous, few spines. Fruits medium size, firm, conic, easily picked. Heavy yielding, very hardy.
Phylis King	Mid season. Canes vigorous, semi-erect. Fruits large, bright red, slightly acid. A good cropper.
Prestige	Early season. Canes medium size, nearly thornless. Fruit large, red. Very heavy cropper.
Purple	Mid-late season. Canes moderately vigorous. Fruits medium sized, dark purple, excellent flavour. Fair cropper.
Pyne's Royal	Mid season. Canes vigorous, semi-erect. Fruits large, conical, dark red, plug easily. Crops quite well.
Qualicum	Mid season. Canes vigorous, upright. Fruits conic, red, pleasant flavour, easily picked.
Rakaia	Mid season. Canes moderately vigorous, semi-upright. Fruits large, dark red, easily picked. Fair to good cropper.
Red Cross	Early season. Canes vigorous, semi-erect. Fruits medium sized, round, light red, very good flavour. Heavy cropper.
Redbrook	Canes high yielding, hardy. Fruits large, bright red, sweet.
Redsetter	Mid season. Canes moderately vigorous. Fruits firm, large, easily seen, good flavour. Crops well.
Resa (Lucana)	Very early season. Canes weak. Fruits medium-large, firm, bright red, good flavour. Yields low.
Reveille	Early season. Canes vigorous, upright, strong, freely suckering. Fruits large, bright red, good flavour. Very hardy.
Reward	Early season. Canes vigorous, semi-erect. Fruits medium sized, bright red, firm, sub-acid. Crops well.
Rival	Mid season, over a long period. Canes vigorous, stout. Fruits large, conical, red, firm, slightly acid. Cropping very good.
Royal Scot	Very early season. Canes vigorous, stout. Fruits large, deep salmon-red, firm, good flavour – does well in wet weather. Cropping good.
Royalty	Late season. Canes vigorous, productive, few suckers. Fruits large, firm, round, purple, very sweet, good quality.
Rubaca (Niniane)	Mid-late season. Canes moderately vigorous, very strong. Fruits medium size, firm, bright red, round-conic, good flavour.
Rucami	Mid season. Canes vigorous, thick with long strong laterals. Fruits large, red, firm, aromatic acid flavour. Moderately productive.
Rumiloba (Rumilo)	Late season. Canes very vigorous, upright. Fruits large, broad, red, aromatic flavour, easily harvested. Medium to high yielding.
Rusilva (Brabant)	Mid season. Canes moderately vigorous, thin, nearly spineless. Fruits round, light red, firm, sour, aromatic. High yielding.
Rutrago (Rucanta)	Late season. Canes vigorous, very strong, erect. Fruits medium size, firm, red, vary aromatic, sweet-acid, easily picked. High yielding.
Saint Walfried	Mid season. Canes vigorous. Fruits very long, bright red, juicy, good flavour. Heavy cropper.
San Diego	Fruits medium sized, good quality. Used in warm regions.
Schonemann	Late season. Fruits large, firm.

Selwyn	Early season. Canes upright, slow to establish. Fruits medium sized, red, soft, difficult to pick.
Sentry	Mid season. Canes vigorous, moderately tall, few thorns. Fruits medium-large, firm, red, good flavour, easily picked. Very winter hardy.
Skeena	Canes sturdy, upright. Fruits medium-large, conical, bright red, firm, good quality. Heavy cropper.
Sodus	Mid season. Canes sturdy, vigorous, upright, very few thorns. Fruits large, firm, purple, sweet, fair flavour. Heavy yielding. Hardy and drought resistant.
Souris	Early-mid season. Canes with few spines, self-supporting. Fruits small. Very hardy.
Success	Mid season. Canes erect, heavy yielding. Fruits medium-large, purple, sweet. Very cold hardy.
Sunrise	Very early season. Fruits large, firm, bright red, v. good flavour. Heavy cropper. Hardy.
Taylor	Mid-late season. Canes vigorous, tall, sturdy. Fruits large, very firm, red, very good flavour; ripen over a long period. Good cropper.
Titan	Early season. Canes moderately vigorous, tall, stout, nearly spineless, sparsely suckering. Fruits very large, sweet, juicy, bright red, mild flavour; ripen over a long period. Very heavy cropper.
Tulameen	Mid and late season. Canes vigorous, fairly upright, spine free except at base. Fruits very large, red, firm, of good flavour, easily picked; ripens over very long period. Very productive.
Vene	Early ripening. Fruits small, round, glossy dark red, soft. Hardy.
Veten	Early-mid season. Canes moderately vigorous, erect. Fruits large, conic, dark red, acid. High yielding.
Waiau	Mid-late season. Canes semi-upright and arching, numerous. Fruits large, red, firm, quite difficult to pick. Good in warm winter regions.
Wawi	Fruits small-medium sized, firm, good flavour. High yielding.
Willamette	Early season. Canes vigorous, tall. Fruits large, very firm, deep red, tart flavour. Requires mild winters. Very productive.
Wyoming	Canes strong, very tall, non-suckering. Fruits purple-black, mild flavour. Quite hardy and heavy cropping.
Yellow Antwerp	Mid season. Canes moderately vigorous. Fruits yellow, quite large, rounded, very good flavour. Heavy cropper.
Zenith	Late ripening over a long period. Canes erect, long, thick. Fruits medium size, red, short, easily picked.

Raspberry flowers are loved by bumblebees

Autumn fruiting (primocane or everbearing) cultivars

Most of these start cropping at the beginning of September in England unless noted otherwise, and continue well into October/November or until the first frosts.

Spineless (or very nearly so) cultivars: Alkoopina, Amity, Autumn Cascade, Autumn Cygnet, Autumn Treasure, Favourite, Galante, Joan Squire, Polana, Polka, Princess, Red River, Redwing.

				August		September			October						
Cultivar	Vigour	Type	Spines	M	L	E	M	L	E	M	L	Colour	Flavour	Size	yield
Alkoopina			no			✓	✓	✓	✓	✓	✓	yellow		m-l	
Allgold/Golden Bliss		↑		✓	✓	✓	✓	✓	✓	✓	✓	yellow	mild	lge	m-h
Amity	vig		no			✓	✓	✓	✓	✓	✓	dark red		med	mod
August Red		↑			✓	✓	✓	✓	✓	✓	✓	red	exc	lge	
Autumn Bliss		↑		✓	✓	✓	✓	✓	✓	✓	✓	red	mild	lge	m-h
Autumn Britten						✓	✓	✓	✓	✓	✓	dark red		lge	m-h
Autumn Cascade			no		✓	✓	✓	✓	✓	✓	✓	dark red	good	m-l	mod
Autumn Cygnet			no		✓	✓	✓	✓	✓	✓	✓	red		med	m-h
Autumn Treasure	mod	↑	no		✓	✓	✓					red	good		
Bababerry	v.vig					✓	✓	✓	✓	✓	✓	red	good	lge	
Bogong						✓	✓	✓	✓	✓	✓	red	exc	lge	high
Dinkham		↑		✓	✓	✓	✓	✓	✓	✓	✓	dark red	v.good	med	
Double Delight		↑			✓	✓	✓	✓	✓	✓	✓	red	good	s-m	mod
Durham	vig				✓	✓	✓	✓	✓	✓	✓	red	good	med	
Erika	vig	↗			✓	✓	✓	✓	✓	✓	✓	red	good	lge	
Fallbrook		↗				✓	✓	✓	✓	✓	✓	red		s-m	
Fallgold	mod					✓	✓	✓	✓	✓	✓	yellow		lge	
Fall Red	vig	↑				✓	✓	✓	✓	✓	✓	red	exc	lge	
Favourite	vig	↑	no			✓	✓	✓	✓	✓	✓	red	good	lge	high
Galante		↑	no			✓	✓	✓	✓	✓	✓	red	good	lge	high
Golden Bliss		↑		✓	✓	✓	✓	✓	✓	✓	✓	yellow	mild	lge	m-h
Golden Harvest	vig					✓	✓	✓	✓	✓	✓	yellow	good	m-l	m-h
Golden Summit					✓	✓	✓	✓	✓	✓	✓	yellow		med	high
Goldie	vig	↑				✓	✓	✓	✓	✓	✓		mild	med	

				August		September			October						
Cultivar	Vigour	Type	Spines	M	L	E	M	L	E	M	L	Colour	Flavour	Size	yield
Hailsham	vig	↑				✓	✓	✓	✓	✓	✓	red	v.good	lge	m-h
Heritage	vig	↑					✓	✓	✓	✓	✓	dark red	mild	med	
Himbo		↑				✓	✓	✓	✓	✓	✓	red	good	lge	
Hollins	mod					✓	✓	✓	✓	✓	✓	light red		med	
Indian Summer	vig					✓	✓	✓	✓	✓	✓	red		lge	
Joan J	mod		no			✓	✓	✓	✓	✓	✓	dark red	good	med	hgh
Joan Squire	vig		no			✓	✓	✓	✓	✓	✓	red	exc	lge	high
Jo Mello	mod					✓	✓	✓	✓	✓	✓	red		med	
Kiwigold	vig	↑				✓	✓	✓	✓	✓	✓	yellow	mild	med	
Latham	vig	↑				✓	✓	✓	✓	✓	✓	dark red	exc	lge	
Lord Lambourne	vig					✓	✓	✓	✓	✓	✓	gold		med	v.high
Nordic							✓	✓	✓	✓	✓		good	med	high
Oregon 10-30						✓	✓	✓	✓	✓	✓		good	med	
Perron's Red	vig	↑				✓	✓	✓	✓	✓	✓	red		lge	
Polana		↑	no		✓	✓	✓	✓	✓	✓	✓		good	med	
Polka	vig	↑				✓	✓	✓	✓	✓	✓	red	good	lge	
Princess			no	✓	✓	✓	✓	✓	✓	✓	✓	red	good	med	high
Red Everbearing						✓	✓	✓	✓	✓	✓		good	v.lge	
Red River			no		✓	✓	✓	✓	✓	✓	✓	red	good	med	
Redwing	vig		no		✓	✓	✓	✓	✓	✓	✓	dark red	good		m-h
Rossana	vig							✓	✓	✓	✓	red		med	
Ruby	mod					✓	✓	✓	✓	✓	✓	red	mild	v.lge	
Sceptre	vig					✓	✓	✓	✓	✓	✓	red	good	lge	high
September	vig			✓	✓	✓	✓	✓	✓	✓	✓	red		m-l	high
Southland	mod					✓	✓	✓	✓	✓	✓	red		med	
Stonehurst		↑		✓	✓	✓	✓	✓	✓	✓	✓	purple		med	high
Summit	vig				✓	✓	✓	✓	✓	✓	✓	red		s-m	high
Sweetbriar		↑				✓	✓	✓	✓	✓	✓	red		med	
Zeva	vig			✓	✓	✓	✓	✓	✓	✓	✓	dark red	v.good	v.lge	v.high

Alkoopina	Canes spineless. Fruits yellow, medium-large, firm, easily picked. Also crops on one-year-old canes.
Allgold	See Golden Bliss.
Amity	Canes vigorous, self-supporting, nearly spineless. Fruits medium sized, very firm, dark red, ripens a week before Heritage. Moderate bearing.
August Red	Canes erect, compact, productive. Fruits large, red, exc. flavour. Very hardy.
Autumn Bliss	Ripens mid-August onwards. Canes very prolific, fairly erect, moderate height, doesn't need much support. Fruits large, red, firm, mild flavour, easily picked. A good reliable cropper.
Autumn Britten	Fruits large, dark red, firm. High yielder.
Autumn Cascade	Ripens mid-late August. Canes spineless. Fruits medium-large, dark red, firm, good flavour. Moderate yielder.
Autumn Cygnet	Ripens late August. Canes spineless, self-supporting. Fruits medium sized, red, soft, uneven, easily harvested. Good cropper.
Autumn Treasure	Upright self-supporting variety, thornless canes and large fruits.
Bababerry	Canes extremely vigorous. Fruits large, red, good flavour. Needs a warm growing location; drought tolerant.
Bogong	Fruits large, red, firm, intense aromatic flavour, easily picked. High yielding.
Dinkham	Ripens from mid August. Canes upright, very productive. Fruits medium sized, dark red, very firm, very good flavour; easily picked.
Double Delight	Ripens from late August. Canes erect, thick, compact. Fruits small-medium sized, bright red, firm, good sweet-acid flavour. Moderate cropper.
Durham	Ripens late August. Canes vigorous, healthy, sturdy, compact. Fruits medium sized, firm, red, good flavour. Fruits both in summer and autumn; very hardy.
Erika	High yielding, large fruits of excellent flavour.
Fallbrook	Canes semi-erect. Fruit small-medium sized, bright red, sweet; ripens over a long period.
Fallgold	Canes moderately vigorous, productive. Fruits large, round, yellow, sweet, freeze well. Very hardy.
Fall Red	Canes vigorous, sturdy, upright. Fruits large, very firm, bright red, excellent flavour. Very hardy.
Favourite	Canes vigorous, erect, spineless. Fruits large, red, long, good flavour, keeps well. High yielding.
Galante	Canes prolific, very erect, spineless. Fruits large, red, good flavour, keeps well. A very heavy cropper.
Golden Bliss (Allgold)	Yellow-fruited sport of Autumn Bliss.
Golden Harvest	Canes vigorous, sturdy, sucker prolifically. Fruits medium-large, bright yellow, good quality. Good cropper.
Golden Summit	Ripens late August. Canes slightly spiny. Fruits medium sized, conic, firm, golden. Heavy cropper. Developed for machine harvesting. Tolerant of heavy soils.
Goldie	Canes vigorous, upright, sturdy, very productive, spread rapidly. Fruits medium sized, sweet, golden, very firm, mild flavour; hold well on canes when ripe. Fairly tolerant of heavy soils.
Hailsham	Canes vigorous, erect. Fruits large, round, bright red, very good flavour. Good cropper.
Heritage	Ripens from mid September. Canes vigorous, upright, sturdy, very productive, spread rapidly. Fruits medium sized, sweet, dark red, very firm, mild flavour; hold well on canes when ripe. Fairly tolerant of heavy soils.
Hollins	Canes moderately vigorous. Fruits medium sized, light red, easily picked. For warm winter areas; also crops on one-year-old canes.
Indian Summer	Canes vigorous, hardy, productive. Fruits large, conic, aromatic, crumbly, very sweet, bright red.
Joan J	Fruits on very young canes, sweet fruits of good flavour.
Joan Squire	Canes vigorous, spreading, spineless. Fruits large, firm, red, excellent flavour. Very productive.
Jo Mello	Canes moderately vigorous, sturdy, erect. Fruits medium size, bright red.
Kiwigold	Canes vigorous, upright, sturdy, very productive, spread rapidly. Fruits medium sized, conic, sweet, yellow, very firm, mild flavour; hold well on canes when ripe. Fairly tolerant of heavy soils.
Latham	Canes vigorous, upright, heavily productive. Fruits large, round, deep red, very firm, very good texture and aromatic flavour.
Lord Lambourne	Canes vigorous. Fruits medium size, golden-apricot colour, juicy, fairly sweet. Crops very heavily.
Nordic	Ripens from mid September. Fruits medium size, tough skinned, good quality. Very productive and hardy; also produces fruit on one-year old canes.
Oregon 10-30	Fruits medium sized, good quality. Bears fruit continuously through summer and autumn in warm areas (where it is adapted).

Perron's Red	Canes vigorous, numerous, fairly erect. Fruit large, conic, red, medium firm.
Polana	Ripens late August. Canes numerous, erect, scarce spines. Fruits medium size, compact, aromatic good flavour.
Polka	Polish selection, very heavy cropping with large fruits of good flavour. Virtually thornless, good disease resistance.
Princess	Ripens from mid-August. Canes with few spines. Fruits medium sized, red, good flavour. High yielding.
Red Everbearing	Early ripening. Fruits very large, good flavour.
Red River	Ripens late August. Canes short, stout, sparsely spined, very hardy. Fruits medium sized, glossy red, good sweet-acid flavour.
Redwing	Ripens from late August. Canes stout, vigorous, short spines. Fruits dark red, sweet, moderately firm, good flavour. Good cropper; good on heavy soils. Hardy.
Rossana	Ripens late September. Canes vigorous, of moderate height, productive. Fruits medium sized, conic, bright red, moderately firm. Quite hardy.
Ruby	Canes moderately vigorous and productive. Fruits very large, bright red, conical, firm, sweet, mild flavour, holds well when ripe.
Sceptre	Canes strong, self-supporting. Fruits large, red, crumbly, of good flavour, ripening September onwards; heavy cropping.
September	Ripens from mid August. Canes vigorous and numerous, need thinning. Fruits medium-large, rounded, bright red, sweet, sub-acid, small-seeded. Hardy, heavy bearer; good on dry sites.
Southland	Canes moderately vigorous, rapidly suckering. Fruits medium sized, conic, sweet, firm, bright red. Heavy cropper. Heat and drought resistant.
Stonehurst	Ripens from mid August. Canes upright. Fruits medium sized, reddish-purple, round, partly hidden by leaves but easily picked. Heavy yielder; also fruits on one-year-old canes.
Summit	Ripens late August. Canes vigorous, slightly spiny, strong laterals. Fruits small-medium sized, round, firm, red. Heavy cropper. Developed for machine harvesting. Tolerant of heavy soils.
Sweetbriar	Canes upright. Fruits medium sized, rose red, firm, conic, easily picked. Also fruits on one-year-old canes.
Zeva	Ripens from mid August. Canes vigorous though slow to establish, medium height. Fruits very large, conical, dark red, soft, crumbly, very good flavour. Very heavy cropper.

Cultivation

Raspberries need shelter from strong winds, which can damage fruiting laterals. A sunny position is optimum, although plants grow and crop well in light partial shade as long as the soil does not become too dry.

The optimum soil is well drained, retentive of moisture in summer, and slightly acid. Poorly drained clay soils and chalky soils are much less suitable.

Plants are usually planted in rows, which are 1.8m (6ft) apart, with plants spaced at 38cm (15ins) in the row. The canes should be planted shallowly about 5-7.5cm (2-3ins) deep, and roots spread out horizontally to encourage suckers. Over-deep planting inhibits suckering and production of new canes. In forest garden situations raspberries can be planted as clumps in any configuration, and allowed to sucker and move to their ideal preferred locations.

After planting, canes should be cut to a bud at 22-30cm (9-12ins) above soil level. If possible, mulch the row with a layer of organic material.

On exposed sites, canes must be supported to prevent wind damage to the canes and fruit, by using posts, canes or a post and wire system.

Established plants should also be kept weed-free by using organic mulches – hoeing can damage the shallow roots and suckers. Cultivation is not an alternative apart from very shallow hoeing, as cultivation will damage the roots of the plants.

Summer fruiting cultivars: as soon as fruiting is finished, it is normal to cut the old canes down to ground level (not leaving any stubs) to allow room for the new young canes which will crop the next year. However if you are growing in a less intensive way, cane removal is less necessary: fruiting canes will die the following winter, and the following year will break and compost by themselves, or can easily be broken off if in the way. Suckers may need controlling.

Autumn fruiting cultivars: all canes should be cut down to ground level in late winter. During the summer, sucker removal may be required.

Raspberries need lots of potash for fruiting and some nitrogen for cane production. For sustainable growers, there will often be enough nitrogen from mulches etc. The potash is easiest supplied by mulching raspberry rows with high potash leaves,

Raspberry bush

e.g. comfrey or with wood ash.

Raspberries flower late in the spring, and thus usually escape frost damage. Pollination is by insects (including bees and flies); self-pollination can also occur. All raspberries are self-fertile.

Fruit should be picked when they are dry and well coloured but still firm. Raspberries have one of the highest respiration rates of any fruit, and are very perishable. They start cropping quickly and give good yields. Established plants on average yield 2-3kg per metre row (1.5-2lb per foot row for summer fruiting varieties;,0.6kg per metre row (0.5lb per foot row) for autumn fruiting varieties.

Raspberries are susceptible to many virus diseases carried by aphids (see below) and in unsustainable monocultures are likely to have a cropping life of only 10 years before becoming unproductive. In sustainable systems where there are lots of aphid predators, productive life can be much longer.

Raspberry cultivars are easily propagated by digging up suckers – such canes should be healthy with no sign of leaf discolouring indicating virus diseases. This method should only be used for a few years after planting healthy stock.

Plants can be grown from seed, though cultivars will not come true as most are quite highly bred. Seeds require cold stratification and can be sown in early autumn or stratified over winter and sown in spring.

Pests and diseases

Viruses: These are usually spread by aphids (above ground) or nematodes (below ground), and sometimes by pollen. Typical symptoms are pale green or yellowish patterns, mottling or blotching on leaves, which may be distorted. Fruiting usually reduces significantly.

Cane blight (*Leptosphaeria coniothyrium*): A disease of wounds, causing withering of leaves and dieback of fruiting canes through infection at ground level; rarely causing serious damage.

Spur blight (*Didymella applanata*): Causes lesions on canes, then leaves can brown and shrivel. The buds in the infected area are frequently killed or weakened but the cane itself remains alive. Can be serious in wet springs, where plants are overcrowded or where nitrogen application is too high.

Cane spot or anthracnose (*Elsinoe veneta*): Sometimes a serious disease of black and purple raspberries, and susceptible red raspberries. Sunken spots appear on canes, initially purple then turning grey; these enlarge, crack and girdle canes, sometimes killing them; fruit can be infected and distorted, and a tip dieback is also common.

With all these diseases, affected canes should be removed and burnt or buried; canes should be thinned to allow for good air access; and light levels should be improved if possible by pruning or removing overhanging branches, shrubs etc.

Raspberry beetle (*Byturus tomentosus*): The most serious pest in Europe, where it is responsible for 'maggoty' fruit. The raspberry fruitworm (*B. unicolor*) causes similar damage in North America. Female beetles, 5mm long and brownish, lay their eggs in the flowers and the young grub tunnel into fruit, eating as they go. When fully grown, grubs drop to the soil and pupate before hatching into adults that hibernate in the soil over winter. Growing in a diverse system usually means there are plenty of predators around and the problem remains minor.

Related species

Blackberry (p.22).

REDCURRANT / WHITECURRANT, *Ribes rubrum*

Zone 6, H6
Deciduous
Edible fruit

Origin and history

Cultivated varieties of redcurrants were first mentioned in Germany in the early fifteenth century; by the late sixteenth century they were commonly grown in Holland and had appeared in Britain where they soon became common in cottage gardens. By the nineteenth century, new varieties were being bred in North America. Their popularity remains high in Holland, where many of the recent varieties have been bred.

Commercial quantities of redcurrants are grown in Russia, Scandinavia and Eastern Europe. Nearly all are used for processing, for the fruit handle badly and are difficult to market fresh in good condition. Whitecurrants, on the other hand, are only grown by amateurs as their yields are lower.

Description

The redcurrant is a deciduous shrub found in hedges and woods throughout Northern Europe. Cultivars are essentially drawn from three wild species, *Ribes rubrum* from Northern Europe to Siberia, *Ribes sativum* (synonym *R. vulgare*) from temperate Western Europe, and *Ribes petraeum* from mountainous areas of Europe and North Africa. Other minor *Ribes* species have also been involved in breeding new cultivars.

These three species differ slightly from each other: *R. rubrum* is an erect shrub about 1m (3ft) tall; *R. sativum* is spreading, with drooping flower trusses, and often with brittle branches which break in exposed locations, and is the most productive of the three, with the largest fruit; while *R. petraeum* is a vigorous shrub with large buds, late flowering, less productive and has the tartest fruit. Older varieties are often derived purely from one of these species, while most newer varieties are hybrids. A further species, *R. multiflorum* from Eastern Europe, has been used in cross-breeding in recent years: this is late flowering and has resistance to leaf spot.

In general, redcurrant cultivars grow to about 1.5-2m (5-7ft) high – occasionally twice that – and unlike the blackcurrant, their maple-like, lobed, mid-green leaves lack glands and are not strong smelling when rubbed. Inconspicuous white flowers in early spring (April-May) are followed by 5-15mm (0.2-0.6ins) round fruit; the fruits are usually red, but sometimes white or yellowish-white. Fruits are borne in bunches (strigs) from spurs of branches aged 1-10 years, and ripen 70-100 days after flowering. Whitecurrants are the same species, simply with white or yellowish-white fruit which tend to be borne less abundantly

Redcurrant

than red varieties. Red and whitecurrants are fairly long-lived (25 years plus).

Uses

Ripe fruit is great raw; although not usually overly sweet, they are rarely tart enough to be considered as lemon juice substitutes. They are also good cooked in tarts, pies and puddings.

Redcurrants make excellent preserves, including jams and jellies; they can be mixed with other fruit. They are high in pectin so jams/jellies containing them set well. Although jellies were always traditionally made, jams are equally good and the small seeds do not detract from the final product.

The fruits are excellent for home wine making, and also freeze well.

The seeds, like those of blackcurrants, yield a valuable oil (gamma-linoleic acid) which is extracted from dried and ground residues left from production of juices, preserves etc. The refined oil is a valuable ingredient in cosmetic, dermatological, dietetic and pharmaceutical preparations.

The leaves can be used to dye yellow and the fruit pink to black.

Varieties/Cultivars

There are many cultivars of red and whitecurrants, although a relatively small selection are available commercially. Despite the differences in bush habit and season of ripening, there is in practice little difference between fruit of different varieties in terms of taste and acidity. Whitecurrants generally give lower yields compared with redcurrants, and these white-fruited varieties are reputed to have lower vitamin C levels. There are also a few 'pinkcurrant' varieties.

Redcurrants

Cascade	Early season. Fruit large, slightly sweet, small strigs.
Cherry	Early season. Fruit very large, deep red; good crops on vigorous bushes.
Earliest of Fourlands	Large, bright red, juicy fruit in long strigs, ripening very early. Upright vigorous bush, very productive. Resists leaf spot. Leafs out early in spring, flowers mid season.
Fay's Prolific	(Synonyms Chenonceau, Comet, Fay, Grand Ruby, Wilder) North American cultivar, a sprawling bush of moderate habit with brittle branches, susceptible to leaf spot. Flowers early; fruit large, dark red, thick skinned, easy to pick on loose medium-long strigs, early ripening with excellent sweet flavour; good yields. Leafs out mid season.
Jonkheer Van Tets	A leading Dutch cultivar, a seedling of Fay's Prolific. Dark red large fruit, good flavour, easy to pick on long trusses; thin skinned so may split in wet weather; heavy yields. Early ripening. Upright, vigorous growth, somewhat brittle branches, mildew and aphid resistant, early flowering.

Ripe redcurrants

Junifer	Very early season. Early flowering, heavy cropper. May be prone to frost damage.
Laxton's No.1	Early-mid season. Heavy crops of bright red, medium-large sized fruit borne in long bunches, easily picked, good raw; good flavour, small seeds. Early-mid season ripening; flowers late so avoid frosts. Susceptible to leaf spot. Vigorous, upright and slightly spreading bush, early to leaf out. A reliable cropper.
Raby Castle	Fruit small-medium sized, on moderate length trusses, hangs well; moderate to heavy yields, late ripening. Small, compact bush, leafs out mid-season, flowers late; susceptible to mildew; very cold hardy.
Red Dutch	Very old cultivar, very cold hardy and resistant to leaf spot. Moderately productive, fruit small, good flavour, on long strigs.
Red Lake	Mid season. American cultivar now popular in Europe. Very large, dark red, juicy fruit of good flavour with thickish skins on long strigs, easily picked; heavy cropper, fruit hangs well when ripe, seeds moderately large. Upright and moderately vigorous growth. Mid season ripening, flowers late so avoid frosts. Very cold hardy.
Redstart	(Synonym Malling Redstart) Medium sized fruit produced on moderate length strigs; good acid flavour. A heavy, reliable cropper; moderately vigorous, upright with compact growth; late ripening, mid-season flowering. Sometimes grown as a stooled bush.
Rolan	Mid season. Large fruit borne on long strigs.
Rondom	Late season. A leading Dutch cultivar. Late flowering; fruit medium sized, red, acid, not very juicy, firm skinned, easy to pick, hangs well on moderate length trusses. Resists leaf spot and mildew. Late season. Very productive (heavy yields) and hardy; strong branches, upright, vigorous.
Rovada	Cross of Fay X Heinemann's Röte Spätlese. Late to very late ripening. Heavy crops of large fruit on long strigs.
Stanza	Good flavoured, medium to large, deep red, firm fruit, heavy cropper; short trusses but easy to pick. Mid to late season, late flowering. Vigorous bush.
Wilson's Long Bunch	Crimson fruit, medium sized, good flavour, in medium-long strigs. Semi-erect, slightly sprawling bush of moderate vigour, low to moderate yielding, susceptible to leaf spot and mildew. Late to leaf out, very late flowering and ripening.

Pinkcurrants

Pinkcurrants

Rosa Hollandische	(Synonym: Hollande Rose) Fruit reddish-pink. Vigorous bush, moderately productive.
Rosetta	Mid season. Medium sized fruit borne on long strigs.

Whitecurrants

Blanka	Late season. Very heavy cropping, ripening in August.
Weisse Langtraubige	Mid season. Fruit medium to large, aromatic, good flavour.
White Dutch	Very old cultivar. Mid season. A sprawling bush, fruit small, milky-yellow, excellent flavour on medium strigs. Moderate yields, bush of moderate vigour.
White Grape	Medium to large, creamy-white fruit of good flavour in long strigs; moderate yields. Mid season ripening. Spreading bush of moderate vigour, cold hardy.
White Pearl	Large yellowish-white fruit borne in large strigs. Mid season. Moderate vigour but light yielding.
White Transparent	(Synonym Transparent) Large, transparent yellowish, rather acid fruit on long strigs; light to moderate yields, mid to late ripening. Strong, vigorous, upright bush.
White Versailles	Large, pale yellow fruit with a good sweet flavour on medium length strigs. Moderate yields. Early to mid season ripening. Large, vigorous, upright bush.

Ripe whitecurrants

It is much easier and quicker to pick whole bunches (strigs) of fruit rather than individual currants, though there may be a few which are unripe and cannot be used. Don't pick the fruit immediately they have turned red, but wait a few days for the full flavour to develop. Ripe fruit hangs well on bushes, for two weeks or more. The fruits are easier to pick if their strigs have clear lengths at the bases – some cultivars are noted for this habit. Machine harvesting is used for large plantations in Europe.

Ripe redcurrants are attractive to birds, and plants may need to be netted to protect the ripening crop.

Cultivation

Redcurrants thrive in a wide range of soils, but they do like shelter from strong winds (some varieties have brittle branches). They are very tolerant of shade, being woodland plants, and continue to fruit well in semi-shade. Soil pH should be acid to neutral (5.5-7.0), and good drainage is important.

Plants are usually grown as multistemmed bushes, planted about 1.2-1.8m (4-6ft) apart, although they can be grown as cordons or fans: cordons are planted at 38-45cm (15-18ins) apart and fans at 1m (3ft) apart. Cordons and fans grow well on north walls, fruiting very well there in conditions of only 15% of normal light conditions. Fruit ripening is delayed in such conditions by up to a week or two after the same variety in sunny conditions, and also may be less well coloured and flavoured (less sweet).

Redcurrants are not heavy feeders and their main requirement is for sufficient potassium to maintain good flowering and thus fruiting. Using comfrey or wood ash can achieve this in sustainable systems.

Most redcurrants have self-fertile flowers, though a few cultivars set more fruit when cross-pollinated. Bees aid in pollination and should be encouraged where possible; flies also pollinate.

Pruning is less essential than many other fruit bushes because the shoots continue to fruit for many years. Established bushes should be pruned lightly, by removing thin and overcrowded branches.

Average yields from established bushes are about 4-6kg (9-13lb) per year, with cordons producing about 0.5-1kg (1-2lb) per plant per year.

Varieties are propagated by hardwood cuttings. These are taken over winter (best in November), and should consist of 25-30cm (10-12ins) cuttings of new growth, preferably about 1cm thick.

Redcurrants are one of the most suitable of all the common bush fruit to use in agroforestry systems in the understorey. They thrive in much poorer soils than most fruit, require less inputs, continue to fruit well in low light conditions and are long-lived.

Pests and diseases

The only serious pest is that of birds eating the ripe fruit, especially pigeons and blackbirds. Netting may be required to exclude them.

Aphids (notably the redcurrant blister aphid, *Cryptomyzus ribis*) are common in spring when they cause new leaves to blister and curl and stunt new growth. Bushes are rarely damaged, and in sustainable systems where predator-attracting plants are grown, there are no problems.

Related species

Blackcurrant (p.28).

ROSES, *Rosa* species

Zones 2-9, H4-7
Deciduous (most)
Edible fruit, Flowers for perfumery, cut flowers etc., Bee plants

Origin and history

Members of the Rosaceae family have long been used for food, perfumery and medicine. Rose hips, the fruit of rose species, are used in many countries, being a rich source of vitamins and minerals, and can be consumed in many food products including jams, jellies, marmalades, teas, powders, baked goods, ice creams, yoghurts, candies, pulps, nectars, juices, wines, liqueurs etc.

Description

A large family of mainly deciduous shrubs, sometimes climbing or trailing, with spiny branches, large five-petalled flowers and reddish fruit. Many ornamental forms have been bred all over the world.

Uses

All rose fruit, called hips, are edible, but the size and quality varies widely between species. Hips contain inedible seeds and hairs in the centre, so must be utilised or processed in a way that removes these.

The larger-fruited species, for example *Rosa rugosa*, have hips large enough that the ripe flesh can be eaten raw from around the core of seeds and hairs, with the fruit flesh having a very good sweet flavour.

The form of vitamin C in rose hips is very stable even through cooking processes. In some countries, like the UK, traditionally a syrup was made from rose hips, to use as a vitamin C-rich tonic. Rose hips can also be dried and the dried fruit (and powder made from them) used for making herb teas.

Rose water (usually made by steeping petals in water) is widely used in Middle Eastern and South Asian cuisine. The petals themselves are also used as a food flavouring.

Rose hip seed oil is extracted and used in some skin care products. Several species of rose are grown commercially for the flower petals, from which essential oils are distilled and used in perfumery, toiletries, aromatherapy etc. The main species used are Damask rose (*R.* x *damascena*) and *R.* x *centifolia*. Others are grown commercially for the cut flower crops.

Rosa rugosa is a very good soil stabiliser, with a suckering root system, though it can spread with great vigour on well-drained sandy soils. Sometimes used as a dune stabiliser, but nowadays more regarded as a pest along coastlines because of its spiny dead branches. On more normal soils it is not invasive and can make a very useful low hedge at 0.5m (1ft 7ins) high or so.

All roses are also very good bee plants.

Rosa rugosa, apple rose

Varieties/Cultivars

The principal selection criteria for efficient harvesting and processing of fruit are usually considered to be (1) fresh fruit weight – i.e. the larger the better; and (2) the percentage of dry peel or the ratio of peel to seed mass. Although there is plentiful information on the former, there is rather little on the latter. All rose hips can be utilised, though of course there are bound to be flavour and vitamin/mineral compositions variations. The following table lists a selection of species, including most with the very largest fruit.

The flowers of *Rosa rugosa* are one of those used commercially

Species	Origin	Common name	Max height (m)	H.zn	RHS	Fruit
R. acicularis	North temperate regions	Prickly rose	1	2	H7	15mm (0.6ins) long
R. arkansana	USA	Low prairie rose	1	4-5	H7	15mm (0.6ins)
R. arvensis	Europe	Field rose	2	6	H6	6-20mm long (0.2-0.7ins)
R. banksiae	China	Banks' rose, Banksia rose	5+	7	H6	6mm (0.2ins)
R. blanda	Eastern North America	Meadow rose, Labrador rose	2	2	H7	10mm (0.4ins)
R. bracteata	China, Taiwan	Macartney rose	3+	7	H6	35mm (1.3ins) diameter
R. britzensis	Kurdistan		3	6	H6	to 30mm (1.1ins) long
R. californica	California		3	5-6	H6	10-15mm (0.4-0.6ins)
R. canina	Europe	Dog rose, Doghip	3+	3	H7	12mm (0.5ins)
R. carolina	Eastern North America	Carolina rose, Pasture rose	1.5	4-5	H7	
R. caudata	Western China		4	6	H6	20-25mm long (0.7-0.9ins)
R. centifolia	China	Cabbage rose, Holland rose	2	5	H7	12mm (0.5ins)
R. chinensis	China	China rose	1	7	H6	
R. coriifolia	Europe-Asia		1.5	5	H7	
R. corymbifera	Europe-Asia		3	6	H6	12-20mm (0.5-0.7ins)
R. cymosa	China			8	H4	
R. damascena	Asia minor	Damask rose	2	4-5	H7	25mm long (0.9ins)
R. dumalis	Europe-Asia		2	4-5	H7	
R. eglanteria	Europe, Asia	Sweet briar, Eglantine	2	6	H6	10-20mm (0.4-0.7ins)
R. foetida	Southwest Asia	Austrian briar	1.5	4	H7	12mm (0.5ins)
R. gallica	Central Europe	French rose, Apothecary rose	1.5	5-6	H6	12mm (0.5ins)
R. gigantea	Southwest China	Manipur wild tea rose	10	9	H4	
R. gymnocarpa	Western North America	Wood rose	3	6	H6	6-10mm (0.2-0.4ins)
R. hardii	(Hybrid)		2	8	H4	
R. hemsleyana	China		2	6	H6	

Species	Origin	Common name	Max height (m)	H.zn	RHS	Fruit
R. highdownensis	(Hybrid)		3	6	H6	
R. laevigata	China, Taiwan	Cherokee rose	5+	7	H6	18mm (0.7ins)
R. luciae	Japan, China, Korea			7	H6	6mm (0.2ins)
R. macrophylla	Himalaya		4	7	H6	25-30mm (0.9-1.1ins) long
R. majalis	Europe, Asia	Cinnamon rose	3	6	H6	10-15mm (0.4-0.6ins)
R. manca	Western North America					
R. micrantha	Europe, Asia		3.5	6	H6	12-18mm (0.5-0.7ins)
R. moschata	Asia minor	Musk rose	4	6-7	H6	
R. moyesii	Western China	Moyes rose	3	5-6	H6	50-60mm (1.9-2.3ins) long
R. multiflora	Japan, Korea		3	5	H7	6mm (0.2ins)
R. nitida	Eastern North America		1	3-4	H7	10mm (0.4ins)
R. nutkana	Western North America	Ash leaved rose, Nootka rose	2+	4	H7	15-20mm (0.6-0.7ins)
R. oxyodon	Eastern Caucasus		2	6	H6	35mm (1.3ins) long
R. paulii	(Hybrid)			4	H7	
R. pimpinellifolia	Europe, Asia	Scotch rose, Burnet rose	1	4-5	H7	
R. pisocarpa	Western North America	Mortar rose	2.5	6	H6	8mm (0.3ins)
R. roxburghii	China	Burr rose, Chestnut rose	2.5	5-6	H6	30-40mm (1.1-1.5ins)
R. rugosa	North China, Japan, Korea	Ramanas rose, Rugosa rose	2.5	2	H7	25mm+ (0.9ins+)
R. sericea	Nepal		2.5	6-7	H6	8-15mm (0.3-0.6ins)
R. setipoda	Central China		3	6	H6	25-75mm (0.9-2.9ins)
R. sherardii	Europe		2	6	H6	12-20mm (0.5-0.7ins)
R. spinulifolia	(Hybrid)		3	6	H6	
R. sweginzowii	China		5	6	H6	to 25mm (0.9ins) long
R. tomentosa	Europe		3	6	H6	18-25mm (0.7-0.9ins)
R. villosa	Central/Southern Europe	Apple rose, Soft-leaved rose	2	5-6	H6	25mm (0.9ins)
R. virginiana	Eastern North America	Virginia rose	1.5	3-4	H7	
R. webbiana	Himalayas		2	6	H6	15-25mm (0.6-0.9ins)
R. wichuriana	Japan, Korea, China	Memorial rose		5-6	H6	15mm (0.6ins)
R. wintoniensis	(Hybrid)		2	6	H6	
R. woodsii	Central and Western North America	Wood's rose	2	4	H7	10mm (0.4ins)

Properties and health benefits of rose hips

In general, the importance of rose hips in nutrition comes from their vitamin content since they contain C, P, B1, B2, E, K and U vitamins, and are very rich in calcium, phosphorus and potassium.

More specifically, they have the highest vitamin C content (417-3062mg/100g) amongst fruit and vegetables, with light-coloured mature fruit having a higher content than dark-coloured hips. Rose hip pulp is used for vitamin C enrichment of some fruit and vegetable juices. Vitamin C is important in collagen synthesis, boosts the immune system against common cold and flu, strengthens arteries along with polyphenols, potentially lowers the risk of cancer due to antioxidant properties, helps dietary iron to function in the body, works in adrenaline synthesis and lowers blood cholesterol.

Minerals also play an important role in human metabolism and health. Calcium is necessary for healthy bones and teeth and potassium is needed to maintain the acid-base balance of body fluids and in metabolism regulation. Rose hip pulp contains 940-1380 ppm calcium, 3370-9340 ppm phosphorus, 7950 ppm potassium and 560-1240 ppm magnesium.

Rose hips contain high levels of nine carotenoids including beta-carotene, which is red in colour but is known to produce yellow colours in various foods; since it does not change the flavour or taste of the food, it has the potential for being used as a natural food colourant. Beta-carotene also has provitamin A activity and can be used for vitamin A enrichment of foods. Because carotenoids have high antioxidant activity, they are capable of protecting components in food including fruit from oxidation. They exert this antioxidant activity by stopping free radical chain reactions and by quenching singlet oxygen. Relatively high levels of the carotenoid lycopene have been reported in rose hips, which could contribute to the prevention of cardiovascular diseases and cancer.

The flavonoids in rose hips act as antioxidants on free radicals and prevent lipid peroxidation (which is implicated in arteriosclerosis, cancer and chronic inflammations). Bioflavonoids having vitamin P properties have been found in rose hips at levels of 1100-3320mg/100g fruit. A recent survey of a variety of dietary plants found that rose hips showed the highest total antioxidant properties.

Rose hips are a rich source of phenolic compounds, with some varieties having as much as 3200-4900mg/100g total phenolics. Rose hips improve the flavour of wine significantly and contribute with a high level of phenolic compounds.

Rose hips are also a good source of pectin. Pectin is an important hydrocolloid in the food industry and is used to improve consistency since it acts as a thickening agent. Its haemostatic, antiseptic and cell renewal properties allow for its usage in treatments of cuts and burns, and it can be safely given to patients with ulcers due to its anti-inflammatory properties, ability to lower blood cholesterol, and binding capabilities in metal poisoning.

Malic, citric and acetic acids impart the characteristic flavour of rose hips, which are also a good source of easily digestible carbohydrates (7.55-21.29% reducing sugars, 1.08-2.1% saccharose and 8.68-22.44% total sugars).

Rose hips are not a rich source of protein but the pollen of *Rosa laxa* has been found to contain a total of 18 amino acids, of which 15 are free and at least eight are essential amino acids. Glutamic acid makes up 13-14.6% of the total amino acids, and is known to play an important role in cerebral tissues during biochemical metabolism, and is involved in the synthesis of physiologically active substances and acid detoxification.

Seed oils have been proven to be more stable when they contain natural vitamin A and C, carotenoids and flavonoids. Seed oil extracted from roses has been found to contain unsaturated fatty acids, and can be used efficiently against contact dermatitis and in food products. Rose seed oil contains approximately 50% linoleic, 20% arachodonic and 19% oleic acids, and thus has a higher oxidative stability than other unsaturated oils. This oil could conceivably be used as a gourmet oil, adding a special flavour to food products.

Two recent clinical studies on rose hips have been reported. In the first, a probiotic drink containing *Lactobacillus plantarum*, fermented oats and rose hips was fed to volunteers. An increase in the amount of short-chain fatty acids was observed – these fatty acids lower the colonic pH and control proliferation of pathogens and colon cancer. The second study involved patients diagnosed with osteoarthritis. When these patients were fed a standardised rose hip powder (prepared from the hips and seeds of *Rosa canina* fruit), inhibition of leukocyte functions that cause cell injury in osteoarthritis was observed along with a reduction of the pain level in 64% of patients.

Cultivation

Rose bushes require relatively low levels of maintenance and grow in most regions.

In many areas of the world, rose hips are still harvested by hand for commercial trade, for example in Chile, where about 6,800 tonnes of dried rose hips are exported annually, mainly to Germany and other European countries. The species harvested in Chile are mainly *Rosa canina*, *R. moschata* and *R. rubiginosa*, with most fruit harvested from wild plants, using homemade harvesting tools called 'rasquetas' (literally 'scratcher'). An adult can harvest up to 100kg per day. Trucks collect the fruit and take them to processing factories, where the hips are dried, and then the fruit flesh is separated from the seeds. The seeds are used as energy for the drying and for the extraction of seed oil.

Recent field trials in Chile have used dog rose (*Rosa rubiginosa*). The highest yields, both for irrigated and non-irrigated fields, were obtained with plants set out at 3 x 0.75m (10ft x 2.5ft), i.e. 4,444 plants per ha. For this species, expected yields are: 0.1-0.2kg (3.5-7oz) fruit/plant in the second year; 1-1.5kg (2.2-3.3lbs) fruit/plant in the third year; 3kg (6.6lbs) fruit/plant in the fourth year.

Work was carried out in Sweden in the 1990s to develop techniques for commercial scale production, with some 130 ha (325 acres) of plantations established, mainly using selections of *Rosa dumalis* and *R. rubiginosa*.

Swedish research recommends the rose plants being planted 0.7m (28ins) apart in the row, with rows 3-4m (10-13ft) apart for mechanical harvesting. The close plants in rows results in them supporting each other. Early ripening cultivars (in August) are less damaged, since the plants can grow and recover after harvesting, whereas later ripening cultivars suffer from winter damage in Sweden. Young plants are vulnerable to browse damage from rabbits and deer, so plantings must be protected for the first few years. Good weed control, however, is obtained by grazing cows without damage to plants when they are 2-3 years old.

Dog rose (*Rosa canina*)

High labour costs and relatively low prices for the unprocessed rose hips makes it necessary to use mechanical harvesting for commercial rose hip production in Sweden. Mechanical harvesters use the 'shake and catch' method similar to that used for other small fruit.

Plants start to fruit in the second year after planting. The first mechanical harvest is made 3-4 years after planting. Highest yields are from plants 4-6 years old.

Every second year, the sides and top of the bushes should be pruned with a tractor-mounted hedge trimmer (or on a smaller scale with a hand operated hedge trimmer) to ensure a suitable plant shape. Plants that have become too large or too old to yield properly can be rejuvenated by cutting back to 5-10cm (2-4ins) above the ground. Rose hip plantations can thus have a good longevity.

With mechanical harvesting, the power needed to separate the rose hips from the branches is much higher than that needed for blackcurrants. Unharvested rose hips can remain on the branches in the following season and can seriously decrease the quality of the new harvest.

Storage of hips

Recent studies have shown that ambient air-drying, also drying at 50°C (122°F) and 75°C (167°F) all preserve the antioxidant activity in rose hips at a high level. Boiling the hips in water for 2-10 minutes (also microwaving for two minutes) also preserves the antioxidant activity at a high level.

Vitamin C levels in hips start to fall as soon as the hips are harvested, and they should be processed for storage or utilisation within a few hours if possible.

Fruit on sweet briar (*Rosa rubiginosa*)

Pests and diseases

In Sweden, the most severe pest is the rose fruit fly (*Rhagoletis alternata*), which is a common tephritid fly in Central Europe, and it damages the fruit of wild and cultivated *Rosa* species. The rose fruit fly can cause serious damage in plantations. Adults emerge from June to August; females then lay an egg under the skin of a nearly ripe rose hip. The egg hatches into a larva which eats within the rose hip.

In commercial fields, the apple blossom weevil (*Anthonomus rubi*) may cause damage to flowers. The larvae nip the flowers which can reduce fruit yields.

Wild and ornamental roses are affected by the same fungal diseases, one of the most serious being black spot caused by *Diplocarpon rosae* and characterised by black spots on the leaves. Infected leaves produce large quantities of ethylene and the plants defoliate. Powdery mildew (*Sphaerotheca pannosa*) can reduce flower production and cause a weakening of plants; it can also attack the fruit. Leaf spot (*Sphaceloma rosarum*) causes a serious spotting of leaves, causing them to yellow and sometimes defoliate. Rust is caused by the genus *Phragmidium* and attacks the leaves, stems and fruit, but is not usually very serious.

SALTBUSH, *Atriplex* species

Zones 7–8, H4–5
Evergreen
Edible leaves

Origin and history

A family of annuals, perennials and shrubs from many parts of the world, normally from dry, sandy seashore or desert environments. The name saltbush refers to the fact that members of this family accumulate and store salt in their leaves.

The saltbushes referred to below are grey-leaved shrubs from the Mediterranean and North America, tolerant of high salinity or alkalinity and drought. Although not the hardiest of plants, they have numerous uses including edible ones.

Description

The *Atriplex* shrubs have silvery alternate leaves and whitish small flowers. Some species are dioecious.

Uses

These shrubs all have edible salty leaves – excellent in salads.

Mediterranean saltbush (*Atriplex halimus*)

Leaves of *Atriplex halimus*

Varieties/Cultivars

Atriplex canescens – Saltbush, grey sage brush

Evergreen dioecious shrub to 2m (6ft) high from western North America (Washington to Texas, Mexico). Narrow grey leaves up to 5cm (2ins) long. Hardy to zone 7 / H5.

Can be used for hedging in mild coastal gardens. *A. canescens* is markedly resistant to burning and can be used as a firebreak in dry climates where bush fires can be a risk.

The leaves are edible – raw or cooked, with a salty tang. Quite good, and can be harvested all year (lightly in winter).

The seeds can be eaten – ground into a flour and cooked. Male and female plants are needed for seed production. Seeds are about 6 x 4mm in size.

Atriplex confertifolia – Shadscale

Evergreen dioecious spiny shrub to 1m (3ft) high, sometimes more, from western North America. Hardy to zone 7 / H5.

The leaves are edible – raw or cooked, with a salty tang.

The seeds can be eaten – ground into a flour and cooked. Male and female plants are needed for seed production.

Atriplex halimus – Mediterranean saltbush, Sea orach

Evergreen grey-leaved shrub to 2.5m (8ft) high from Southern Europe, found on cliffs and salt marshes. Leaves less narrow than on *A. canescens*. Hardy to zone 8 / H4.

Can be used for hedging in mild coastal gardens. It is also a sand dune stabiliser and grazing animals relish the foliage.

Edible leaves – raw or cooked – an excellent edible leaf with a salty tang. Can be used all year (lightly harvested in winter).

The seeds can be eaten – ground into a flour and cooked. Seeds are about 4 x 3mm in size.

Atriplex lentiformis – Quail bush

Evergreen shrub 1-3m (3-10ft) high, sometimes more, from southwestern North America. Hardy to zone 8 / H4.

The leaves are edible – raw or cooked – with a salty tang.

The seeds can be eaten – ground into a flour and cooked.

Cultivation

These species are very tolerant of wind, salt spray, alkaline soils and dry soils. They demand full sun and grow fine in most well-drained soils. In a damp climate like the UK, good drainage is essential, as waterlogging can kill them. They dislike too much fertility. Any frost-damaged growth should be cut back in spring. Bushiness is likely to be encouraged if young shoots are pinched out for harvest.

The leaves themselves are not very large so harvesting can be slow – if whole branches are stripped with your hand then leaves will not usually regrow, so it is better to prune off longer branches and strip them when leaves are wanted.

Propagate by seed (not dormant but slow germinating) or cuttings in summer: half-ripe cuttings in July/August work well. Also cuttings of mature wood in November/December.

SASKATOON, *Amelanchier alnifolia*

Zone 2, H7
Deciduous
Edible fruit

Origin and history

The Amelanchiers are a group of some 25 deciduous shrubs or small trees with edible fruit, most originating from North America. Saskatoon (also known as regent serviceberry, western serviceberry, alder leaved serviceberry – and a European company has recently patented the name 'Greatberry' for it) is the most promising of the species for fruit production, and decades of breeding work in Canada has led to a good selection of varieties with larger fruit and heavier yields.

Description

Saskatoons are very hardy and adaptable plants, found in the wild at woodland edges, stream banks and in hedges. They are slender upright plants, with slender branchlets. The size varies with variety, from 2-5m (6-16ft) high. May sucker a little but not nearly as much as some of the other Amelanchier species.

Leaves are simple, alternate, oval and turn red in the autumn before they fall.

Showy white flowers are borne on the previous year's growth, opening around the same time as the leaves unfold in April and May. Pollination is via bees and other insects; plants are self-fertile.

Fruits are blueberry-like, 10-18mm (0.25-0.75ins) across, rounded, purple-black, sweet and juicy with low acidity, borne in clusters of 6-12. The seed size is relatively large. In warm climates, may dry on the plant into 'raisins'. Fruit tends to ripen evenly and the crop can usually be picked all at once.

Uses

Fruits of saskatoons are edible: sweet and juicy, good to eat raw or cooked. Fruits contain some 10% sugars and are good sources of potassium, magnesium, manganese, iron and calcium. Fruit can also be used in jams, fruit leathers and for making wine.

The nutrient content of the fresh fruit per 100g is:

Energy	85 cal	Potassium	162mg
Fibre	5.9g	Sodium	0.5mg
Sugars, total	11.4g	Vitamin C	3.6mg
Calcium	42mg	Vitamin A	11 IU
Magnesium	24mg	Vitamin E	1.1mg
Iron	1mg	Folate	4.6mcg
Manganese	1.4mg	Riboflavin	3.5mg

Saskatoon flowering in spring

It is a good hedging plant, providing good bee forage in the early spring, and the fruits are attractive to birds and other wildlife.

Varieties/Cultivars

Although most of these originate from North America, some breeding work has taken place in Eastern Europe so some originate from these programmes.

Beaverlodge	Large, juicy fruit, good flavour.
Bluemoon	Ukranian selection, grows 2.5m (8ft) high. Fruit 12mm (0.5ins) across, sweet, juicy.
Bluff	Shrub to 5m high, moderately suckering. Fruit medium sized, good flavour.
Buffalo	Shrub to 4m high, moderately suckering. Fruit large, excellent flavour.
Elizabeth	Shrub to 4m high, few suckers. Fruit very large, good flavour.
Forestburg	Shrub to 3-3.5m (10-12ft) high, tolerates drought, with few suckers. Fruit very large, good flavour, very heavy yielding. Mid-late season ripening.
Gypsy	Large, juicy fruit; good flavour.
Honeywood	Multi-stemmed shrubs to 3-4m (10-14ft) high, with few suckers, bearing at an early age. Large dark purple fruit in heavy clusters; excellent flavour. Late season ripening.
JB30	Shrub to 3.5m high, few suckers. Fruit large, good flavour, ripens over a long period. High yielding.
Killarney	Shrub 4-5m high. Fruit medium size, high yielding.
Krasnojarskaya	Vigorous upright tall shrub. Heavy cropping, recommended for home gardens and commercial plantations in Poland.
Lee #3	Compact shrub growing 1.5-3m high, few suckers. Fruit very large, intense flavour, very fleshy with few seeds.
Mandam	Medium sized shrub. Crops well, recommended for home gardens and plantations in Poland.
Martin	Medium size bush to 2.5-3m (8-10ft) high, moderately suckering. Fruit very large, excellent flavour, high yielding. Early season ripening.
Moonlake	Shrub to 3m high. Large fruit, good flavour; sporadic bearer. Late flowering.
Nelson	Bush to 1.5m (5ft) high, moderately suckering. Fruit large, very good flavour, high yielding. Mid-late season ripening. Late flowering.
Northline	Upright shrub to 2m (6ft) high, freely suckering. Fruit slightly pear shaped, medium sized and with an excellent flavour. Very heavy yielding. Late season ripening.
Obelisk	Ornamental variety, very narrow and upright, small fruit.
Paleface	Very productive shrub to 2m (6ft) high. Large, white, mild flavoured fruit. Doesn't sucker.
Parkhill	Hybrid with *A. stolonifera*. Productive, upright bush to 1.5m (5ft) high, with few suckers. Fruit large, fair quality, moderate yielding. Mid season ripening.
Pearson II	Shrub to 3m high, many suckers. Fruit medium sized, good flavour. High yielding.
Pembina	Upright bush, 2.5-3m (8-10ft) high, suckering only a little. Large, oval, sweet fruit with an excellent flavour borne in long clusters. Very vigorous and high yielding. Mid season ripening.
Prince William	Hybrid with *A. canadensis*. Multi-stemmed shrub to 2.5m (8ft) high. Heavy bearer of 12mm (0.5ins) purple-blue fruit with a very good flavour.
Regent	Hybrid with *A.stolonifera*. Hardy, bushy shrub 1.2-2m (4-6ft) high; suckering a little, moderately productive with sweet medium sized fruit of fair flavour (somewhat seedy). Bears after two years. Mid-late season ripening.
Sleyt	Eastern European selection.
Smoky	Spreading bush, 2-2.5m (6-8ft) high, suckers widely, bearing large, red-purple, round fruit (to 18 mm, 0.75ins) 2-3 years after planting. Fruit well flavoured; ripens mid season. Single bushes may yield up to 45kg (90lb) of fruit. Very cold and drought resistant.
Sturgeon	Shrub to 3m (10ft) high; good flavoured, large fruit in large clusters. Productive.
Thiessen	Small roundish tree or open bush to 5m (16ft) high, moderately suckering. Very large fruit, excellent flavour, high yield. Early season ripening.
Timm	Medium sized tree, fruit in its second year. Large fruit are sweet with a good flavour.

Cultivation

Saskatoons tolerate part shade, though they fruit better in sun, and thrive in almost any soil, preferring a moist fertile soil. They are drought tolerant and also tolerate alkaline soils. Pruning is usually unnecessary.

Named cultivars start fruiting within 3-4 years, reaching full production after eight years. Many commercial orchards use seedlings from named cultivars of *A. alnifolia* due to cheaper propagation costs, but seedlings do come true to type. Orchards are planted with 4m rows and plants at 1m in the rows; after eight years, light pruning consisting of removal of older and weaker branches is beneficial. Commercial orchards in Canada (and more recently Europe) obtain fruit yields of 4 tonnes/acre (10 tonnes/ha).

Propagation is usually by seed or cuttings, although any suckers could be removed and low branches can be layered. Unusually, seedling plants usually come true to type (i.e. genetically identical to the mother plant).

Seed should be removed from the fruit by maceration, and should not be allowed to dry out. Best sown immediately and allowed to experience summer warmth then winter cold. Dry seed requires a 3-5 month period of cold stratification, and germination may improve by preceding this with a scarification or four-week warm stratification.

Softwood cuttings, 7-12cm (3-5ins) long, taken in late May or June under mist with hormone rooting powder, can work well.

Pests and diseases

Saskatoons are tough and adaptable plants and don't often suffer from insect pests or diseases. Of course, as a commercial monoculture, pests like aphids can be problematical, and various fungi can attack plants.

Birds are the main pest, attracted by the fruit, particularly due to their early season ripening and purple colour (one of the most attractive to birds!). You may need to scare birds off while the fruit is ripening.

Related species

There a number of other Amelanchier trees and shrubs. The tree forms (*A. canadensis*, *A. laevis*, *A. lamarckii*) are described in *Trees for Gardens, Orchards and Permaculture*.

Saskatoon 'Pembina'

SIBERIAN GINSENG, *Eleutherococcus senticosus*

Zone 5, H7
Deciduous
Roots used medicinally

Origin and history

Siberian ginseng, as its name indicates, is principally found in Siberia, although it is also found in China, and is widely used medicinally in both regions. Its roots are used in place of ginseng (*Panax* spp.) Other common names are wujia, eleuthero root, tough-me-not, and devil's shrub. A common synonym for it is *Acanthopanax senticosus*.

Description

Siberian ginseng is a hardy deciduous shrub belonging to the family Araliaceae with erect, little branched and slender prickly stems, growing to 2.4-4.5m (8-15ft) high.

Leaves are dark green with hairy veins and three or five oval-oblong, finely toothed leaflets each some 7.5cm (3ins) long.

Flowers are spherical umbels 4cm (1.5ins) across with purplish male and yellow female flowers terminating the shoots. Each individual plant produces three types of flower – male, female and bisexual – which open in July. Flowers are cross-pollinated, mainly by wild bees.

Pollinated flowers develop into black oval berry-like fruit 8-12mm (0.3-0.5ins) in diameter when mature.

Long, round, woody, pliable roots spread horizontally at a shallow depth and produce abundant suckers.

Siberian ginseng is found in forests through Siberia, to the Sakhalin Islands, Japan, Korea and China. It grows in thickets, small groups or clumps, at the edges and within broad-leaved and evergreen forests.

Uses

Young leaves are edible raw – good for salads.

The roots are used medicinally; the leaves and stem bark also contain some of the major chemical components. In China, the fresh flowers are used to make a tea; fresh and sliced dried roots are made into a tea; dried roots are made into tincture and powder.

The root and the root bark are adaptogen, anti-inflammatory, hypoglycaemic, tonic and vasodilator. It is taken internally during convalescence and in the treatment of menopausal problems, geriatric debility, physical and mental stress etc. It works by strengthening the body's natural immune system. It has also been used to combat radiation sickness (e.g. was used after Chernobyl) and exposure to toxic chemicals.

Production in Russia in the 1960s and 1970s required over 100 tonnes of the root, which provided over two million doses of the herbal extract for human consumption. The by-products of the plant – from roots, leaves and branches – were used in animal food products. Its use in Russia is fairly recent, but it appears to have been used for over 2,000 years in China.

Siberian ginseng has even found its way into commercial drinks in Russia – a soft drink called 'Bodrust' (meaning 'vigour') and a vodka 'Golden Horn' both being produced. The latter reduced the undesirable hangover effects of too much vodka, though it discoloured the product.

Many pharmacological attributes are ascribed to Siberian ginseng. It is classed by some as an 'adaptogen' (like true ginseng). It has strong anti-oxidant properties, and it is a non-toxic, non-specific, regulator of various organ systems. It thus increases the capacity of the body to adapt to a wide range of biological and physical stresses. Regular use is supposed to restore vigour, memory, good appetite, and to increase longevity. Several Russian studies support the supposed value in increasing endurance and concentration; Russian cosmonauts have frequently used it on their trips, and it is used by divers, rescue teams, athletes, soldiers etc. Other studies have shown it to increase the life span of mice (longer than true ginseng) and to retard cancer development, as well as having antiviral properties. It does seem to have more universal effects on the immune system than true ginseng, and is sometimes judged more effective and reliable.

Siberian ginseng accounts for over 3% of the American medicinal herbal industry – valued at some $370 million per year (2005 prices).

Varieties/Cultivars

The only cultivars in trade outside Russia and China appear to be ornamental cultivars, for example variegated leaf forms. These can be used in all the same ways, but variegated forms are likely to be less vigorous and yield a lower harvest of roots.

Cultivation

Commercially, Siberian ginseng is harvested from its natural habitat in Russia and northern China, but is in danger of being overharvested and endangered. Recommended practices are now to leave some roots in the soil for future regeneration.

Recent experimental cultivation in Japan and Canada has

Siberian ginseng

shown that there are no difficulties in cultivating the plant out of its natural habitat, where it has semi-shade, and rich, moist, sandy loam soils. Poor soil and air pollution are tolerated. There is a thornless form, *F. inermis*.

Plants should be sited in semi-shaded conditions, and need a well-drained but fertile soil. Seedlings require 3-4 years to flower and set seed themselves; cuttings and suckers probably less. Plants respond well to some nitrogen, and might benefit by being sited near to nitrogen-fixing trees or shrubs.

Siberian ginseng roots are usually dug in autumn or early spring, but can be dug at any time during the winter, conditions allowing. The roots are dried whole, then chopped and stored for later use. The dry root wholesales for about £8-16/kg ($10-20/lb). Commercial production in Russia yields 300-600kg/ha (268-536lb/acre) depending on location and environment; highest yields are from broad-leaved forests thinned by felling or fire with a good undergrowth.

Propagation is by several methods. Seeds require warm then cold stratification (four months warm followed by two months cold) to germinate well; there are about 40 seeds/g (1100/oz). Hardwood and softwood cuttings can also be taken – softwood taking best, in late June. Suckers can be dug from the parent plant in winter.

Pests and diseases

There are none of note out of its native region.

Related species

It is not related to ginseng (*Panax* spp.), the name coming from its similar reputed medicinal effects.

SPICEBUSH, *Lindera benzoin*

Zone 5, H7
Deciduous
Flavourings

Origin and history

The spice bush, also known as wild forsythia and fever bush, is native to eastern USA, and is sometimes grown for its early spring flowers, aromatic foliage, and autumn colour. However it is a long used spice plant, noted especially for the allspice flavour of the bark and fruit.

Description

The spice bush is a deciduous, highly aromatic, rounded, multi-stemmed shrub growing 2-3m high (occasionally more) and similar width.

Shoots are smooth and bear leaves 6-15cm (2.3-5.9ins) long by 2-8cm (0.7-3ins) wide, on short stalks. The leaves turn a rich yellow colour in autumn.

The flowers are pale yellowish-green, small (to 5mm/0.1ins in diameter), borne in small clusters on one-year-old wood in April (well before leaf emergence). The species is dioecious, with male and female flowers on different plants, hence both sexes of plant are required for fruiting.

Fruits are to 7.5mm (2.9ins) across, ellipsoid, bright red, ripening August to September. They contain a single seed.

Uses

The young leaves, shoots and fruit contain aromatic oils and make a fragrant tea. The shoots are considered to taste best while flowering in spring, as the nectar adds considerably to the flavour. Pioneer families kept the cut twigs in their kitchens – the 'spice sticks' were used to flavour soups.

The fresh and dried/powdered fruit (with and without the seed) is used as a good substitute for allspice. The crushed leaves have a lemony aroma and make a nice tea. They can also be dried, ground and used as a spice in their own right. The young bark is pleasant to chew. The fruit can be made into a delicious jelly. A beverage similar to ginger ale can also be made from the fresh berries.

The shoots and leaves were used medicinally for a wide range of ailments by several Native North American tribes, including colds, fevers etc. Recent research has shown that extracts from the bark have strong antimicrobial effects.

Analysis of the essential oils reveals numerous components, but the main ones are:

- Fruit – alpha and beta-phellandrene, odour characterised as fresh-citrusy, peppery-woody/minty. These are also found in some Eucalyptus species and angelica (alpha) and fennel and Canada balsam (beta).
- Crushed leaves – 6-methyl-5-hepten-2-one, odour characterised as "oily-green, pungent-herbaceous, grassy, diffusive, with fresh and green-fruity notes". This compound is used in commercial fruit flavourings in small amounts. Beta-

Spicebush (*Lindera benzoin*)

caryophyllene, odour characterised as clove-like. Also found in cloves and black peppers. (e)-nerolidol, odour characterised as woody-floral. Also found in neroli.

- Crushed stems – 1-8 cineol, odour characterised as camphoraceous-cool. Also the main constituent of most Eucalyptus oils, also found in rosemary.

All these essential oils are classified as safe in general usage.

Varieties/Cultivars

There are a few ornamental cultivars which can be used in the same ways.

Cultivation

Lindera benzoin has a slender open habit and is very happy in part shade or dappled sunlight. It prefers a moisture retentive, fertile, acid soil (pH 4.5-6.0). Plants are quite vigorous and suffer little from pests or diseases. Spice bush is notably resistant to honey fungus.

Spicebush flowers on bare branches in early spring

Pruning need only consist of removing dead wood in spring. Branches to be harvested for the bark or shoots can be cut in spring – do not remove more than about 40% of the top growth in a single season. Plants regenerate well from cutting back over a period of a few years.

Fruits are easily harvested, usually in September, as they form in bunches.

Propagation is usually by seed or cuttings. Seed is best sown in autumn if fresh and ripe, otherwise cold stratified. Semi-ripe cuttings are taken in July, or cuttings of mature side shoots, September/October, 12cm (4.7ins) long, with a heel. Layering of low branches can also succeed.

Pests and diseases

There are none of note.

SUMACHS, *Rhus* species

Zones 3-6, H7
Deciduous
Edible fruit, Dyeing, Bee plants

Origin and history

Sumachs (also spelt sumacs) are deciduous or evergreen trees, shrubs and climbers, some from cooler regions but mostly from the subtropics and tropics, with some 250 species in total. They are often grown ornamentally for their striking foliage and rich red autumn colours.

The genus *Rhus* contains many useful trees and shrubs, and some of which are very poisonous. The poisonous species are sometimes separated into their own genus, *Toxicodendron*, and can cause severe skin irritation from the sap; they are not included in the section below and should not be cultivated unless you are sure you want them, and that you can stop them spreading. It is fairly easy to distinguish the poisonous species: they have panicles of flowers and fruit arising from leaf axils, and the fruits are smooth, whereas non-poisonous species have compound terminal panicles and fruits covered with acid crimson hairs. The

Staghorn sumach (*Rhus typhina*)

sap from some of these poisonous species has sometimes been tapped and used as a varnish or lacquer. The poisonous species include *R. ambigua*, *R. coriaria*, *R. diversiloba*, *R. radicans* (poison ivy), *R. succedanea*, *R. sylvestris*, *R. toxicodendron* (poison oak), *R. vernix* (poison sumach) and *R. verniciflua*.

Description

The species covered here are all hardy shrubs with compound leaves arranged spirally, and spikes of flowers followed by dense clusters of small reddish fruit (drupes). The drupes of several species are lemony in flavour.

Uses

Leaves of all species are rich in tannins. They can be collected as they fall in autumn and used for tanning, as a brown dye, or as a dyeing mordant.

Seeds of all species are rich in oil. This oil when extracted has a tallow-like consistency and can be used to make candles.

Many of the species below have edible fruit. They are acid/lemony in flavour and quite small, hence the traditional use of soaking them in water to make a lemon-flavoured drink, which can be sweetened as required; the flavour of fruit is best during dry weather. The fruits contain flavonols, phenolic acids, hydrolysable tannins, anthocyanins and malic acid. Seeds of the non-poisonous species are an important wildlife food for birds.

Flowers are pollinated by bees; in good weather they can be a major summer nectar source, with the golden honey often scented and bitter when new but maturing to an excellent flavour by the autumn. The flowers are also a nectar source for many butterflies in North America.

Sumach wood is generally light and soft, and not particularly useful; it is occasionally used for small furniture or cabinets. Woody prunings make a quick-burning kindling when dried.

Varieties/Cultivars

Rhus aromatic – Lemon sumach, Fragrant sumach

A low suckering downy shrub, growing to 1.2m (4ft) high from eastern North America. Trifoliate leaves are aromatic when bruised. Sometimes found in open woods, so it should tolerate light shade. Tolerates drought and poor soils. Hardy to zone 5 / H7 or colder. Flowers yellow, in April, fruits are round, red, downy, dry, 6mm thick; seeds ripen in September. A very low growing form, var. *arenaria*, grows on sand dunes in the mid-east of North America.

Uses

- The small fruits are edible, raw or cooked. They can be made into a lemon-flavoured drink by soaking in cold or hot (not boiling) water for 10-30 minutes. They can also be mixed with flour and used in cakes, porridge etc.
- Medicinally, the leaves are astringent and diuretic, formerly used for colds, bleeding, stomach aches. The root bark is also astringent and diuretic. The fruits were chewed for stomach aches, toothaches etc.

Fragrant sumach (*Rhus aromatica*)

- The leaves contain up to 25% tannin; the bark is also a good source.
- The split stems are used in basketry.
- The extensive root system makes the plant useful in preventing soil erosion.

Rhus chinensis – Chinese gall

A small broad-headed tree or large shrub, growing to 6m (20ft) high from China and Japan. Hardy to zone 8 / H4. It needs a hot summer to ripen its wood, and suffers dieback below -7°C (19°F) in winter. Flowering occurs in August, and fruits are rounded, flat, orange-red and downy.

Uses

- The fruits are edible when cooked, with an acid flavour. They can be used as a rennet substitute.
- Many parts are used in Chinese medicine, including fruit, leaves, roots, stem bark, seeds and root bark; galls on the plant are also used. Extracts have recently been confirmed in their antiviral behaviour.
- The roots and leaves have an anti-insect effect against cotton aphids (*Aphis gossypii*), rice leafrollers (*Cnaphalocrocis medinalis*) and rice field insects.
- A blue dye is obtained from galls on the plant. They contain up to 77% tannins and can be used as an ink.

Rhus copallina – Dwarf sumach, shining sumach

A medium sized downy shrub, usually growing to 2m (6ft) high and wide, from eastern North America. Hardy to zone 5 / H7. Flowers from July-September; seeds ripen October-December. Fruit are 3-5mm (0.1-0.2ins) long with little flesh, but are borne in dense panicles.

Uses

- Fruits are edible, raw or cooked, with an acid flavour. Often made into a drink by soaking in water.
- Roots, bark and fruit were all used medicinally by Native Americans.
- Fresh leaves usually contain 10-25% tannins, while dried leaves average 32%.
- Red and black dyes are obtained from the fruit.
- Can be used against soil erosion due to the extensive root system.

Rhus glabra – Smooth sumach

A shrub growing 3m (10ft) high and wide, from many parts of North America. Hardy to zone 3 / H7. Flowers in July-August, the seeds ripen in September-November. Plants are fast growing and sucker profusely, individual stems not being very long-lived.

Uses

- The fruits are edible, raw or cooked, with an acid lemony flavour. They are usually soaked in water for 10-30 minutes to make a lemon-flavoured drink, sometimes with added sassafras. They can also be chewed, with the seeds as well, to quench the thirst and leave a pleasant taste in the mouth.
- Many parts have been used medicinally, including the root bark, roots, leaves and fruit. Recently, extracts have been found which exhibit antibacterial, antiviral and antitumour properties.
- All parts of the plant are antibacterial against tomato wilt (*Pseudomonas solanaceum*). Parts of the plant have also been used as a rodenticide.
- Fresh leaves usually contain 10-25% tannins, dried leaves average 27%; the shoots and roots are also rich in tannins.
- A black dye is obtained from the fruit, and an orange or yellow dye from the root.
- The leaves were smoked by many Native American tribes.
- The extensive root system makes the plant useful for soil stabilisation and it can be used as a pioneer species for establishing woodlands; it is also used in North America in windbreaks.

Rhus potaninii

A small to medium sized round-headed tree, usually growing 5-8m (16-28ft) high and to 8m (28ft) across, from central and western China. Hardy to zone 5 / H7. Flowers in June, though it rarely flowers in Britain.

Uses

- Parts are used medicinally as an antiseptic, astringent and haemostatic.
- An indelible black ink is obtained from galls on the leaves.

Rhus x pulvinata

A hybrid of *R. glabra* x *R. typhina*, making a wide-spreading shrub growing 3m (10ft) high. Hardy to zone 3 / H7. Flowers in July-August, with seeds ripening September-November.

Smooth sumach (*Rhus glabra*)

Tolerates most soils, including chalk and poor sandy soils. Often grown ornamentally, there are some named varieties; 'Red Autumn Lace' (sometimes called *R. glabra* 'Laciniata') is a female form which fruits freely. Freely suckering, with individual stems not very long-lived.

Uses

- The fruits are edible, raw or cooked, with an acid lemony flavour. They are usually soaked in water for 10-30 minutes to make a lemon-flavoured drink.
- Many parts have been used medicinally, including the root bark, roots, leaves and fruit.
- Leaves usually contain 10-25% tannins; the shoots and roots are also rich in tannins.
- A black dye is obtained from the fruit, and an orange or yellow dye from the root.
- The extensive root system makes the plant useful for soil stabilisation and it can be used as a pioneer species for establishing woodlands.

Rhus punjabensis

A small to medium sized tree, growing to 12m (40ft) high, from the Himalayas, central and western China. Hardy to zone 6 / H7. Flowers in June. The form *sinica* is most commonly grown in Britain.

Uses

- The fruits are edible, raw or cooked. Usually soaked in water for 10-30 minutes to make a lemon-flavoured drink.

Rhus trilobata – Skunk bush

A small to medium sized shrub from western North America, growing to 1.8m (6ft) high; closely allied to *R. aromatica*. Leaves have an unpleasant scent. Hardy to zone 4 / H7. Flowers in March-April; the fruit are round, red, downy and 6mm (0.2ins) thick.

Uses

- The fruits are edible, raw or cooked. Usually soaked in water for 10-30 minutes to make a lemon-flavoured drink. They can also be dried, ground and made into a jam.
- Several parts were used medicinally by Native Americans, including fruit, leaves, bark and roots.
- Several dyes can be obtained from the fruit, shoots and leaves: yellow with alum mordant, mid-brown (chrome), olive tan (copper), bright yellow (tin), grey-green (iron), beige (no mordant).
- The shoots are tough and slender, and used in basketry – often stripped of bark and split into several strands.
- The species is used in North America for windbreaks and screen plantings.

Rhus typhina (*R. hirta*) – Stag's horn sumach

A large shrub growing to 6m (20ft) high and wide, from eastern North America. Hardy to zone 4 / H7. Tolerates poor soils and drought. Suckers very freely, though individual shoots are fairly short-lived. Shoots are velvety. Flowers in June-July; fruit are red, downy.

Uses

- The fruits are edible, cooked in puddings (they are sour) or soaked in water to make a lemon-flavoured drink.
- Several parts have been used medicinally, including the bark, roots, leaves, flowers, fruit and sap (N.B. sap can cause a rash on some people). Recently, extracts have been found which exhibit antiviral and antitumour properties.

Fruit head of smooth sumach (*Rhus glabra*)

- The leaves contain up to 48% tannins, but average 25%; the bark, especially from roots, and the fruit are also rich in tannins.
- The leaves contain several insecticidal compounds which are effective against aphids. A solid obtained by steam distilling the leaves contains these compounds, as does an ethanolic extract of the leaves. The extract, when applied to leaves of the food plant, was very effective within a few minutes against the black bean aphid (*Aphis fabae*), the green peach aphid (*Myzus persicae*) and the mustard beetle (*Phaedon cochleariae*). The extract also has a fungicidal effect, which is moderately effective against fireblight (*Erwinia amylovora*). The stems and leaves are antifungal against fusarium wilt (*Fusarium* spp.) and antibacterial against tomato wilt (*Pseudomonas solanaceum*). The plant has also been used as a rodenticide.
- A black ink can be made by boiling the leaves and fruit. Several dyes can be obtained from the fruit and leaves: greenish-gold with alum mordant, chestnut brown (chrome), brassy gold (copper), bright yellow (tin), charcoal grey (iron), tan (no mordant). A yellow dye can also be obtained from the roots.
- The young shoots were hollowed out and made into pipes for use as flutes and to tap the sap of sugar maples.
- The extensive root system makes this valuable as a windbreak screen and soil stabiliser.

This is an excellent bee plant, producing lots of pollen and nectar.

Other species which are only hardy to about -5°C (23°F) (USDA zone 9 / RHS H3) include *R. integrifolia*, *R. microphylla*, *R. ovata* and *R. sempervirens*, all shrubs from southwestern North America. They all have edible fruit, soaked in water to make a drink as with many other species.

Cultivation

The sumachs are easily cultivated; most species like a well-drained soil and full sun; a few tolerate some shade. Most species described here are deciduous.

Although windy sites are tolerated, plants have brittle branches which can break in strong winds.

Most species have a suckering habit and will form thickets if allowed.

Flowers are pollinated by bees. Most species are dioecious, so male and female plants are required for seed; a few species are monoecious. All the species described below are dioecious unless otherwise indicated.

Sumachs are very tolerant to cutting and will respond vigorously to regular coppicing.

Propagation is usually by seed or by digging suckers – several species can sucker widely (and sometimes be a nuisance). Seed usually needs some cold stratification.

Pests and diseases

Plants are susceptible to coral spot fungus (*Nectria cinnabarina*) but resistant to honey fungus (*Armillaria* spp.).

TEA, *Camellia sinensis*

Zone 8, H4
Evergreen
Beverage plant

Origin and history

Tea has a very long history from China of being used to make teas. Originally from around western China, now cultivated across Asia and elsewhere.

Description

An evergreen shrub to 6m (20ft) high but usually kept as a 1-1.5m (3-5ft) shrub in cultivation.

Glossy mid-green leaves and white flowers.

Uses

One of the most widely grown beverage plants on the planet.

After picking, the leaves of *C. sinensis* soon begin to wilt and oxidise unless immediately dried. An enzymatic oxidation process triggered by the plant's intracellular enzymes causes the leaves to turn progressively darker as their chlorophyll breaks down and tannins are released. This darkening is stopped at a predetermined stage by heating, which deactivates the enzymes responsible. In the production of black teas, halting by heating is carried out simultaneously with drying. Without careful moisture and temperature control during manufacture and packaging, growth of undesired moulds and bacteria may make tea unfit for consumption.

Tea is generally divided into categories based on how it is processed. At least six different types are produced:

- White: wilted and unoxidised;
- Yellow: unwilted and unoxidised but allowed to yellow;
- Green: unwilted and unoxidised;
- Oolong: wilted, bruised, and partially oxidised;
- Black: wilted, sometimes crushed, and fully oxidised;
- Post-fermented (dark): green tea that has been allowed to ferment/compost.

Varieties/Cultivars

Hundreds of varieties exist throughout Asia, however few are in cultivation in Europe or North America.

Cultivation

Plants are usually kept shrubby by the harvesting process. Every two weeks or so the growing tip along with 2-3 young leaves are pinched out and harvested for use.

Pests and diseases

None of note. Hardiness is likely to be the main issue.

Related species

C. oleifera is cultivated for the seed, from which camellia oil is extracted. This is an edible culinary oil used by a large number of people in Asia. Although this species is of similar hardiness, it needs a warmer climate to produce seed. Active breeding programmes in China are aiming to improve yields.

Young leaves of tea

TEA TREE / MANUKA, *Leptospermum scoparium*

Zone 8, H4
Evergreen
Beverage plant, Bee plant

Origin and history

It originates from New Zealand, where the Maori have many traditional uses for the plant, now best known for manuka honey.

Description

Evergreen aromatic shrub growing to 2-5m (7-16ft) tall, with dense branching and small leaves with a short spine tip. The flowers are white, occasionally pink. The wood is tough and hard.

Uses

It is cultivated in New Zealand for manuka honey, produced when honeybees gather nectar from its flowers, and for the pharmaceutical industry.

Leaves are steeped in water to make a tea-like beverage.

The wood was often used for tool handles and for carving.

Manuka sawdust imparts a delicious flavour when used for smoking meats and fish.

An essential oil is produced by steam distillation of its leaves.

Varieties/Cultivars

Some ornamental cultivars are available.

Cultivation

Grow in a sheltered site unless in a very mild climate or near to the sea. Plant in a well-drained soil in full sun. Prune by pinching back shoot tips – will not sprout from old wood.

Propagate by seed (not dormant) or summer cuttings.

Pests and diseases

None of note.

Manuka

TREE LUPIN, *Lupinus arboreus*

Zone 7-8, H5
Evergreen
Nitrogen-fixing, Bee plant, Soil stabiliser

Origin and history

Tree lupin is a small-medium evergreen shrub from southwestern North America, naturalised in southern England.

Description

Grows to 3m (10ft) in height and spread. Bright yellow flowers are followed by 7cm (2.7ins) long seed pods, containing brown 5mm (0.1ins) seeds (not edible). Short-lived, especially when growing on rich soils. Plants can self-sow when in a suitable position.

Uses

A very good nitrogen fixing plant.

Plants are used in land reclamation schemes to stabilise sandy soils and dunes. Because they are fast growing and tolerant of maritime exposure, they quickly provide shelter for other plants as well as enriching the soil with nitrogen.

Bee plant.

A bright yellow dye is obtained from the flowers.

Varieties/Cultivars

Some ornamental cultivars exist.

Cultivation

Needs sun and a well-drained acid to neutral soil; tolerates maritime exposure.

Propagate by seed.

Pests and diseases

There are numerous minor pests and disease.

Related species

Some annual Lupinus species (notably *L. albus* and *L. angustifolia*) are cultivated for the edible seeds. Most lupin seed contains toxins but varieties have been selected with low to zero toxicity, and these are grown commercially as a protein source.

Tree lupin

TRIFOLIATE ORANGE
Poncirus trifoliata (Citrus trifoliata)

Zone 5-6, H6-7
Deciduous
Edible fruit

Origin and history

Trifoliate orange is closely related to the citrus family, but unlike them it is deciduous and hardy in temperate climates. It is native to northern China and Korea; and common in Japan through cultivation. Its fruit look like small oranges or lemons, and are edible when suitably prepared. Common names include trifoliate orange, bitter orange, hardy orange, Japanese bitter orange, Japanese bitter lemon, fuzzy lemon.

Description

The trifoliate orange, the only member of *Poncirus*, is a deciduous shrub or small tree up to 5-6m (16-20ft) high, much branched and with stout green spines up to 6cm (2.5ins) long. It becomes a dome-shaped bush of tangled and twisted olive-green stems.

Leaves are trifoliate, small, compound, with three elliptic, somewhat leathery leaflets each 2.5-6cm (1-2.5ins) long.

Flower buds are formed in leaf axils in early summer, then overwintering before opening or with the leaves the following spring. Flowers are white, solitary, short-stalked, scented, 25-50mm (1-2ins) wide with flat spreading petals.

Fruits are round to somewhat pear shaped, 3-5cm (1-2ins) in diameter, starting green but ripening to a dull lemon-yellow colour, fragrant when ripe and covered with fine down. The peel is soft, thick (5-10mm / 0.19-0.39ins), rough and with copious oil glands; the pulp is sparse with very acid juice, with numerous ovoid seeds.

Uses

Fruits are acid and bitter when raw but can be cooked and made into a marmalade; the fruit peel can also be used as a flavouring.

The tart juice is slightly bitter but is an excellent substitute for lemon juice in cooking. Each fruit yields only about a teaspoon of juice but as a mature tree produces two buckets or more of fruit (10kg+, 22lb+), the total juice yield is fairly good. The juice yield is best if fruits are stored for two weeks after harvesting before being processed, when the yield is about 20%. The juice is rich in vitamin C. Watch out for the resin in the skin which gums up knives!

The fragrant young leaves are cooked and used as a flavouring.

The fruit (dried and unripe) and stem bark have uses in traditional Chinese medicine.

Poncirus trifoliata is often grown for its ornamental qualities: the attractive interlacing network of stiff thorny branches and sweetly-scented flowers in late spring/early summer.

The thorny and bushy nature makes it a fine impenetrable barrier and hedge – completely stockproof.

The other main use is as a frost resistant rootstock for *Citrus* species: its use enhances the cold-hardiness of the citrus cultivar grafted as a scion, and is somewhat dwarfing on light soils (by up to 50%) but not on heavy soils; it is also resistant to root-knot nematodes which attack some citrus species, and tolerant to *Phytophthora*. It is mainly used for satsuma mandarins and sweet oranges; it is the main rootstock used in Japanese satsuma plantings.

The flowers are attractive to bees in April and May.

Varieties/Cultivars

Cultivars have been bred mainly for their use as rootstocks; little information is available on fruit quality.

Flying Dragon	A dwarf cultivar with corkscrew-shaped shoots and very small leaves. Used as a dwarfing cold hardy rootstock, resulting in citrus trees only some 25% of full size (about 2m / 6ft high).
Karlic, Skoroplodnaya, Skorospelka	Used as rootstocks in Georgia (former USSR); dwarfing and precocious.
Pomeroy, Rich 16-6	Rootstocks of moderate vigour.
Rubidoux	Of moderate vigour, used as a rootstock which is slightly dwarfing.

Cultivation

The trifoliate orange grows in any well-drained, fertile soil, preferring a sunny location but tolerating light shade. Both acid and alkaline soils are tolerated (pH 5.0-8.3). In Britain it tends to make a spreading, dome-shaped shrub about 2-3m (6-10ft) high and the same across, growing 20-30cm (8-12ins) per year. It is healthy in Britain (preferring the west) and fruits freely in southern England; fruits ripen September-November and fertile seed is produced after warm summers. Plants are self-fertile. Yields of up to 14kg (30lb) of fruit per plant have been recorded in North America.

Ripe fruit of trifoliate orange

Pruning is not normally required, but dead or damaged wood can be pruned out in spring; hedging plants can be clipped in early summer. Note that flowers are produced on the previous year's wood, so clipping plants will reduce their fruiting capacity.

Plants are relatively short-lived, usually declining after about 25 years.

The easiest method of propagation is by seed. The seeds are not dormant, though may benefit from a short period of chilling, and are best sown in spring in warm conditions. Seed stored over winter should be kept dry and cold. Germination takes about a month. First year growth is 20-38cm (8-15ins). Seedlings are usually true to type; seeds are often polyembryonic (i.e. contain several embryos) and several shoots may develop from a single seed.

Pests and diseases

None of note.

Related species

Hybrids of *Poncirus trifoliata* with *Citrus sinensis* (sweet orange) are called citranges, and are quite cold hardy hybrids with fruit of better quality.

LEMON VERBENA, *Aloysia triphylla*

Zone 8, H4
Evergreen
Beverage plant

Origin and history

Lemon verbena (previously *Lippia citriodora*) is native to South America. It was brought to Europe by the Spanish and the Portuguese in the seventeenth century and cultivated for its oil.

Description

An aromatic shrub or subshrub growing to 2-3m (6-10ft) high. The pointed leaves are slightly rough to the touch and emit a strong lemon scent when bruised.

Sprays of tiny purple or white flowers appear in late spring or early summer. It is evergreen in above-zero locations, but is sensitive to cold, losing leaves at temperatures below 0°C (32°F), although the wood is hardy to -10°C (14°F).

Uses

Lemon verbena leaves are used to make a lemon-flavoured tea, with fresh or dried leaves.

The leaves are used to add a lemon flavour to fish and poultry dishes, vegetable marinades, salad dressings, jams, puddings, Greek yoghurt, etc. The leaves are also used in liqueurs and potpourri.

Cultivation

Plant in full sun in a well-drained soil. Needs protection from cold drying winds. In cold winter temperatures, mulch around the base of the plant with a deep, loose mulch.

Plants can grow lax and leggy in time. Pruning is recommended in spring to encourage a bushy form.

Propagate by summer cuttings.

Pests and diseases

Can be susceptible to whitefly when grown in greenhouses.

Lemon verbena

WILLOWS, *Salix* species

Zone 2-6, H6-7
Deciduous
Basketry

Origin and history

The willows comprise a large number of trees and shrubs, mainly from the Northern Hemisphere. Here we are only considering some of the shrub willows and their uses.

Shrub willows are common to moist and wet areas, not only along watercourses. Like all willows, their light fluffy seeds can travel great distances in the air.

Description

Shrub willows are mostly multistemmed plants growing 2-6m (6-20ft) high. Leaves are long and narrow. Fluffy catkin flowers are followed by downy seeds that are wind dispersed over long distances.

Uses

All willows contain medicinal compounds in the inner bark. Willow bark contains salicylic acid, flavonoids and tannins (up to 20%) and is anti-inflammatory, analgesic, febrifuge, antirheumatic and astringent. Salicylic acid was the forerunner of aspirin and has many of the same analgesic and anti-inflammatory actions – unlike aspirin, it does not thin the blood or irritate the stomach lining.

The shrub willows are mainly used for basketry.

Basketry varieties/Cultivars

All species of shrub or tree willows can be used for basketry, however some are better than others and the main species

Osier (*Salix viminalis*) regrows strongly after cutting, like all willows

Basketry willows

Baskets have been used for millennia and remain one of the few everyday items which are still handmade, even if the cheap types usually found for sale are mass produced using moulds for uniformity. In temperate regions, the most common materials used for basketry are stems from willows (*Salix* spp.) and here we concentrate on the cultivation of willows to produce basketry materials. Willows are some of the easiest plants to grow and only a small patch is needed to supply the needs of a family and garden.

In almost every case where today one uses cardboard, plastic or plywood as packing materials, 200 years ago this need would have been met by basketwork. Fruit and vegetables were gathered from fields in baskets; and fish, poultry and dairy produce were all packed into baskets for the journey to town markets. Bulky items like manure or rubble were transported in baskets, and many other items were made from willow such as beer strainers, travelling trunks, etc.

Basket willow cultivation

In Britain until the 19th century, withy beds were collections of mixed varieties in which the growing plants were cut off a year after planting at a height of 30-120cm (1-4ft), allowing a head of shoots to spring from a single stem or stool. The advantage of this system was that the stools, after cutting each year, remained above weeds and perhaps animals, so that the new shoots were not so prone.

In more recent years, the favoured system is to cut the stools back as near to the ground as possible (within 5cm / 2ins). This encourages long straight rods (canes) which are clean of branches, and also maximises the lifetime of the stool.

It is a misconception that willows grow best in wet or boggy conditions. Although they may well tolerate such conditions, they grow best in any soil of reasonable fertility and good drainage (apart from very light sandy soils). Having said that, they are ideally suited to a damp patch in the garden/field that may be less suited for other crops.

Planting

Willows grow very easily from cuttings, and new beds are always established by planting cuttings straight into their final positions. The cuttings are 20-30cm (8-12ins) lengths of willow cut from the thick ends of good-sized rods – a diameter of 8-15mm (0.3-0.6ins) is preferable. They are planted by hand (or mechanically on a large scale) at a spacing of 30-45cm (12-18ins) each way in lines (especially for mechanised harvesting) or in other arrangements, e.g. staggered. A third of the cutting is left above soil level. More vigorous species/varieties (e.g. *S. viminalis*) are best planted at the wider spacing (45cm / 18ins), moderately vigorous species (*S. purpurea*, *S. vitellina*) at 35-40cm (13-15ins), and least vigorous species (*S. purpurea*) at 30cm (12ins).

If planting into bare (unmulched) ground, it is very important that the ground is clear of weeds: lush weed growth is probably the most common cause of new plantings failing. It is highly recommended that the cuttings are planted through a thick organic mulch like bark. This will save considerable work in the first few years.

Harvesting and maintenance

If the bed is unmulched, it is essential to control weeds for the first two years at least. In the first year, usually only a single rod will grow from each cutting, hence the foliage is not very dense and weeds are not well suppressed. After two years, the foliage will suppress weed growth once the annual growth has reached a height of 1m (3ft), but before this (i.e. in spring and early summer), weeds must still be controlled: lush grasses can easily overtake the young shoots and swamp them.

The first harvest takes place the winter after harvest, after leaf fall, between November-February. For a low cut, trim the rods as close to the ground as possible – don't worry if you can't see buds beneath the cut. Secateurs are the best tool on a small scale; a hook is used by larger growers. The first year's canes are often branched and of poor quality. The following year (year 2), a dense mass of rods will arise from each stool. These are harvested at the end of the season again, and the cycle continues. After harvesting, there is little visible except a knotty mass underfoot. Take advantage of the open conditions to remove weeds, particularly grasses and perennials like nettles.

A willow bed does not need feeding; allow the leaves to decay around the plants. It should last 30-50 years or more before growth reduces substantially. The higher the density of planting, the shorter the life of the bed. An area of $10m^2$ ($100ft^2$) should be sufficient for 3-4 baskets per year.

Using the willow rods

When willow is bought for basketmaking, it has usually been stripped, making it smooth and easier to make into fine baskets. This process is very hard work on a small scale, and totally unnecessary: unstripped willow can be used to make baskets, which, although inevitably rougher, are just as strong and useful as finer willow baskets. Hand stripping willow rods is easiest if the rods are cut in spring (April) and stripped immediately.

To use unstripped willow, it is best dried for a few months after cutting – lean it against a sheltered wall or fence. After a couple of months it can be used without soaking for basketry. Note that rod colours will fade.

Bay willow (*Salix pentandra*) showing seeds and fluff. Coppiced willows for basketry don't flower so you rarely see this.

used number only a few. But even from these, several hundred named varieties have been selected in Europe, North American and Asia.

Salix alba vitellina (synonym *S. vitellina*) – Golden willow

Vigorous species with yellow-orange rods. Rods are tough and flexible, suitable for rougher work and still used in American basketry. Very hardy, to zone 2 / H7.

Salix daphnoides – Violet willow. Europe

Moderately vigorous, with brownish-purple rods. Cultivars include 'Meikle'. Hardy to zone 5 / H7.

Salix eriocephala (synonym *S. cordata*, *S. rigida*). North America

Moderately vigorous shrub. Produces very tough, flexible rods. Several clones grown for basketry in North America; 'Green USA' is very vigorous with dark brown rods, tolerates poor dry soils. Hardy to zone 6 / H6-7.

Salix eriocephala x *petiolaris* 'Americana'. Hybrid

A shrub to 3m (10ft) high with reddish-brown rods. A widely used cultivar in American basketry, very hardy and tolerates poor soils. Hardy to zone 5 / H7.

Salix gilgiana. Japan, Korea

A vigorous shrub, sometimes grown in Japan for basketry rods. Hardy to zone 6 / H6-7.

Salix kinuiyanagi. Japan

Very vigorous shrub, widely cultivated in Japan for basketry; closely related to *S. viminalis*, and used for coarser baskets like osier. Hardy to zone 6 / H6-7.

Salix koriyanagi. Korea

Moderately vigorous shrub with yellowish-grey rods. Grown extensively in Japan for basketry. Rods are fine, flexible and durable – used for fine quality baskets. Hardy to zone 6 / H6-7.

Salix miyabeana. Japan

Vigorous shrub close to *S. purpurea*, with light grey rods. Sometimes grown in Japan for basketry rods. Hardy to zone 6 / H6-7.

Salix x *mollissima* (*S. triandra* x *S. viminalis*). Hybrids

A group of clonal hybrids resulting from cross-breeding in osier beds. Several used for basketry, including 'Black Spaniard' – very vigorous, stout, brittle. Hardy to zone 6 / H6-7.

Salix pentandra – Bay willow. North and Central Europe

Vigorous shrub with glossy reddish or brown shoots; produces stout, osier-type rods. Two cultivars grown in North America for basketry are 'Lumley' (moderate vigour) and 'Patent Lumley'. Hardy to zone 5 / H7.

Salix purpurea – Purple willow, Purple osier. Europe, Russia, naturalised in North America

Low or moderately vigorous shrub, producing very flexible, tough, thin rods, usually 1-1.5m (3-5ft) long, suitable for small baskets. Rods are often tinged with red or purple. Numerous basketry cultivars exist, including: 'Brittany Dicks', 'Dark Dicks', 'Dicky Meadows' (rods reddish, wide spreading from stool, very good quality, popular in North America), 'Franz Geel', 'French', 'Goldstones' (vigorous, golden-orange rods), 'Green Dicks' (vigorous, rods reddish), 'Lancashire', 'Leicestershire', 'Purple' (moderate vigour, was widely grown in North America), 'Red Buds' (rods wide spreading from stool, very good quality, popular in North America), 'Welsh'. Hardy to zone 5 / H7.

Salix triandra (synonym *S. amygdalina*) – Almond-leaved willow. Europe, Asia

A species of moderate vigour – this and its varieties are much in demand by basketmakers. The rods are of good quality, olive brown to black, often growing 1.5-3m (5-10ft) high (average 2m / 6ft) annually, with diameters at ground level up to 10mm (0.4ins). Basketry cultivars include: 'American Green' (moderate vigour, was widely grown in North America), 'Black German', 'Black Hollander' (rods dark reddish-brown), 'Black Maul' (the most popular variety; rods dark brown, almost black), 'Black Top', 'Dark French', 'Grisette Noir', 'Light Newkind', 'Stone Rod', and 'Whissander' (rods slightly stiffer, mid-brown). Hardy to zone 5/H7.

Salix viminalis – Osier. Europe, Asia, naturalised in North America

This species and its varieties tend to produce a very vigorous growth, suitable for heavy coarse agricultural baskets. The rods, yellowish to olive-green, often grow 3-4m (10-13ft) high annually, with diameters at ground level up to 15mm (0.6ins). It thrives beside water. Basketry clones include: 'Aquatica Gigantea', 'Black Rod', Black Osier', 'Black Satin', 'Brown Merrin' (very vigorous, rods mid-brown), 'English Rod', 'Gigantea Korso', 'Irish Rod', 'Mealy Top', 'Readers Red' (moderate vigour, red rods), 'Stricta', 'Superba', 'Utelescens' and 'Yellow Osier' (very vigorous, rods yellowish-green). Hardy to zone 4 / H7.

Cultivation

Easy to cultivate, shrub willows grow in any reasonably moist soil in full sun.

Propagate via cuttings. Hardwood cuttings 30cm (12ins) long in winter are easiest although cuttings at any time of year have a good chance of succeeding. First year growth starts slowly and weed control is essential otherwise new cuttings can be swamped and killed by weeds.

Pests and diseases

There are many minor pests and diseases but most trees in a diverse planting remain healthy. Monocultures of willow varieties are much more susceptible to rust and other diseases and should be avoided.

WISTERIAS, *Wisteria* species

Zone 4-8, H4-7
Deciduous
Nitrogen-fixing, Bee plants

Origin and history

A small group of deciduous, twining, woody climbers found in temperate China, Japan and eastern North America. They are usually found on low, moist, fertile alluvial soils. Fast growing and long-lived, the profuse fragrant flowers have led to their widespread ornamental use.

Description

Vigorous deciduous climbing twining shrubs up to 12m (40ft) high with showy flowers.

Uses

All species are nitrogen-fixing and bee plants.

All used for wall screening/façade insulation and ornamentally.

There are various (old) reports of parts of some species being eaten – seeds, flowers and leaves – but these are not included here as all parts are known to contain alkaloids.

Varieties/Cultivars

Wisteria floribunda – Japanese wisteria

From Japan, growing up to 8m high; hardy to zone 4.

A fibre and cloth is obtained from the bark.

Wisteria x *formosa*

A hybrid of *W. floribunda* and *W. sinensis*. Grows to 8m high; hardy to zone 5.

Uses: A fibre and cloth is obtained from the bark.

Wisteria sinensis

Wisteria frutescens – American wisteria

From eastern North America, growing 12m high; hardy to zone 5.

Uses: Edible flowers – raw in salads, also said to be excellent when dipped in batter and fried in oil as fritters.

Wisteria japonica

From Japan and Korea, hardy to zone 8.

Uses: Façade insulation.

Wisteria sinensis – Chinese wisteria

From China, growing up to 10m high; hardy to zone 5. Naturalised in France. Tolerates part shade. Very tolerant of pruning, plants can regenerate from old wood.

Medicinally, the seed is diuretic and is used in the treatment of heart ailments.

A fibre from the stems can be used to make paper; the fibre is about 1.3-3.7mm long. Stems are harvested in the summer, the leaves removed and the stems steamed until the fibre can be stripped. The fibres are cooked for two hours with lye and then put in a ball mill for three hours. The paper is a buff colour.

Wisteria venusta – Silky wisteria

From Japan, growing 10m high; hardy to zone 5. Cultivated as a fibre plant in Japan.

A fibre obtained from the bark is used for cloth and thread.

Wisteria villosa

From China.

Uses: Edible flowers.

Cultivation

Give a well-drained, moist soil and full sun or light shade; can become chlorotic on alkaline soils. They prefer a sunny south or southwest facing position, sheltered from cold winds and from early morning sun on frosty mornings.

Propagate by layering, basal cuttings in summer, or by seed.

Pests and diseases

Plants in this genus are notably susceptible to honey fungus. A number of minor diseases can also affect plants. Birds sometimes consume the flower buds.

YELLOWHORN, *Xanthoceras sorbifolium*

Zone 4, H7
Deciduous
Edible seeds / nuts

Origin and history

The yellowhorn (also called the shiny-leaf yellowhorn and the northern macadamia) is a large shrub (sometimes a small tree) native to northern China, where it grows in thickets on dry hill slopes. The name refers to the horn-like growths between the petals.

Description

Yellowhorn grows in the wild to a height of 6m (20ft) and width of 2.5m (8ft), upright at first but becoming rounded with age; in Britain it rarely exceeds 3m (10ft) in height. The young branches are shiny and very pithy.

The leaves are alternate, up to 30cm (1ft) long with 9-17 deeply-toothed leaflets each 4-5cm (1.6-2ins) long, dark green above and paler green beneath. They persist into the autumn, falling very late.

White-petalled flowers, 2-3cm (0.8-1.2ins) across, are produced in dense racemes to 25cm (10ins) long in May at the same time as the leaves emerge. They are flushed yellow, later carmine at the base, and are sweetly scented.

Fruits are top shaped, 4-6cm (1.6-2.4ins) across at the top, leathery thick-walled capsules, which enclose 8-10 round brown seeds. The seeds are 8-15mm (0.3-0.6ins) across.

Uses

The seeds are edible with a Brazil nut flavour and crunchy texture. They can be eaten raw or can be roasted and shelled, or (like chestnuts) the shelled seed can be ground into a flour and used in any of the ways that chestnut flour can be.

An edible oil can be obtained from the seeds – indeed, the yellowhorn is one of China's domestic oil trees.

Other minor edible uses include the flowers and leaves; both have been eaten boiled as a famine food, but they are not recommended!

The inner bark and thick fleshy roots are yellow and can probably be used for dyeing.

Cultivation

Likes a well-drained fertile soil and a sunny position, though most soils (including chalk) apart from wet ones are tolerated. Ideally likes a continental climate with cold winters and hot summers; late spring frosts and cold winds at flowering can be

Yellowhorn

damaging, and in temperate climates the new wood does not always fully ripen, leading to dieback and fewer flower buds. In the UK it prefers conditions in the south and southeast; elsewhere the protection of a wall may be needed for flowering to occur.

Plants are usually slow to become established and grow to about 2.5m (8ft) high in 10 years. Flowers are produced on the previous year's wood. In the wild, flowering is very abundant but the rate of fruit set is very low (only 2-6%); measures to dramatically improve this, and thus the seed yield, in China include the application of fertiliser after seed harvesting, encouraging the growth of spurs and the development of flowers/young fruit the next year; and irrigating in dry weather.

Propagation is mainly via seed or root cuttings. The seeds require six weeks of cold stratification, and germination occurs within 4-6 weeks. There are approximately 1340 seeds per kg (610 seeds per lb).

Root cuttings can be taken in December or January; 3cm (1.2ins) long pieces of root are planted horizontally in pots under cover. A good percentage usually take.

Division of suckers is possible in winter.

Yellowhorn seeds

Pests and diseases

Susceptible to attacks by coral spot fungus (*Nectria cinnabarina*), particularly if the wood is not fully ripened. Affected wood should be cut out.

PART 2 | CHOOSING SHRUBS

Choosing shrubs for your particular site and region need not be a difficult task. Broken down into stages it could go like this:

Find your climate hardiness zone (USDA or RHS version)

This is a measure of winter hardiness and all the shrubs in this book have hardiness rating.

You can simply find a map of hardiness zones and locate yourself on it, however this should always be a starting point and not necessarily the final result.

The real figure for your site might be different: if very exposed or higher in altitude than most of the land around, you may be in the next colder zone than the norm, and similarly if you are in a very sheltered general location you may be in the next warmer zone.

Your plantings can also change your hardiness zone over time, making shelter and warm spots for more tender species, which are likely to be easier to introduce over time.

In most places the winter minimum temperatures are gradually rising due to global heating. How much and at what rate varies from place to place, and of course there is much unpredictability looking into the future. But already in most places you can plant species that would not have survived 50 years ago due to winter cold.

If you live in a mild climate (e.g. USDA zones 7, 8 or 9 like Britain) then most of the shrubs in this book are possible.

What conditions can you offer?

The conditions you have can have a big influence on which shrubs might be suitable.

- Light conditions – full sun, part sun, shade. Most species do best in sun; they vary a lot in shade tolerance.
- Soil drainage conditions – well drained, moist, wet. Most species do best in a moist but well-drained soil. Few can tolerate wet conditions.
- Soil pH conditions – acid, neutral, alkaline. Most species prefer acid to neutral conditions.
- Wind conditions – exposed, sheltered. Most species do best in shelter but pioneers tend to be very tolerant of exposure.

Most shrubs are self-fertile but if not, they will need a partner to cross-pollinate with to produce fruit. You may have one already but if not then you'll likely need to plant two or more of these species.

Remember that the conditions may change from what you started with. So shade and shelter tends to increase in most plantings over time; in more ecological systems, like forest gardens, the soil will change over time, with organic matter levels increasing, drainage improving, pH levels stabilising and so on. So even if you rule a plant out to begin with (or you try it and it fails), you may be able to reintroduce the same species after five or 10 years and have it succeed.

Find out what others near you grow

This can be invaluable, especially with plantings over the last 10-20 years. People nearby may have done a lot of the work in finding out what does well where you are, and you therefore can save yourself work and planting failures.

Example: USDA zone 6 (e.g. most of Germany), moderate shade

If you have challenging conditions from the start, for example shade as with this example, it will be easier if you start with a list of the shade-tolerant shrubs:

Shrubs tolerant of light shade (3-4 hours sun per day)	Shrubs tolerant of moderate shade (1-2 hours sun per day)
Aronia berries	American elder
Blueberries	Bamboos
Bog myrtle	Blackberries
Cranberry	Chilean hazel
Currants (other)	Chocolate vines
Fuchsia	Elaeagnus (evergreen)
Grape vines	Flowering quinces
Honeyberry	Gaultheria
Kiwi fruits	Gooseberry
Nanking cherry	Highbush cranberry
New Zealand flax	Japanese wineberry
Northern bayberry	Magnolia vines
Raspberries	Oregon grapes
Saskatoon	Redcurrants
Spicebush	Siberian ginseng
Trifoliate orange	
Wisterias	

Moderate shade here is defined as the position receiving only 1-2 hours of sun per day in the growing season. Be aware that almost all fruiting shrubs will be less productive in shade, although some (like gaultheria, gooseberries and redcurrants) can still produce near-full crops.

For this example, from the list above, some species can be ruled out as not hardy enough: Chilean hazel and evergreen Elaeagnus.

Now choose from the remaining species that suit your purposes: so if you want a vegetable then bamboos (for shoots); for fresh fruits then maybe gooseberry or redcurrants; for fruits to process then perhaps flowering quinces or highbush cranberry. And so on.

Example: USDA zone 8 (e.g. much of England), wet site

A wet site is perhaps the most challenging of all. Very few shrubs tolerate constant wet soil; a few more tolerate wet soil for much but not all of the time. So start with a list of wet soil-tolerant species:

Tolerant of wet soil
American allspice
Bog myrtle
Cranberry
New Zealand flax
Northern bayberry
Willows

You can see immediately that the list is short. Of these, only bog myrtle and willows tolerate constantly wet soil; the others can tolerate long spells of waterlogging. So you need to know your site well enough to make a judgement about the degree of wetness of the site, then in a zone 8 region, any of the above species are potentially useable.

Example: USDA zone 3 (e.g. parts of Scandinavia and northern North America), exposed site

In this situation, refer to lists of species which tolerate the cold winters and which tolerate exposure:

Shrubs hardy to zone 1-3	Shrubs tolerating exposure
American elder	American elder
Bog myrtle	Aronia berries
Bush cherries	Bog myrtle
Cranberry	Brooms
Currants (other)	Elaeagnus
Drimys	Goji berry
Elaeagnus (some)	New Zealand flax
Gaultheria (some)	Northern bayberry
Gooseberry	Pea shrub
Highbush cranberry	Willows
Honeyberry	
Juniper	
Lingonberry	
Nanking cherry	
Northern bayberry	
Pea shrub	
Roses (some)	
Saskatoon	
Spicebush	
Sumachs (some)	
Willows (some)	

The shrubs that are very hardy but also tolerate exposure are few: American elder, bog myrtle, northern bayberry, pea shrub, willows. It just goes to show that it is very difficult to grow food plants in an exposed position! But of course, once shelter has been established in this example, the other hardy species will all become possible in time.

Example: USDA zone 7 (e.g. much of Western Europe), heavy soil

Heavy soils, with a high percentage of clay, may initially seem difficult to work with, but in fact, as long as they do not remain wet for too long in winter, many species are possible:

Shrubs tolerating heavy soils
Aronia berries
Barberries
Blackberries
Blackcurrants
Bog myrtle
Brooms
Cranberry
Currants (other)
Elaeagnus
Flowering quinces
Gooseberry
Grape vines
Highbush cranberry
Honeyberry
Japanese wineberry
Kiwi fruits
Magnolia vines
Northern bayberry
Oregon grapes
Redcurrants
Roses
Saskatoon
Siberian ginseng
Spicebush
Trifoliate orange
Willows

In this example, with hardiness zone 7, all the species in the list above are possible, so simply make your choice depending on what crops you want.

Tables for choosing shrubs by climate type and zone

You can also use the tables below, starting with climate type and then hardiness level. This then leads to lists of shrubs that have the best chance of being well suited to your conditions. Use these lists as a starting point, as your own specific conditions may well require them to be narrowed down further.

Climate types

These climate classifications are based on the Köppen system with adaptations that make them more applicable to plant adaptations.

DRY	SEMI-ARID	Continental climate, hot summers, cold winters, annual rainfall around 250mm (10ins). Irrigation required. North America: Great plains of the Midwest USA Zone 3 – page 223 Zone 4 – page 223 Zone 5 – page 223 Zone 6 – page 223 Zone 7 – page 223 Zone 8 – page 224
MILD MID-LATITUDE	HUMID SUBTROPICAL	Hot humid summers and mild winters, large storms in winter and thunderstorms in summer. North America: Southeastern USA Zone 6 – page 224 Zone 7 – page 224 Zone 8 – page 224
	MARINE TEMPERATE	Mild and rainy all year, close proximity to ocean (50-100 miles), very humid. Europe: Western half of Britain, western Ireland, western France North America: Pacific Northwest of the USA and southwest Canada Zone 7 – page 224 Zone 8 and 9 – page 225
	TEMPERATE	Mild and rainy all year, 100-250 miles (80-160km) from ocean, humid. Europe: Eastern half of Britain, eastern Ireland, eastern France, Belgium, Netherlands North America: Inland Pacific Northwest of the USA Zone 7 – page 225 Zone 8-9 – page 226
MILD MID-LATITUDE contd	MEDITERRANEAN	Hot and dry summers, mild wet winters. Irrigation required. Europe: Western Spain, southern France, Portugal, Italy, Greece, southeastern Mediterranean North America: Southwest coast of the USA (+ see below) Zone 8-9 – page 226
	DRY MEDITERRANEAN	Hot and dry summers, dry mild winters. Irrigation essential. Europe: Southern and mid Spain North America: Southwest coast of the USA (+ see above) Zone 8-9 – page 226-227
COLD MID-LATITUDE	CONTINENTAL	Warm summers and cold snowy winters. Europe: Germany, Eastern Europe, Scandinavia North America: Northeastern USA, Canada Zone 2 – page 227 Zone 3 – page 227 Zone 4 – page 227 Zone 5 – page 227 Zone 6 – page 228 Zone 7 – page 228
	HUMID CONTINENTAL	Hot summers and cold snowy winters. Europe: Few parts of southeastern Europe North America: Mid-eastern USA Zone 4 – page 228 Zone 5 – page 228 Zone 6 – page 228

Shrub lists for different climates

Treat these lists as an initial list for your climate. Some of the shrubs on your zone's list may only just be hardy where you are, so you may still need to source hardier selections, or varieties to suit your particular situation. You may have a pest or disease that is not around in other regions of similar climate so you may need to find a resistant variety. So although most shrubs on your list should be able to grow where you are, there may be some that cannot!

SEMI-ARID – ZONE 3

The majority of these tree crops will require irrigation in semi-arid conditions.

Fruit shrubs

American elder (*Sambucus canadensis*)
Barberries (*Berberis* spp.)
Bush cherries (*Prunus* spp.)
Currants and gooseberries (other) (*Ribes* spp.)
Elaeagnus (*Elaeagnus* spp.)
Gaultheria (*Gaultheria* spp.)
Gooseberry (*Ribes uva-crispa*)
Highbush cranberry (*Viburnum trilobum*)
Honeyberry / Haskap (*Lonicera caerulea*)
Juniper (*Juniperus communis*)
Lingonberry (*Vaccinium vitis-idaea*)
Nanking cherry (*Prunus tomentosa*)
Roses (*Rosa* spp.)
Saskatoon (*Amelanchier alnifolia*)

Nut shrubs

Pea shrub / Peatree (*Caragana arborescens*)

Other shrubs

Bog myrtle (*Myrica gale*)
Northern bayberry (*Myrica pensylvanica*)
Sumachs (*Rhus* spp.)
Willows (*Salix* spp.)

SEMI-ARID – ZONE 4

As for semi-arid zone 3 plus:

Fruit shrubs

Arctic / Siberian kiwi (*Actinidia kolomikta*)
Blueberry (*Vaccinium* spp.)
Chokeberries / Aronia berries (*Aronia* spp.)
Hardy kiwi (*Actinidia arguta*)
Magnolia vines (*Schisandra* spp.)

Nut shrubs

Yellowhorn (*Xanthoceras sorbifolium*)

Other shrubs

Bush clovers (*Lespedeza* spp.)
False indigo (*Amorpha fruticosa*)
Genista (*Genista* spp.)
Wisterias (*Wisteria* spp.)

SEMI-ARID – ZONE 5

As for semi-arid zones 3-4 plus:

Fruit shrubs

Chinese date (*Ziziphus jujube*)
Chocolate vines (*Akebia* spp.)
Goji berry (*Lycium barbarum*)
Trifoliate orange (*Poncirus trifoliata*)

Other shrubs

Brooms (*Cytisus* spp.)
California lilacs (*Ceanothus* spp.)
Carolina allspice / Spicebush (*Calycanthus floridus*)
Spicebush (*Lindera benzoin*)

SEMI-ARID – ZONE 6

As for semi-arid zones 3-5 plus:

Fruit shrubs

Fuchsia (*Fuchsia magellanica*) – marginal
Grape vines (*Vitis* spp.)
Pineapple guava (*Acca sellowiana*) – marginal

SEMI-ARID – ZONE 7

As for semi-arid zones 3-6 plus:

Fruit shrubs

Kiwi fruit (*Actinidia chinensis/deliciosa*)
Myrtles (*Myrtus* and related spp.)
Passion fruits (*Passiflora* spp.)

Other shrubs

California allspice / Spicebush (*Calycanthus occidentalis*)
Chaste tree (*Vitex agnus-castus*)
Daisy bush (*Brachyglottis greyi* and hybrids)
New Zealand flax (*Phormium tenax*)
Saltbush (*Atriplex* spp.)
Tree lupin (*Lupinus arboreus*)

SEMI-ARID – ZONE 8

As for semi-arid zones 3-7 plus:

Nut shrubs

Chilean hazel (*Gevuina avellana*)

Other shrubs

Caper bush (*Capparis spinosa*) – marginal
Drimys (*Drimys* spp.)
Lemon verbena (*Aloysia triphylla*)
Tea (*Camellia sinensis*)
Tea tree / Manuka (*Leptospermum scoparium*)

HUMID SUBTROPICAL – ZONE 6

Fruit shrubs

American elder (*Sambucus canadensis*)
Arctic / Siberian kiwi (*Actinidia kolomikta*)
Barberries (*Berberis* spp.)
Blackberry and hybrid berries (*Rubus* spp.)
Blackcurrant (*Ribes nigrum*)
Blueberry (*Vaccinium* spp.)
Bush cherries (*Prunus* spp.)
Chinese date (*Ziziphus jujube*)
Chocolate vines (*Akebia* spp.)
Chokeberries / Aronia berries (*Aronia* spp.)
Currants and gooseberries (other) (*Ribes* spp.)
Elaeagnus (*Elaeagnus* spp.)
Flowering quinces (*Chaenomeles* spp.)
Fuchsia (*Fuchsia magellanica*)
Gaultheria (*Gaultheria* spp.)
Goji berry (*Lycium barbarum*)
Gooseberry (*Ribes uva-crispa*)
Grape vines (*Vitis* spp.)
Hardy kiwi (*Actinidia arguta*)
Highbush cranberry (*Viburnum trilobum*)
Honeyberry / Haskap (*Lonicera caerulea*)
Japanese wineberry (*Rubus phoenicolasius*)
Juniper (*Juniperus communis*)
Magnolia vines (*Schisandra* spp.)
Nanking cherry (*Prunus tomentosa*)
Oregon grapes (*Mahonia* spp.)
Pineapple guava (*Acca sellowiana*)
Raspberry (*Rubus* spp.)
Redcurrant / Whitecurrant (*Ribes rubrum*)
Roses (*Rosa* spp.)
Saskatoon (*Amelanchier alnifolia*)
Trifoliate orange (*Poncirus trifoliata*)

Nut shrubs

Yellowhorn (*Xanthoceras sorbifolium*)

Other shrubs

Bamboos
Brooms (*Cytisus* spp.)
Bush clovers (*Lespedeza* spp.)
California lilacs (*Ceanothus* spp.)
Carolina allspice / Spicebush (*Calycanthus floridus*)
False indigo (*Amorpha fruticosa*)
Genista (*Genista* spp.)
Spicebush (*Lindera benzoin*)
Sumachs (*Rhus* spp.)
Willows (*Salix* spp.)
Wisterias (*Wisteria* spp.)

HUMID SUBTROPICAL – ZONE 7

As for humid subtropical zone 6 plus:

Fruit shrubs

Kiwi fruit (*Actinidia chinensis/deliciosa*)
Myrtles (*Myrtus* and related spp.)
Passion fruits (*Passiflora* spp.)

Other shrubs

California allspice / Spicebush (*Calycanthus occidentalis*)
Chaste tree (*Vitex agnus-castus*)
Daisy bush (*Brachyglottis greyi* and hybrids)
New Zealand flax (*Phormium tenax*)
Saltbush (*Atriplex* spp.)
Tree lupin (*Lupinus arboreus*)

HUMID SUBTROPICAL – ZONE 8

As for humid subtropical zones 6-7 plus:

Other shrubs

Drimys (*Drimys* spp.)
Lemon verbena (*Aloysia triphylla*)
Tea (*Camellia sinensis*)
Tea tree / manuka (*Leptospermum scoparium*)

MARINE TEMPERATE – ZONE 7

Fruit shrubs

American elder (*Sambucus canadensis*)
Arctic/Siberian kiwi (*Actinidia kolomikta*)
Barberries (*Berberis* spp.)
Blackberry and hybrid berries (*Rubus* spp.)
Blackcurrant (*Ribes nigrum*)
Blueberry (*Vaccinium* spp.)
Bush cherries (*Prunus* spp.)
Chinese date (*Ziziphus jujube*) – marginal
Chocolate vines (*Akebia* spp.)
Chokeberries / Aronia berries (*Aronia* spp.)
Cranberry (*Vaccinium macrocarpon*)
Currants and gooseberries (other) (*Ribes* spp.)
Elaeagnus (*Elaeagnus* spp.)
Flowering quinces (*Chaenomeles* spp.)
Fuchsia (*Fuchsia magellanica*)
Gaultheria (Gaultheria spp.)
Goji berry (*Lycium barbarum*)

Gooseberry (*Ribes uva-crispa*)
Grape vines (*Vitis* spp.)
Hardy kiwi (*Actinidia arguta*)
Highbush cranberry (*Viburnum trilobum*)
Honeyberry / Haskap (*Lonicera caerulea*)
Japanese wineberry (*Rubus phoenicolasius*)
Juniper (*Juniperus communis*)
Kiwi fruit (*Actinidia chinensis/deliciosa*)
Lingonberry (*Vaccinium vitis-idaea*)
Magnolia vines (*Schisandra* spp.)
Myrtles (*Myrtus* and related spp.) – marginal
Nanking cherry (*Prunus tomentosa*)
Oregon grapes (*Mahonia* spp.)
Passion fruits (*Passiflora* spp.) – marginal
Pineapple guava (*Acca sellowiana*) – marginal
Raspberry (*Rubus* spp.)
Redcurrant / Whitecurrant (*Ribes rubrum*)
Roses (*Rosa* spp.)
Saskatoon (*Amelanchier alnifolia*)
Trifoliate orange (*Poncirus trifoliata*)

Nut shrubs

Pea shrub / Peatree (*Caragana arborescens*)
Yellowhorn (*Xanthoceras sorbifolium*)

Other shrubs

Bamboos
Bog myrtle (*Myrica gale*)
Brooms (*Cytisus* spp.)
Bush clovers (*Lespedeza* spp.)
California allspice / Spicebush (*Calycanthus occidentalis*)
California lilacs (*Ceanothus* spp.)
Carolina allspice / Spicebush (*Calycanthus floridus*)
Chaste tree (*Vitex agnus-castus*)
Daisy bush (*Brachyglottis greyi* and hybrids)
False indigo (*Amorpha fruticosa*)
Genista (*Genista* spp.)
New Zealand flax (*Phormium tenax*)
Northern bayberry (*Myrica pensylvanica*)
Saltbush (*Atriplex* spp.) – marginal
Siberian ginseng (*Eleutherococcus senticosus*)
Spicebush (*Lindera benzoin*)
Sumachs (*Rhus* spp.)
Tree lupin (*Lupinus arboreus*) – marginal
Willows (*Salix* spp.)
Wisterias (*Wisteria* spp.)

MARINE TEMPERATE – ZONE 8 and 9

As for marine temperate zone 7 plus:

Fruit shrubs

As for marine temperate zone 7, with some species less marginal.

Nut shrubs

Chilean hazel (*Gevuina avellana*)

Other shrubs

Caper bush (*Capparis spinosa*) – marginal
Drimys (*Drimys* spp.) – marginal
Lemon verbena (*Aloysia triphylla*) – marginal
Tea (*Camellia sinensis*) – marginal
Tea tree / Manuka (*Leptospermum scoparium*)

TEMPERATE – ZONE 7

Fruit shrubs

American elder (*Sambucus canadensis*)
Arctic / Siberian kiwi (*Actinidia kolomikta*)
Barberries (*Berberis* spp.)
Blackberry and hybrid berries (*Rubus* spp.)
Blackcurrant (*Ribes nigrum*)
Blueberry (*Vaccinium* spp.)
Bush cherries (*Prunus* spp.)
Chinese date (*Ziziphus jujube*) – marginal
Chocolate vines (*Akebia* spp.)
Chokeberries / Aronia Berries (*Aronia* spp.)
Cranberry (*Vaccinium macrocarpon*)
Currants and gooseberries (other) (*Ribes* spp.)
Elaeagnus (*Elaeagnus* spp.)
Flowering quinces (*Chaenomeles* spp.)
Fuchsia (*Fuchsia magellanica*)
Gaultheria (*Gaultheria* spp.)
Goji berry (*Lycium barbarum*)
Gooseberry (*Ribes uva-crispa*)
Grape vines (*Vitis* spp.)
Hardy kiwi (*Actinidia arguta*)
Highbush cranberry (*Viburnum trilobum*)
Honeyberry / Haskap (*Lonicera caerulea*)
Japanese wineberry (*Rubus phoenicolasius*)
Juniper (*Juniperus communis*)
Kiwi fruit (*Actinidia chinensis/deliciosa*)
Lingonberry (*Vaccinium vitis-idaea*)
Magnolia vines (*Schisandra* spp.)
Myrtles (*Myrtus* and related spp.) – marginal
Nanking cherry (*Prunus tomentosa*)
Oregon grapes (*Mahonia* spp.)
Passion fruits (*Passiflora* spp.) – marginal
Pineapple guava (*Acca sellowiana*) – marginal
Raspberry (*Rubus* spp.)
Redcurrant / Whitecurrant (*Ribes rubrum*)
Roses (*Rosa* spp.)
Saskatoon (*Amelanchier alnifolia*)
Trifoliate orange (*Poncirus trifoliata*)

Nut shrubs

Pea shrub / Peatree (*Caragana arborescens*)
Yellowhorn (*Xanthoceras sorbifolium*)

Other shrubs

Bamboos
Bog myrtle (*Myrica gale*)
Brooms (*Cytisus* spp.)

Bush clovers (*Lespedeza* spp.)
California allspice / Spicebush (*Calycanthus occidentalis*)
California lilacs (*Ceanothus* spp.)
Carolina allspice / Spicebush (*Calycanthus floridus*)
Chaste tree (*Vitex agnus-castus*)
Daisy bush (*Brachyglottis greyi* and hybrids)
False indigo (*Amorpha fruticosa*)
Genista (*Genista* spp.)
New Zealand flax (*Phormium tenax*)
Northern bayberry (*Myrica pensylvanica*)
Saltbush (*Atriplex* spp.) – marginal
Siberian ginseng (*Eleutherococcus senticosus*)
Spicebush (*Lindera benzoin*)
Sumachs (*Rhus* spp.)
Tree lupin (***Lupinus arboreus***) – marginal
Willows (*Salix* spp.)
Wisterias (*Wisteria* spp.)

TEMPERATE – ZONE 8

As for temperate zone 7 plus:

Fruit shrubs

Some less marginal.

Nut shrubs

Chilean hazel (*Gevuina avellana*) – marginal

Other shrubs

Caper bush (*Capparis spinosa*) – marginal
Drimys (*Drimys* spp.) – marginal
Lemon verbena (*Aloysia triphylla*) – marginal
Tea (*Camellia sinensis*) – marginal
Tea tree / Manuka (*Leptospermum scoparium*) – marginal

MEDITERRANEAN – ZONE 8-9

Fruit shrubs

Barberries (*Berberis* spp.)
Blackberry and hybrid berries (*Rubus* spp.)
Blackcurrant (*Ribes nigrum*)
Blueberry (*Vaccinium* spp.)
Chinese date (*Ziziphus jujube*)
Chocolate vines (*Akebia* spp.)
Chokeberries / Aronia berries (*Aronia* spp.)
Currants and gooseberries (other) (*Ribes* spp.)
Elaeagnus (*Elaeagnus* spp.)
Flowering quinces (*Chaenomeles* spp.)
Fuchsia (*Fuchsia magellanica*)
Gaultheria (*Gaultheria* spp.)
Goji berry (*Lycium barbarum*)
Gooseberry (*Ribes uva-crispa*)
Grape vines (*Vitis* spp.)
Honeyberry / Haskap (*Lonicera caerulea*)
Japanese wineberry (*Rubus phoenicolasius*)
Juniper (*Juniperus communis*)
Kiwi fruit (*Actinidia chinensis/deliciosa*)
Magnolia vines (*Schisandra* spp.)
Myrtles (*Myrtus* and related spp.)
Nanking cherry (*Prunus tomentosa*)
Oregon grapes (*Mahonia* spp.)
Passion fruits (*Passiflora* spp.)
Pineapple guava (*Acca sellowiana*)
Raspberry (*Rubus* spp.)
Redcurrant / Whitecurrant (*Ribes rubrum*)
Roses (*Rosa* spp.)
Saskatoon (*Amelanchier alnifolia*)
Trifoliate orange (*Poncirus trifoliata*)

Nut shrubs

Chilean hazel (*Gevuina avellana*)
Yellowhorn (*Xanthoceras sorbifolium*)

Other shrubs

Bamboos
Brooms (*Cytisus* spp.)
Bush clovers (*Lespedeza* spp.)
California allspice / Spicebush (*Calycanthus occidentalis*)
California lilacs (*Ceanothus* spp.)
Caper bush (*Capparis spinosa*)
Carolina allspice / Spicebush (*Calycanthus floridus*)
Chaste tree (*Vitex agnus-castus*)
Daisy bush (*Brachyglottis greyi* and hybrids)
Drimys (*Drimys* spp.)
False indigo (*Amorpha fruticosa*)
Genista (*Genista* spp.)
Lemon verbena (*Aloysia triphylla*)
New Zealand flax (*Phormium tenax*)
Saltbush (*Atriplex* spp.)
Siberian ginseng (*Eleutherococcus senticosus*)
Spicebush (*Lindera benzoin*)
Tea (*Camellia sinensis*)
Tea tree / Manuka (*Leptospermum scoparium*)
Tree lupin (*Lupinus arboreus*)
Wisterias (*Wisteria* spp.)

DRY MEDITERRANEAN – ZONE 8-9

Fruit shrubs

Barberries (*Berberis* spp.)
Blackberry and hybrid berries (*Rubus* spp.)
Blueberry (*Vaccinium* spp.)
Chinese date (*Ziziphus jujube*)
Chocolate vines (*Akebia* spp.)
Elaeagnus (*Elaeagnus* spp.)
Fuchsia (*Fuchsia magellanica*)
Gaultheria (*Gaultheria* spp.)
Goji berry (*Lycium barbarum*)
Grape vines (*Vitis* spp.)
Kiwi fruit (*Actinidia chinensis/deliciosa*)

Magnolia vines (*Schisandra* spp.)
Myrtles (*Myrtus* and related spp.)
Passion fruits (*Passiflora* spp.)
Pineapple guava (*Acca sellowiana*)
Raspberry (*Rubus* spp.)
Roses (*Rosa* spp.)
Trifoliate orange (*Poncirus trifoliata*)

Nut shrubs

Chilean hazel (*Gevuina avellana*)
Yellowhorn (*Xanthoceras sorbifolium*)

Other shrubs

Bamboos
Brooms (*Cytisus* spp.)
Bush clovers (*Lespedeza* spp.)
California allspice / Spicebush (*Calycanthus occidentalis*)
California lilacs (*Ceanothus* spp.)
Caper bush (*Capparis spinosa*)
Carolina allspice / Spicebush (*Calycanthus floridus*)
Chaste tree (*Vitex agnus-castus*)
Daisy bush (*Brachyglottis greyi* and hybrids)
Drimys (*Drimys* spp.)
False indigo (*Amorpha fruticosa*)
Genista (*Genista* spp.)
Lemon verbena (*Aloysia triphylla*)
New Zealand flax (*Phormium tenax*)
Saltbush (*Atriplex* spp.)
Spicebush (*Lindera benzoin*)
Tea (*Camellia sinensis*)
Tea tree / Manuka (*Leptospermum scoparium*)
Tree lupin (*Lupinus arboreus*)
Wisterias (*Wisteria* spp.)

CONTINENTAL – ZONE 2

Fruit shrubs

Bush cherries (*Prunus* spp.)
Cranberry (*Vaccinium macrocarpon*)
Currants and gooseberries (other) (*Ribes* spp.)
Elaeagnus (*Elaeagnus* spp.)
Highbush cranberry (*Viburnum trilobum*)
Honeyberry / Haskap (*Lonicera caerulea*)
Lingonberry (*Vaccinium vitis-idaea*)
Nanking cherry (*Prunus tomentosa*)
Roses (*Rosa* spp.)
Saskatoon (*Amelanchier alnifolia*)

Nut shrubs

Pea shrub / Peatree (*Caragana arborescens*)

Other shrubs

Bog myrtle (*Myrica gale*)
Northern bayberry (*Myrica pensylvanica*)
Willows (*Salix* spp.)

CONTINENTAL – ZONE 3

As for Continental zone 2 plus:

Fruit shrubs

American elder (*Sambucus canadensis*)
Barberries (*Berberis* spp.)
Gaultheria (*Gaultheria* spp.)
Gooseberry (*Ribes uva-crispa*)
Juniper (*Juniperus communis*)

Other shrubs

Sumachs (*Rhus* spp.)

CONTINENTAL – ZONE 4

As for continental zones 2-3 plus:

Fruit shrubs

Arctic/Siberian kiwi (*Actinidia kolomikta*)
Blackcurrant (*Ribes nigrum*)
Blueberry (*Vaccinium* spp.)
Chokeberries / Aronia berries (*Aronia* spp.)
Hardy kiwi (*Actinidia arguta*)
Magnolia vines (*Schisandra* spp.)
Raspberry (*Rubus* spp.)

Nut shrubs

Yellowhorn (*Xanthoceras sorbifolium*)

Other shrubs H3

Bush clovers (*Lespedeza* spp.)
False indigo (*Amorpha fruticosa*)
Genista (*Genista* spp.)
Wisterias (*Wisteria* spp.)

CONTINENTAL – ZONE 5

As for continental zones 2-4 plus:

Fruit shrubs

Blackberry and hybrid berries (*Rubus* spp.)
Chinese date (*Ziziphus jujube*)
Chocolate vines (*Akebia* spp.)
Flowering quinces (*Chaenomeles* spp.)
Goji berry (*Lycium barbarum*)
Japanese wineberry (*Rubus phoenicolasius*)
Oregon grapes (*Mahonia* spp.)
Trifoliate orange (*Poncirus trifoliata*)

Other shrubs

Bamboos
Brooms (*Cytisus* spp.)
California lilacs (*Ceanothus* spp.)
Carolina allspice / Spicebush (*Calycanthus floridus*)
Siberian ginseng (*Eleutherococcus senticosus*)
Spicebush (*Lindera benzoin*)

CONTINENTAL – ZONE 6

As for continental zones 2-5 plus:

Fruit shrubs

Fuchsia (*Fuchsia magellanica*) – marginal
Grape vines (*Vitis* spp.)
Pineapple guava (*Acca sellowiana*) – marginal
Redcurrant / Whitecurrant (*Ribes rubrum*)

CONTINENTAL – ZONE 7

As for continental zones 2-6 plus:

Fruit shrubs

Kiwi fruit (*Actinidia chinensis/deliciosa*) – marginal
Myrtles (*Myrtus* and related spp.) – marginal
Passion fruits (*Passiflora* spp.) – marginal

Other shrubs

California allspice / Spicebush (*Calycanthus occidentalis*)
Chaste tree (*Vitex agnus-castus*)
Daisy bush (*Brachyglottis greyi* and hybrids)
New Zealand flax (*Phormium tenax*)
Saltbush (*Atriplex* spp.)
Tree lupin (*Lupinus arboreus*)

HUMID CONTINENTAL – ZONE 4

Fruit shrubs

Arctic/Siberian kiwi (*Actinidia kolomikta*)
Blueberry (*Vaccinium* spp.)
Chokeberries / Aronia berries (*Aronia* spp.)
Hardy kiwi (*Actinidia arguta*)
Magnolia vines (*Schisandra* spp.)
Raspberry (*Rubus* spp.)

Nut shrubs

Yellowhorn (*Xanthoceras sorbifolium*)

Other shrubs

Bush clovers (*Lespedeza* spp.)
False indigo (*Amorpha fruticosa*)
Genista (*Genista* spp.)
Wisterias (*Wisteria* spp.)

HUMID CONTINENTAL – ZONE 5

As for humid continental zone 4 plus:

Fruit shrubs

Blackberry and hybrid berries (*Rubus* spp.)
Chinese date (*Ziziphus jujube*)
Chocolate vines (*Akebia* spp.)
Flowering quinces (*Chaenomeles* spp.)
Goji berry (*Lycium barbarum*)
Japanese wineberry (*Rubus phoenicolasius*)
Oregon grapes (*Mahonia* spp.)
Trifoliate orange (*Poncirus trifoliata*)

Other shrubs

Bamboos
Brooms (*Cytisus* spp.)
California lilacs (*Ceanothus* spp.)
Carolina allspice / Spicebush (*Calycanthus floridus*)
Siberian ginseng (*Eleutherococcus senticosus*)
Spicebush (*Lindera benzoin*)

HUMID CONTINENTAL – ZONE 6

As for humid continental zones 4-5 plus:

Fruit shrubs

American elder (*Sambucus canadensis*)
Barberries (*Berberis* spp.)
Bush cherries (*Prunus* spp.)
Elaeagnus (*Elaeagnus* spp.)
Fuchsia (*Fuchsia magellanica*) – marginal
Grape vines (*Vitis* spp.)
Honeyberry / Haskap (*Lonicera caerulea*)
Juniper (*Juniperus communis*)
Nanking cherry (*Prunus tomentosa*)
Pineapple guava (*Acca sellowiana*) – marginal
Roses (*Rosa* spp.)
Saskatoon (*Amelanchier alnifolia*)

Other shrubs

Sumachs (*Rhus* spp.)
Willows (*Salix* spp.)

Late flowering fruit and nut shrubs to miss spring frosts

These shrubs all leaf out and flower late and rarely suffer from spring frost damage to flowers.

American allspice (*Calycanthus* spp.)
American elder (*Sambucus canadensis*)
Bamboos
Barberries – some (*Berberis* spp.)
Blackberry/hybrid berries (*Rubus* spp.)
Blueberry (*Vaccinium* spp.)
Bog myrtle (*Myrica gale*)
Brooms (*Cytisus* spp.)
Bush clovers (*Lespedeza* spp.)
California lilacs (*Ceanothus* spp.)
Chaste tree (*Vitex agnus-castus*)
Chilean hazel (*Gevuina avellana*)
Chinese date (*Ziziphus jujuba*)
Chocolate vines – some (*Akebia quinata*)

Cranberries (*Vaccinium macrocarpon*)
Daisy bush (*Brachyglottis* spp.)
Elaeagnus – some (*Elaeagnus* spp.)
False indigo (*Amorpha fruticosa*)
Fuchsia (*Fuchsia magellanica*)
Gaultheria (*Gaultheria* spp.)
Genista (*Genista* spp.)
Goji (*Lycium barbarum*)
Grapes (*Vitis* spp.)
Highbush cranberry (*Viburnum trilobum*)
Honeyberry / haskap (*Lonicera caerulea*) – not late, but frost resistant flowers
Japanese wineberry (*Rubus phoenicolasius*)
Juniper (*Juniperus communis*)
Lingonberry (*Vaccinium vitis-idaea*)
New Zealand flax (*Phormium tenax*)
Northern bayberry (*Myrica pensylvanica*)
Pea shrub (*Caragana arborescens*)
Raspberry (*Rubus* spp.)
Roses (*Rosa* spp.)
Siberian ginseng (*Eleutherococcus senticosus*)
Sumachs – some (*Rhus* spp.)
Willows (*Salix* spp.)

Fruit and nut shrubs for short season climates

These shrubs all flower and ripen their crops within about five months and by the end of September.

Arctic / Siberian kiwi (*Actinidia kolomikta*)
Blackberry and hybrid berries (*Rubus* spp.)
Blackcurrant (*Ribes nigrum*)
Blueberry (*Vaccinium* spp.)
Bush cherries (*Prunus* spp.)
Chokeberries / Aronia berries (*Aronia* spp.)
Currants and gooseberries (other) (*Ribes* spp.)
Gaultheria (*Gaultheria* spp.)
Goji berry (*Lycium barbarum*)
Gooseberry (*Ribes uva-crispa*)
Hardy kiwi (*Actinidia arguta*)
Honeyberry / Haskap (*Lonicera caerulea*)
Japanese wineberry (*Rubus phoenicolasius*)
Lingonberry (*Vaccinium vitis-idaea*)
Nanking cherry (*Prunus tomentosa*)
Oregon grapes (*Mahonia* spp.)
Raspberry (*Rubus* spp.)
Redcurrant / Whitecurrant (*Ribes rubrum*)
Roses (*Rosa* spp.)
Saskatoon (*Amelanchier alnifolia*)

Shade tolerant shrub crops

These shrubs all tolerate partial shade quite happily (in terms of growth). However, few shrubs fruit better in shade than in more open sunny conditions, and the amount of fruit usually decreases with increasing shade.

American elder (*Sambucus canadensis*)
Bamboos
Barberries (*Berberis* spp.)
Blackberry and hybrid berries (*Rubus* spp.)
Chokeberries / Aronia berries (*Aronia* spp.)
Currants and gooseberries (other) (*Ribes* spp.)
Drimys (*Drimys* spp.)
Gaultheria (*Gaultheria* spp.)
Gooseberry (*Ribes uva-crispa*)
New Zealand flax (*Phormium tenax*)
Oregon grapes (*Mahonia* spp.)
Raspberry (*Rubus* spp.)
Redcurrant / Whitecurrant (*Ribes rubrum*)
Siberian ginseng (*Eleutherococcus senticosus*)

Supplier list

Europe

Alba Trees
Lower Winton, Gladsmuir, East Lothian EH33 2AL, UK
www.albatrees.co.uk

Agroforestry Research Trust
46 Hunters Moon, Dartington, Totnes, Devon TQ9 6JT, UK
www.agroforestry.co.uk

Blackmoor Nursery
Blackmoor, Liss, Hampshire GU33 6BS, UK
www.blackmoor.co.uk

Buckingham Nurseries
14 Tingewick Road, Buckingham MK18 4AE, UK
www.buckingham-nurseries.co.uk

Burncoose Nurseries
Gwennap, Redruth, Cornwall TR16 6BJ, UK
www.burncoose.co.uk

Chris Bowers and Sons
Whispering Shrubs Nurseries, Wimbotsham, Norfolk PE34 3QB, UK
www.chrisbowers.co.uk

Cross Common Nursery
The Lizard, Helston, Cornwall TR12 7PD, UK
www.crosscommonnursery.co.uk

The Citrus Centre
West Mare Lane, Pulborough, West Sussex RH20 2EA, UK
www.citruscentre.co.uk

Cool Temperate
Newtons Lane, Cossall, Nottinghamshire NG16 2YH, UK
www.cooltemperate.co.uk

Crug Farm Plants
Griffith's Crossing, Caernarfon, Gwynedd LL55 1TU, UK
www.mailorder.crug-farm.co.uk

Deacons Nursery
Moor View, Godshill, Isle of Wight PO38 3HW, UK
www.deaconsnurseryfruits.co.uk

Frederic Cochet
48 Ch De St Pierre, 07200 Aubenas, France
www.cochetfrederic.com

Flora Toskana
Schillerstr. 25, 89278 Nersingen, Germany
www.flora-toskana.de

Ken Muir
Honeypot Farm, Rectory Road, Weeley Heath, Clacton-on-Sea, Essex CO16 9BJ, UK
www.kenmuir.co.uk

KORE Nursery
Warren Fields Farm, Trellech, Monmouth, Gwent NP25 4PQ, UK
www.korewildfruitnursery.co.uk

Mallet Court Nursery
Marshway, Curry Mallet, Taunton, Somerset TA3 6SZ, UK
www.malletcourt.co.uk

Otter Farm
www.otterfarm.co.uk

Pépinière Coulié
Le Sorpt, 19600 Chasteaux, FRANCE
www.coulie.com

La Pépinière du Bosc
Route de Lodève, 34700 Saint Privat, France
www.pepinieredubosc.fr

PflanzenSpezl
Germany
http://pflanzenspezl.de
Ross Markt Strasse 11, 97616 Bad Neustadt, Germany

Perrie Hale Forest Nursery
Northcote Hill, Honiton, Devon EX14 9TH, UK
www.perriehale.co.uk

Pépinières Louis Gauthier
187 chemin des paluds, 13670 St Andiol, France
http://pepinieres-gauthier.fr

Reads Nursery
Douglas Farm, Falcon Lane, Ditchingham, Bungay, Suffolk NR35 2JG, UK
www.readsnursery.co.uk

Welsh Fruit Stocks
Bryngwyn, Kington HR5 3QN, UK
www.welshfruitstocks.co.uk

North America

Aarons Farm
PO Box 800, Sumner, GA 31789, USA
www.aaronsfarm.com

Bay Laurel Nursery
Bay Laurel Garden Center, 2500 El Camino Real, Atascadero, CA 93422, USA
www.baylaurelnursery.com

Burnt Ridge Nursery and Orchards
432 Burnt Ridge Road, Onalaska, Washington 98570, USA
www.burntridgenursery.com

Chestnut Hill Outdoors
15105 NW 94 Ave, Alachua, FL 32615, USA
www.realtreenursery.com

Cummins Nursery
1408 Trumansburg Rd, Ithaca NY 14456, USA
www.cumminsnursery.com

Digging Dog Nursery
31101 Middle Ridge Rd, Albion, CA 95410, USA
www.diggingdog.com

Dave Wilson Nursery
19701 Lake Road, Hickman, CA 95323, USA
www.davewilson.com

Edible Landscaping
361 Spirit Ridge Ln, Afton, VA 22920, USA
http://ediblelandscaping.com

England's Orchard
2338 Highway 2004, McKee, KY 40447, USA
www.nuttrees.net

Forest Farm
14643 Watergap Rd, Williams, Oregon, USA
www.forestfarm.com

Far Reaches Farm
1818 Hastings Avenue, Port Townsend, WA 98368, USA
www.farreachesfarm.com

Grandpa's Orchard
P.O. Box 773, Coloma, MI 49038 USA
www.grandpasorchard.com

Hardy Fruit Shrubs
P.O. Box 5754, Sainte-Julienne, Quebec, Canada, J0K 2T0
www.hardyfruittrees.ca

Hidden Springs Nursery
170 Hidden Springs Lane, Cookeville, TN 38501, USA
www.hiddenspringsnursery.com

Mckenzie Farms
2115 Olanta Hwy, Scranton, SC 29591, USA
www.mckenzie-farms.com

Mori Essex Nurseries Inc
1695 Niagara Stone Rd, R.R.#2, Niagara-on-the-Lake, Ontario, Canada, L0S 1J0
www.moriessex.com

One Green World
6469 SE 134th Ave, Portland, Oregon, 97236-4540 USA
www.onegreenworld.com

Piroche Plants Inc
20542 McNeil Road, Pitt Meadows, BC, V3Y 1T9, CANADA
www.pirocheplants.com

Quackin' Grass Nursery
16 Laurel Hill Road, Brooklyn, CT 06234, USA
www.quackingrassnursery.com

Rolling River Nursery
P.O. Box 332, Orleans, CA 95556, USA
www.rollingrivernursery.com

Raintree Nursery
391 Butts Road, Morton, Washington, 98356, USA
www.raintreenursery.com

Tripple Brook Farm
37 Middle Road, Southampton, MA 01073, USA
www.tripplebrookfarm.com

Ty Ty Nursery
4723 US Hwy. 82 West, TyTy, GA 31795, USA
www.tytyga.com

Photo acknowledgements

Under Creative Common license at http://commons.wikimedia.org/wiki/File:

Page	
3	Salicyna
5	Nonenmac
6	Citron
11	64
13	Arnstein Rønning
18	Kenraiz
29	H Zell
34	Albval
35	Nonenmac
45	Hajotthu
45	Daderot
47	H Zell
48	Kenraiz
48	Forest & Kim Starr
50	Nova
51	Nova
53	by Cillas
54	Lazaregagnidze
55	Jactinto 18
56	Clematis
57	Wouterhagens
58	Tina1
59	McZusatz
60	Daderot
63	YukioSanjo
64	Philmarin
66	Alpsdake
67	Kenraiz
68	Alpsdake
71	Goku122
72	Romaine
73	B.navez
76	GaardenierMortsel
81	Koljian
83	Rudolphous
83	Hedwig Storch
85	Ryan Hodnett
88	Consultaplantas
89	Dalgial
92	Gmihail
93	Warburg 1866
94	Magnus Manske
97	Josve05a
98	Dryas
100	H Zell
101	Tuenspaans
105	AfroBrazilian
107	neurovelho
107	Oyvind Holmstad
108	Deaceane
109	Silverije
115	Martin Bahmann
120	Salicyna
121	Kenpei
123	Nova
124	Zooclub
125	Josve05a
127	VisbyStar
129	Kawkazmlekiem007
130	Sten
131	Qwert1234
131	Nova
132	Warden

133	Bff
133	Nova
134	Tashkoskim
137	Meneerke Bloem
138	Rosa-Maria Rinkl
139	Zysko serhii
140	Silcyna
141	Yujeo
142	Steve Law
143	Giancarlodessi
144	Giancarlodessi
146	Josve05a
147	WildBoar
148	Meisam
149	Forest & Kim Starr
152	Kenraiz
153	Famartin
154	Denis.prevot
155	David Monniaux
156	HubiB
158	Consentida
159	Ryan Hodnett
160	Ural-66
161	Anna reg
162	Arn
163	Daderot
165	Tortie tude
166	Cillas
167	Kollányi Gábor
172	Fischer.H
175	Aiwok
181	Franco Folini
182	Hedwig Storch
183	Toubib
189	MayaSimFan
190	Rasbak
191	Lidine Mia
192	Kenraiz
193	Wsiegmund
195	123tuhkjatolm
197	Salicyna
198	David Stang
200	AnRo0002
201	Salicyna
203	Kenraiz
204	ThayneT
206	Tournasol17
207	Kenraiz
209	BlueBreezeWiki
210	Cillas
211	Selso
213	Molekuel
215	Fanghong
217	XAthenchen
217	Xanth sorb3

Bibliography

Trees for Gardens, Orchards and Permaculture
Martin Crawford; Permanent Publications; 2015.

Creating a Forest Garden
Martin Crawford; Green Books; 2010.

How to Grow Your Own Nuts
Martin Crawford; Green Books; 2016.

Edible Forest Gardens
Dave Jacke and Eric Toensmeier; Chelsea Green; 2005.

The Carbon Farming Solution
Eric Toensmeier; Chelsea Green; 2016.

The Encyclopedia of Fruit and Nuts
Jules Janick and Robert E Paull; CABI; 2008.

Ultimate Fruit and Nuts
Susanna Lyle; Frances Lincoln; 2006.

Plants for a Future
Ken Fern; Permanent Publications; 2000.